AUTOBIOGRAPHY

AUTOBIOGRAPHY

MORRISSEY

G. P. PUTNAM'S SONS

New York

PUTNAM

G. P. PUTNAM'S SONS
Publishers Since 1838
Published by the Penguin Group
Penguin Group (USA) LLC
375 Hudson Street
New York, New York 10014

USA • Canada • UK • Ireland • Australia
New Zealand • India • South Africa • China

penguin.com
A Penguin Random House Company

Jacket design by Jason Ramirez
Jacket photograph © Paul Spencer

ISBN 978-0-399-17154-3

Printed in the United States of America
1   3   5   7   9   10   8   6   4   2

AUTOBIOGRAPHY

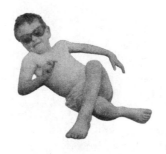

My childhood is streets upon streets upon streets upon streets. Streets to define you and streets to confine you, with no sign of motorway, freeway or highway. Somewhere beyond hides the treat of the countryside, for hour-less days when rains and reins lift, permitting us to be amongst people who live surrounded by space and are irked by our faces. Until then we live in forgotten Victorian knife-plunging Manchester, where everything lies wherever it was left over one hundred years ago. The safe streets are dimly lit, the others not lit at all, but both represent a danger that you're asking for should you find yourself out there once curtains have closed for tea. Past places of dread, we walk in the center of the road, looking up at the torn wall-papers of browny blacks and purples as the mournful remains of derelict shoulder-to-shoulder houses, their safety now replaced by trepidation. Local kids ransack empty houses, and small and wide-eyed, I join them, balancing across exposed beams and racing into wet black cellars; underground cavities where murder and sex and self-destruction seep from cracks of local stone and shifting brickwork where aborted babies found deathly peace instead of unforgiving life. Half-felled by the local council, houses are then left slowly crumbling and become croft waste ground for children to find new excitements with no lights for miles. Fields are places in books, and books are placed in libraries. We, though, are out here in the now, unchecked and un-governed; Manchester's Victorian generation having coughed to their deaths after lifetimes of struggle, and these waterlogged alleys have occasional shafts of greeny-yellow grass jutting between flagstones that have cracked under duress like the people who tread them. Here, behind the shells of shabby shops, that foul animal-waste waft from which no one can fail but to cover their mouths as they race past. These back-entries once so dutifully swept and swilled and donkey-stoned to death by the honest poor now have no future, for this now *is* their future, that moment when time runs out. Like us, these streets are left to their own stark destiny. Birds abstain from song in post-war industrial Manchester, where the 1960s will not swing, and where the locals are the opposite of worldly. More brittle and less courteous than anywhere else on earth, Manchester is the old fire wheezing its last, where we all worry ourselves soulless, forbidden to be romantic. The dark stone of the terraced houses is black with soot, and the house is a metaphor for the soul because beyond the house there is nothing, and there are scant communications to keep track of anyone should they leave it. You bang the door behind you and you may be gone forever, or never seen again, oh untraceable you. The ordinary process of living takes up everyone's time and energy. The elderly muse in bitter ways and the kids know too much of the truth already. Unfathomably, as we fester, there are casinos and high-living elsewhere; first-class travel and money to burn. Here, no one we know is on the electoral roll, and a journey by car is as unusual as space travel. Prison is an accepted eventuality, and is certain to turn you into a criminal. Penalties assessed, arrears called in, and dodging life's bullets is known as survival. It is only ever a question of *when*. In the midst of it all we are finely tailored flesh – good-looking Irish trawling the slums of Moss Side and Hulme, neither place horrific in the 1960s, but both regions dying a natural death of slow decline. The family is large and always admired, the many girls for their neatness and quiet glamor, and always attracting the leisurely stride of local boys. Naturally my birth almost kills my mother, for my head is too big, but soon it is I, and not my mother, on the critical list at Salford's Pendlebury Hospital. I cannot swallow and I spend months hospitalized, my stomach ripped open, my throat pulled wide, my parents are warned that I am unlikely to survive. Disappearing beneath a mass of criss-crossed blanket stitches, I grip onto the short life that has already throttled me. Once I am discharged from hospital, my sister Jackie, older by two years, is interrupted four times as she attempts to kill me, whether this be rivalry or visionary no one knows. We are not vulgarians, yet here we are, in rent-demanding Queen's Square backing onto the high walls of Loreto Convent, with its broken glass atop lest we, below, get any fancy ideas. The family is young and amused and all Irish-born but for my sister and I. The lineage leaps back to Naas, where Farrell Dwyer and Annie Brisk begat Thomas Farrell Dwyer who, somewhere, found Annie Farrell. Battling against the schoolmasterly dullness of detestable poverty, we Irish Catholics know very well how raucous happiness displeases God, so there is much evidence of guilt in all we say and do, but nonetheless it is said and done. My parents are both from the Crumlin area of Dublin, adjoin-

Free in our pleasures, Jackie and I at Queen's Square, 1965

Jackie and I, 1966, wondering how we can possibly leave
the world better than how we found it

ing streets at that, from large families of struggle. My parents are both striking lookers, and it is they who sail to Manchester as the great extended hordes follow, and soon three houses on Queen's Square are occupied by the maternal side of the family, by whom my sister and I are raised. We rarely see my father's side, but they too are splattered about Manchester, full of boys instead of girls, high in number and eager for glee. The Irish banter is lyrical against the Manchester blank astonishment. Walled in by cold-water dwellings, we huddle about the fire, suitable to our calling. Around us, the tough locals welcome this large Irish band as we roar and rage through the 1960s, pinned together by pop music, and by the suspicious absence of money (which, in fact, no one anywhere seems to have). Nameless turnings suggest nothing beyond, and we trudge to school ankle-deep in slush, half-thawed and half-frozen, musing on *My boy lollipop* by Millie Small. The school looms tall and merciless in central Hulme, as the last of the old order, a giant black shadow of ancient morality since 1842, invoking deliberate apprehension into every wide-eyed small face that cautiously holds back the tears as he or she is left at its steps – into long echoing halls of whitewashed walls, of carbolic and plimsoll and crayon blazing through the senses, demanding that all cheerful thought must now die away. This bleak mausoleum called St Wilfrid's has the power to make you unhappy, and this is the only message it is prepared to give. Padlocks and keys and endless stone stairways, down unlit hallways to darkened cloakrooms where something terrible might befall you. There are floors unused and cellars untouched in rooms unloved by ancestors who were certain that wisdom must lie in a keen self-loathing. St Wilfrid's is an asylum, of sorts, for Hulme's pitiful poor, and although it had been declared due for demolition in 1913, it grinds on, fifty years later, dragging we small children with it, plunging us into its own rooms of gloom. Children tumble in soaked by rain, and thus they remain for the rest of the day – wet shoes and wet clothes moisten the air, for this is the way. Our teachers, too, are dumped, as we are, in St Wilfrid's parish. There is no money to be had and there are no resources, just as there is no color and no laughter. These children are slackly shaped and contaminated. Many stragglers stink, and will faint due to lack of food, but there is no such thing as patient wisdom to be found in the sharp agony of the teachers.

Headmaster Mr Coleman rumbles with grumpiness in a rambling stew of hate. He is martyred by his position and is ruled by his apparent loathing of the children. Convincingly old, he is unable to praise, and his military servitude is the murdered child within. His staff stutters on, minus any understanding of the child mind. These educators educate no one, and outside of their occupations they surely lament their own allotted spot? No schoolteacher at St Wilfrid's will smile, and there is no joy to be found between the volcano of resentment offered by Mother Peter, a bearded nun who beats children from dawn to dusk, or Mr Callaghan, the youngest of the crew, eaten up by a resentment that he couldn't control. When, in 1969, he spies a copy of the disc *Hare Krishna mantra* by the Radha Krishna Temple on my desk, his face cracks into a smile. He orders a record player from a musty and musky war-ruined stockroom, and he plays the record five times to an unwashed class whose nits sway in rhythm. Music, you see, is the key.

Mr Callaghan is momentarily unlocked, and is free of himself and his cauldron of spite for at least as long as the music plays. When it is over, his facial muscles collapse to their familiar soupy sourness. Favouring the girls, Miss Redmond lowers her eyes dispassionately at the pickpocket boys, for they are a dismal mass of local color. Miss Redmond smiles lovingly at Anne Dixon, a curly-haired girl whose mother is what the gibbering world term a Lollipop Lady. Miss Redmond is aging, and will never marry, and will die smelling of attics. The post-volcanic black worn by the school nuns and their monastic sheepish priests shapes the subtle effects of oppression; they know their time has gone, and the spinster-faced have seen the door close for the last time. Before them, a new race of youth with their lives yet to be lived, and the contrast between time gone and time to come burns dangerously. An inordinate number of teachers are unmarried, or possibly untouched by human hand, and this shows in the disdainful twist to the mouth. *'You touch me and my mum'll be down,'* I warn Miss Dudley. I am nine years old. Herself a sexual hoax, her lips thin and tighten as she drags me along the corridors of horror to the drooled gruel face of Mr Coleman.

'You!' he shouts at me, as if, at nine years old, I had already scarred England. But there will be no beating for any case that steps this far over the line, assuming the psychological; it is only the meddlers with pulpy hands who are whacked, and usually with a thin leather strap (and these are small children of eight and nine years). I am well turned out, soft to the eye, soft of voice, and absent of the Jackson Crescent muddiness, and this calls for a certain

consideration. Many years later I will foolishly return to these rooms with a television crew, and I will find myself sitting once again with Miss Dudley, speaking through her teeth in a new darkness of advanced age. Miss Dudley recalls Jeane, my mother's almost-too-pretty younger sister, who, like sisters Mary and Rita, also served time at St Wilfrid's. As the cameras roll, I sit smiling with Miss Dudley, as a mortician might inspect a corpse, for practical and understanding we both might be in the now, but there is really no way of forgetting. I think back to that day when fat Bernadette wrapped a leather belt around her neck and proceeded to pull it tightly in both directions, thus possibly killing herself as she sat at her wonky desk in the classroom of B2. *'I'm gonna do it!'* she shouts at Miss Dudley, who casually reaches into her shopping-bag for her newspaper which she then unfolds on her battered desk – completely ignoring damaged and needy Bernadette, who is still shouting *'I'm gonna do it!'* Miss Dudley seems irritated only by the fact that she is taking so long.

When rakish and clanking Brian clumps to the ground in Assembly, he is carted away silently by grim-faced school staff, and the word goes around that Brian hasn't had food for seven days. But there is no gentle therapy for these deprived and confused inner-city slum kids, and there is no response to anything they say other than violence and more hurt. It piles up. This is the Manchester school system of the 1960s, where sadness is habit-forming, and where shame is cattle-prodded into kids who are in pursuit of bliss amid the unrelenting disapproval. Look around and see the gutter-bred – all doing as well as they can in circumstances that they are not responsible for, but for which they are punished. Born unasked, their circumstantial sadness is their own fault, and is the agent of all of their problems.

'*Ooh, doesn't this smell nice?*' says my sister Jackie as she stretches towards me with an open jar of Pond's cold cream. As I lower my head to take a sniff, Jackie rams the jar of cream fully onto my nose. Jackie cackles loudly at this, as I scream and wave my hands. Aproned and full of *Jesus, Mary and Joseph!* declarations, Nannie charges from the kitchen with a handful of black pepper which she then rams up my nose with the hope that I'll sneeze the cold cream out instead of sniffing it brainwards. Life is thus. On another night, singing and swirling in front of an open fire as tea-time telly chortles and Nannie sets the table, I trip and fall towards the fire, burning a two-inch square area of skin off my wrist. A heavy bandage is worn with pride for months to come, teaching me all I shall ever need to know about attention and style. Jeane is asked to watch me one afternoon whilst everyone disappears to grapple with life's grim duties, and she feeds me rice pudding for lunch with a spoon so large that it locks in my throat and I can't pull it out. I panic, and run away from Jeane, who I am certain is trying to kill me.

My best friend is Anthony Morris, whose mother Eunice had been friends with my own mother. Anthony looked not unlike me, but with a small mole on his right cheek. A local nuisance with attractively badly cut hair, he invented little jokes and little bouts, wooing and spurning with a cold stare of sailor-blue eyes. We are the same age and the same height and the same weight and the same everything in an urchinular and picaresque Manchester way. Anthony lives in the new flats at the junction of Cornbrook Street and

Chorlton Road, where Moss Side creeps up on Old Trafford. The flats still stand today, but were a nine days' wonder
of progress only because of their flashy chutes and rooftop
views. It didn't take long for the lifts to jam and the land-
ings to stink, and for people to flee the flats like burning
rats. There is much excitement one day when Granada
Television film the famous Violet Carson, in cathode character as Ena Sharples, gazing mournfully from a mid-floor
veranda, misty-eyed with old thoughts, as I squeeze in
amongst the gathered crowd. The photograph becomes
the jacket of a hardback book by H. V. Kershaw. These
new flats had also been filmed for the opening credits of
television's *Coronation Street* throughout the 1970s, panning
from the flats over to Cornbrook Street and beyond to
Harper Street, where I had lived as a newborn, swept up
into someone's arms from Davyhulme Hospital.

It was with Anthony Morris that a torrent of nervous
energy unleashed itself in the ripped-out houses in the
dangers of faltering light. It was he who told me the reason
why girls fluttered around me at St Wilfrid's, and what it
was that they wanted. He told me this because I didn't
know, and even when I knew, I was less interested than
when I didn't know. I had no idea that it was anything other
than a mere spout. Many years later, by 1974, Anthony
has jumped to stern custodian manliness, and for once
his vicious glare is aimed at me: '*You like all those queers,
don't you?*' he bites. By this he means my merging musical
obsessions, and my heart sinks down into a new darkness.
There is nothing I can salvage from this accusation, and
the eyes pool, as I lose.

From left side to right side, Queen's Square's bookends

are the Bretts and the Blows, two overlarge and knowing Manchester families. Sitting on a thousand secrets, they are central to everything, vitalized and full of life – not rough, but happy – escapist and impossible to match. Both families welcome ours, the Dwyers, with doors always open in a way that modernists assume never actually happened. The Blows live at the end house in the square, rammed up against the high wall of Loreto, their annual November 5th bonfire drawing in all of the Square's residents, unifying the leathery old with the darting young. Even Mr Tappley, who lives alone under his flat cap, creeps out to watch, determined to be unimpressed. Life is taken as it is, and Roy Orbison sings *It's over* all the way to number 1.

Nannie Dwyer is Bridget McInerny of Cashel birth, the family ringleader, my mother's mother, chiefly a personality and the center of everything. Nannie remains of Moore Street in Dublin, of astounding memory and continual disgust; her past as the leader of Dublin's first all-female Queen's Theater Revue had been unexpectedly nipped in the bud by the unexpected bud of Dorothy, followed by Elizabeth (my mother), Patricia, Ernest, Anthony, Jeane, Mary and Rita, and from thereon self-deflationary battles with life's important truths, plus the usual Irish companions of shame, guilt, persecution and accusation. Nannie is afraid, and appears older than her years. Her every hysterical observation is steeped in the fear of God (a God who will not save her at the end of it all), and although her life is entangled in love, Nannie doesn't know it, or cannot show it. Nannie is married to Esty, but she does not like men, or indeed any gooey evaluation of family life. At Christmas dinners Nannie will eat last, setting a place for everyone but herself, yet she will rise first to clear away and wash the dishes. Most fun when most grave, she will play the upright piano for anyone who will listen, her too-long finger nails clipping across mock-ivory until Uncle Liam inevitably tells her that she is murdering music, and thus Nannie will step aside as *Pretty flamingo* by Manfred Mann lashes the lino. A few years older than Jackie and I, Rita screams at music, and every male singer is 'gorgeous'. Family life is chaotic and full of primitive drama as everything is felt intensely. There are no electronic distractions and all human endeavor takes place face to face. We are stuck in the wettest part of England in a society where we are not needed, yet we are washed and warm and well fed. The dull-yellow street lights have none of the eye-crossing dazzle of modern illuminating flash. We are fascinated by shop fronts that remain lit up into the night, often the only form of light for miles. The switching on of street lights each evening tells us all that we ought to be at home, or heading there, for where else? There is nowhere else to be. It is the Nelson Riddle intro of *The Untouchables* that orders me directly off to bed each night, and I wonder what it is about the frozen Eliot Ness that I shouldn't see. The clumsily cut transition of *The Wolf Man* from sane to savage sends me darting with fright, and *Dr Who*, with its lasered x-ray synth swirl, disturbs me just as much. The happy bubble of television shows me the earth and its fragile moments of fantasy, and I, with all the petulance of the pipe dream, am allowed to engage. In childhood and early youth there is no such thing as 24-hour television, and the two and a half available channels play the national anthem at each evening's *Close Down*, which shows a ticking

Nannie at the age of hope, and still Bridget McInerny
of Tipperary

Mother, always nearest the heart. Staten Island, 1975

clock – as if ushering us up to bed with the burden of our own thoughts. Television is the only place where we banish ourselves from the community of the living, and where the superficial provides more virtue than the actual. We watch in order to find ecstasy, for at last we can survive in some-one else. Our conclusions are our own, yet the landscape is infinite. Cross-legged, I sit on the floor and lean into the screen for *Champion the Wonder Horse*, where a boy and his horse find sunlit adventure in an America that permits everything, just as *Skippy* introduces us all to Australia, where a boy and his pet kangaroo find similar sunlit adven-tures in a world where adults are understanding and have time to explain and to sympathize with the peach-cheeked kids – none of whom resemble anyone that I know. Quick-sand and rattle-snakes are passing dangers, but both boys in these shows never remain at the same point for very long, and are rarely discontented or fenced in. Where, I wonder, can such stylishly fitted jeans be found? Not in Manchester Play Streets, where children can only encumber. Where are there such boys who are fully and entirely content with simply *being*? Not in Manchester by-streets, which are exactly what they sound like. Schoolboy misadventures with *Just Jimmy* are the British version of boy-prank sub-terfuge, as Jimmy Clitheroe apple-raids, catapults, conkers and water-pistols his mother's nerves to blustering fussi-ness. These, though, are giant leaps on from the slapstick of *Mr Pastry's Pet Shop*, *Deputy Dawg*, and the pop puppet piglets *Pinky and Perky*. *Fireball XL5* calls my bluff, and each day brings five full minutes of *Captain Pugwash*, where paper characters shift across a screen of painted backgrounds, and where only left-to-right eye movements signify reactions aboard the sea-faring Black Pig. The French *Belle and Sebastian* once again shows the world beyond England as a better place for kids, and I am already ripe for disappearance. Funniest of all is *Batman*, so glamorous against our homegrown *Ask the Family* stodge or *Candid Camera* humiliations. Television is black and white, so therefore life itself is black and white. Gasps of color can be found only at the Odeon, the Gaumont, the New Oxford, the Trocadero or the Imperial, where the cinema screen gives you the hope of other people's happiness. Television flickers and fleets, and must be watched closely lest what you see is never seen again. Whatever you see you will never forget. I know so little compared to Canada's *The Forest Rangers*, whose lead boy is unleashed and free and stylish in his manly kindness. I sit on a stool by the fire and I watch the kids called the Forest Rangers who moralize and are never accountable, and who are too self-assured to ever think cruel thoughts. They heartily shake the hands of adults – something I have never once been called upon to do. Turn and look at me – in affectionate childhood distress, the last in the asylum, by a frosty Manchester fire. Could there be hope? *Animal Magic* offers none at all, and conjuror David Nixon smiles an honest half-smile. *Orlando* is played by Sam Kydd, a boat-builder on London's docklands where kids run wild and are given credit for being funny. *It's a Knockout* offers international games in madcap costumes, and *Honey Lane* is the damp bed-sit drama of East End market traders – our squatty England against America's *The Big Valley*, where, even in the Old West of 1870, Victoria Barkley has no trouble kitting herself out in Christian Dior. An annual flash of glamor is the *Eurovision Song Contest*, whose voting system is heart-stopping, as is the Grand National turf accountant's dream of *Miss World*, as all of England places their bets on the beauty of young women whose full human potential is limited to one frozen expression; their bodies are for others, but not for themselves. Live from the Lyceum Ballroom (could I possibly know that, several lifetimes hence, I would one day become a someone on that very stage?), *Miss World* is unmissable high drama, a spectacle of heaven in Eva Reuber-Staier (Miss Austria 1969), and Marjorie Wallace (Miss USA 1973), never-to-be-forgotten world rulers. Breathing lulls throughout *Miss World* trans-missions as British families ram into chocolate-strewn settees for a genuine glimmer of glamor, where cabaret battles the convent as the finalists huddle together back-stage awaiting the announcement of the juicy winner in a severed condition of meaningless tragedy. The seconds prior to this announcement cause wet heaps of tension throughout Britain. It is magnificent, and its results are the talk of the entire country. In telly-land, *Miss World* and the *Eurovision Song Contest* are the highlights of each passing year, not only because they are competitions, but because we who know so little are allowed a view of the greater world. I recall Miss Brazil in 1970 waving at the camera as she walked into the final, and it was she alone who made me wonder about Brazil. I recall Spain beating the United Kingdom by one vote in the dying seconds of the very last count in the *Eurovision Song Contest* of 1968, and thus I wondered about Spain – my jotter on my knee, my own private scoring system profoundly at odds with the final result. There is no such thing as *Mr World*, perversely enough.

Little Big Time with Freddie Garrity shows kids in a pop-opera fizz, and slaps us all back to where we live and how we live. The wretched kids who sing on *Opportunity Knocks* make my heart bulge with jealous rage, and I know I must molder in silence for many tears to come. *Tarzan* is Ron Ely, a dimple-smile of warmth from a man who lives without electricity and sanitation, with a chest broad enough to safely land a 747 on. Tarzan is a far cry from *Torchy the Battery Boy*, but he emphasized once again that all action and adventure with moments of meaning happen in a place called elsewhere, and never in the sad soil of Manchester. James Darren wears the same sweater in every episode of *The Time Tunnel*, but he's the one for me to be, and it is he I shall be when bedtime casts out all light. *Thunderbirds* are an international rescue service operating from a private Pacific island, where doll-brothers Scott, Virgil, Alan, Gordon and John are anything but problem kids. How could a boy possibly be named Virgil? Thunderbirds launch their space and sea crafts with a shout of 'F.A.B.!' and their fearless London Agent is Lady Penelope. They are, of course, animated puppets, yet they are as real as I am. But how real am I? The introduction for supersub *Stingray* warns how *'anything can happen in the next half hour'*, and, of course, it usually does. Troy Tempest and his partner Phones battle the evil Aquaphibians – terror fish who menace the oceans. Marina is a mute girl from an undersea world who swims her way through the seductive opening sequence making even the misfortune of muteness seem well worth having. *Mystery and Imagination* is sixty foggy minutes of rattling drama so unsettling that I can sleep only with the bedroom door open wide to the landing light – the light! the light! the light! – my heart's lighthouse.

My sister and I would play every day in the attic with great blocks of chalk and strips of colored Plasticine. Mother is a critical guide, and Dad is playful although fist-ready with the outside world. He is constantly called upon when family feuds demand the physical, and he is always there and always unafraid in the days when physicality ironed matters smoothly, and recipients backed down without offence. Often the scrapper spirit is thought crude, but it solves the problem when there is no one else to protect. Mother is Mother, and never Mum (or the ghastly Manchester 'Mam'); she is glamorous foremost, and then she is other things. Dad plays amateur-league football and enjoys a laugh, whereas Mother does neither, yet her glamor stops traffic whenever she walks me to school. Wolf-whistles follow us as we walk through Hulme, past the fastidious little BBC where Billy Fury and the Beatles have played, and past the Hulme Hippodrome where Mother will work for a while – a hall of theater cocktails and glamorous speculations. The new Hulme Library is where Jackie and I prowl each day once St Wilfrid's pulley raises its drawbridge, and books transport the mind until Mother appears to cart us homewards. Around the flashy library, the cobbled streets of terraced houses are dark cabins with their lights out, with windows like eyes facing downwards, awaiting the chop. Asphalt, dust and diesel fuel wrap around the dismal Victorian grandeur, for someone in a distant place has decided that this close-knit community must be dispersed, and that the wishes of the hard-working elderly, who would much rather remain where they have

Dad, at Queen's Square, with historical records for historical record

always been, must be ignored. With all of its consequences, redevelopment has its cold and set way through Bold Street and Preston Street, and all the way to Royce Road where perilous St Wilfrid's shall not be moved. Bonsal Close and Burchill Close are both encroaching, and Hulme is set to be re-made with curved Bath-style crescents, the like of which we puddle-doused pygmies are certain to enjoy. I approach school each day with renewed fear, over the asphalt, treading underfoot the flattened remains of people's lives, and bigger and blacker the school edifice rises above its bludgeoned parish like a rat refusing to die. We small kids see no warm lights to welcome, and no hope in the literal darkness. The flashy new maisonettes that elbow their way across Hulme are tatty and stained within their first year. Winding our way around them, we are scuttled off to Leaf Street Public Baths, so thankless and cold and pitifully cheap; the chlorinated stench turning the stomach. It is here we shall be taught how to swim – in ice-cold water where shadowy old Manchester once allowed its street-traders a sanitary dip in a slipper bath, or use of its crack-tiled showers. Now lifted out of humiliation by the Manchester Education Committee, the authoritarian and patronizing attitude frightens all of the children, who see the experience as excessively destitute. Leaf Street Baths opened in 1860 as the first public baths in England to house a Turkish bath. Its iron columns and exposed drainpipes dripping with condensation proved fully resistant to heavy bombing in 1941, and its 75-foot pool and public wash house scrubbed and soothed the Hulme poor until 1976, when, surrounded by sunless derelict streets, there were no longer any rain-sodden locals to take the icy plunge, and the tired doors bolted their last. At Trafford Park Baths I had gone to watch my father swim. Whilst cheering from the sides, I am pushed into the deep end by a brutally sallow teenage boy, whom my father then neatly chinned. I was small and I couldn't swim, and the panicked roll to the corn-plastered depths terrified me for years after. This ringing hum of panic returned at Leaf Street Baths on our induction day, and I refused to jump into the pool. Ever-present Miss Dudley made no effort to understand the secret agony of a troubled child, and I was lifted up and thrown into the water in an act that, these days, would count as extreme physical and psychological assault. 1960s working-class education remained in 1930s desolation. In the great public buildings of Lancashire there were few rights for children, and there was thought to be no need to protect children against violence or assault from educators since such things were not thought likely to take place, and human history moves along.

The industrial city has a teeming imagination, and Manchester was rife with what were known as tramps. Of these, too, most small children were frightened. The tramps were always men, usually in de-mob suits, no longer required as World War Two cannon-fodder, they have survived the manic eccentricities of Churchill and Hitler and are now untreated sewage of the urban dark, throwing strange shadows in city squares. They always approach children and they always ask for money, their faces discolored with dirt and their clothes brewing with meth-stench. In the midst of their wretchedness it is said that such tramps are happy only in the company of men, and in seeking such an impossible domestic arrangement they gather with their like under battered roofs in deep cellars, huddled around low fires, awaiting the rise of the bolt on the bath-house door. It is said that tramps are allowed use of Leaf Street Baths, where I and others float in dismal dignity. Many children cry because the tiles beneath their feet are so cold and pockmarked with stains, and my experience of St Wilfrid's is sealed as a secret agony. There is no chirpy friskiness as we wind our way back along Jackson Crescent, Miss Dudley's pale frown a map of lovelessness. As each member of the family leaves the school for standardized secondary placings – Jeane first, and then Mary, then Rita, followed by Jackie – I am the last of the flock, further alone in an area now bereft of its narrow and once-crowded streets, and stripped of its maze of illuminated corner-shops. Dark crimes return to a wasteland where there is now no street lighting since there are now no streets. There is no street traffic, and the hum of Stretford Road is distant. It has all been wiped away, and the church once pressed upon by houses now looks like a pathetic creature of pointless endurance. The Three Legs o' Man and the Unicorn call in the last of the old crowd, who will tell you that life was so much better when things were slightly worse. There is a sense that something terrible has happened to this district even though they of scant resources welcome the promise of luxury – miles away from the knots of houses and narrow passageways of old. See the slums and the tramps and read of murdered children – beyond, where the bleak moor lies. An ultraviolet magnetic shock goes through the blood as the parents of the missing children over-hope. A swarm of misery grips mid-60s Manchester as Hindley and Brady raise their faces to the camera and become known to us all;

nineteenth-century street life right here and now, with 1970 but a spit away. It is factual Hindley and Brady, and not our spirited Lake poets or cozy tram-trammeled novelists, who supply the unspoken and who take the travelling mind further than it ever ought to have gone, sealing modern Manchester as a place of Dickensian drear. Of Hindley and Brady there would be nothing to give you heart in their complicity, as children of the poor, who had lived short and shaky lives, were led away to their tortured deaths, and the social landscape of Manchester warps forever with further reason to cry. Tormentedly, everyone appears to know someone who knew Myra Hindley, and we are forced to accept a new truth; that a woman can be just as cruel and dehumanized as a man, and that all safety is an illusion. Nannie rails against Hindley and Brady with a hatred skirting terror, and our thunderclouds part only for the obsessive details of football results and the success stories of our world-famous local teams. Arbitrarily illiterate, football players remained in the stuckness of their own dull social units until George Best spoke and teased and joked and made sense. Best was clever and witty, and he had found a variety of ways to make his life glamorous. The old mold of the at-home regular fellow smashed forever as Best diversified the image of the football player, now suddenly capricious and disorderly but led by no one. Demonstrating the life of success, Best is of course penalized for enjoying too much, yet he is a revolution effecting overwhelming change on how sport is viewed because he is blatantly contemptuous of the press and of governing sporting associations whilst also, incidentally, being an extraordinary player. Catch him if you can. Conventionalized noblesse oblige such as Bobby Charlton would show disapproval of Best because Best is the shocking new against Charlton's 1950s pipe-smoking discipline. It is the physical and facial glamor of George Best that gains him so much love and hate, for everybody wants what he has. My father takes me to see George Best play at Old Trafford, and as I see the apocalyptic disturber of the peace swirl across the pitch, I faint. I am eight years old. Squinting in the sun, it is all too much for me, and I remember my father's rasp as he dragged my twisted body through the crowd and out into the street, causing him to miss the rest of the match. Another form of church, football was all that stood between earth and God. Mike Summerbee's central Manchester boutique was destiny fulfilled, and George Best's space-ship house in Bramhall attracts more visitors than Lourdes. *But I?* Am I to be saved? And, if so, for what reason?

Watches and clocks are set to mark the sound and vision of ice-cream vans, whether Gerrards or Mr Whippy. This is still the old and weathered Manchester where people carry deep bowls to ice-cream vans, and load them with scoops, or carry dinner-plates to fish and chip shops where their supper is dumped onto their own trusted china which is then covered by a tea-towel for the walk home. All that you consider hip and happening will also tumble into nostalgia just at that moment when you finally come to realize where everything is, and how things ought to be. It is a race to the grave.

Nannie drops a knife and shouts *'Man to the door!'* – a somber and fearful predicament in a family and house where men usually represent trouble. 1967's major investments are *Simon Smith and his amazing dancing bear* by Alan

Price (who sings 'well excepted everywhere', which surely ought to be 'well accepted everywhere'), *Peek-a-boo* by the New Vaudeville Band, *Bernadette* by the Four Tops. *Everything I am* by Plastic Penny has the line 'got my feet on the ground | you've found some good in me', and the sad lilt jabs. I am fascinated by *I've been a bad, bad boy* by Paul Jones, because it is so loud and so strange, and there it is at number 6 in the charts, hooray. These small black discs are the first things that are truly mine; my choice, paid for with my own scraps of cash, reflecting my own stubbornness. In a dream, I watch them spin and spin, calling out, pointing the way. These are the days when very few people collect records, so therefore whatever they might buy defines their secret heart. Everyone scratches their name on the paper labels because in the event of the discs being brought to parties it's important that the owner leaves with whatever they arrived with. This becomes irrelevant in the 1970s when the value of records is beginning to be understood, and any defacing will reduce trading prices. In the 60s, of course, it doesn't occur to anyone that they might one day sell their collection, for who would want such throwaway items?

In our abyss, Jeane falls in love with Johnny, who is teen-aged and tattooed and dispossessed. Johnny governs Jeane's heart, and the family becomes a battleground since Johnny swells disfavor within everyone. The tornado of Nannie's life erupts further as Johnny clambers up the drainpipe to bang on Jeane's bedroom window; Dad chases Johnny and beats him up; Johnny laughs it off with Hulmerist ferocity; Jeane becomes pregnant with the first of three; Nannie's house is broken into – filchings are sorrows, and buckets in the front parlor collect the rain. One bright Saturday afternoon I patrol Alexandra Road with Nannie and Jeane, and here comes Johnny in the oncoming traffic, hands in pockets, tattooed neck and Rat Pack sunglasses. He swiftly uppercuts Jeane as he zaps past, Nannie falls into a mad Irish panic, and we race backwards towards Loreto Convent where, for reasons unknown to me, Nannie bangs on the door of the nuns' lodge begging holy assistance. We are within their high, spiked walls, and a slum nun greets us but blocks the doorway with her overfed bulk. Nannie pleads for refuge, pointing to Jeane's battered face, and fearing the threat of immediate stabbing. Imprisoned in her own clothes, the nun knows only the world of make-believe, and she slams the door in our faces. In fear and trembling, Nannie leads us back home through a maze of mean and narrow streets, paralyzed by the thought that Johnny might strike again. But he doesn't, and instead, Jeane reunites herself with the lover who punched her face in public, but who also has the power to make her happy.

1965 had brought Grandad's death, so suddenly at 52. In the dark November air his eyes close for the last time, his still body discovered by Jeane. Grandad is called Esty and is loved by all, now as then. Mother and Ernie attend the mortuary to identify Grandad, and as they leave, Ernie says *'Well, if I look that good when I go,'* and six weeks later, Ernie is dead at 24. Leaving his office job around the Tib Street area, Ernie heads for home only to collapse and die in the street, and we are all lost, faith denied, but with no one groping for an answer. The deaths of Grandad and Ernie are so keenly felt that no one can mention their names for the ten years that follow. Lying in hospital

Carrying the soul of the world, Ernie is standing where he stood,
born one May 22nd in Dublin, and time moves too fast

with a broken leg, Nannie is told that her second son has died, and as Mother had identified her father's body, she then identified her brother's body in the same mortuary six weeks later. Mother turns against the church as her father and her last surviving brother are lowered into the same grave in gravely unpleasant Southern Cemetery. Life is now beyond logic, and a new nightmare fleshes out against the commands of the church. Mother screams loudly at an immobilized priest, and all of our lives thus far are lost in the lap of memory. Manly in bearing, Ernie was my true uncle, my Mother's favorite, and just three years her junior. In one photograph (because this is what people become), he cuts a warm figure as he holds up a picture of James Dean. Ernie would prophesize how he, like James Dean, would die at 24, which he did, in the year that his favorite song, *All over the world* by Françoise Hardy, crept into the charts. I shared my birth date of May 22nd with Ernie, a harmonica in a box scrawled with Ernie's handwriting my eternal possession once he is no more. Throughout his short and angered life he ached, like most people, to find something of value to do, and he cursed Manchester, and he cursed England through mists of pain, and he cursed the Christian Brothers who had blackened his eyes once too often in the name of heavy-handed holiness. Ernie sank into the army for identity, but lost his, and returned home to Manchester, unhappily. Nannie's first boy, Anthony, had a pitifully short Dublin life, slipping away after nine difficult months of exertion, buried unpleasantly at Mount Pleasant in a grave full of strangers (even in death another family might be willing to take you in). How do these things happen?

Was this 1712? In the 1990s we locate Anthony's grave, neatly placed in a cemetery loaded with secrets, and I am convinced even now that he is not too deep to be rescued and raised to his parents' plot in Manchester, but such meddling is fearfully dismissed by family members who can barely manage the truth of the horror as it stands, without lifting child-size coffins into the air. Nannie moves from Queen's Square to a condemned house at 10 Trafalgar Square, a short walk just further along Augustus Street. The execution of Queen's Square is delayed no longer, and our lives are flattened before our eyes – as if the local council couldn't wait a minute longer for we pack rats to gather our trappings and transistors. During my final year at St Wilfrid's I am called upon by Mr Coleman to accompany a boy named Patrick Keane to his home, twenty minutes away in darkened Duke Street. Patrick is ill and cannot be left to walk by himself. Once we arrive at the terraced house, so shadowed in somberness, Patrick lets himself in with his own key as he waves me away, smiling and fully cured of the sullen glop of St Wilfrid's.

I return to school and Mr Coleman seeks me out for a full medical prognosis. I explain that Patrick is now home and seemed very well. *'You!'* roars Mr Coleman. *'You idiot!'* he swells, eyes frenzied with over-reaction, *'and what if he collapses? Why did you leave him alone in that house?'* Mr Coleman's punished face reveals the monster for all to see. I am eleven years old and had crossed many main roads and junctions to ease the journey to Duke Street, but in the fashion of the day, the fault of desertion was all mine, without my own safety being an issue. The duty forced upon me, and the rocketing hysteria of Mr Coleman, both answered a vital question, and I would never again assume that any figure of authority automatically held any intellectual distinction. I am unafraid.

Minus her husband and her son, Nannie settled into 10 Trafalgar Square even though the local council had already chalked it off as unfit for human habitation. Every house has a face, and the eyes of 10 Trafalgar Square were already closed. The square itself was not unattractive, and prior to the seething rot of 1968 it surely sheltered the faithful very pleasantly. Backing onto the lodging houses and breweries of Moss Lane, events piled up around the Trafalgar Square house – in which we all somehow lived, or passed through, as the family began to fray and snap. I would spend many nights sleeping at the foot of Nannie's bed, the impossibly loud tick of her alarm clock preventing any rest, yet Nannie is gone to the world with a satisfied Embassy wheeze whistling in rhythm to the bedside clock, her night-light pointing the way to cough-sweets, holy water, milk of magnesia, and Germolene – the vital accoutrements for anticipated midnight peril.

On a driving jaunt to Liverpool with Dad at the wheel, we are smashed into by an amber-gambler, and passenger-seat Mary has her face shattered with glass. Seated nervously in Liverpool General, we hear Mary's screams as stitches are forced into and pulled out of the left side of her face. Weeks later we are in a second crash as a blown tire forces the car to swirl and whirl across Wilbraham Road in Whalley Range, in a playful roustabout with death, leaving the car about-face in someone's garden. The gentle house-holders of old take us in to sooth our nerves, whereas today's indignation generation would pellet writs at us from upper windows.

The oldest of the Dwyer sisters is Dorothy, and she works in central Manchester and has a life. She is generous and vocational and dances whenever she can – making the first flutter to virtuous and green Stretford, where real air might be breathed. Number 17 Norwood Road is a house of distinction, leading to Edge Lane, so prim and unhurried all those years ago. Dorothy is closest to Nannie, being Nannie's firstborn, but with so much clash and clamor passing through Trafalgar Square the shrillness never dies. Friday evening always brings Dorothy to Trafalgar Square, and never is she without an imaginative gift or goody bag that will amuse me for days. Teenaged Mary stands with the back of her legs to the open fire, balancing on the hearthstone, the fireguard folded away. Her blonde teased hair is part-beehive and, as the second youngest, she, too, is led by music and makeup and the itch of life beyond. In the half-light, I follow Mary out of the square as she meets whomever it is she meets, and I do the same secret-agent undercover work with Rita as she slips out at darkening 6 PM to a youth club on Bangor Street, where the untamed restives smoke cigarettes and flirt their fractious proposals. Here, the local scruffs loiter to amuse themselves in youth club fashion, bursting with the secrets of yearning maturity and rough serenade. All Manchester boys are mad, and they shout, and they laugh loudly, and courtship is a question of aggression rather than gallantry. I am unwanted at the youth club – being far too yearling young, and Rita orders me home. Luring me is the advent of a new crowd who have no connection to school, and who frighten and

Rita, born one August 13th in Dublin, yet everywhere in the heart, and here, at Trafalgar Square, Old Trafford

fascinate me in equal measure. Who is this gang, known only to Rita, who shout as they bolt into the blackness of sleeping Tamworth Street? I return to Trafalgar Square, to Nannie and the central focus of the television set, under which sits the cat with her litter of newborns. But already the houses on the square are being abandoned. With parlor-leaks and darting mice Nannie will hold on, fuming and fussing at the fractured lives of her six daughters, and cursing my mother for working and buying glamorous clothes. Nannie bricks together the traditional Christmas for all to gather and disagree. My sister and I head out to the Pot Shop and the Jubilee Shop, both crumbling and cluttered corner shops wheezing their last goodbyes to an indifferent world, their elderly and bluntly rude shopkeepers plagued and tormented by the lengthy time it takes my sister and I to methodically choose our sweets.

Rita now works at Seventh Avenue in Piccadilly and buys expensive Planters cashew nuts. Mary works at a Granada showroom, but is ready to leave it all behind. Crumlin summers of childhood are spent on Clonard Road, fagged out on the beach and dead beat by 5 PM. Safe and wide, the dry streets of Crumlin are empty of cars, and the houses cackle with the droll of the extended family. Bustle and fluster pad out these Dublin days, but as each year passes my sister and I are less willing to leave Manchester. Ireland is our soaring past – ruddy and cheerful, yet somehow the past. My parents will never let it go, and it is not difficult to understand why. All around us the Irish deputation mourn the loss of the land, and how British liberality hobbles in comparison to the hearty warmth of Dublin's outstretched arms. Dublin kids are active and animated, quick and streetwise, and always in force. A nearby sweet kiosk is operated by a man who is blind, and we watch in awe as his hands follow each request.

Dublin Catholics are spiritual but not saintly, faithful but not strict, godly but not exact. Devout and good, they are also loosely at large with a blunt and sincere grasp of what the human frame requires. I feel no pull towards the church, but I understand that there is nothing else. Catholicism has you tracked and trailed for life with an overwhelming sense of self-doubt, and every church churns with painful pews and mourners' stalls. Jackie enlists at the harrowing Cardinal Vaughan School in Stretford, now that we have mobilized from Queen's Square to Kings Road. Here in Stretford we are the young intruders against the settled late-middle-aged Mr and Mrs brigade – each gentle and smiling long-standing residents for whom the war was just yesterday. Firswood is lending libraries and parks in almost-posh Lancashire, each New Year's Eve bringing swarms of neighbors to their garden gates to shake each other's hands – well wishes and smiles as time rips at them in its march. In the background, Old Trafford factories hoot their salutes, for people were thankful to have made it through. Nannie remains back at Trafalgar Square, housing the homeless, sometimes Jeane, sometimes cousin Eileen Sullivan (who arrives unexpectedly and will then be discovered dead in Nannie's back bedroom). Sometimes Jackie and I are the refugees, as Rita flits in and out with her secretive social whirl. There is only ever a sense of change and of slipping away, but never a sense of security or stability. Tomorrow is already a jigsaw. Nannie's cousin John Joe Rahilly will arrive from

Dublin and will anchor himself around the house in his irremovable heavy overcoat. He is another pleasant slice of yesteryear Dublin, a lifelong bachelor who will propose marriage to Nannie without regard to the ancestral bloodline. We had waved goodbye to Mary at Manchester Airport, a US emigrée in her nineteenth year, and to never again be a Manchester lass. We all cry uncontrollably as Mary's flight is called – a loved branch hacked away.

As Nannie's brood reduces, hers is suddenly only one of two houses occupied in Trafalgar Square, the rest all boarded up, their duty done. Even during the day we are surrounded by the dark. The back of the house leads across to a builder's yard, where one Saturday afternoon a group of Moss Side boys are stoning a rat to its death. The rat is large and Manchester-tough and manages to crawl halfway up the wall of the builder's yard, but the mob is relentless and suddenly the rat falls back on itself and surrenders to death in the rubble, whereupon the boys stroll off, itchy for the next amusement. Nannie is alarmed because, hearing a scuffle in the abandoned house next door, she has unwisely investigated and discovered a man standing naked before her – the sight of which delivers a knockout blow of senselessness, leaving Nannie tranquilized with gibberish for the rest of the day. Our lifeblood Alexandra Road is also now boarding itself up, so that we now rely exclusively on the gasping Off Licence – a beacon of bacon with the wonder of Wonderloaf. It is important never to walk by the forsaken houses lest a strong arm should pull you in and you become minced meat. When Nannie is offered a flat in Gorse Hill, it is Minnie, a mousy Victorian woman in her eighties who will now be the very last lone resident of Trafalgar Square.

I, of course, stand alone with Nannie as she says her goodbyes, and it is too much to bear as the small and shrunken Minnie waves us off from her cramped corner-house, to return within as the last lit lightbulb of life in this already forgotten corner, where she will climb the darkened stairway to rest her head – not from the whirring day, but from a lifetime now closing, all the madcap marriages and births of Trafalgar Square now gone, the swirl of life now meaningless in the friendless dark. The only tap running is hers, and the awaiting move is to a new flat that time or fatigue will scarcely allow her to enjoy as history overtakes her. It is with the wave that she gives on that day to Nannie and I that her light fades, and even though I hardly know her, I am in tears at the pitifully wizened figure giving a salute of good luck, all life spent, with nothing remaining but the brusque knock of a stranger intruding with instructions of where to go, how to sit, and how to die. Absurdly, Nannie has placed Blackie the cat in a brown paper shopping bag with string handles in readiness for the bus journey to Gorse Hill, which is possibly thirty minutes away. I am explaining to Nannie that this idea will not work, but she looks away each time I protest. On Cornbrook Street, Blackie leaps from the bag and tears her way back down the street in the direction of the junkpile scrap heap of written-off Trafalgar Square. I am, once again, fraught with shock, but Nannie marches on. '*No!*' she says, '*leave her. Minnie will feed her.*' I know this is not true, and that nothing and no one will look after either Minnie or the cat.

Nannie's cousin Jody Keating is a small huffing and

puffing Irish woman of rasping tobacco-voice, who rolls in on a cloud of Embassy and reflects as only the Irish can in five parts curse and five parts prayer. It is kitchen-table mourning for time gone, and for people of hushed scandals half-forgotten. It is recognition that they, now, have shifted to the end of the queue, and are suddenly life's trusted historians when once they were gadabout girls of slender means. The Sandymount of my mother's birth, the Pearse Street of childhood, and over to North Great George's Street where the half-told is tale enough. Jody and Nannie are the last of the old crowd, and guardians of morality. Inside, Jody is dark and unhappy. At 11 years old, her only son Billy had accidentally set fire to himself in the backyard of their doleful terraced house in Rye Street in Chorlton-on-Medlock. Moving slowly, Jody nonetheless manages good humor and charitable smiles, returning by bus to Rye Street's ghosts and outcasts in a house of visitations and imaginary sobs of children. Crime historians would later name Rye Street as having been patrolled by Hindley and Brady, and although Billy had escaped them, his remains now lay in Southern Cemetery (close to those of Ernie and Grandad), beneath a featureless stone inscribed *Our Billy*. Years on, there is no one left for whom Billy is 'ours', and the only flowers frequently left at his grave are from me.

The magical properties of recorded noise had trapped me from 1965 onwards. Song made a difference to everything, and permitted expressions that otherwise had no way through. The Paul Marsh record shop on Alexandra Road had been my Eton, a temple of Holy Scriptures and evangelical hope. Nothing else could be worth knowing, and the whole world fell away as I surrendered to the words on the page and the voice that sang. Paul Marsh is a small shop with exposed wooden floorboards; pop singles lodged upright in pigeon-holes behind the counter and LPs conveniently racked for small boys to study in occultish ways. *Record Song Book* is an expensive magazine that prints the lyrics of famous or bubbling songs of the month, and I practice with invented melodies on the songs that I haven't heard. It is only the singing voice, I decide, that tells us how things became how they are, and *You've lost that lovin' feelin'* by the Righteous Brothers had led me to the light. In this duet between Bill and Bobby, the language of despair becomes beautiful, and the final forty-five seconds hit such call-and-respond excitement that I am now in danger of feeling too much. Bobby's rooftop falsetto is the fire in the belly, whilst Bill's deep-chested leveling is the full invasion. Suddenly everything else in life is in question. From yesteryear I discover *Good timin'* by Jimmy Jones, and I am beginning to feel something that no one else has brought to my attention. Tony Orlando's surfs-up voice leaps on *Bless you*, and I am spirited away watching and watching as these discs spin, calling up to me. How is the voice imprinted on the cheap plastic? Paul Marsh is revelation and prophecy, and every effort is made to evoke enough pity from anyone with cash to take me along Alexandra Road and to pause at this temple. My very first disc had been *Come and stay with me* by Marianne Faithfull, acquired after howls of insistence from beneath the kitchen table. The howls worked and my parents gave in, and the five-and-six eased my soul like God could only know. *Top of the Pops* began its life in Manchester, and although we are not easily intimidated we allow *Top of the Pops* to tell us where it's at. All human activity is fruitless when pitted against the girls and boys singing on pop television, for they have found the answer as the rest of us search for the question. I will sing, too. If not, I will have to die. But again and again it is the sight of the Righteous Brothers singing *You've lost that lovin' feelin'* (to each other?), gazing into their own separate distances. I cherish each glimpse that television allows – so unrepeatable, and God forbid that anyone should talk too loudly or meddle with the sound. Yes, there he goes again – Cherub Bobby swooping up into a female scream, and visual art unravels before me. At a crofted fairground on Stretford Road the sights and sounds and smells are alive with harm and hellborn pleasures. I catch sight of Margaret, who is in my class at St Wilfrid's and who has a red birth mark on her right cheek, and I wave a wave that she returns, but the brimstoned boy that she is with rockets towards me and lands me an upper-cut so fierce that I am unable to see for a full minute. When my senses return, I am voluntarily rescued by Billy O'Shea, who is also from my class and who whomps the boy with a swing that I am assumed unable to deliver. Smiling Billy returns this duty some weeks later at school when I find myself singled out for a ferocious whack in the yard. As a blow lands, I fall, and from nowhere Billy O'Shea shazzams and rips the head off the ass-backwards assailant. And the world turns.

Before leaving for America, Mary had once again escorted me to Paul Marsh, where I had chosen *Rainbow valley* by the Love Affair, a group led by impish Steve Ellis, who has a mannish voice. I am thrilled to death whenever the Love Affair appear on television, as I am with the

Foundations, who are led by Clem Curtis in cheap-looking high-waisted trousers, smiling all the way through *Back on my feet again* with a chorus that never ends. *Lazy Sunday* by the Small Faces is an urgent investment, and their singer is Steve Marriott, another puckish working-class runt, yet naming Noël Coward as his hero, and the canvas for investigation broadens out. Sandie Shaw had a vacantly indifferent expression, not especially willing to please. I like her single *You've not changed* because of its barking brass and simple lyric. She, though, is almost lifeless – a Saturday afternoon girl at Marble Arch. Lulu trips up over her own niceness, with drama-school wide-eyes and cutely dimpled nods to the camera, rolling her Rs on *I'm a tiger*, a brilliant slab of froth. Mary and Rita own the most entrancing single in *Heart* by Rita Pavone, a boyish Italian girl with a rising belt of vocal power. The room spins and spins. Jeane favors Elvis Presley and Billy Fury, whilst Rita repeats the same *as-I-peer-through-the-window-of-lost-time* Supremes single over and over again – twenty times on any given night, until Nannie's nerves erupt, disgorged and worn. Sometimes I dance around the room with Rita as *I'm livin' in shame* wags its finger, until the day Dad tells me I look embarrassing, so I stop. Rita writes '*Wilson for ex-premier*' on all of her discs. The self-help manual passed around to all is *The Best of Timi Yuro*, a long-player in a black sleeve from which the New York-Italian singer glares with petite toughness. Timi Yuro was born Timothy, and although she is not as well known as Dorothy's beloved Shirley Bassey, Timi Yuro's voice rattles the bannisters with little effort. I scramble from cheap record player to cheap record player. It is considered odd that a boy so young should care so much. At

Norwood Road, Dorothy and Liam own a fancy stereo-cum-cocktail cabinet, misused, I thought, by the rack of James Last LPs. Here and there my eyes and ears are caught only by the solo singers; town-crying to all people at all times, television troubadours minus jingle-jangled nodding musicians. The song bears witness, the body weaves, and there are no camera cuts to blandly smiling session-players when all we want to see is the sculptured singer – alone, carrying all, sub-plot and sub-text, the physical auto-biography; simultaneously, subjectively and objectively at the same time. There is no way out for the solo singer; introduction, statement, conclusion, quick death – all con-veyed in the pop sonnet, with no winking glance over to guitarists in order to ease the setting. There are visions of divine things: Tommy Körberg sings *Judy, my friend*, Matt Monro sings *We're gonna change the world* and Shirley Bassey sings *Let me sing and I'm happy*. I still don't know what it's all about, but like the science of signs, I am called to, because the song is the art of using language as persuasion, and with that allowance and this hope, I want to cry. I am caught and I am devoted to a fault. Snobbery jumps in. If I can sing, I am free, and no legislation can stop me. Sacha Distel, of course, has everything except a strong voice, whilst Matt Monro has a propelling voice, but not the physical poetry. Shirley Bassey fires a certain bolstered timbre that lifts her out of the Rose and Crown, and the Maria Callas history-of-human-torture facial expressions certainly appear to be additional value for money (even if, during brief interviews on television, she is unable to relax, as if desperate to con-ceal an extensive lack of personality). The Lord giveth and the Lord taketh away, and no singing artist seems to be in possession of the complete bundle. Even the royal Elvis Presley does not write the songs that he sings – not that this matters much, yet it is noted how someone with such masterly vocal direction must await the patchwork and paste of songwriters in order to alight the gift.

Loudly and wildly the music played, always pointing to the light, to the way out, or the way in, to individualism, and to the remarkable if unsettling notion that life could possibly be lived as you might wish it to be lived. *Top of the Pops* makes the inevitable journey to London, where it stays forever. I rage with jealousy at the disembodied audience of zombies who show unearthly indifference in the presence of Shocking Blue. No illness of any ferocity could sway my interest during *Top of the Pops*, a rare flash of glamor in our oh so very pale lives, a heart-stopping rundown of the Top 30, followed by jaw-dropping paralysis as our personal favorites step into view. Now you see them, now you don't. What *was* that? Eat it up and dream about it later, or wake up and dream as the years shuffle like cards. Facts blur with hallucination as T. Rex edge in from somewhere interplanetary, giving an elbow thrust to Pickettywitch and the galvanizing Tom Jones. T. Rex are a question I had been saving up for a long time, and the singer is of pleasantly soft speaking voice, and my little radio crackles with interference regardless of where the station happens to be. The year 1970 is loutish stoops in studlike gear, shuddering catchphrases and racist television comedies of half-wit mispronunciations; Ruffle Bars and T-Bars, and my parents are neither friends nor lovers to one another, and nothing in our lives is tidy or designed. With a detachable head, I paddle my own way through it all. As my parents clash on every subject, Jackie takes sides and cries in between. I make several bolts for freedom clutching only *The Otterbury Incident*. First, I run to Lostock, where Jeane and Johnny now have their own flat, but I am in the way here, too, and Johnny promptly hitches me onto the crossbar of his bicycle and takes me back home – all along Barton Road, a journey of days, and how I sat there throughout can only indicate the hardiness of the times.

I make several dashes to Dorothy and Liam, now living in the snootiness of willowy Wilmslow, where Liam's GPO advancements have upgraded their lifestyle to a beautiful cottage on Mill Brow. I also make a midnight dash to Nannie, who whacks me across the head and then asks questions. My father still took Jackie and I to the Bluebird Café on Back Piccadilly, shaded somewhere behind Chelsea Girl, for a weekly watery-grey set menu of chips with everything, for Jackie and I would eat nothing else. No multinational menus were yet on the Manchester horizon, and anything with a hint of flavor was considered exotic. In the mid-1970s my parents would quietly divorce, Dad having disappeared two days before Christmas amidst loud assumptions that he has other lives elsewhere.

Throughout these years I am a largely bedridden child unwilling to keep death at bay. Hope remains only via television, which shows me what might happen to me should I manage to live to be fully grown. *Lost in Space* offers the full flavor of studio-bound American allure as a handsome and well-balanced family hurtles through an extensive range of hostile planets in search of Alpha Centauri. The Robinsons are never short of food or hair products, and, whereas the family is gratingly sane, they are offset by Dr Zachary Smith, who is waspish and wicked and full of childish snips and snaps – each rapier rejoinder accompanied by arched brow and *Ah! Wilderness* eyes slung to the gallery. It is to the fourth wall (audience or camera) that actor Jonathan Harris plays, each startled reaction given directly to the unseen viewer. I would much rather be Major Don West (Mark Goddard), who is of track and field physical, but who is a juvenile groundling compared to the Elizabethan riches of Dr Smith, who, in his maggoty bitterness, provides all of the fun, and whose command illuminates the very smallest of actions. Bio-mechanical Major West hardly ever speaks, whereas Dr Smith's mouth won't close under any circumstances, and there he is – forever downstage and close to the camera, his joys and sorrows child-like (that is, undeveloped) and full of pantomime pranks; part circus, part *Peer Gynt*, and a thigh-slap away from *Annie Get Your Gun*. I cannot miss *Lost in Space*, where the secrets of masculinity are meted out in the ping-pong clash between Dr Smith and Major West; Mrs Danvers facing a wide receiver's grit in two worlds that can never meet. The masculine man hates the feminine man because soft is the enemy of hard. Dr Smith's voice is the caustic cattiness of a tetchy dowager rising in pitch as each line ends, hands a-flutter with *away with you, my child* intolerance. Major West, on the other hand, will kick to kill. My notepad resting on my lap takes the scribbles of unspoken truth: effeminate men are very witty, whereas macho men are duller than death. The divide bristles – West permanently at a Denver Bronco's training session, and Smith playing with full nobility up and out to the studio lights – a *Twelfth Night* jester allowed his moment. At 30, the prematurely grey Richard Bradford is the star of *Man In a Suitcase*, a discredited CIA agent now loitering about London waiting for the phone to ring (usually from a youngish blonde female whose father, The Major, is under shocking duress). As McGill, Richard Bradford mumbles his lines, is never witty, and gets by purely on the red-blooded toughness of his Tyler, Texas door-ramming physique, which provides all answers and never once fails him. Bradford is a figure of glamor, although his girlfriends are infrequent or short-term. He rests his cigarette down by placing it upright like a pencil, never slanted into an ashtray, and his charging physicality renders sparkling wordplay unnecessary. He lives alone, unexcited, disinterested, world-weary and ungiving, yet it is this dry-as-dust approach that makes him fascinating. Men, you see, are either one thing or another, but never both, and the world loves a man who can fight. Suddenly, *Department S* comes close to the unthinkable; a witty Sebastian Melmoth who is also swift to deploy expert judo at the drop of a Ming vase. Peter Wyngarde plays Jason King with impeccable Old Vic control, and dazzling Shaftesbury Avenue command. King is Knightsbridge to McGill's Notting Hill, even though Peter Wyngarde had been born in Marseilles. Although King's dapperness is a host of Burlington Arcade giveaways and Aix-en-Provence getaways, his Interpol partner Joel Fabiani (playing Stewart Sullivan) would thrash you in a game of squash – or squash you in a game of thrash. King is Beerbohm Tree smoking Sobranie, because Wyngarde is legitimate theater whom television is lucky to have, and whose techniques and intentions are infallibly precise (although the exact style of his delivery

is by no means conventional). Wyngarde might occasionally rush into a following line without punctuated pause
(enjambement?), but whatever he attempts by way of
delivery is so meticulous that he leads the way as the governing center of *Department S.*

Fabiani was the flipside of Wyngarde's coin, being ex-US
Navy, wiry Californian tough, and married to a woman.
Completing the TV team is Annabelle Hurst (played by
Rosemary Nichols), a most correct and well-educated
computer-whiz British bird of polite wit; a tea-room and
commando-trained lacrosse champ whose sexuality is only
a detail. Of course, such women did not exist then, or now.
In the wings, the child-like inquisitor does his best to
understand whatever unravels before him on the screen
(because the screen is certainly bigger than I am), with
Sullivan as the true human ideal, yet the talent to amuse is
Jason King's – utilizing chopsticks with eye-crossing speed
and reading from Italian menus with an expert's sigh. *'Mine's
the car with the Swiss number plates,'* he instructs hoteliers, and
Europe is his casino. This charmless child is ready for bed,
constructing a melting-plot wherein the broth blends
Sullivan and King with an added dash of *77 Sunset Strip*, and
the final creation might very well be Mary Shelley's.

> I don't care what the price is
> I'll make the sacrifices
> I'll bear the sorrow
> Just let it be me.

By the grace of God I am a part of the local gang whose
spearhead and protectionist is Lillian, who is all funfair

worldliness at 16. Lillian organizes international excursions for a gaggle of kids to faraway, far-flung ranges such as Navigation Road or Jackson's Boat. For a small weekly sub Lillian arranges everything, and the clued-up boys and girls of Stretford follow her in a trance, for Lillian could be as hard as nails – Susannah York's Childie, but with grisly grit, cropped-off mousey hair, suede jacket and tight jeans. Touch her and you might not get your hand back. Yet Lillian is all heart and love, but fearless in the face of foe. Gangs are fashions passion in ragamuffin 1971, and some out-of-towners invade our untouchable Longford Park patch. Lillian warns a buckish bully that she can finish him off without actually touching him. Laughing at her, he opens his wastrel mouth wide, and with expert aim Lillian unleashes a wad of phlegm that scores an impressive bulls-eye in the back of his throat. Shaken and repulsed, he and his teen firebrands turn tail into the Chorlton mist. Firmly, I am under Lillian's wing, and she loves the kids that make up the gang. Thin and lively, she will take a stand against any boy bigger or older, and never once would she hesitate. The one spoiler is Leslie Messenger, who is teeth-grindingly jealous of the attention given to me by the girls, and one afternoon he springs upon me, as Sunday's dull-ness swarms the park with dingy, dreary, unkillable families. For what will be the second time, I floor Leslie, he all bluff and little-man threats, yet soft to the touch in the heel of the hammerlock. I do not know where my uppercuts come from, but there they are, an orbit of finishing blows rising from somewhere deep within, overtaking the final push that panics the body into do-or-die strength. It is a vigorous high, but it is not my sphere, and nor do I want it.

1971 brings a partial eclipse at 9:40 AM, plunging the skies of Britain into 69 per cent blackness; Nannie drops to her knees and prays for salvation at what she is certain is the end of the world. Alas, it is not.

No rampantly challenging mind could overlook the lost cultures as mapped out in British film, wherein the restricted horizons of the expendable working-class thrillingly show us how British life got to where it is now – in your private modern cuckoo-land. A gas-lit hallway in a tired lodging house and I am pulled in, with Mum forever fussing about the table setting tea. Distorted by nostalgia, we see in the family and in the local community everything an honest soul might need in order to live out their time on the human gridline, and we see the obvious punishments for anyone who would insist upon more than their lot. In my favorite films of the 1940s, 1950s and 1960s, the working class are usually portrayed as children enacting pointless working-class crimes. We always see the police as adults, representing a conscience for the daft scrubbers in pubs and dance halls – who are not rich, and therefore cannot behave themselves. Decent folk always allow themselves to be controlled by the police, because the police are never known to be either devious or wrong. The laboring-class boys of grey flannel are instinctive in their behavior because they are, in fact, in possession of nothing at all other than instinct; science and diplomacy are tools unused. The shadowy social films of lost Sunday television are *Oliver Twist* (1948) (in which career-criminal Bill Sikes says *'There's light enough for what I 'ave to do!'*), *London Belongs to Me* (1948), *The Blue Lamp* (1950), *I Believe in You* (1952) and *Sapphire* (1959). In *The Painted Smile* (1962), the statuesque womanhood of comely Liz Fraser attempts to frame an uncomplicated Tony Wickert for the murder of her boyfriend in the recurring British theme of happiness not to be found. In all working-class films of the 1960s, life's winner is the boy with the gleam in his eye – roughs of self-recognition and blessed profiles. They will not accept conservative limits, and their selfish motivations or their crude nerve are both justified by the fact that they give nothing but look everything. By contrast, a Shakespearian saint with a disjointed face is never thought interesting enough for film. In *Two Left Feet* (1963) there is the unusual glimpse of hard and pretty Michael Craze rutting lustily for his pal David Hemmings.

Calling on friends, their back doors swing open with a swoosh of smells. The tangs of the unfamiliar are the malodorous hallmarks of the humans within – no scented candles yet, although the rarity of air fresheners can be found somewhere in the newly landed supermarkets of Maypole, Seymour Meade or the Co-op.

Putrid smells reduce me to a pitiful pile, and none are more vomitarian than school dinners. All foods of miasmic fragrance disturb me, and the mere hint of garlic induces the shakes, as fish cooked or uncooked causes gut-wrenching panic. This boy of 1971 has an abnormally limited palate – a working-class host of relentless toast, and the inability to expand beyond the spartan. Somewhere, Tin Tin sing *Toast and marmalade for tea* – which certainly suits me. I remain bedevilled by a dangerously sparse intake of food until my late thirties, when pasta and pizza throw the line. In place of food, my senses existentially turn to old high walls of red brick, and I lie awake at night weighing the fascination. There will never be an end or a conclusion to this dazed attraction, and even now, decades on, I cannot find any written acknowledgement of the trance such things pull me into. Whatever detains the eye is understood by no one, least of all me. My eleventh year brings my becloaked stage debut at the local community center. In the play *On Dartmoor* I am Ulrick, a sulky child with a stupid voice. Unseen, I persistently shout down from an imaginary bedroom. The audience laugh, but my father does not. *'You were very embarrassing,'* he tells me, as I appear all-smiles, and my air-balloon collides. Two years on, at Stretford Stadium I represent the school in the 400 meters dash (of sorts), legs muddied, face wet with rain, I clamber in at fourth place. My father is standing by the finishing-line. As I approach him he says, *'You didn't win,'* and he looks away, and life decomposes in a bucket. Perhaps I *didn't* win but it didn't help anyone to point it out.

Barry Ryan sings *Eloise* and rises to number 3 with a song that is five-and-a-half-minutes long – an eternity in radio space. It is an overly dramatic epic of clash and plea, a 48-piece orchestra wrapped in cliff-bound sirens, racing to an *out-of-my-mind* screaming vocal. It is an unusual disc, and Barry Ryan is from Leeds, the adopted city of Alan Clarke and Billy Bremner. None of the family had passed the 11-Plus exam, and henceforth cannot be saved, our futures doomed by an undotted i. We transmute from the gothic horror of St Wilfrid's to the next phase in a familiar theme, and unto an even darker place go. If, like Oliver Twist, I had known, I would have screamed all the more louder, and not even *Something here in my heart* by the Paper Dolls could save me now.

St Mary's Secondary Modern School on Renton Road in Stretford may indeed be secondary, but it is not modern. An unattractive slim slab of glass, St Mary's is life's second bolt of frightening lightning, and it hits the target with five confined years that will answer no purpose – a school of notoriously mean disciplinarians whom one hopefully survives despite everything. Now comes the hour to choose between being acceptable to others or being acceptable to one's own self, for we must kill our true selves off in order to survive. I had no idea that life could get worse, or that schoolteachers could be more contemptuous than those of wilting St Wilfrid's, but the snarling stupidity at St Mary's is deathless, and its wearisome echo of negativity exhausts me to a permanent state of circumstantial sadness. Vincent Morgan is the Headmaster whose voice is a sigh, whose carriage is militantly empirical, and although a spectacle of suffering, he is mysteriously tuned in to God. Well past middle-age, he is rigorous in grey suit and gleaming black shoes, the sag of cruelty in his face a clue to the torrential capacity for violence. Sealed up like an envelope, he is unable to act with kindness or humanity, for he has neither, and there is evidently nothing to humanize him. For five years I witness the monumental loneliness of Vincent Morgan as he busies himself day after day with the beatings of small boys. And it goes on, and on, and on, and on – leading nowhere, achieving nothing. By 9:40 each morning, we shall all have witnessed several humiliating beatings at St Mary's, and this is how we begin our day of knowledge. As Vincent Morgan concludes his morning prayer in assembly – in which he gives thanks – he will then point to up to twelve boys seemingly at random, who must step aside and prepare to be lashed, such being the heart of a man of Christian forgiveness. In its motive and conclusion, it is pathetic. Yet it never subsides. Inevitably, I am sooner or later marked out as one of the turkey twelve, drawn to Vincent Morgan's attention for reasons that he shall never be called upon to explain. Standing in line, my rage is for the smaller boys alongside me who, after one of six swinging whacks with a thick leather strap, have trouble standing, and whose small hands crack under the powerful military might of Morgan's excited slam. Undersized and freshly plucked from junior school, these boys are still children and are no match for the satanic attack launched by this heaving and burning artilleryman. What could it possibly all be for? Only once do I ever see a boy square up to Vincent Morgan with the measured advice that he should '*Fuck off*', and it is that moment once again when the gunshot is so unexpected that it baffles the bully. My only possession is a brave front, since I have never known how to fight, and even as Vincent Morgan whacks and whacks and swings that leather belt with the full and mighty force of his entire body, something in his face tells me that he alone pays for all of this misery. Marooned, Vincent Morgan walks to and from school every single day by himself, an umbrella neatly propped on an arm that crosses the front of his body with marksman preparation. He has no friendship with the other teachers, and is only ever visible as the one of perpetual flogging. The fruitlessness of such overactive repulsion, in modern times, would of course suggest the starkest sexual overtures ... for what else? What *job* did he think he was doing? And ... for whom? And if there is no reason to show interest in these boys for any other cause (as there clearly isn't), then why be so concerned about administering their punishment? Why isn't their punishment ignored along with their hopes and dreams?

The tough and tearless boy who had advised Vincent Morgan to *'fuck off'* was Michael Foley, and as star witness I slung my glass into the sea. At last, an individual! Handsomely G.I.-faced Foley is the only boy of wit and glamor in the entire school, and luckily for me he is in my class and easy to befriend. He cannot, though, turn zest and spark to anything at all other than girls' knickers, and a friend for life fades in time. He works on the bread vans each Saturday morning, and entices me to give it a go, rising as I must at 6 AM to be poetically active by 6:30 – an experience so frightening as to not be tackled twice. In my short conversations with Vincent Morgan I am struck by his game of persuasion, trying to convince me that whatever I say to him by way of reply has no value. I am dented by his technique of always making the cross-examined feel 'less', as I am also pierced by his bullying trick of speaking only in intimidating questions: *'and what's all this, then?'*, *'and who told you that you could do that?'*, *'and who do you think you are, exactly?'* – and irrespective of however you explained yourself he would always come back with a question-reply so that he maintains ground as the inquisitor, keeping you answerable, yet failing to account for your actions. The words are a trick to make the victim passive. Without question, the boys lined up before Vincent Morgan, ready to be corrected by his floggings, were England's dregs, and they could only be taught failure *by* failures, illumination by violence.

Whether at St Mary's or St Wilfrid's, I am spared the indignity of ever staying for school dinners, although I cannot escape the daily waft of dead pig and foul fish sandblasting both buildings and clinging to the senses for a lifetime. Once the dinner vans arrive, the school corridors are polluted by floating venomous toxins, unbearable to inhale so surely deadly to consume, and by late afternoon the leftovers will splodge and stink and spill and surge from huge bins awaiting collection. We are decades away from food awareness or any consideration of animal compassion, and stories circulate throughout St Mary's of small stones in mashed potatoes and of mince that moves. Yet it is uncivilized to complain, and a Mr Bumble always hovers somewhere, and although you pay for your dinner you are not invited to shape the menu. The condition of England at the time was such that supported the predicament of taking whatever is dished out, whether this be food or violence. In order for there to be winners there needed to be losers, and the winners were already seated at fully heated Stretford Grammar. Somebody, it had been ordained, must be available to bang nails into wood for a living, and here we were.

By their unlucky presence, the teachers surely felt a similar way about themselves. Not for them some first-class establishment where laughter and success intermingled – they, too, have been thought to be not much cop, their dreams undone by the emphatic grainy-blackness of St Mary's, unexpurgated and without serenade. Injuries of time marked the school as tired and tatty, yet trying to be technical. Exactly why I am here, and what it is I am meant to do, is beyond me. Each day is an array of invectives, thrown at the boys who are united in their understanding that they have been dumped, and are being dumped upon. Each day is Kafka-esque in its nightmare, and the school offers nothing at all except a lifelong awareness of hate as a general truth. Encouragement is not on any curriculum, its place filled by the shit-without-wit repartee of such as Mr Kijowski, physical education instructor ostensibly, yet whose constant stream of hate suggests that if he is not frightening someone then he is nothing. Young and un-married, he is obsessed with homosexuality – that it should be traced and uncovered, named and shamed. This tirade goes on and on for more years than could be thought pos-sible, and I am not surprised that I am regularly the butt of his bombast, and yet the most obvious homosexual behavior reveals itself in Mr Kijowski himself, as each PE lesson closes and the obligatory communal showering is enforced. This is always the time when Mr Kijowski will conduct any sub-plot to demand that all showering boys *'freeze'* and remain still until a fantasized misdemeanor of some kind is admitted to, with the familiar threat that *'No boy will move until the culprit owns up,'* as Mr Kijowski pushes his way through this cramped room of naked boys. Mr Sweeney is also a physical education teacher, and un-married, but is less obsessively homosexualist, although it is commonly noted how he stands and stares and stands and stares at showering boys when neither standing nor staring is necessary. One day during five-a-side, I flip for-wards and crash down on my right hand. This stirs a blip of compassion from Mr Sweeney, who then takes me into his private office, whereupon he proceeds to massage my wrist with anti-inflammatory cream. At 14, I understand the meaning of the unnecessarily slow and sensual strokes, with eyes fixed to mine, and I look away, and the moment passes. Shortly thereafter, drying myself off after a shower, Mr Sweeney leans into my mid-region to ask, *'What's that scar down your stomach, Steven?'* – but his eyes are lower, and these are the moments that cause you to check certain words in dictionaries, and for the first time you are forced to consider yourself to be the prize, or the quarry.

Air from 1947 hangs in the school stockrooms where outmoded textbooks stockpile against unwanted plaques anointing proud achievements of boys long-since gone, like a roll-call of the war dead. The slowness of days drills the brain, especially around 2:30 in the afternoon, when time never seems to move, and the 3:40 bell hangs lifelessly until the last drop of nausea has been wrung from the brow. Chalk and stale sweat catch whatever air escapes into these barren vaults, and a yellowing world map is all that the eye can rest upon, with not one continent available to you or meant for you. It is impossible to imagine a time when we shall feel free of all of this dissonance, and it is impossible to meet the situation halfway. Sadly, it is also impossible to simply just get on with it. My eyes lock permanently on the view from the windows, as I long to the point of tears to be released from this prison maze, or this maze prison, where I am ridiculed simply for just turning up. Mr Pink is reading aloud a story entitled *Boris the Wig-maker.* He stops suddenly and burns in my direction as my eyes watch the black rain banging against feeble windows.

'Steven, who exactly was Boris?'

'I'm sorry, I'm not interested,' I quickly reply, but very softly.

'Right!! Stand up!!' Warhorse Mr Pink charges to a

cupboard to grapple for his treasured leather strap, and I am ordered to stand and take four whacks of the belt across my hands. I am then ordered to sit down, and, his turbulent rush fed, he continues to read to the class. I return my gaze to the rain. It is all so utterly stupid. I am at this point struck by the understanding that this freakish use of the leather strap is the answer for all teachers who find themselves in a situation that they simply cannot deal with, or answer. It is *their* weakness, not ours. Simply because I quite honestly admitted to having no interest in *Boris the Wig-maker*, how does a violent charge with a leather strap provide an answer?

Occasionally we suffer the disdainful presence of a local priest, young and patronizing, with a name never to be recalled. Oddly, he seems to fix his curiosity upon me, possibly because I sit aloof, possibly because I do not contribute to polite laughter, possibly because of the newly tended weave in my hair.

'And what do YOU like in life?' he asks me, ready to play the patronizing game at my expense in order to raise a giggle from the rest of the class, thus rendering him popular for a few perverse minutes.

'Mott the Hoople,' I answer truthfully.

'Oh, I see,' he smirks, greater and grander than us all, *'most boys like girls – he likes Mott the Hoople.'*

The Catholic priest looks to the rest of the class having given them their cue for courteous laughter. But no laughter comes, and the priest looks back at me with his face of hate – as if to warn me that there will come another time when he shall score.

The topsy-turvydom of 1972 had brought an explosion of music and art and newness into my life and I was now in full self-development mode and desperate to be free of censure. There was no one with whom to discuss these understandings, and certainly any interest in art and self-expression through music was something to keep hidden throughout the cracked corridors of St Mary's. I had bought the *Starman* single by David Bowie, which had climbed to number 42 in the chart, and I catch this epoch of self-realization for the first time on television as the exotic and shapely Ayshea Brough celebrates newly distributed color television with her show *Lift Off with Ayshea*. As David Bowie appears, the child dies. The vision is profound – a sanity heralding the coming of consciousness from someone who – at last! – transcends our gloomy coal-fire existence. David Bowie is detached from everything, yet open to everything; stripped of the notion that both art and life are impossible. He is quite real, impossibly glamorous, fearless, and quite British. How could this possibly be?

'*STOP biting your finger-nails,*' Mr Pink shouts at Michael Foley.

'*I can't. It's a habit,*' explains Michael.

'*RIGHT!!*' shouts Mr Pink, who then grabs his leather belt and the ritualized violent whacks across Michael's hands ensue. Again, it is pathetic to witness, and pathetic to endure.

An excitingly arch London magazine called *Film and Filming* has versed me in the Warholian, with all of its guiding principles of self-determination and autonomy. I cried for poetic language and I cried out to find those who were unafraid, those free agents, unbigoted and unshackled. I didn't want to live unseen, camouflaged within the crowd.

I knew then that life could only ever be changed for the better because somebody somewhere had taken a risk — often with their own life. As an educational establishment, St Mary's contained only the traditional values of negativity, and there would not be a single hour spent within its walls when I could feel either relaxed or untrammeled. It simply wasn't allowed. In their God-fearing, chanting morality, the teachers of St Mary's only managed to convey nihilism and limericks. Look for one boy who left the place feeling spiritual and complete. You will never find him. My face had by now taken on the demeanor of continual deep regret, which only music could soothe. The new poets were not by the Lakes, but suspending disbelief in recording studios where words and sound mix the literal with the perceptual and the conceptual. In 1971 I had watched helplessly as Buffy Sainte-Marie made her debut on *Top of the Pops* singing her own composition *Soldier blue*; a mannish white working shirt, and what were surely blue jeans, dogged determination in her brownish face, and the truth of it all in her eyes.

> Oh soldier blue, soldier blue,
> Can't you see that there's another way to love her?

The 'her' is the land, and 'the other way' is minus bombs and military artillery. Or so I assumed. Serious artists rarely make the stages of *Top of the Pops* because the show is essentially light entertainment, yet this song of great depth has risen to number 7, and, light or not, the BBC are duty-bound as a public service to air any song elected by the public. In the market-driven mush of British pop, there is no continual place for Buffy Sainte-Marie with her carrion calls of loss and injustice. But there she is, and here am I, and the secret of song unravels. I discover *Moratorium* on the flipside of *Soldier blue*, and this song has a fighting vocal over a lengthy stream of words that include the line '*Fuck the war – bring our brothers home*', and I weigh my new love against the Willesden weediness of Greyhound, whose singer's voice is ready to crack and fold at any second. Trojan Records had also presented the Pioneers with *Let your yeah be yeah*, attempting to match the impassable scatology of *Double barrel* by Dave and Ansell Collins, or the freeing stringed swoop of *Young, gifted and black* by Bob and Marcia. It seemed to me that it was only within British pop music that almost anything could happen. Every other mode of expression seemed fixed and predictable and slow. Sportsmen used the same seven words in every interview, and were largely incapable of surprise (Cassius Clay and George Best the eternal exceptions). The music of 1971 had given the lost strangeness of *I will return* by Springwater, the eco-protest of *Don't let it die* by Hurricane Smith, and the liberating sadness of General Johnson's voice on a wild roll of Chairmen of the Board singles. From nowhere comes the California cobra chords of *Run run run* by Jo Jo Gunne and *Heaven must have sent you* by the Elgins – wide variables on an open pitch, all adapting to different listeners – the well and the ill. All of this starts me, and I cannot stop. If I can barely speak (which is true), then I shall surely sing.

'*If you MUST sing every night, would you please sing something that we know?*' says elderly Mr Coleman from next door, which was of course a polite way of telling me to shut up, as each night I sang myself to sleep. T. Rex had raged into perfection with their trio of *Jeepster* (number 2 for six weeks!), *Telegram Sam* (number 1) and *Metal guru* (number 1), an extraordinary rush of success magnifying the importance of Marc Bolan as a rattling sea change. Wearing makeup and an extreme mantle of pride, Bolan didn't seem to have any life other than song. He is struggling to break in America, but it doesn't work in a country whose fiercely conservative patterns cannot allow a small and effeminate man to attempt to direct and influence their unknotted Ivy League WASPS. Marc Bolan's lyrics are steeped in the quietly insane world of the gothic English novel, and are too deeply eccentric to survive any explanation. On earlier records, Bolan sounds as if singing in Olde English – incomprehensible to the modern ear. Yes, but the Bible speaks of '*a whole earth of one language*', and this is something that only pop singers can manage. Certainly, politicians cannot.

T. Rex are my first concert and my dad and sister drop me off at daunting Belle Vue on June 16th 1972, watching me waddle away alone in my purple satin jacket – a sight ripe for psychiatric scrutiny. I am now determined, and newly emerged from *Groovin' with Mr Bloe* by Mr Bloe. England was already set to change trains from Marc Bolan to David Bowie, whose *Starman* single had shaken everyone with its *somewhere-over-the-rainbow* chorus and Blue Mink's *Melting pot* bridge. Full-page advertising for David Bowie's new Top Rank tour causes me to laugh excitedly as I see the now famous shot of spike-thin Bowie half-propped on a high stool, wearing tight white satin pants tucked into plastic boxer-boots, one hand on hip, the other hand pointing the way to somewhere, quite fanatically homo-sexual. The face is damned-soul-as-savior-of-society, preacher and reformer, now free of his own unhappy child-hood and willing to help you through yours should Black Sabbath and Deep Purple prove insufficient. I crawl from the cultureless world to Stretford Hardrock in September 1972, where David Bowie is showcasing the venue. At mid-day he emerges from a black Mercedes, every inch the eighth dimension, teetering on high heels, with all the wis-dom of our ancestors. Smiling keenly, he accepts the note of a dull schoolboy whose overblown soul is more ablaze than the school blazer he wears, and thus I touch the hand of this inexplicably liberating reformer; he, a Wildean visionary about to re-mold England, and I, a spectacle of suffering in a blue school uniform. Two months later I am at the same venue for Roxy Music, who are still promoting their first LP but who are exhibiting the sleeve of their second LP in the foyer – an advanced flash for those who can't wait. I creep into the soundcheck (quite easily, since the obscurity of the band does not necessitate any form of security), and I speak to saxophonist Andrew Mackay as he plays a pinball machine in the Hardrock lobby. It is a netherworld encounter for Mackay, but a great joy for the pesky boy. There is new meaning to everything as Roxy Music inexplicably jump to number 4 with their first single, *Virginia plain*, a pursed-mouth whirl of low noise and words used for sound value only. There is no chorus and nothing is repeated. The song is madcap in construction, and singer Bryan Ferry is an honored northern guest – escapist but shy, a slither of glamor rippling like the sea. Roxy Music are resolutely odd, and Agatha Christie queer; the smile of

Ferry is Hiroshima mean, as he shuffles crab-style from stage right to stage left ... like someone who's had his food dish removed. It's a voice of cold metal, just barely skin deep. I eagerly catch his first Radio One interview wherein he falls asleep at the drone of his own replies. Eno, on the other hand, uses words that no one else can spell and is wrapped in so much sexual allure that *Top of the Pops* cameras avoid him for fear of frightening the frighteningly drab majority. The technical detachment of Roxy Music is, briefly and possibly accidentally, a radical experience, one that they swiftly dispense with once they establish a large audience. But before they lose their strangeness they are magnificent, and the drabness of true artifice comes alive. Also billed for this night at the Hardrock are the New York Dolls, who have yet to make a record, but about whom the press had already written so much. Bumped up against the front of the stage, I, and others, sigh heavily as it is announced that the New York Dolls will not appear due to the sudden death of their drummer three days earlier in London. In these limping, impeded days of 1972 there is no way that such news could reach our social quarter, since our houses and our lives are shut down from instant communications.

In this year I also see Mott the Hoople and Lou Reed live, and my senses never return. Lou Reed is unimpressed by applause, and lives a life detached from custom. His stare is cold and his romanticism is brutal. His songs are half-sung melodies of menace. He might drop dead any second, and is therefore the real thing. Examined ravenously like a museum exhibit, Lou Reed is evidently spiked to excess, and strangely loveable. This feared raggle-clatter of pop species is changing everything. The womanly David Bowie is attacked by the *Daily Mirror* as being 'a disgrace' – although *how* he is a disgrace, or *why*, is not explained. Bowie's extraordinary effect of menace upon British culture is largely forgotten now, but I watched it break like a thundercloud in 1972, and its presence was as volcanic as that which later would be termed Punk. An even darker force controlled the personalities of the New York Dolls, who are younger than Bowie and who are more-or-less transgender in appearance. *Melody Maker* announces them as 'the world's first homosexual rock band', which, of course, is what they are not. On face value, the Dolls are menacing rent boys who are forcing the world to deal with them. Their arms drape lovingly around one another in photographs at a time when young men are assumed to want to look like Bobby Moore, Jimmy Greaves or Terry Venables. *Disc* magazine gives a warning on its front page: *Lock up your sons, it's the New York Dolls!*, as singer David Johansen lurches forwards in color. The suggestion that your sons rather than your daughters might need to be protected from a male rock band had never previously been considered. The cautionary headline from *Record Mirror* is ARRIVAL OF THE DOLLY BOYS, and David Johansen advises the same magazine: *'We're not butch'* – an astonishing confession in rock's macho Zeppelin age.

TACKY, TACKY, TACKY shouts another Dolls headline, and in 1973 the Dolls' first 45, *Jet boy*, and their first studio album are very heavily promoted in all of the British music papers. The Dolls meet with all of the obvious condemnations, for this is still an era of darkness and drowned dreams. The New York Dolls were chaotic because they

An impressive display of exotic sanity, the New York Dolls, 1973,
out of the order of nature, a secret told to me alone

were themselves; their own creation, and not connected to the glam-rock theatrical puns of Slade's twinkie-blinks or the Sweet's *Charley's Aunt* winks. Malodorously 24-carat, the Dolls are legless realism – wired and rigged honest trash scraped up off New York's back alleys, banished from the communities of the living. The flesh awakens with *Jet boy*, premiered one lunchtime on the *Johnnie Walker Show* on Radio One. What seems like promotion is actually a May-day bleep.

The Spanish arm of their record label are so offended by the Dolls' appearance that they refuse to show any photographs of the band on their debut LP, and instead release it minus any shots of the most visual and striking band of the modern age. With relief, I catch the Dolls on their now-famous *Old Grey Whistle Test* television appearance, and whereas both of my parents watch unimpressed, pride and joy electrify my body as the revenge motif dates every other modern pop artist in an instant. Snarl matches visual art and the Dolls were mine. I heard and saw a high-wire act of tough noise and fantastic pop lyrics, and I heard an invitation to anyone man enough to challenge them. Offhand and uncivil, the Dolls were ready to run the game, featuring in a *Circus* magazine article under the title *New York Dolls and what's it to ya?* In comparison, everyone else suddenly seemed like a travelling salesman. The Dolls were a social unit, great fun, grave fun, salty and completely off the deep end. The opposite to polite and antiseptic, there wasn't actually any visible line to avoid stepping over, and *'We have new drags for England that will blow the mind off the Queen herself,'* laughed David Johansen, adding, *'Oh we love all those queens … everybody's alright by us.'* Fast-forward forty years and such comments might not seem so harum-scarum, but this was 1973 – with the Carpenters on top of the world looking down on creation, and with Donny Osmond hanging on as the pickle puss face of America. How could people like the New York Dolls *even exist?* And as a musical unit! And where exactly did this leave Dr Hook and the Medicine Show? The morning after the *Whistle Test*, I present 50 pence at Rumbelows in Stretford Precinct and I ask for the New York Dolls single.

'*See,*' said one fat assistant to another, '*I told you someone would buy it.*'

At last I am someone! The 45 purchased has the middle section of the song cut out and fades quickly, in an arrangement I have never since discovered on any pressing of this record. The confusion with the Dolls is that their scum-sucker rough-trade drag contrasted with the truth of their wise-guy personalities. The Dolls were actually the toughest band on earth, and their appearance proved it. Unfolding before us, they raised the game one hundredfold so that even Alice Cooper – supremely devilish on his *Billion Dollar Babies* coup de maître – was suddenly a broad on Broadway to the Dolls' own Bellevue Hospital. Pomp-rock had degraded everything and left audiences immobilized and horizontal in trench coats and woolly sweaters. The Dolls were the slum of all failures, had nothing to lose, and could scarcely differentiate between night and day. For the Dolls, it could never be dark enough. Their raw existence vibrated with expectations of disaster, yet their organs are not tormented. Mockery and practical defeat may very well be their reality, and musical success doesn't even appear to be their aim. On an infinitesimal scale, Dolls songs are about life happening against us – never with or for us – and as agents of their own troubles they relate everything to themselves. Their eyes are indifferent. They have left the order of this world. Jerry Nolan might even kill you. Because they feel excluded they have no reason to account for their own actions. *Trash* scorches the skin. Flayed alive, the Dolls may look beautiful, but they are withering fast, and around them we see Johnny Carson, Paul Newman, Cassius Clay, Robert Redford, David Cassidy, as males within the paragraphs of law. The Dolls endure the consequences of how they look, afflicted by existence yet not responsible. David Johansen laughs, but is irritated by everything and anything, since life clearly signifies nothing, yet he can always save the day with an eloquent phrase. The detachment of Johnny Thunders and Sylvain Sylvain is open to nothing, and you mustn't ask more of Arthur Kane than just being alive. *Well.* The Dolls are the last frontier of task and adventure for the discontented mind. The objective is only in being. Their excess of drugs and alcohol increased the fire and sword of their swagger – now is the golden hour, and tomorrow could be too late. *Vietnamese baby* may very well be a song of universal meaninglessness, but the Dolls have no cause to disguise their madness, and isn't sex the one and only reason why all of us are actually alive? Appearance is a new debate in rock music, and the counter-culture of the New York Dolls is an infinite landscape. But who can cope with such a landscape having been kenneled for so long? The uniform of bad denim still shrouds most of the million-sellers on the US chart, but bassist Arthur Kane, with his hand resting on guitarist Sylvain Sylvain's knee, ventures further than the universe allowed. This did not happen with the Eagles. Squinting, the Dolls were in endless puberty, deeply close to one another, as thick as thieves, a private gang of deep-seated buddies whose companionship and familiarity revealed a mutual affection that rendered them loveable in a way that Wings or the Moody Blues just weren't. The word 'doll' had only ever previously been tagged to a female – of beauty queen or Venus nectar. The New Oxford helps with *'doll: attractive woman, beautiful woman'*, which is possibly why we have no recollection of James Cagney ever turning to George Raft with *'Say, you're quite a doll,'* (not on camera, at any rate). Their chosen name, the New York Dolls, was as provocative and inflamed as being called the New York Fags; and really, this is precisely how the Dolls were initially deciphered, anyway. Knowing what we now know – that the Dolls chased the bearded clam at every opportunity – simply triples their social effect. And this is how history is made.

Jerry Nolan on the front of the Dolls debut album is the first woman I ever fall in love with; the hussy-slut positioning of the legs is playmate call-girl, and the pink drum kit just might be a rock 'n roll first. When had drummers ever looked this way and played so hard? You have witnessed a lunar-landing even before you start to listen, and within the courtesan cover you discover a fit of throttling lunacy from a band that fear no foe or woe. The Velvet Underground had been born weary, had found hell within themselves, and they couldn't care less if they made you suffer, because their message was simple: you will never have anything. The Dolls were laughing all the way to a speedy grave. That they were even alive at all, and had managed to endure on a planet that even I had felt certain was as flat-tire as fuck, was a shock to anyone having been raised, as I was, on smiling nice-boy singers. How had the Dolls found each other? Searches for 'like-minded musicians' seemed, to me, to be so unfeasible as to be hardly worth attempting. Pugs who played musical instruments in 1973 were either older than dirt, or moth-eaten techies. In the swell-elegant world of success it was always the case that most bands of dapper style nonetheless also contained members whose natural ugliness let the team down. The New York Dolls were the first band who equaled each other in demeanor and effect; in essence, the most perfect-looking pop group – minus that hesitant component who wasn't quite sure of his connection to the others.

High-toned, I carry the Dolls LP sleeve into school, where I attempt to reproduce its front cover in blotchy Manchester Education Committee goo-paint as an art presentation. Art teacher Miss Power (for teachers, *Miss* told us that she was not legally bound to a man, *Mrs* told us that she *was* legally bound to a man, whilst *Mr* slyly protected the secret) was so highly strung that she frequently raced from the classroom in tears of rage at someone not present. On this particular day, spotting the New York Dolls sleeve resting on my desk in that's-my-boy sniffiness, Miss Power grabbed the LP sleeve and held it aloft for the entire class to examine:

'LOOK AT THIS!' she demanded of everyone, *'LOOK AT THIS!'* and everyone looked at this. *'THIS is sickness. These are MEN making themselves sexual for OTHER MEN.'*

And on she went, terribly upset. She appealed to the class for support, but none came, and although I expected a fierce larruping for abstaining from dullness, none came, and Miss Power had merely outed me as a prostitute; a midnight cowboy in flannel-grey. I felt quite pleased that something might disconnect me from the vacant clam-brains seated around me, but it wasn't Miss Power's fault that she did not know that the Dolls' appearance had girls – not boys – flocking to mingle with them, and that the Dolls gratefully obliged in a modern world uncharted by Miss Power, who was nonetheless certain that her own life had a moral superiority that the New York Dolls ought to be wise enough to follow. But the world within (and without) St Mary's was not yet ready, and even when the Dolls' *Frankenstein* was bravely spun on the school's *nearer-my-God-to-thee-am-I* record player by Miss Judge for an English language dissection (for I was not the type to give up until blood spurted out – my own, if necessary), none of the listening lads of 1973 had anything to say by way of autopsy until Andrew Lempiki spoke up quite brilliantly with:

'I thought they were birds.'

Unfathomably, I had several cupcake grapples in this year of 1973, with no experience worth repeating, yet somehow having dropped myself further into each bungee jump than I thought allowable. Plunge or no plunge, girls remained mysteriously attracted to me, and I had no idea why, since although each fumbling foray hit the target, nothing electrifying took place, and I turned a thousand corners without caring. Plainly I was not interested, being chosen but not chooser. In King's Lane a sporty Welsh girl lands me such a powerful clenched-fist blow that I fall to the ground deafened.

'*What was THAT for?*' I said, sightless with soreness. '*Because I like you and you won't look at me,*' she said — as if what she had done might improve the situation. It didn't. Far more exciting were the array of stylish racing bikes that my father would bring home (from the Stylish Racing Bike Sanctuary, no doubt; we were wise *not* to ask). The bikes were often too large for me, but all the better to risk the sharp corners and mud-splattered daredevil routes of Turn Moss. Something within me loved the manic race through the darkened warrens of Longford Park, battered by rain, drenched but alive, taking iceberg corners too quickly, rising aloft from the seat down wing-and-prayer slopes. Night after night like an unowned dog I would tear through the park, a creature in human form, all perilous bolt inviting danger, the bike dancing controlled flips as I gulped jets of rain — more danger, more fun. In comparison, what had girls to offer? Nothing but a mangled jungle of tangled hair presented as the jackpot payoff. Honeypots sprawled like open graves, their owners doing nothing at all other than *letting you.* The call of duty is all yours — to turn on and get off; to hit the spot and know the ropes; to please and be pleased; as the owners of such Bermuda Triangles do … *nothing.*

The lonely season was best, and I much preferred time wasted with my closest friend Edward Messenger in these childish days that lacked any profound distinction between the sexes. But I am already a popular menace, and Edward's older brother Leslie wants something that I've got, and shortly thereafter a famous bout took place in the Messengers' garden on King's Lane, wherein I emerged victorious (but un-gloating) from my first punch-up with

Leslie, and it all becomes too muddled, and life's divides take hold. Prior to this, King's Lane had been a second home for me – one less complicated than my own. Edward's mother Jean loved Steve McQueen and was a strong woman of northern bluntness, yet untroubled by my constant presence. The house is northern cheerfulness and cooking smells and Sandy the dog being lovingly bullish. Leslie calls his younger brother 'Ebward' for reasons ungraspable, and somewhere in the middle their sister Annette is a smiling face beneath limp brown hair, just waiting to be old enough to *do something*. It's a good home to go to, and Edward and I unleash make-believe as our teeming imaginations race over and through each King's Lane garden like gundogs; a disorderly chase through stinging nettles with horrified protests from elderly dwellers who have tended and tended all of their lives. Maddening church bells stop play each Sunday as I, but not Edward, am called to attend church. Mothers who never let go of their sons, and sons at pains to grow, are all I see in the crammed churches, and I ache to return to King's Lane horseplay – which had always moved on by the time I was finally unshackled from God. I slept at the Messenger's house many times – at the opposite end of Edward's bed. In the fashion of the day, nothing encourages openness, and we instinctively never widen our understanding of anything, and the fetish of secrecy begins, for isn't it touch alone that changes you? Ten years later we pass one another in the street, and we nod as we pass, because that's what northern males do, and can only do.

At Kings Road my appointed boyhood lot is injured birds and broken typewriters; a bulging box-bedroom of

American paperbacks bought carefully at the Grass Roots shop on Newton Street, where a fascinating flood of feminist literature signposts the way, as we wait for a genius to state the obvious. The shelves of Grass Roots raise consciousness through the roof, and the staff is fittingly unfriendly in an aura of root vegetables and patchouli oil ... as Jill comes tumbling after. Books on non-sexist language flip my life for the better, and I understand feminism to be a social savior because it liberates everyone without exclusion, whereas masculinism damns itself by measuring a man's health by the amount of sexual gratification he receives. If a man is measured by however he approaches a swimming pool, or whether or not he confidently fills whatever chair he decides to sit in (as opposed to perching nervously on its edge), then I continue only as a clanking Edward Ardizzone sketch, miles from obvious definition, and alive only because the 3p stamp connects me to those beyond the barbed wire.

Robinsons Records on Blackfriars Street offers a vast warehouse of extraordinary stock – pristine pressings lovingly racked and dazzlingly stacked, tearfully beyond my budget. I stand for hours flipping each sleeve, examined and memorized, domestic and American, always, always out of reach. On John Dalton Street there is Rare Records, whose records are not rare at all, but whose air is the leathery and old giving way to the young sounds. Rare Records is the last to offer listening booths, yet it is cosmopolitan enough to display the first album by Jobriath – somehow assuming that a pained wretch will part with £2.10 for the pleasure; thus I sense my cue. Although masterfully talented, Jobriath has already been laughed off the face of the planet (*this* one, and quite possibly other planets, too) as a beautiful blunder whose lyrics read like an exchange of under-the-dryer face-pack gossip. On every level, the press work against him, and his name is generally only heard as a punch line. My duty is to run to his rescue, and thankfully he makes it all worthwhile – some songs commanding, some even imperative – but he is already being snuffed out and no amount of carbon-dioxide foam can extinguish the flames. On Lever Street, the cramped Virgin Records is heavy on prog and student notice boards, and always first with American imports – unaffordable at £5.25 when £2.25 is the general retail ceiling. When HMV appears on Market Street its stock is stylishly shrinkwrapped, and this out-dazzles Virgin's unvarnished and bending manhandled presentations. Piccadilly Records is awkwardly run-of-the-mill, yet it is here that £2.29 secures the New York Dolls' first LP as the main window of the shop blazes with thirty Dolls sleeves stapled together in a dramatic traffic-stopping mosaic, 50 million unimpressed shoppers running by with a speed suddenly increased by the sight of Arthur Kane. Like a lost lark I drag all curiosities back to the sanctity of my bedroom where the door closes and *James Dead is not Dean* art fills wall and headspace as neat boxes of 7-inch discs explain me to any passing psychiatrist. I have no other identity and I wish for none. These were times when all were judged squarely and fairly on their musical tastes, and a personal music collection read as private medical records. You should, after all, judge a book by its cover, and any poor fool anointed by heavy rock or smocky folk begged and pleaded for a public hanging. Music was rarely heard anywhere – never on television apart from *Top of the Pops*, *Disco 2*, *Lift Off with Ayshea*, or the unreliably placed *Old Grey Whistle Test*. Department stores, television commercials, lifts, escalators, airports, shopping areas had yet to discover the advantages of pop noise. For me, there was no one available with whom to discuss these urgings of the heart, because nobody could understand how the head could ring persistently with song. In 1972 I had played *All the young dudes* by Mott the Hoople to my father, and as it spun innocently before us on orange CBS, he stands to leave.

'*Ooh no, I'm not having that,*' were his words as he vanished in disgust. What exactly he wasn't having I still do not know. He walks around the house singing *Four in the morning* by Faron Young, or *Scarlet ribbons* by somebody else. My sister and my mother never sing, but my sister and I were united in the glorification of the social problem film – a fly-by television treat never to be missed, especially the school-as-cesspit honesty of *Spare the Rod* (1961), *Term of Trial* (1962), *Up the Down Staircase* (1967) or *To Sir, With Love* (1967), wherein slum kids are shown to endure in sufferance the pointlessness of secondary education (for what use is anything at all that is secondary?). *The Blackboard Jungle* (1957) had been the first to free teachers – spouting resentment at the no-hope kids who were, by birth, three rungs below scum – and boundaries of frankness snapped. Jackie and I would watch as many films as we could, long before the days when television channels refused to transmit monochrome films for fear that no one would watch.

Back at St Mary's, my life harnessed and travestied beyond belief, there is only one teacher whom I physically fear, yet this is not the fear of bulk or brawn because rakish Mr Chew has neither, but he is manically loud and always upset, and it is this offhand agitation as he marches squarely around the classroom that disturbs me to such a degree that I close the book on mathematics and successfully avoid the subject for five years. Instead, I curve left rather than right as everyone swarms to his calling, and I skip every lesson simply by sliding out a side door that leads to the bike sheds. This is the rear of the skanky and stinky canteen – where none dare pass – and where I am never to be detected, or missed as absent. As long as Mr Chew has his trapped audience before him, he is in *Measure for Measure* delight. Nothing, I have decided, could waste precious life more than trigonometry and logarithms. Meriting equally fully plumbed hatred is Mr Hawthorn, who wastes each woodwork lesson by roasting and scorching every boy before him; no intellectual distinction, yet a fascinating study in volatility, Mr Hawthorn is pitiful to watch – every word uttered without hope, his Eric Morecambe spectacles completing the nightmare unleashed. No one laughs at his jokes, because they are not funny, and they are always hurtful. Mr Chesworth runs the metalwork class, but he does not teach it because his irritability causes the boys to close down and back off. His favorite trick is to creep up behind a boy and then pull the boy's head back by the hair, to which the rest of the class fall silent at the vocational hatred.

A single minute is not allowed to pass without fiery physical attack from teacher to boy. With no identifiable human being behind the agonized persona, such teachers are restored only by the general truth that the trapped audience before them cannot squeal, for no one would listen. The classroom is their stage, and each day is their theatrical execution – to our joint disadvantage. What gives these teachers the green light for such relentless physical harm? And who, without seeing it, could ever believe it? Warped with trial–sentence–death affixed to their brows, the teachers of St Mary's block the route to education, because, after all, why bother? The rabble before them are refuse – future postmen at best, largely unemployable, unfit, and ripe for life's incinerator. Ruggedly rugger-grunting Mr Thomas's concentrated insults are his only connecting moments with the boys stuck in his company – boys who surely hammer-rammer his nightly dreams.

'Does your mother know you're truanting?' Mr Pink leans from his car window as I sidle along the street. I had discovered that if you were to walk out of the school building with concentrated quietism that you would be neither stopped nor thought to be suspicious, and this I did regularly for days of self-exile in Longford Park – awaiting signs of 3:40 movement when it would be safe to be seen on civilian streets. All of the vile merging forces of St Mary's reduced me to nobody, and it could only be by fleeing the wreckage that I saved myself. To know this was to be guilty – guilty of *something*. To vary facial expression could lead to a beating, and boys would be forced to hang from the wall-bars in the gym with their bodies facing outwards as Mr Kijowski kicked a football towards them, targeting the stomach whilst demanding that they do not raise their legs in self-protection. It is barbarism. On days of whipping rain we are nonetheless forced outside into a wet yard for what was known as 'break time' as – blatantly beyond logic – we are

herded out into the rain with all of its obvious detriments. We are then brought back into the school, ravaged and soaked by the bad weather. During several lessons, I stand up and protest against this mayhem, explaining how no one should be forced to go out into a blizzard of rain that will leave them drenched for the rest of the day. But no matter what one thought one knew, if the boys remained inside the building then the teachers must lose their own 'break' in order to watch them, and it was for this reason only that dry kids were ordered outside into cloud juice.

'*Yes*,' snaps Miss Power, '*and YOU'RE another one not content with the hair color given to you by Christ.*' Baffled, I immediately imagined Christ setting my hair beneath a blow-dryer, but of course this is in fact Miss Power's boorish way of drawing attention to my 14th-year adventure of hair of canary-yellow streak. Kath Moores, a close friend who lived in Dukinfield, had whisked the yellow streak through my hair from left corner front to right corner back. The effect was impressive and suddenly I was famous. No awards for confidence or originality ensued. Previously unknown in the mob-rule dehumanization of St Mary's history, I stood before their world as a frozen target; a boy with a dyed yellow streak in his hair paying a deathly price for a stab at living artistry. In these days of Arthur Scargill and Brian Clough, somehow a schoolboy with inventively colored hair disgusted art teacher Miss Power. What kind of 'art' was she teaching, anyway? *The art of non-expression?* Swashbuckling Mr Thomas sniffs out burgeoning transsexuality as I sit front row in his history class, and of course he cannot miss the opportunity to sneer, leer and jeer. Under St Mary's roof, 1974 magically rings with the intolerance of 1850. My hair is, after all, my own, and nobody else's. Mr Thomas, for example, doesn't have any – or very little. The abyss in which I live hasn't the wit to save itself from savage ignorance, and I now feel assured that I am not in the company of my own species (or, at least, I *hope* I am not, for if I am, then I am *they*). Dear God, let time pass quickly, and let this end. Let me be older and let this mediocrity pass as a dream – one in which the utmost was done to bury me alive.

'Morrissey, you were absent last week – where were you?' asks Mr Barry.

'I went to Preston to see Roxy Music,' I explain in perfectly level tone.

'Ooooooooooh, no you don't!' booms Mr Barry, full of civic bureaucracy and clan-in-the-right. This recalcitrant malaise! Punish the boy! *Punish! Punish! Punish!* The price you pay for the quest of art. But Roxy Music will drop quickly from the emotional radar soon, as singer Bryan Ferry announces that his favorite food is veal – second only to foie gras in savage cruelty.

The terrors of releasing the self and enjoying the self swamped the school corridors. With undercurrents of sorrow, teachers are unable to give heart or encouragement, and it must all be beaten back, and the disease spreads into the kids who must bear it for the rest of their lives – as here I am, now, writing this. My mother is asked into the school to explain my fragmentary absences. I see her walk across the yard in a stylishly short black coat, her hair an insignia of pride, her accessories skilfully impressive. But she is nobody's fool. Exuding feminine goodness, her set expression is determined and fearless. Mr Barry looks up from his desk and bullishly throws in: *'She's great looking your mum, isn't she?'* I can only imagine what will pass between my mother and the war-ruined husk of Vincent Morgan.

Whilst it is obvious that school teaches me nothing useful, its unsettlement is relieved by sports – all of which I find easy. By accident I am enlisted to represent the school in track events for the 100 meters and the 400 meters for which, unthinkably, I receive schoolboy medals. For this, my Saturdays are marked out by solitary excursions to woebegone stadiums in child-gorging Gorton or dishearteningly dented Denton. I am obliged to make my own way, and I am obliged to feel honored and to dream of the 14-second dash, or the one-minute 400. I arrive in the always wet and windy north Manchester, where other boys vary in nationality against the virtual whiteness of St Mary's. Frozen amongst the pugilistic roughnecks whose kits don't fit, I await the starting pistol, always relieved to let loose on a grey granite track with its wet chalky smells. The school-doom factories of north Manchester are as pitiful as those of St Mary's south; foul-smelling changing rooms – their tiled floors alive with disease, or awash with disinfectant that is more dangerous to the skin than the athlete's foot that it sandblasts. How to change into your kit without bare feet touching the floor, lest contamination paralyze you for life or chew your legs off? Bullish and half-grown juvenescents shout under cold showers, and dare you muster the nerve to stand alongside them and show whatever it is you've got? The little mannish machine affects indifference to nudity, and personal comments can only be made via gibberished jokes that will allow mutual study. Female nudity is generally easy to find – if not actually

unavoidable – but male nudity is still a glimpse of something that one is not meant to see. In mid-70s Manchester
there must be obsessive love of vagina, otherwise your life
dooms itself forever.

The star of the fifth year sports is Pete Gregg, who is
kitted out in readiness wherever I'm sent, but his is a manly
body of muscle against my whipper-snapper, featherlite
twister. I am a torrent of nervous dash, whereas he is solid
control and hefty granite legs. However, as I struggle down
Oldham Road, out of life's loop, I know that Jason King
and Stewart Sullivan and Annabelle Hurst are zig-zagging
across Europe solving the unsolvable, and my pain
magnifies.

Of some interest to me are the limericks of Edward Lear
and the bordering-on-bathos of Walter de la Mare. There
is even more meaning in the scanty lines of Hillaire Belloc:

> Pale Ebenezer thought it wrong to fight,
> but Roaring Bill (who killed him) thought it right

and in this year of 1974, knowing nothing of Hillaire
Belloc (in fact, I walk into a bookshop in St Anne's Square
asking for 'anything by Hillary Belloc'), I had no idea that
a complete poem could be as short as two lines (couplet?):

> I'm tired of love; I'm still more tired of Rhyme.
> But Money gives me pleasure all the time.

Naturally, Hillaire Belloc's name is never mentioned in the
unhappy classrooms of St Mary's School for the Daft, and

I find it difficult to track down any information on the rhymist who thought it quite enough to say:

> The chief defect of Henry King
> Was chewing little bits of String

Belloc sets me out on the hunt for humorous verse, a search as yet largely unmapped. Naturally, I find Dorothy Parker loitering, who offers:

> If, with the literate, I am
> Impelled to try an epigram,
> I never seek to take the credit;
> We all assume that Oscar said it.

And, of course, in the world of words, there is only one Oscar. Now begins a whirligig of dramatic shock as I am awed beyond reason by the poet who gives the whole person, and jabs sharply. They can tell you everything you need to know about your own sorrow, and about the joy and sadness that is usually found side by side. My senses sharpen at the words of Stevie Smith:

> Some are born to peace and joy
> And some are born to sorrow
> But only for a day as we
> Shall not be here tomorrow.

Smith had recently passed away after a lifetime of bleeding to death. She appeared to live like a never-opened window, with hardly any right to be, except to pass on a shivery touch of flu. She lived with her aunt in a Victorian pile in Palmers Green, all so painful yet full of life; absent from life – yet all of it right on top of her; fencing adversity with spilled ink; 50 per cent blotting-paper and 50 per cent loose tea.

With a face of distressed concrete, W. H. Auden drops into view:

> Give me a doctor, partridge plump,
> Short in the leg and broad in the rump,
> An endomorph with gentle hands
> Who'll never make absurd demands
> That I abandon all my vices
> Nor pull a long face in a crisis,
> But with a twinkle in his eye
> Will tell me that I have to die

In 1973 W. H. Auden dies, the words silenced, the heart finally given a rest, all in life's shocking order. I do not know much about him, but there is so much wisdom in the unfolding words; flinching at the narrow-minded and sighing at the petty irritants. He had been interviewed on television, and I could sense the air of genius even before he spoke – as if a person's greatness need never be pointed out, for it is there, anyway, in the silent being. Invisible behind a fog of cigarette smoke, W. H. Auden has a face of concentrated power, a voice that comes from somewhere deeper than the body, and a life too full and intense. W. H. Auden has lived through the lifetime that it takes in order to find all the right words. There is a stroking sensuality to the voice, and the richness of tone wards off the listless Yorkshire giggle of interviewer Michael Parkinson.

Here, for me alone, is a glimpse of genius of the highest intellectual distinction which nobody could possibly be qualified to question. I am gradually beginning to grasp the meaning of W. H. Auden – with his eyes too large for their sockets, and his mouth stuck in the wrong part of his body. A half-asleep voice of broadcasting tones is carefully warning you that the only way to deal with him is to back down. More affable and screen-friendly is poet laureate John Betjeman (1906–1984), who is a monument to the sadness of human virtue:

> I made hay while the sun shone.
> My work sold.
> Now if the harvest is over
> And the world cold
> Give me the bonus of laughter
> As I lose hold.

Betjeman puts it all as well as it can be put, in language of simple rhythm, fastidiously straightforward. There is no egocentricity with Betjeman, who is always helpful and at ease, and who is hopeful and is happy with his gift. But, clutching his teddy bear, Betjeman evidently frustrates the will of prickly poets who look on his celebrity as a dry well of formulated thoughts. Even with the misfortune of always knowing what is coming next, Betjeman is without agitation or propaganda. His only connection with fleshy life is through a small door kept locked, and therefore his view of England's condition is often sugary. Yes, well, I see it now. The crate in the basement contains a living poet who is burdened by an increasing sense of their own idiocy, with pride and self-pity securely as one. The will surrenders to the resolve and dignity of the written word, and I, the gentle self, step forward, pattering up the ramp, one half of an incomplete person, knowing with certainty that I cannot live – yet wondering if I could possibly write? Slight and weary and full of angularity, my heart is never un-broken, but I am unable to call out. I have a sudden urge to write something down, but this time they are words that must take a lead. Unless I can combine poetry with recorded noise, have I any right to be? Yet, let it begin, for who is to say what you should or shouldn't do? In fact, everyone tries to knot your desires lest your success highlight their own failure. Better, it is thought, that we all swill in the same bucket, just making do. But I have no intention of living backwards, and I have no intention of surviving for eight-een years in order that I might be strangled to death in my nineteenth. I will never be lacking if the clash of sounds collide, with refinement and logic bursting from a cone of manful blast. Here, from the weeds, the situation worsens since each abiding art-form lacks one essential ingredient – and that ingredient is the small and bowed passionate I. Since there is no living being as recipient of my whispers, and since there are no certainties that one shall ever appear, then the off-balance distortion of my everyday feelings *must* edge into the un-cooperative world *somehow.*

In what could be termed sheer panic I buy a drum kit, and suddenly I am in mortal danger of doing something productive. The kit fills the bedroom, for the house itself is far too small, and of course a drum kit cannot be played softly. I stare at this mountain of glamor far more often than I slip onto its stool, because each time I thwack out my Paul Thompson formulations I am tearfully useless, and there is no one to ask. Inside my head there is mocking laughter – a little boy play-acting as people passing the house look up to the window as the pitiful search for scrambled rhythm sounds like someone dismantling bits of furniture. Instead, I will dream the dreams of others, as shimmer by shimmer, the kit and my hopes are dismantled – unable to touch the desire it arouses. Indulgence is rarely projected freely from this particular body, and only the act of waiting registers the truth of the feelings within. Unfortunately, what I am waiting for is *myself*, as others hahahaha on streets where squabbles threaten and desire is dread.

Robert Herrick (1591–1674) writes in what is termed 'duple rhythm', which is a ploy of two syllables per line – almost like two tapping feet responding to each other:

> Thus I
> Passe by,
> And die:
> As one,
> Unknown,
> And go.

The secrets of the female form are Robert Herrick's poetic pleasures, and he writes repeatedly to his 'mistress' Julia:

> Julia, when thy Herrick dies,
> Close thou upon thy poet's eyes;
> And his last breath, let it be
> Taken in by none but thee.

Although they who write modern pop songs could never deliver lines as strong as Robert Herrick's, there is no one else appointed to attempt such, just as there is no one else so freely delegated. Blend noise and words and save the world. I say this not to myself, but to an imaginary upstart – out there, somewhere – for even the lyrics in the songs that I love are by no means fine art; they merely fit well beside the dexterity of voice and instrument. Stripped of sound, the lyrics of most pop songs are artful dribble; artful as in Dodger, and dodger as in wily. I am caught by what *could* be and *should* be, as the sagging-roof poetry of Shelagh Delaney's rag-and-bone plays say *something* to me about my life. Showing a very considerable understanding of life is Melanie Safka, who is from Queens, New York, and is fortified with such songs as *I really loved Harold, Some say I got devil, Johnny boy, Tuning my guitar, I don't eat animals* and *Close to it all*. It is folk music, it is pop music, but it is also using recording as a lecture platform, and the sincerity in the voice is overwhelming.

My mother had decided to call me Steven after the American actor Steve Cochran, who had died in 1965, the year of Grandad's and Ernie's deaths. No biographies of Cochran have ever existed, but his extraordinary face and gangster swagger leap forwards with sexual antagonism and vendetta smiles. In *Tomorrow is Another Day* (1951), *Slander* (1957) and *I, Mobster* (1958) he is malevolently magnificent, hooded by virulent beetle-brows and brute lure. At 48 he had a heart attack and died whilst adrift off the California coast with a yacht full of young females. A post mortem probably wasn't necessary.

Nellie is my father's sister, and in 1973 she innocently

asks me: *'Have you considered being a butcher when you leave school?'* Nellie is thoughtful – and very kind, but her question is met with a silent howl. Why would I want to butcher *anything?* Her home town of Dublin offers Patrick Kavanagh, who died in 1967 at 62:

> On Pembroke Road look out for my ghost
> Disheveled with shoes untied,
> Playing through the railings with little children
> Whose children have long since died

and, wrongly, unnecessarily, this child weeps, full of the foolish embarrassment that his father has clearly marked out. New air is discovered in the words of A. E. Housman (1859–1936), scholar-poet, vulnerable and complex. On the day of his twelfth birthday his mother dropped dead, sealing a private future of suffering for Housman, who was said to be a complete mystery even to those who knew him. With no interest in applause or public recognition, Housman published three volumes of poetry, each one of great successful caress, each a world in itself, forcing Housman into the highest literary ranks. A stern custodian of art and life, he shunned the world and he lived a solitary existence of monastic pain, unconnected to others. The unresolved heart worked against him in life, but it connected him to the world of poetry, where he allowed (in)complete strangers under his skin. In younger years he had suffered from the unrequited love of Moses Jackson, the pain of which was so severe that it doomed Housman for the rest of time. All of his work would be governed by this loss, as if life could only ever offer one chance of happiness (and perhaps, for every shade and persuasion, it does?):

> When the bells justle in the tower
>   The hollow night amid,
> Then on my tongue the taste is sour
>   Of all I ever did

Housman suffered throughout his life, and therefore (and not surprisingly) his life became an unyielding attempt not to cooperate. The black horizon never shifted, and his emotional lot never mellowed.

> He would not stay for me; and who can wonder?
>   He would not stay for me to stand and gaze.
> I shook his hand and tore my heart in sunder
>   and went with half my life about my ways.

At his Wildean lowest, Oscar's personal sadness had never slumped to such leaden fatigue; Housman suffered and accepted, death always close in his mind's eye – but not regrettably so.

> I did not lose my heart in summer's even,
>   When roses to the moonrise burst apart:
> When plumes were under heel and lead was flying,
>   In blood and smoke and flame I lost my heart.

> I lost it to a soldier and a foeman,
>   A chap that did not kill me, but he tried;
> That took the sabre straight and took it striking
>   And laughed and kissed his hand to me and died.

The published poetry makes the personal torture just barely acceptable. The pain done to Housman allowed him to rise above the mediocre and to find the words that most of us need help in order to say. The price paid by Housman was a life alone; the righteous rhymer enduring each year unloved and unable to love:

> Shake hands, we shall never be friends, all's over:
> I only vex you the more I try.
> All's wrong that ever I've done and said,
> And nought to help it in this dull head:
> Shake hands, here's luck, goodbye.
>
> But if you come to a road where danger
> Or guilt or shame's to share,
> Be good to the lad that loves you true
> And the soul that was born to die for you
> And whistle and I'll be there.

It's easy for me to imagine Housman sitting in a favorite chair by a barely flickering gas fire, the brain grinding long and hard, wanting to explain things in his own way, monumental loneliness on top of him, but with no one to tell. The written word is an attempt at completeness when there is no one impatiently awaiting you in a dimly lit bedroom – awaiting your tales of the day, as the healing hands of someone who *knew* turn to you and touch you, and you lose yourself so completely in another that you are momentarily delivered from yourself. Whispering across the pillow comes a kind voice that might tell you how to get out of certain difficulties, from someone who might mercifully detach you from your complications. When there is no matching of lives, and we live on a strict diet of the self, the most intimate bond can be with the words that we write:

> Oh often have I washed and dressed
>   And what's to show for all my pain?
> Let me lie abed and rest:
> Ten thousand times I've done my best
>   And all's to do again.

I ask myself if there is an irresponsible aspect in relaying thoughts of pain as inspiration, and I wonder whether Housman actually infected the sensitives further, and pulled them back into additional darkness. Surely it is true that everything in the imagination seems worse than it actually is – especially when one is alone and horizontal (in bed, as in the coffin). Housman was always alone – thinking himself to death, with no matronly wife to signal to the watching world that Alfred Edward was now quite alright – for isn't this at least partly the aim of scoring a partner: to trumpet the mental all-clear to a world where how things *seem* is far more important than how things *are*? Now snugly in eternity, Housman still occupies my mind. His best moments were in Art, and not in the cut and thrust of human relationships. Yet he said more about human relationships than those who managed to feast on them. You see, you can't have it both ways.

Who on earth is Patrick MacGill, who in 1916 wrote:

Over the top is cold, matey –
You lie on the field alone.
Didn't I love you of old, matey,
Dearer than the blood of my own.
You were my dearest chum, matey –
(Gawd! but your face is white)
But now, though reliefs 'ave come, matey,
I'm goin' alone tonight.

I'd sooner the bullet was mine, matey –
Goin' out on my own,
Leavin' you 'ere in the line, matey,
All by yourself, alone.
Chum o' mine and you're dead, matey,
And this is the way we part
The bullet went through your head, matey,
But Gawd! it went through my 'eart

Partial disclosures of male closeness fascinate me, because it's something that is nowhere in the life around me. All males are adversaries in muggy Manchester, and it is now my grim intent to break spells. Meanwhile, I live my life in slow motion. And what drove Oscar wild?

Lily-like, white as snow
    She hardly knew
She was a woman, so
Sweetly she grew.
Coffin-board, heavy stone
    Lie on her breast;

I vex my heart alone,
    She is at rest.
Peace, peace; she cannot hear
    Lyre or sonnet;
All my life's buried here
Heap earth upon it.

As the world's first populist figure (first pop figure), Oscar Wilde exploded with original wisdom, advocating freedom for heart and soul, *and for all* – regardless of how the soul swirled. He laughed at the squeezers and the benders and those born only to tell others what to do. Tellingly, a disfigured barrister and a half-wit in a wig destroyed Wilde in the end, and in doing so one lordly barrister and one lordly judge deprived the world of further works from Oscar Wilde. Solitary confinement was deemed judicially right for the man who had brought more positive change and excitement and fun to the London literary world than anyone else – dead or alive. With childish exuberance, an abstract High Court judge with the full force of jealousy issued a judgment equivalent to the death sentence, oh so inflamed and burdened by correctness was Justice Wills. Out of sheer envy of Wilde's genius, Wills got at that genius as best he could, for judges in high-profile cases want to be remembered *somewhere* (anywhere!) in history's grubby footnotes. Rather than say something helpful, the judge's only way to out-shadow Wilde was to present a sentence that was internationally gasp-worthy in its excess, and thus came the ruling that killed off the writer who has yet to be matched or equaled, even now, one hundred and ten years after Wilde's death. The law is often wrong, but Justice Wills –

who killed Oscar Wilde with the most severe sentence that the law allowed – knew exactly what he was doing, and acted with the dubious belief that Wilde must be destroyed in order to save the world from homosexuality. It was only by this that Justice Wills nailed his place in history. Float the Wills name through judicial records and you will find it unconnected to anyone but Wilde. It is important to judges to believe that their chosen profession is a difficult one of 'difficult' decisions, but this is how they themselves describe it only in order to make a plea for any impoverished decisions that they might clumsily make along the way. But it is they who choose their profession and it is they who allow themselves to be led by the unrestricted freedom that their profession allows. How does British society identify wayward judges? It doesn't, because it isn't allowed to. Identification can only be made by yet another judge, who is unlikely to point the finger at a colleague lest suspicion is returned from whence it came. When is a judge ever asked to account for his own words? Never. Barbarity might mount upon barbarity, but the British public has no legal right to question a judge on the grounds of bias – not even in a democratic society. But what if a judge *could* be proven to have been biased? One would need to convince another judge of this first, and no judge would ever be prepared to blow that particular whistle. If one fell, they'd all fall.

In her agony my sister walks home from school each day near to tears. She, too, cannot take one shadow more of her teachers – most of whom are children of the 1920s. Jackie is hounded and hawked by one teacher in particular, whose name is Miss Lewis, whose obsessive persecution of Jackie has a daily determination that never tires. The world has now moved on, quite naturally, from the draped and hooded heap of black that were 1970s schooldays, and the harrowing harassment by 1970s schoolteachers of children in their charge would now quite rightly be identified as criminal behavior. The Manchester Education Committee themselves were their own critical guide, which equals the Metropolitan Police dealing with complaints against their own officers (well, there are *unlikely* to be any charges made). The Manchester kids of my circumstances learned a sense of humiliation as a priority before they learned anything else, and it is perhaps this that separated them from the generation that followed, and we all find ourselves antiquated at some stage due to the irascible march of time. My years at St Mary's may have damaged me forever, but warm to the skin was that final July when St Mary's slithered its last heave of hatred, and freedom held out its hand for me to take it. Full of faulty development, I walked away, not an hour richer, with boyhood's fire doused, yet determined not to drown.

Jon Daley walked along Great Stone Road towards the Hardrock wearing silver knee-length boots, tight sky-blue jeans, blouse open to expose hairless body and flat belly, his spiked yellow hair expertly snipped, his eyebrows shaven off; nail polish and thin silver bracelets completing the dare. He looks sensational, as if plucked from the interplanetary beyond, living the trans earth Bowie reflection as beautiful creature – fearless and resolute. So striking is he that a passing lorry slows down beside him and gruff voices call out in order to throw Jon off balance (well, this *is* the north) – a compliment, of sorts, since it proves just how much you are getting at people, pinging their own self-doubts. Jon doesn't flinch. In this year of *Aladdin Sane*, Jon is the cover artwork in living form. The afternoon sun burns as Jon makes his way alone. I have no hesitation in approaching him – so fascinating is his appearance against the walls of Old Trafford Cricket Ground. We instantly have much to discuss, although my own slavishly dull school uniform is wretched compared to Jon's intergalactic grace. Jon is five years older than I, but shorter and thinner, and lives at 12 Reather Walk in Miles Platting (or Collyhurst – if you must) with his extremely Irish parents and his two giddy sisters. He is, without doubt, my first glimpse of modern art in motion. In fact, he works for a catalogue company somewhere beyond Piccadilly train station, and he tells me that he generally minds his own business. I am astounded at his survival in child-eating Collyhurst, so unforgiving and Jack Smethurst blunt. As I approach Jon's house an enormous dog bounds towards me from nowhere, jumps up on my head and knocks me to the ground, and then runs off with a mouthful of my left trouser leg.

'*Oh, hello,*' smiles Jon. Somehow he sails through – laughed at by children and pitied by adults. How does he do it? And where, in Newton Heath, are silver knee-boots to be found? Well, evidently *somewhere*. Although the brain is well-stocked and the conversation plentiful, Jon has no friends at all. We meet every weekend in central Manchester (or 'in town', as locals will say) and we walk for hours; through Back Piccadilly and Tib Street's under-belly where blind mice are stacked pathetically in pet shop windows – ready to be sold as your pet snake's soup. Wherever we walk, heads turn to examine Jon, who is neither loudly burlesque nor gay-faced, but is instead quietly unassuming and mildly oblivious to the cage of Manchester. Every inch of the city center is marked, every sunless side street, every tired shop front measured; from Grey Mare Lane eastwards, over to scuttling Salford, and everything in between. For almost two years Jon and I will be occupied with each backland enclave of Victorian Manchester (especially since Manchester remains almost exclusively Victorian), like Betjemanesque church-steeple fanatics we wonder at door cases of Corinthian plaster, or at narrow seventeenth-century passages, and we lust over neo-gothic rain-sodden yards. On tiptoe we would stretch to examine bits of glass on fortress doors, anciently engraved as the last of the old land. A timber staircase down an alley off Great Ancoats Street leads us nowhere; helpless against Edwardian decay and war damage. The scars of Hitler remain evident in 1970s Manchester where businesses somehow continued in rooms of drear on semi-derelict streets. Beyond leftover Shudehill and the deathbound dark shadow of Victoria Station, Jon and I would encircle Strangeways prison, still leaned on by slum streets and courtyards, and we wonder at the bored-stiff inmates, lost in a cauldron of quiet questions. We would sit in sunless turn-of-the-century pubs and ponder the slowness of distant days – of bodies dumped by the Quality Street Gang, ghosts and outcasts and diseased lovers of 1888 – and how we too are part of the process of time frittering away. Queen Victoria had visited Manchester in the 1840s and had remarked upon its destitution as despair previously unseen, and she also remarked upon the sickly look in the faces of Manchester folk (even though she herself was without doubt the most unfortunate-looking woman on the planet). Manchester repaid her unflattering comments with a fat, black statue in Piccadilly Gardens. Why did they bother? What had she ever done for Manchester but criticize it? 1840 was a time when Manchester's poverty and violence outstripped even London's hard-as-nails East End inferno.

One day a large wooden gate falls open into a walled yard somewhere amongst unmarked backstreets behind Deansgate, and there before us stood what was the original outdoor set for television's *Coronation Street*. It is a grubby façade of pretend houses and a shabbily stark corner shop – carelessly stacked with yellowing cornflakes boxes with their brand names sloppily hidden behind hastily applied gaffer-tape. Misdirected, we walk in, squinting at the magical properties of television. The eye is detained by the smallness of the set and the surprising lack of realism. Behind us, the *Coronation Street* cast suddenly arrives in readiness for exterior shots, on a street where cobbles face the wrong direction, and where each house has identical off-white net curtains.

'Have you noticed how the post-box is facing a different direction in each episode?' smiles Julie Goodyear (who plays Bet Lynch).

'Yes,' I lied.

Julie Goodyear is dressed in her faux-leopard brassiness, and is linking Peter Adamson (who plays Len Fairclough). I am suddenly faced with Bernard Youens (who plays Stan Ogden), who looks at me oddly.

'Oh, you are a nuisance, aren't you,' he comments, which

confuses me since I hadn't actually said anything apart from one simple-soul 'yes'. Jon and I realize that we are assumed to be extras for the afternoon shoot, which centers on Margot Bryant (Minnie Caldwell) struggling around on feeble feet. Hours pass, and nothing seems to happen, so we advance to leave, but I am stopped by a woman tumbling with a bundle of scripts.

'Can you handle a bicycle well?' she asks.

'Very,' I say.

'We need a boy for Saturday. It's a 7 am start, no dialogue.'

On Saturday I am prompt for my first television appearance: an Edwardian drama of a brooding England rife with tuberculosis and fraught romances against the typical northern landscape of tug-of-war family ties and money worries. Ushered into the Granada TV makeup room I am forced into a chair where my shagpile moptop is shorn to the bone without my consultation. I am horrified, and then, thirty seconds later, I am thrilled. Habitual-criminal mismatched tweeds, a worn and torn debtors' prison vest, the obligatory pit-boots and pickpocket's waistcoat ... and the screen is mine. I am ordered to cycle through a conventional industrial scene of the frozen north of 1913 whilst in the foreground lovers tiff about whatever it is lovers tiff about. The day is naturally overlong, the weather naturally arctic, but the cycling chimney-sweep pulls it off. Avril Elgar is the main star of this production of *The Stars Look Down*, and I, a spot on the horizon, cycling in search of the Hollywood Bowl – a punctured bicycle on a hillside desolate. Even if you don't blink at all you will miss me.

When Lou Reed played the Palace Theater in 1973 I had befriended Hazel Bowden and Kath Moores, who are part of an east Manchester sect steeped in all the right noises. They all bound off to Leeds to see the New York Dolls, and they spend the night with the Dolls at the Dragonara Hotel – not as sleeping partners, but just sitting around saying not very much, as David Johansen throws Arthur Kane's famous above-knee-length boots out of the hotel window and on to the street below – just for a hoot. Hazel wears a beret, is 1940s skinny, speaks in a full whisper, drinks whiskey, smokes impressively, and holds the eye. Hazel appears not to care about anything at all – which is a relief, of sorts. Michael Foley is impressed with this new glamorous syndicate and wants to get closer to the pizzazz of Elnette and Russian cigarettes. As we follow Roxy Music into the Midland Hotel in 1973 (where we are most certainly not wanted), Hazel returns insults to a passing roughneck who bats back the compliment with a bone-crunching whack to Michael's face. It is an unfortunate but recurring Manchester wrangle wherein the female starts the trouble but is then protected by her femininity when combat kicks off, and the innocent boy-stander (Michael) gets the one–two punch to the blindside. I watch all a-wobble as Michael's face expands.

Hazel was careless but greatly likeable. She was scatter-shot but loyal. She was tough but funny, and anything is forgiven of anyone who makes us laugh. Kath Moores and her Dukinfield friends were all lascivious young women, and they liked their men to look like the Dolls or Bowie. They despised the macho Boddington's-eloquent chat-up drunks of which Manchester produced nothing but. Male beauty was Mick Ronson or Jerry Nolan, and any man wearing makeup rang all the right bells. For me, it is a relief to be with people who are not shockable, although my own style is Antique Market baggy trousers and cord jackets of men long dead. I know only lodging-house thrift, and I do not ever attempt glamor in this city of gangs. From this time, it is Hazel Bowden who attempts to prolong our friendship, baffled as I am, since her life in Romiley is nothing like mine – with all of its redundantly difficult circumstances. I like Hazel whilst understanding nothing about her.

Suddenly and without necessity, Jon Daley takes up the sport of shoplifting. He favors the larger stores such as Lewis's, Kendals and Debenhams, but for one so eloquent he cannot explain why he does what he does. Often he would throw the stolen items away, and would always be in possession of enough money to cover the cost of whatever he had just lifted. I do not ever accompany Jon on his excursions, but the impressive spoils were often laid out before me with poacher's pride. Oasis on Market Street is regularly marked out by Jon, where Stolen From Ivor offers a cubicle curtain so large that Jon can make anything disappear. These are not yet the years of imposing security guards or intrusive CCTV cameras. Behind Lewis's stands a fancy art-supplies shop called Megsons, where the materials are unaffordably dazzling and priced out of my range (for, as ever, I have no range). Jon manages to haul in a host of notebooks, heavy paper, fancy pens, wax pastels, and water-soluble Caran d'Ache – all free of charge to those who have no intentions of paying in the first place. It is funny, but probably wrong. At some faraway track at Wellacre School, Jon arrived one day to watch me run for St Mary's (although I was actually running *from* St Mary's).

He is a standout oddity in an exhaustingly straitlaced crowd (for *what else* in Sale in 1974?), and I begin to understand how things must seem. Wellacre are roughish posh boys with Garden of Eden facilities, and none of the put-up-and-shut-up regimented mildew and mold of St Mary's. I am jealous and I stay jealous.

It is Hazel Bowden who stays close to Jon in the fading days of friendship, long after Jon and I find we have less to say to each other. There is a natural phasing out without a falling out, and it is Hazel who tells me that Jon has been killed in a horrific motorway crash. Driving alone to Birmingham, Jon is crushed by a tailing juggernaut that fails to brake. The story makes the national television news, and, as it does, this period of my life loses itself to the lap of memory. I stand at Jon's grave at Moston cemetery and I see that his name is spelled with an 'h', and that both of his parents are encased on top or beneath him. It is too much to bear, and in this dank November air I hear voices of people who are not there.

From St Stephenson Square I take a beetroot Ribble bus north to Accrington, near where Anji Hardy lives, in Haslingden. It's always a slow and laborious journey, and a chill drizzle never fails on arrival. The short and cold streets of Haslingden are full of cramped clumsiness and the slate-landscape of out-of-time Lancashire. An eternity of repetitive streets of Victorian terraced houses rest on one another for fear of being wiped out, their windows like empty eye-sockets hiding secrets in back bedrooms and dingy parlors. How, I wonder, would Lou Reed cope with this? In its midst, Anji Hardy uses her madcap humor as an excuse for everything, and every single day is an orgy of hysterical sensation. Inertia was unwelcome in the house that Anji shared with her Scottish mother; a house oddly laid out with large, bare bedrooms over-run with mice. (I never see one myself, but Anji assures me.) I climb into the single bed in the dreary back room and my feet slip into a mass of knitting needles; Anji's humor is there to be relished. She rarely leaves the house, but when she does we allow ourselves to be thrown about by Haslingden's unfailing winds. This is a forgotten and daft-as-a-brush town where locals might say '*I were agate*' to emphasize surprise. It is true that nothing happens in Haslingden, and only fantasies sap Anji's strength, although there is occasionally a strong and unsmiling teenager who often appears in the house, and I assume that his trousers are apt to come undone, for why else is he there? He works for Holland's Pies, and will tell no more than that. I don't ask, anyway. In the town center everything looks awful; pigs' feet are displayed in shop windows, and tripe is listed proudly on café menus. One day we bump into four of Anji's girlfriends, and they are pleasant and tough and unvarnished. They are mad about boys and are typical girls of their day, of intense expression and Boots makeup.

My repartee goes no further than music, and I ask them who they listen to. All four reply at once:

'*Glitter Band and t' New York Dolls.*'

'*What?*' I say, falling backwards gently.

'*Glitter Band and t' New York Dolls. We've seen t' Glitter Band four times.*'

I push a little, and the fresh young life of Haslingden tell me that they have pictures of the Dolls on their bedroom walls – amongst the usual run of unnameable others. They tell me that they had all bought the Dolls album in Accrington. This outer reality hits me like a discovery of tombs in Luxor, for I had no idea that truly ordinary Lancashire girls might take on the New York Dolls when press reports make it clear that the Dolls are out of bounds to anyone other than the sexual outcast. In fact, David Johansen himself had said, *'We have come to redeem the social outcast.'*

Attempting to expand my horizons further, Anji's mother asks me to meet her one day in central Manchester. I do so, and she leads me to a doorway by the Britons Protection pub just below St Peter's Square. As she hands me a lit cigarette, we are ushered into a private club. I am 15 years old, a pale mask of clumsiness, holding a cigarette that I cannot smoke, and here is something interesting. We are the only two white faces in a darkened cellar where we are encircled by up to thirty black men, none young, all locked in 1960s speakeasy tight pants and tight shirts, like immigrants of 1955 looking for digs and a job on the docks. The music is soft Blue Note jazz, and the air is south of the midriff, and everyone is relaxed behind bolted doors. Anji's mother is a familiar face here. She is life-loving and ready to laugh, and it is time to wonder what and who one really is.

Anji's nightly telephone calls to Kings Road are marathon, and even the most vague generalities of her day are spiced with such absurd account that the two hours kneeling in an unheated hall, ears numb and jaw aching, are always worth the labor.

'Oh, I went to the doctor today,' begins Anji.

'*Y-e-e-s?*' I say, impatient for Part Two.

'*He said I've got six weeks to live,*' she breezes, almost throw-away. I laugh because everything in Anji's delivery is funny – and she knows it.

'*Yeah – leukemia ... hang on, there's someone at the door ...*'

Some weeks later Anji's life has met its deadline, liberating laughter leading her every step to the grave, never losing her edge for an instant, bearing sadness with dignity, and always explaining herself so well, at peace with death as she was with life, the black earth of Haslingden entombing seventeen years of best endeavor and generosity. I see her now – peeling potatoes in the sun and laughing her head off.

For reasons too terrifying to analyze I had found myself walking around Macclesfield town center one sorry-assed Saturday in 1975. Such jaunts are typical of those scattered days when you aren't quite sure what to do with yourself and you appear to be the bounty that nobody especially wants. These are Saturdays when the content is always the same, and the search for a listener is fruitless. Lured into Boots the Chemist I pass ten minutes flicking through their routine selection of best-selling long-players only to inexplicably find *Horses* by Patti Smith, unfathomably racked as an import at five pounds. Precisely why such a record was for sale (on import!) in such a frowsy frumps' paradise as Boots the Chemist is something that foxes me to this day. The distinction of this LP was that it had recently been reviewed by Charles Shaar Murray for the *New Musical Express*, and then a week later it had been re-reviewed with equal exhilarating commotion. It was, in fact, the only album I had ever known to be re-reviewed. The galloping joy of Charles Shaar Murray urged me to take the risk. Cross-legged by a dying fire later that night, and with only a side-light for company, I allowed *Horses* to enter my body like a spear, and as I listened to the bare lyrics of public lecture, I examined the genderless singer on the heavyweight album sleeve. So surly and stark and betrayed, Patti Smith was the cynical voice radiating love; pain sourced as inspiration, an individual mission drunk on words – and my heart leapt hurdles, scaling and vaulting; something won and overcome. Unfulfilled as a woman, impotent as a man, Patti Smith cut right through – singing and looking and saying absolutely everything that would be thought to go against the listener's sympathy. But the reverse happened, and the wisdom of centuries shook me and told me that, however heavy-hearted and impossible you might feel about yourself, you can still bestow love through recorded song – which just might even be the *only* place where you have the chance to show yourself as you really are since nothing in your disposed life gives you encouragement. The fact that you do not look like a pop-star-in-waiting should not dishearten you because your oddness could become the deciding wind of change for others. There is nothing obvious about Patti Smith, least of all any obvious biological conclusions, and this gives its own erotic reality in a shyness of arrogant pride. The past snaps. I have never heard or seen anything like Patti Smith previously, and I have never heard truth established so sincerely. The female voice in rock music had rattled with fathomless depths of insincerity, whereas Patti Smith spoke with a boy's bluntness, and she looked for squabbles wherever she went. *Horses* pinned all opponents to the ground. It shook the very laws of existence, and was part musical recording and part throwing up. Its discovery was the reason why we could never give up on music, and its effects were huge. 1976 slapped the face of the world with the first album by the Ramones, who were so negatively disposed that it seemed difficult to imagine them attracting anyone at all. At first I felt galled by *Ramones* because I had so earnestly wanted the Dolls to be the ones to reshape the planet, and here were the Ramones moving in with their own style and with songs that sweat blood – all trashcan-in-the-sun New York. The Ramones told me there was nothing I could do to prevent the Dolls from becoming fagged-out back-numbers, and as I catch the Ramones' first Manchester gig (at the Electric Circus in Collyhurst) my mouth is a big round O. It is mesmeric. The Ramones are models of ill-health, playing backwards, human remains washed ashore, so much condensed into a single present-ation, and it is outstanding. Change! Change! Change! It doesn't happen by being the same as everybody else. *Now* I could accept all the suffering that came my way as long as the Ramones were in the world. Singer Joey looked as if he had been murdered in a hospital bed. I've found my twin. The following year Jackie and I would see them at the Lyceum in London, and I would spend the night on Birmingham's New Street Station in order to witness Patti Smith at the Birmingham Odeon. In a dream state I watch her explode as she takes on the lesbian contingent at the front who are calling to Patti to 'come out' (where to? from what?), and they heckle her in almost every song. By extreme contrast I see David Bowie in 1976 at Wembley.

He is already cold in form and un-giving, and as I spend the night hanging around Euston Station awaiting the first train back to Manchester, I am lost in Bowie's loss. It is Patti Smith, though, who rings as the first musical artist who promises nothing, and who gives nothing other than the sordid actuality of fact.

The frayed threads of Iggy and the Stooges on 1973's *Raw Power* were, as with the Dolls' debut, a disconcerting reply to the macho men of rock. Lipsticked Iggy was tougher than them all, and each night on stage he sang and he moved as if he might possibly die at any moment, whilst also diving offstage like a wild schoolboy who can do nothing in secret. Iggy does not so much sing as relieve himself. *Your pretty face is going to Hell* has a quality of emotion in line with Paul Robeson, and this is why I am still writing about it forty years on. I am not writing about *Goats Head Soup*. All of the body is thrown into the vocal delivery; bare-chested in tight silver pants, Iggy defined the new manhood that the world so badly needed, lest we die beneath the wheels of Emerson, Lake and Palmer. No one represents Iggy other than Iggy, and commercial success is not necessary to Iggy's own success. He heads the secret stream of inspiration granted to the active few. Mainstream success can often be the worst thing that can befall a true artist. Imagine David Bowie without his EMI America years — better to be absent and inactive in Hannover, or better my lover dead. Iggy was a face and a voice that had not been stated before his time. He recorded *Raw Power* as a moment of life that could never again be lived. It spat at you. Ask a boy from Michigan to be Elgar; he can't. Ask a boy from Michigan to be Iggy; he can't.

Iggy Pop, Lou Reed and Patti Smith have secrets that have never been lost because the inquisitive mind can't get in. This trinity is decorative art with an incredible understanding of effect. Their contribution to thought marks them out as our very own Goethe, Gide and Gertrude Stein, and it tells us that we all might come to whatever it is we seek – with flickering irony. They pawn everything of themselves into the current moment. The daring brilliance of early Lou Reed takes its place with the literary greats partly because he denied all tradition in his writing and physical presentation. With his Velvet Underground, life itself was the movable stage; lowbrow, imaginer, maker, self-regarding, susceptible to the will to corrupt. It is a proud sign of bad breeding, and of carrying within us everything we seek outside of us. You have their insolence at hand still, and now, but when the morgue yawns for them, their harsh expressionism will clank its way into hagiography as the new saints, and you will understand their meaning to be far greater than whatever seems logical during their lifetime.

At last I am face to face with Marc Bolan – as his flutterers flutter about him in the lobby of the Midland Hotel in Manchester. I am nothing and look nothing.

'*Could I have your autograph?*', I ask softly.

'*Oooh, no,*' he says, and slowly walks away to nowhere – unavailable to the outside world. I nod with all the shyness of adolescent modesty, as if understanding the catastrophic trouble I had brought upon him by asking. His new album will enter the chart at number 50, and mental illness is artistic activity is mental illness is artistic activity. On this day of buried disappointments, the show-biz version of Marc Bolan probably relishes the socially trapped condition, yet there is no one here but I – a member of his audience to whom he once turned for confirmation of what he was, and I gave to him as he gave to me. Ah, but not today – shadow close, swift as a swallow ...

Back on Manchester's inscrutable streets I find a tatty leaflet stuck on a Peter Street lamppost telling me that the Sex Pistols will play that very night at the Lesser Free Trade Hall. They are not the saviors of culture, but the destruction of it – which suits me quite perfectly, and I manage to see them two more times that year. By their third Manchester visit they have released a single, *Anarchy in the UK*, and everything has tensed up. The music papers are at their peak, and it's almost as if this idea of music has only just started. Their riches are overwhelming, and they seem to be helping everyone to come up with something new. The Sex Pistols are the first British band whose social importance appears to be instantly recognized, and their immediate success is an exhilarating danger to behold. Their singer is a striking Dickensian original; a pop-eyed Wilfred Bramble, but aged 19, and I am fascinated to discover that the Sex Pistols loathe and despise everyone on earth *except* the New York Dolls. I see! Something must've happened over Manhattan. Solitary, I slope from gig to gig, and I find my freedom only in the liberating shouts of others as they sing themselves into view. Nothing is ever enough, and I want my turn. Manchester gigs throw up the same dramatis personae; Paul Morley and Ian Curtis are always in line, both ready to be Elvis, both ready to chronicle the age. Ian stays with his grandmother on Milner Street, which leads off Kings Road, and he telephones me a few times to test my palette of words. He is genuine and is attempting first poems. I continue to live with my mother and sister at 384 Kings Road, with its landing haunted by the previous occupant – an elderly woman who lived and died within these walls. Of course, elderly people were not *always* elderly, and are often new to such a surprising fate. I am suddenly full of sweeping ideas that even I can barely grasp, and, although penniless, I am choked by the belief that something must happen. It is not enough just to 'be'. I am reliant upon the postage stamp, and tactlessly revealing letters are catapulted north and south – anywhere where a considerate soul might lurk. There is such a godsend as 'penpals' – friends known only via letters, and these are easier to construct than any living embodiment. The lineage from Dolls to Ramones seemed like a Himalayan missionary's trek from which a thousand lessons could be applied. But I want no more. I want it to stop now. I cannot continue as a member of the audience. If only I could forget myself I might achieve. I am crumbling from the top downwards – in mad-eyed mode, finding daylight difficult. Unemployable, my life draws in tightly. At 17 I am worn out by my own emotions, and Manchester is a barbaric place where only headless savages can survive. There is no one to take me on, and no one to bother about me. Months go on for years. I explode from intensity. I cannot cope with anything other than my inability to cope. I want to sing. I am difficult and withdrawn – a head, really, but not a body – full of passion within, but none outwardly. There are no sexual guidelines and I see myself naked only by appointment. It is simply a funnel, and there is no one around who suggests otherwise, and my mental horizons are so narrow and no soul is interested in the me that is beneath the chastity belt.

My mother had given me the money to travel to New York in 1976, where I stayed on Staten Island with Mary, who had left Manchester in 1969. Mary was now married with two children (Matthew and Erin), and is welcoming as seven sun-blasted weeks pass. But I cannot muster any lift in spirits, and I spend every day apologizing or saying the wrong thing, and I am born sorry. Mary's large wooden house is dramatically positioned in the midst of a tricky swampland area, where grasping reeds of great height line the sides of each narrow dirt road. The final stretch of hidden laneway leading to the tall and shaky house is permanently covered by large, busy toads, and there is no way to reach the house without leaving a tire-trail of squashed slime as the toads gather in their thousands. *'Look, there's nothing we can do,'* says Mary, as my head drops into my hand. Each journey to and from the house is heart-breaking, and the toads multiply daily in their hundreds and are fixed to the road. This is the only road available, and each night beclouds with sound of toad and cricket. When Mary had first bought the house she had found three pythons living in the basement. Possums lumbered through the trees like fat cats.

'So, what kind of girls do you like?' probes Mary, but too much rattles about my head. Thankfully Hurricane Belle distracts Mary, who is warned by local authorities (authorities in what, I have no idea) to leave the island or face the wrath of any approaching whirlwind. In the event, we

remain behind, boarding up the house and boxing ourselves in, peering out at the lashing reeds as the eye of the
storm circles above. The next day there are apparently dead
bodies across the island, but the toads remain.

I wander into CBGBs, where I find Russell Mael, and I
blush my way through a request for a photograph, and there
I stand – 17, clumsy and shy, with Russell, smiling beneath
the CBGBs canopy. The first five Sparks albums had been
constant companions. I had first heard *This town ain't big
enough for both of us* as Radio One's Record of the Week,
which they played daily at around 5:15. I had no idea who
Sparks were, but I thought the singer – whoever she was
– had the most arresting voice I'd ever heard. In time, of
course, Sparks exploded, the color of madness. Ron Mael
sat at the keyboard like an abandoned ventriloquist's doll,
and brother Russell sang in French italics with the mad
urgency of someone tied to a tree. It was magnificent, and
the ferocious body of sound was a speedboat in overdrive.
The life and death question was: *what is it?* As children the
Mael Brothers probably slept in bunk-coffins in an unused
wing of the house, playing with surgical instruments whilst
other kids of Los Angeles addressed the surf. The strait-
jacket sound of Sparks could never be fully explained, and
even now their historic place is confusing since they belong
apart. Lyrically, Ron Mael is as close to Chaucer as the pop
world will ever get – elevated and poetic, nine parts demon,
and I am very thankful:

> You mentioned Kant and I was shocked ... so shocked;
> You know, where I come from, none of the girls have
> such foul tongues.

The lyrics of Ron Mael and the vocal sound of Russell Mael are solid and original factors, so unique that by the very laws of existence I can hardly believe they exist. The sound registered is very tough, although the faces are fixed in imperishable marble. What *are* Sparks? A miracle, of sorts, and the dead child is momentarily revived.

> You've been waiting for your first encounter
>   – what a let-down.
> I'm just finishing my first encounter – what a let-down.

By the continued grace of my mother, I manage three more trips to America before 1980 enters us all, but by now Mary has moved to the less-interesting Denver, and although my life remains all wrong, I continually dump myself on Mary for seven-week stretches where I am unable to do anything but just get by. The knee-high Arvada snow makes everything look bright and clean, and I rashly place a fruitless ad in the *Rocky Mountain News* in search of musicians as despair mounts upon despair. I apply for a job at the ghastly Pathmark, only to be turned down whilst headless mutants are taken on. I attend an interview at Target but once again I am unconvincing to the mom-and-pop co-op who will employ almost anyone as long as they have at least one fully working eye. It is all too much. *'You have a better chance of being hit by lightning,'* laughs Mary. I cannot burden Mary any longer with my heavy granite shoulders, and I cry myself back to intolerant Manchester. Yanks is a messy record shop somewhere behind the old Gaumont Cinema on Oxford Road. It is a large, damp cellar stacked with cut-price US deletions, and it is here that I ring the till for a few months

— wrapped in a heavy overcoat, as the cellar quite naturally has no heat. A customer hands me a credit card and I have no idea what it is – having never actually seen one. Another hands me a cheque and I drop it into the bin below. My heart and mind are elsewhere – or rather, nowhere. One November night, as work concludes, I climb the cellar steps only to be met by a gang of immovable bulk who punch me to the ground and kick me senseless, hurling me from full Nelson to scissor-hold. I see blackness, and I hope it is death. A ludicrous concept, I struggle towards Piccadilly Bus Station with a twisted mouth. Walking through busy 6:30 traffic – with blood on my face, and with no inter-vention from passers-by – my life in Manchester is defined. I then serve time in another basement as a filing clerk for whom, upstairs, is the Inland Revenue. It is the only way, I am sure, to get the money to return to America because sooner or later *something* must work in my favor.

Several war-torn months are spent kowtowing to the rigors of gabbling clerical ciphers in a fate worse than life. As I understand it, there is nothing else I can do. This is one small rung below prostitution and is fully against sane judgment (because I would actually *prefer* prostitution), but my zest for life is fifty fathoms below sea level and it's all I can do to add this day to yesterday. Let it all seep as one. Each day I enter the building prepared for execution.

'*WHAT is that?*' shouts the senior clerk pointing to my Gabba Gabba Hey t-shirt, and I am thus summoned to the all-powerful 4th Floor Inspector, and I wonder what world I am in as he sits before me – bald and paunched, an off-white shirt of sweat-encrusted armpits.

Sadness can often … just be … fatigue.

At Stretford Jobcenter a fat-assed woman sits before me demanding to know why I left my golden position in the underground warrens of the Inland Revenue. She is a Dunlop bloater of such walrus proportions that I find it difficult to answer her.

'*Look at you,*' she says, '*can't you tidy yourself up?*' and she shifts her full-figured pigginess, with lard-arms waving and jelly-legs struggling … *and I to the appointed place.*

'*Because you left a perfectly good job we cannot allow you any unemployment benefit. Here is a job I want you to take.*' The hippo hands me a card with job details, and I read with disbelief.

'*You are asking me to clean canal banks?*'

'*Yes.*'

'*Clean canal banks?*'

'*Yes.*'

'*As an occupation?*'

'*Yes.*'

I breathe one final prayer of mercy, and I recall Nancy's words in *Oliver Twist*: *I shall put the mark on some of you that will bring me to the gallows before me time* … and the morgue yawns my name. I am cross-examined at Stretford Sorting Office as there are postman vacancies, and this is the most I consider possible. Yet it isn't, *because I am turned down* – deemed physically and psychologically incapable of delivering letters. There is now no escape but death.

I take the train to London to attend an interview with *Sounds* magazine, who are looking for a new writer. Editor

Alan Lewis gives me hope, but the inevitable refusal arrives by post nine days later, and my head once again drops permanently to the side.

Starting a few weeks' employment at the Bupa hospital in Whalley Range I begin my first day's walk to work in heavy snowfall. It takes me an hour to reach the hospital by foot, and I fall flat on my face four times, clinging hopelessly to hedges as I slap to the ground. God is sending me a special message. My work in the sluice room requires me to shake bits of human innards out of post-op doctors' uniforms in readiness for laundry. I will only be here for a few weeks, but I am holding on, poorly adapting yet not quite numb to shame. I am surely a secretive part of some scientific experiment of endurance, or a prank played by God. I represent filth. I am forbidden to live – by religion.

Since *Coronation Street* is our only link to Bel Air, I write to Leslie Duxbury at Granada TV, helpfully explaining how the twice-weekly crawl through northern morals needed a new knight of the pen. I am invited to submit a script, and I whip off a word-slinger's delight wherein young take on old as a jukebox is tested in the Rovers Return. Swords cross, heads bump and horns lock, and the episode fades with Violet Carson addressing the camera, one eyebrow arched, with *'Do I really look like a fan of X-Ray Spex?'* – cue *Thanks-for-the-memory*-style theme tune. It's silly – but, really, *what isn't?* Leslie Duxbury assures me that my talents lie elsewhere and, self-unmade, I turn once again and I look at myself, my entire body ready to be put on ice. On Cross Street, Damien and Jason are looking for a stylist. I am not one, but I apply and I am given a trial run until I fail to differentiate between oily hair and an actual wig. There are rumors of tunnels beneath Cross Street and I start to look for them. I am beginning to give insanity a bad name.

The bus rattled down the Old Kent Road – away from the overdeveloped pink blob of the Elephant & Castle's shopping center. Each inch of the road has spent itself in other eras, everyone once working but now lying in bed, returning to nothingness on ice-cold afternoons in 1977. The famous Thomas a Becket pub completes the cynical view of an area that can no longer look after itself; many doctors, many waiting rooms, and the new life hammers the old life. I make this journey many times throughout the late 70s to visit James Maker, who lives with his parents in a maisonette of ramps and grey slabs on the corner of St James's Road and Catlin Street. I jump off the bus at the Civic Centre, where Tommy Trinder fell from the rafters every Friday night and told it his own way to those unlucky people. James is cluttered in a row of 1950s formulations that have bright living rooms and downstairs bedrooms, walled in by Rotherhithe Road and Raymouth Road. It is the safest side of the tracks that are unsafe on both sides; a mishmash area that wisely manages to keep Peckham at bay, with its distinctly enormous schoolgirls with fat-tire legs. James is a year my junior and digs down deep – Louis XIV wit gallops ahead without a word or gesture lost. Dunhill cigarette smoke blasts the atmosphere, and James lives a life of impotent rage. He is certain that words can be found to describe the entire mess, yet he is also convinced that life has been made difficult on purpose in order to squeeze out the greatness in those of us who

A teenage JAMES MAKER: trouble

flutter wildly at the bars. His look is James Dean mid-blizzard, with a tongue more free than welcome. He will utilize anything at all that might serve the purposeful quest for recognition. We are united. James will tell you that his life had been nothing until the New York Dolls, and he is enslaved to the song *Frankenstein* – the Dolls' slumland melodrama wherein the deeper associations of evangelical pop have a roughhouse scruff-up with the musical dreams of Mahler's 7th Symphony: *'When those plans they don't fit your style, you get a feeling of your own, or two,'* is David Johansen's phonetic poetry – words as collage, using shape as well as sense to convey … um … what? *'Well, I'm asking you as a person …'* Verbal, verbal, verbal, the song is 5:58 of holler-holler, minus chorus, minus repetition. *Frankenstein* has all the magical properties of sheer nerve, ready to blow up any minute. Screw loose and fully-to-the-skull, the guitars of Johnny Thunders and Sylvain Sylvain wrap around spiffy-tuff drums of Tony Lo Bianco's ducking and diving *French Connection* New York City. Steam rises from the streets to meet David Johansen's tourette's, which complements his teenage dementia. The musical seizure of *Frankenstein* is an everlasting hallucination for James Maker, from which there is no joy like hearing loss; mechanical noise, tinnitus, joy. The neutral basis equals medication, and the New York Dolls become the amphet-amine that they themselves are always in search of. The Dolls have a 'when readers write' aura; no one is more like you than we are. It is everlastingly lamented by James and I that *Frankenstein* had not been the opening track on the most important album ever made, instead of the Dolls' foolishly impaired *Personality crisis*, and oh, the moldering debate goes on in a cramped back bedroom at 91 Redlaw Way in 1977, as intuition races ahead of understanding. Our walks through fog-bound south London were always funny and full of the child-rhymer, but we also knew it was the dark turn of righteous oblivion, full of willing stubbornness, feeling short-changed should a day be dull – as if it all, somehow, should be peak after peak.

Unfit for society, James answers the telephone for Mayco Travel – '*9.3.double ohhhh?*' – and writes best when most low, and becomes so attached to his complications that it will take decades to shake them off. '*Mayco Travel was actually a very good job,*' he remembers, '*I had my own chair.*' James would like to become famous in order to make up for past defeats. Since birth his life had been a sterile hell. Mimicry was his only pastime. Above all, he suffered from penis envy – being quite certain that he was not a conscious being. Deserts of boredom dripped by, thinly disguised as years. To pass autumnal afternoons James invented rivals. His only friend was Cheryl Bygrave, who lived along the flats – an equally mutilated existence of futile pains and an exclusive dependency on Freddie Laker Getaways. James would open the door but would not let you in, your rain-soaked demeanor registering nothing. His attitude to everything is obstinately masculine, yet he sees females as rivals in a stillborn play. Indescribable disgust jolted James out of bed each day, and darkness could never become light. One day we go swimming at a typically pitiful public pool in Peckham – the stench of feet agonizing. Roughly brutal kids dive-bomb all around us, and suddenly I notice someone in the pool who is still wearing his socks, and I close my eyes.

Am I even here? James looks at himself far too closely to see anything, and every slice of hardboiled luck comes to him only as compensation for otherwise having nothing to do. No one had ever bothered with James, and even his own sister had considered herself to be an only child. His parents had urged him to never – *under any circumstances* – be himself. When his true self slipped out, he covered his face with his hands, as if scrubbing himself away. He sought a listener – preferably one who might accompany him on piano. Like an unappreciated wife, he became exclusively absorbed in his own reflection – not because he loved himself, but because he didn't. The reflection was always the truth, the mirror had the last word, and James was too vigorous in his self-doubt to ever be doubted. In the Bermondsey of 1977, such behavior registered as abnormality of the hormones, a sadness in a man that develops in construction quite like that of a woman. No aggressive sexual activity is allowed, and so the boy wilts away, timing all wrong. *All wrong.* The mind is overactive yet the body does nothing, and depression can only be conquered if wallowed in. James had no understanding of himself as flesh, and because his life had been so lonely he directs himself towards masculine support – because this is the one thing he's never had. All he really wants is male friendships. When my life saves itself, James's life falls in on top of him. We had become just close enough to infect each other with our disappointments, although James was not without gaslight-flickers of fun – carelessly on Shadwell Dock Stairs, knee-deep in the not knowing, he would gumshoe early-hours Rotherhithe Tunnel in denim jacket and matching jeans offset by lyrically fetching court shoes as trademarked by David Johansen. James would annex anything that could be taken into his intellectually inexhaustible schemes, and he didn't mind being beaten up because of it. In fact, a beating could be considered a good review. At one point he follows me out to Denver not knowing that I have already left, yet he nonetheless arrives and stays, chattering the midnight oil with my family who have no idea what it is that sits before them. James was one of the first people I had ever met who spoke in complete sentences, minus the 'kind of, sort of, like, y'know, actually' redundancies that prop up most people's tautological cobblers. Londoners especially over-used the word 'actually', and usually placed it where it meant nothing. In their living room, James, his mother and his father had their own personal ashtrays, each a free-standing invention that needed to be pressed down like a coffee percolator in order to plunge the ash out of sight. Coming from a smoke-free background this struck me as quite funny. It had been, after all, just another consistently ho-hum evening at Kings Road in 1976 when the telephone rang louder than usual and I answered to hear James Maker's voice:

'*IS that Steven Morrissey?*' – heavy on the IS. Well, it was. I had placed an ad in *Sounds* magazine requesting Dolls acetates in exchange for several large bags of pre-stressed concrete, and James had tracked my telephone number down via a variety of veiled maneuvers involving Stretford Town Hall and a careless local priest. Quite a convincing human being, James was only slightly damaged, but understood by no one, which usually left the body being lowered slowly into the ground. The tongue rattled carelessly on a staircase at midnight, and on his first arrival at Kings Road he spoke directly to my mother:

'*Hello. Are you Scottish?*'

'*No,*' she replied, '*are YOU?*'

'*No,*' he said, and an hour of silence followed.

In affection distress my life briefly matches that of Simon Topping, newly free of school, living with his parents and his sister Joy in Flixton.

'*Do you mean to say that your sister is actually called Joy Topping?*' I ask.

'*Yes,*' he laughs.

Soon the new motorbike rolls up at Kings Road with regularity, and I wonder what it is that he wants. I open the door and he stands before me holding up a copy of Nico's *Chelsea Girl* LP.

'*Have you heard this?*' his Dana Andrews smile at full rev.

'*Translated into nine languages,*' I say, '*... except English ...*' I trail away – not in the least bit funny.

Nonetheless it's Nico's *Chelsea Girl* that fills our afternoons at Kings Road as rain batters the window, a cluttered tea-tray on the floor before us. Simon appears to be the first person who likes me for all the reasons that others usually dislike me. It had been a long hard war. It was enough just to sit there minus the usual nonsense of trying to make myself interesting. Simon takes me to his parents' house in Flixton. I hitch up onto the back of his bike – a fastened position of proximity that throws an entirely new light on seething hurt. Once at his house, I find that my wet shoes (for this *is* Manchester) have dragged acres of grass into the living room, and Simon's mother visibly ages as she looks down at her carpet.

'Oh, I can't stand her,' says Mrs Topping as a Bette Davis film began on television, *'she always acts the same in every film.'*

I'm obliged to chip in with *'Oh? I think she's always completely different in each film,'* so smarty-face says – having lived since the time of Socrates.

Mrs Topping looks disgusted at me and leaves the room. Some weeks later Simon and I are in his grandmother's house just off Barton Road. She has recently died, and Simon has temporarily moved in. It is a typical old Stretford semi, with grandma still very much in evidence: postwar literature, baffling knickknacks, an occasional table, all lovingly in order with that northern aura of making-do. I am quietly lost in sad thoughts when Simon smashes in with:

'My mother says you're a bad influence on me.' I smile weakly. A now familiar reel is about to be unwound. *'She's worried that ...'* he begins, but I cut him off.

'Ooooh, I know ... I know ... I know,' with an exaggerated sigh that could ruin crops and kill off migrating geese. I see before me Christopher Power, a school friend who lived on gasp-worthy Urmston Lane in Edwardian lushness (it may not be now, but it was then); the house a mass of travel and reference books, and a staircase that was neither narrow nor cramped, and how he sat at the foot of the stairs one hazy Saturday after hours of picking rhubarb, and said: *'My mother thinks you're a bad influence on me.'*

By now, I evidently know more than I know. Having accidentally managed everything in life to my own disadvantage, here we are again – with Simon Topping, journeying through yet another closing door. My mind stalled. I decided to dodge the plop of being a wearisome echo of myself, and I said:

'She's quite right. I AM a bad influence.'

Minutes later I am walking home – a wet heap of diffident stoop. I take the stairs at Kings Road, where Nico is always waiting for me, and I drag the river of this day's events as Nico sings in the background like a big bale of black coming towards me through moorland mist. If I had access to a high place, I'd jump from it. Having been killed and eaten by Mrs Topping, I ponder on how I could possibly be considered a bad influence, since I am neither bad nor remotely influential. It is not as if, at this age of 18, I designed dresses under the name Violet Temper. It is not as if I sought a career in exotic dancing, or read jokes aloud at funerals. I had never even once been drunk. My main concern in life was to find somewhere that could make spectacles in less than an hour. I bored my own self into unconsciousness every single day, so how I could exert bad influence mystified me.

Nico was an unclassifiable artist and largely disregarded as a gifted amateur who took far too much refuge in horror. Her youth's beauty dissolved into a lifelong lusty love of heroin that turned her into a shapeless object that moved along the ground like shifting smog. I meet her twice in unlit corners of Manchester danceterias, her frozen eyes wide amongst masses of deep black garments. The voice is a deadly frost that speaks only in mind-boggling twister-teasers, and you feel certain that *Nico is in there somewhere*, amongst the creases. The body is eighty-five parts anti-freeze and fifteen parts first-degree aitch. It is said that Nico introduced her teenage son to heroin, and, as he lay in a hospital bed having overdosed, she rigged up portable recording equipment in order to capture his last breath. Nico herself will be dead at 49, having fallen from her bicycle. Her singing voice is the sound of a body falling downstairs, and she speaks as if the hangman's hands are at her throat. One drizzly night at a crib called Rafters, Nico hoists herself onstage in preparation. Her fortress harmonium stands center-stage like a battleship, ready to wheeze vaporized tones like the last harpooned humpback. Nico aims for her stool but misses and jigs herself sideways. She readjusts and begins the foot-pumping process of awakening her harmonium. There is no *'hello'*, and no *'goodbye'*. I treasure her four studio albums, none of which contain the faintest hint of hope.

Two feature films of nervous vitality lock in my brain and possibly poison it forever. The first is *The Strange One* (1957), where de Paris pathologically infects the entire population of the world with his talent for bully tactics and his persistent offensiveness. Only articulate disdain for humanity saves him, and his rein of terror at a military school in Florida is remarkable solely for lasting as long as it does – even though it seems morally inevitable that he will end up being tied to a tree. His looks and style are far more penetrating than the God-fearing toothsome goofs around him – all of whom he breaks and wounds because they pay him far too much attention (or even because they show him none). De Paris is star quality and is not short on wit, thus I cannot help thinking that the common evil of his childishly dangerous ploys should be accepted by reason of his magnificent oeuvre alone – which in itself is certainly worth having. I think so, anyway. Ben Gazzara plays de Paris perfectly, relishing the humiliation of others. De Paris is too cute to be caught, and his contribution to immortality (what?) is suggested by the number of camera shots where the victim cadets are either kneeling before de Paris and looking upwards, or somehow seen from between the breeched legs of de Paris. If it sounds sordid, it isn't. There are no lines of cruelty on the de Paris face, but we assume that he is that rare thing: a confident sodomite, or a libidinous bully, or perhaps just a talker, or all three. Inexplicably a lone female enters the film in a later scene with de Paris, and she sweeps through the only scene in the film where de Paris looks bored stiff, and we immediately forget that she's even there. It is a plotless situation thrown in to take us off the salacious scent. Phew, thank heavens for that. We're all saved! Could Hollywood bear the eternal burden of a tough fruitcake? No! Anything but that! George Raft? In any case, de Paris must die soon because he is just as real as life, and since he is free of sexual loathing there is slim chance of the obligatory suicide. It takes dominantly handsome Mark Richman, with a civic duty to sexual custom, to turn the nature of suffering back on de Paris, who, yes, is tied to a tree and tortured. For this, we are all purified and we return to the ideal vision of manliness untroubled by that nasty game of thinking. But it is all too late because we already prefer the richer intellect of de Paris to the bullheaded correctness of Mark Richman. But de Paris must perish, because he is neither correct nor dull, and by the closing credits we are left to assume that he is as dead as a pansy from last spring.

But spare a thought for those who rock the boat. They challenge your attention, and even in your rage you find you quite like them for poking at you as if you were a dead mule. *Perhaps you are?*

Watch Charles Lloyd Pack in *I'm a Stranger* (1952) as Mr Cringle – who talks in order to rescue every moment from utterly sterile boredom. Without any effort whatsoever he is magnificent, and he knows his worth as a cast of confused spectators surround him (and surround him they do) in every scene. As with de Paris, it is only a matter of time waiting for Mr Cringle's comeuppance, because that's how society wobbles along – knocking whoever speaks up on the head.

GEORGE WESTCOTT: ... he is a police officer!
MR CRINGLE: [*bored*] ... yes ... it *leaps* to the eye.

Mr Cringle is a solicitor wrapped in folds of heavy tweed, of funny spectacles, a persistently offending theorist. The dominant in his life is the essayist poetry of each uttered reply. He will not allow himself to be overlooked, and he understands the value of effect more than anyone else. He is, of course, Oscar Tame, living on a planet unworthy of himself, yet rapidly game for a laugh. Everything he says might sound like grammatical malice, but he certainly has a heart even if there is rarely cause for it to be used. He only hurts people's feelings by being persistently right. Around him, the cast of James Hayter, Patric Doonan and Greta Gynt are frozen in dullness each time Mr Cringle speaks – which is often. Each scene gives center stage to Mr Cringle – mainly because he is interesting, but mostly because he says things that the other characters do not expect to hear. The smile is used to emphasize the most unpopular part of his commentary – almost as if waiting for a punch in the face. The pleasure of *I'm a Stranger* is the intensity of Mr Cringle's brilliance, because he certainly knows better, and he can rest forever on whatever it is he has just said. Others may have good looks and sexual success, but Mr Cringle's weapon of words carries enough punch to alter the texture of every life around him, partly because, as a fanatic of himself, he has suffered enough to know better. Absurdly miscast, Patric Doonan has supposedly just landed from his home in Calcutta, *'I'm a stranger here,'* he says, *'I don't really understand the ways of this country,'* and he delivers these lines in a very precise British accent that is eight parts Notting Hill and two parts Derbyshire. He has landed in London to claim his inheritance now that an unknown uncle has usefully expired. *'You know how it is with elderly bachelors,'* smiles Mr Cringle, *'they distribute their wealth between duty and conscience – a passport to a better world no doubt.'*

The careful monotony of Inspector Craddock (whom Mr Cringle naturally refers to as Inspector Haddock – if only to be annoying) is, as with all on-screen police figures, utterly insensible, flickering constantly with inefficiency.

'I'm anxious not to take you out of your depth,' Mr Cringle slyly smiles at Inspector Craddock, adding, *'Suspicion is one thing, proof another.'* But we all know the rules of the game, and by the final act of *I'm a Stranger* Mr Cringle is suddenly and inexplicably confused and burned out, as Inspector Craddock – after ninety minutes of inaction – is allowed to win the argument. Whereas Mr Cringle need only be

A teenage LINDER STERLING: trouble

heard for an audience to be held, the sterile and stupid Inspector Craddock takes the curtain bow because he is the dominant spirit of dull human existence as he moves across the screen like a carpenter in search of a piece of wood. Well, so what? Why make anything at all out of such films? Mr Cringle and de Paris – the colorful and exciting disturbers of the peace – are impossible to miss and impossible to overlook as adventurers on thin ice, exhaling a secret stream of inspiration, having far too exciting a message to deliver, and – even worse: *not* without a sense of humor. The arts translate life into film and literature and music and repeat a deadly poison: *the monotonous in life must be protected at all costs.*

But protected from what?

From you and I.

During the soundcheck for the Sex Pistols' third Manchester gig I begin a conversation with Linder Sterling, who is with the group Buzzcocks. Linder is nine parts sea-creature, and alights with all of the conversational atmospherics of someone steeped in machine-gun artistry. Some thirty-five years later, that conversation continues. Born in central Liverpool, Linder is an alcohol-free mangle of Jean Genet, Yoko Ono, Norma Winstone and Margaret Atwood. Pens, pencils, pens, pencils. She lives like an owl in a turret at 35 Mayfield Road in Whalley Range, unable to be reached by anyone but the most persistent. On the day of our first meeting, Linder is romantically paired with Howard Devoto – who sings for Buzzcocks and who looks like a harshly visionary 1960s schoolteacher. Buzzcocks are a close, genial unit, and Linder's sleeve-art will wrap their presentations perfectly. Like Marina swimming away from Troy Tempest and towards Phones, a small gesture from Linder means so much. My conversation cripples itself with the usual *'Me, of all people,'* full heart and empty hands, and I tell Linder that I had seen her at the Sex Pistols nights at the Lesser Free Trade Hall. Linder and Buzzcocks are all older than me, and I am thrilled to at last exchange with a group of genuinely artistic people. Linder sits on a table, her body curved like a question mark. Fagin, who sings for the Sex Pistols, leaps in.

'Is this a rough part of Manchester, then?' he asks, looking away.

'Yes,' says Howard, *'round here people walk about in their underpants,'* and everyone laughs. And it is true. The Electric Circus is surrounded by condemned yet fully inhabited 1930s council traps, from where mutant dwellers of the most hunchbacked and club-footed type swarm out in order to make fun of the pop kids who line up outside the Electric Circus. Manchester's most pickled poor live in these surrounds – non-human sewer-rats with missing eyes; the loudly insane with indecipherable speech patterns; the mad poor of Manchester's armpit. Dickens himself would be lost for words. These Collyhurst locals are like savage asylum escapees, and I tremble like a leaf in a storm. I am 17 and I am here to meet ex-Dolls Johnny Thunders and Jerry Nolan, who now play as the boringly named Heartbreakers, and I approach them knowing that my heart might at very least stop. They allow me to take photographs, but their unsmiling shrugs render conversation unwelcome. The outer reality shakes the inner life awake. Johnny and Jerry mean nothing after all. The Clash

also stand about, waiting to do their soundcheck, but their sound is so turbulent and chaotic that it's difficult to see how a soundcheck might help them. They are dressed in clannish school uniforms, and they look cruel next to the potting-shed pottiness of Buzzcocks. This night of December 9th 1976 is the start of a drawn-out process of easing myself away; no more soundchecks – unless they were my own.

'Are you still ill?' asks Linder, as we meet our weekly meet at Kendals rooftop restaurant, and while a song is born, so too is a lifelong friendship fortified and not weakened by time. The lonely orgasm of Megsons, and the indefatigable plans and plotting over something sticky at the Meng And Ecker café. Linder had begun to release records with her band Ludus, singing of a reality that no one had thus far wished for. In the exploding Manchester scene, she was the only female, and although she fought with fire and sword to render the unreceptive receptive, she is overlooked. The music scene of Manchester is a dark thread of maleness. The Fall have a keyboard player who is female, the Distractions have a bass player who is female, but Linder walks the line alone as the hunter of non-permitted dreams.

I respond to a card stuck on the wall at Virgin Records, and a paper trail leads me to Billy Duffy, a guitarist who lived with his mother in Wythenshawe. I no longer wanted to watch others do what I felt sure I could do so much better, so I present myself to Billy as 'a singer'. Could I now tell reality what to do? Should versus could? Would I continue to take no responsibility for my own life? Is the safe way the only way? Billy was well turned out and had a voluptuously statuesque girlfriend named Karen Concannon. He was also an impressive guitarist, and he looked at me and listened to me with bemused interest. Inside my head a tape looped and looped itself around and around, and it repeatedly told me that I would not be good enough when the time came. It unfolds, and then it happens, and when it does, it seems like it had always been there ... just waiting. From Wythenshawe, back to Stretford, back to Wythenshawe, on dark nights of self-creation, each slab of construction happened quickly, although Billy and I will never be drunken co-confessors. Billy pulls in some random musicians, and I am there at his urging – suddenly in rehearsal rooms loaded with amps and wires and headphones, and the clock strikes. Merging forces meet, and I, too deep to be rescued, sing. Against the command of everyone I had ever known, I sing! My mouth meets the microphone and the tremolo quaver eats the room with acceptable pitch and ... I am removed from the lifelong definition of others, and their opinions matter no more. I am singing the truth by myself, which might also be the truth of others ... and give me a whole life ... let the voice speak up for once and for all ...

'Make a joyful noise unto the Lord ...'

It works! A chest voice of light baritone, and all is ours. Billy wants to call the band the Politicians, or Hearts Go Bop, and my only suggestion is T-Shirt (after a recent LP by Loudon Wainwright) or Stupid Youth, and on and on. A Wythenshawe band called the Nosebleeds have broken up, and Billy enlists their rhythm section for a wrangled spot at Manchester University where a cast of thousands will play, and we are ready with our five songs – but no name. Astonishingly, the night is reviewed in print by Paul Morley for the *New Musical Express*. The band is listed as the Nosebleeds, and I am lumbered with this miscued name in private sufferance forevermore.

The hall had been packed, and with my dark green nylon shirt from the Antique Market I am fired from a canon. It was probably nothing, but it felt like the world. What is this strange, strange feeling as the crowd instantly applauds loudly? It is sexual release – mine, not theirs. Billy plays well, and I sing forcefully in tune, applause booms and I am home. History had trapped me for a long time, and now it must let me go. But my time with Billy is already over. He has been lassoed into joining the excellent Theatre of Hate who are ready for *Top of the Pops*, and rather than bury my face in the mud I am happy for him. And history takes the strangest of turns. I return to the have-nots, with more reason to cry than anyone else on earth, but Billy has left me with a parting suggestion. He tells me of a boy called Johnny Marr, who also lives in Wythenshawe and who '*is a much better guitarist than me*'. The suggestion is thoughtful, but I am not the type to tap on people's windows. Luckily, Johnny Marr *was* the type to tap on people's windows, and Billy had also turned Johnny to face my direction.

The shift of the 1980s had already begun to sound like the end of everything – politically infuriating and musically wretched. The *New Musical Express* continued as a lifeline of gifted writers, but it was difficult to be tempted by the squalid sounds smiling blandly from pop television, who appeared to be signaling a message to those of the Punk era: *Well, you've had your bit of fun, now let's get back to flash cash.* When my old friend Simon Topping appeared on the cover of the *NME*, I died a thousand deaths of sorrow and lay down in the woods to die. Linder and I attended the opening night of the Hacienda Club, which was initially for the secret agony of the secret public, but soon stuffed coaches from Blackburn and Bolton would pull up outside, unloading disfigured disco dancers and goblin-esque pork-pie chubbos with carroty-red curls smelling of pickled pig who claimed the Hacienda as their own public toilet. Making their northern debut, Culture Club stand onstage as the audience visibly back off.

'*C'mon, Manchester,*' says singer Boy George, '*I thought you were supposed to be hip?*' No, we're just automaton snobs with an excess of intolerance – you really *must* forgive us. A few months later Culture Club are number 1 in the singles chart, and, yes, it seems to be *that easy*. Manchester's imagination teems with musical groups crawling out of the literal and the metaphorical darkness. There are new sounds all around, and Linder and I forsake the sculptured mask of the Hacienda for the Beach Club and other dimly lit dumps somewhere behind Shudehill. Teenaged kids with dyed grey hair floodtide the city center, wrapped in heavy overcoats and Lowry gloom. Intoxicated by sunless Hulme – which is now rid of its hard and simple families – art students have made off with all of the cramped cold-water maison-ettes. Of his band A Certain Ratio, Simon Topping tells me: '*We're doing a cover of* Frankenstein *by the New York Dolls.*' I ask Jesus *exactly* how I am expected to take such news. Having spent so long outside the palace gates, I somehow cannot believe it. I had served as a thematic thread for

Simon as he pieced his band together, and I had placed the ad for a drummer for Simon that had produced Donald Johnson, who would become A Certain Ratio's savior. My affection for Simon remained solid, but Major Domo I wasn't. I collected the cash for A Certain Ratio's first-ever gig at the Band On the Wall, but couldn't for the life of me understand why. Heart on backwards, I began to suffer daily panic attacks. My mother is alarmed as my heart seems to be stuck in my throat. I endure the common slipway of prescribed antidepressants when I am really only reacting quite naturally to my humiliating surroundings – plus lack of air. I travel in the van with A Certain Ratio to Liverpool for their debut at Eric's, and although the band look terrific, nothing that isn't my own seems to work for me. Dispassionate and obviously mad, Margaret Thatcher is presiding over political England, raging war on the needy and praising the highborn. She creates more social unrest throughout England than has ever been known – major cities ablaze everywhere as Thatcher turns the police onto the British people. Every public address by Thatcher is a swamp of tormented revenge and madness, with never once a gesture of understanding or kindness. Thatcher is tagged the Iron Lady for being in possession of pigheadedness, perverseness and inflexibility – negatives for the rest of us, yet somehow she is delighted with the tag. Neither iron, nor a lady, Thatcher is a philosophical axe-woman with no understanding of personal error. Power-mad, Thatcher destroys the miners with relish, a damned and unhappy soul smiling victoriously when, under her peace-by-force military instructions, an Argentinian ship full of young teenage soldiers is blown up even though it poses no threat whatsoever to British troops. The *Belgrano* is outside of the Malvinas Exclusion Zone and sailing away from the islands, and Thatcher cannot defend her actions when cross-examined on television by a member of the public.

To give the impression of winning every argument, Thatcher simply drowns out her opponent with a loud, doomsday drone. When a ban on ivory goods is proposed throughout Europe in order to save thousands of African elephants that are being hacked to death, Thatcher's egotistical greed will not allow her to support the ban. When animal protectionists call upon Thatcher to halt the barbaric transportation of calves from England to the European mainland, where, newly wrenched from their mothers, the calves will then be chopped up or locked in veal crates, Thatcher refuses to consider compassionate change, and her demonic influence throws further shadows across the now lost soul of England.

Nannie's lair at 45 Milton Close continues as the family headquarters, as all gather daily to report the depth of changes in their lives. Rita is now manager at Chelsea Girl in Piccadilly and can often be spotted chasing shoplifters through Piccadilly Gardens. Jackie will marry at 25, and deliver Sam and Johnny unto the world; Rita will marry and produce Alex and Joseph at Roebuck Lane in Sale; Dorothy and Liam have begat Fiona and are now orderly and happy at 25 Bramley Avenue in Stretford; Jeane has Tracie, Susan and Elizabeth, and in New Jersey, Pat's progeny are Noeleen, Anthony and Brian, whilst in Colorado Mary will add Patrick to Matthew and Erin – and lo, the world expands. This is the swelling population of the family, the harmony and meter tangled and torn only when my own end-of-the-family-line sadness rises for hushed debate. The male family members have all disqualified me from any inclusion, with no halfway meetings of man-to-man concern. I am adrift. At 21, penniless in a world of plausible excuses, I am alone with my goals. These are difficult years, and if anything loving lay ahead I was already paying a large enough price. At my lowest in these years of signing on, I do not fit in anywhere with the family philosophy, and these days set the tempo of the times – even for the days when the sun re-enters the room. Travestied or not, you must just get through it. I tag along with Anna for a while. She lives on Stamford Street in Old Trafford, is Polish, and wears only authentically Victorian clothes. With seven pounds to my name I suggest to her that we move in together. Wisely, she refuses.

Johnny Marr was born in Ardwick in a Victorian dwelling not dissimilar to my own. Blocked in by dye works and engineering works, timber yards and iron foundries, the Ardwick of the Avis Bunnage era was an area of seasoned street fighters such as the Little Forty Gang, whose dapper style was well known when there was nothing nice to rest the eye on. Johnny was also of Irish parents, who would eventually inch their way south of the city center (for north is not the road that anyone ever travels). In 1982, Johnny appears at Kings Road immaculately be-quiffed and almost carried away by his own zest to make meaningful music. He reminds me of Tom Bell in *Payroll*, an early 1960s film set in Newcastle yet minus one single Geordie accent. Johnny despairs of things as they are and wants to change them, even if, beneath the grit and growl, his favorite group of all-time is Pentangle.

'*We've met before, y'know,*' he says, '*I'm glad you don't remember.*'

Ooh, but I do.

It had been in the foyer of the Ardwick Apollo, where Patti Smith had displayed her radiant stallions gradually lapping into seahorses nervousness. I stood in conversation with Philip Towman (another Wythenshawe musicologist), when Johnny first shoved his face in, and he said, '*You've got a funny voice.*' The comment contained an oblique confession, which said: you don't talk as shockingly bad as I do. In fact, Johnny later confessed that prior to meeting me he had pronounced the word 'guitar' without the t, so Ardwick-mangled the parlance. I couldn't imagine how this would be possible, or how he could be understood. I am shaken when I hear Johnny play guitar, because he is quite obviously gifted and almost unnaturally multi-talented. Since he shows an exact perspective on all things, I can't help but wonder: *What is he doing here with me?* Formulating writing systems and mapping out how best to blend our dual natures – here, against the hiss of the paraffin lamp, and me wrapped in the sanctity of an enormous overcoat acquired in a Denver charity shop for $5. Why has Johnny not already sprayed his mark – elsewhere, with others less scarred and less complicated than I am? It seemed to me that Johnny had enough spark and determination to push his way in amongst Manchester's headhunters – yet here he was, with someone whose natural bearing discouraged openness. Stranger still, we get on very well. It is a matter of finding yourself in possession of the one vital facet that the other lacks, but needs.

There are months to follow when Johnny and I – along with Angie (Johnny's lifelong girlfriend) – concentrate deeply on the realization of the dream. For the first time in my life the future is more important than the past. Angie's view in 1982 (and for the next five years, at least) held a bravely impartial and apolitical quality, and she would never be of the Girlfriend Syndrome who are famously destructive of the band that causes their love life momentary pause. Angie would always be intelligently supportive and ready to block gunfire; an honorable tack far superior to the commonplace and dreaded musician-girlfriend who would habitually cause infallible destruction and petty squabbles at Thatcherite levels. I suggest to Johnny that we call ourselves the Smiths, and he agrees. Neither of us can come up with anything else. It strikes me that the Smiths name lacks any settled association on face value, yet could also suit a presentation of virtually any style of music. It sounded like a timeless name, unlikely to date, and unlikely to glue itself to come-and-go movements: it could very well be Hancock Park of 1947, or Hulme of 1968; it could be primitive or developed – the Smithy poets of bygone Russia, or the servitude of the hard-working, and so on.

Johnny calls in bass player Andy Rourke and drummer Mike Joyce after a few stop-start sessions with other musicians. Andy and Mike are also of Irish stock and are both overly capable of a tough and masterly sound. Mike calls his flashy drumkit 'Elsie', and is the most experienced of all four of us. Both Andy and Mike are very funny, and the four of us look right together. We rehearse assiduously, but each passing week sees either Andy or Mike deciding that they'd rather not be a part of it, and Johnny darts after one or the other brimming with a persuasion that never fails. A damned soul, I play no part in the persuasion since I have no experience of ever persuading anyone to do anything. It is Johnny who pulls Andy back, and it is Johnny who races after Mike, and surgical persistence always wins the day.

A major stroke of luck is the enormous rehearsal room in central Manchester which owner Joe Moss loyally offers to Johnny free of charge. It is this rehearsal space that makes us, and it is here that we are free to re-order the universe; no dabbling, no squabbling, no tinkering about. Mike has recently won a court action against some unfortunate, and he is flushed with cash, but it is understandably not for the Smiths' pot and the burden of getting favors called in lands on Johnny's shoulders. The Smiths' sound rockets with meteoric progression; bomb-burst drumming, explosive chords, combative bass-lines, and over it all I am as free as a hawk to paint the canvas as I wish. It is a gift from Jesus. I sing out to the youth of the slums, and *Hand in glove* and *Still ill* anchor four lives together – four lives unlikely to be anchored together for any other reason.

The sound registered on these rehearsal nights above Crazy Face jeans shop left me with no doubt whatsoever that the Smiths worked on many levels, and let battle commence. Swiftly our set was assembled – each trial run of every song an excruciating torment of excitement; nothing ever failed, nothing ever stumbled. The harsh intensity of every song gave immediate rise to an indescribable

The scar of the stomach for all the world to see. I came with nothing —
all doors closed

stimulation mixed with impatience. Here, at last, it all is. I had been far too ingrained with pessimism to ever allow myself the indulgence of illusion, but suddenly life was close to me, and as I belted out *Miserable lie* with the full of my body I no longer felt like an overgrown forget-me-not. The bedrock of sound from all three instruments was as commando-tough as could be imagined, and with it, I felt as strong as a lion.

Johnny's boy-about-town associations brought our first gigs, and Manchester's weary intelligentsia edged out to form a visual line of those-in-the-know. Richard Boon had operated New Hormones Records on Newton Street, and had managed both Buzzcocks and Ludus, as well as the Beach Club. He would remain a constant throughout the Smiths' journey and was always encouraging (even though his expressionist jargon often swamped logic in far too much existentialism – if only for the Park Drive hell of it). Writer Jon Savage was also there; a friend to me, of sorts, whose flat on Wilbraham Road I would visit on nights of mourning, fascinated by Jon's Punk dissertations, his vintage Jag, and tales of his childhood in Kensington, where he had an entire floor of an Edwardian house to himself – such the indulgence of an only child by comfortable parents. Both Jon and Richard were always a magnificent whirlpool of words. Also present at the first few Smiths gigs was local newshound Anthony Wilson, to whom I had given a copy of the New York Dolls' first album in 1975. *'I've never heard of them,'* he said, so keenly lay his finger on the pulse. Having latched on to the Sex Pistols and Iggy Pop for his television show *So It Goes*, Wilson now assumed the cognoscenti cloak and found

himself blessed with the need to assess, judge and grade
– like a war general plastered with rows of ribbons but
who had never actually seen battle himself. At an early
Smiths night Wilson offers an opinion that no one has
asked for:

'I'm not so sure about Johnny. Hand in glove *is* Rebel rebel.
All this Byrds stuff has been done and done.'

The comment tests me in my new role as Johnny's com-
rade, and I fail because I allow meat-fed Wilson to say his
piece.

Reacting against everything, the Smiths are an instant
touring unit, with Joe Moss as four-stripe commander leading us up and down the M1. We are swiftly reviewed in
glowing terms by the national press, and a Smiths coterie
forms in every British city like an army on the march. The
exhilaration is bracing, since we are very much apart from
any previous factions and actions, trailing no one, and very
much our own campaign. We stood alone and we drove
our own crusade, our touring fortified by front-of-house
engineer Grant Showbiz, whose great wit and inherent
decency strengthened the Smiths' quest. Even when the
walls caved in, Grant remained an eloquent positive. The
groups from Punk's overspill continued to rabble-rouse in
large armies, but the Smiths drew a line under the past with
a detachment that presented a confidential perspective, and
one that would never snap. The vat of agitprop, melody
and self-culture all mish-mashed into a strong autonomous
weapon that seemed on the face of it to be academic, yet
appealed to heavily scarred jostlers. Something other than
safe and dreary success was happening. EMI Records
jumped in first, and paid for three recordings (*What*

difference does it make?, *Handsome devil* and *Miserable lie*), and then they just as quickly rejected the results. Our paltry finances were gathered to record *Hand in glove* under our own steam, which we planned to present to the venerable and wonky Rough Trade Records at their rinky-dink west London tower of power. I am certain that my vocal is not good enough, and I suffer my first professional wobble. Joe Moss finds the cash to allow me to re-record the vocals, and we are all saved. Johnny and I journey to London for an agreed appointment with Geoff Travis, who is the moral conscience of Rough Trade.

Whatever it was that Rough Trade were, they were not a hip label, and by their appearance, Rough Trade personnel in the early 1980s need never have feared sexual assault. Everything was a question of personal identity, and Rough Trade set out to assert autonomy whilst at the same time challenging the established order. They did this largely by pressing records that no one wanted to buy. They were postmodernism up the pole. The dominant culture sought to sell many and very quickly, whereas Rough Trade's service was to new artistic forms and slightly forbidden subject matter. Although the existing Rough Trade catalogue was known to be anti-Everything, it was also anti-listenable, and it would take the Smiths to bring a level of success and glamor to Rough Trade that the label had never dared hope for, and suddenly the smell of money replaced the smell of overcooked rice in the Rough Trade cloisters. The Smiths would pull Rough Trade out of the water – and would continue to do so long after the group had ended. Significant future signings were of groups who mostly wanted to be on Rough Trade because the Smiths once had been, and not because of the hysterical intellectual spinster image that the label had considered so confrontational until *Hand in glove* shattered their afternoons of wok rotas, poetry workshops and *Woman's Hour*. Lugubrious historian Geoff Travis looked bitterly upon the Smiths because, on the day that Johnny and I arrived for our scheduled meeting (clutching *Hand in glove*), Geoff waved us away and didn't want to see us. It was only because Johnny chased after Geoff and pinned him to the swivel-chair in Geoff's private hutch that Geoff very reluctantly listened to the music.

'Well, it's excellent and I'd like to release it immediately,' said the man who, four minutes earlier, wouldn't even say hello. From that moment on, once 'the Smiths' (actually just Johnny and I) were signed to Rough Trade, Geoff removed his Vivian Stanshall cape and made an impressive effort to erase the old-governess spirit of Rough Trade with a tear-less goodbye to their fair-trade essence of hiring dwarfs on stilts to pack and shift; or of rolling along in tight circumstances that favored social awareness, musicians' collectives, the communal vote, homemade bread and an unsexed all-hands-on-deck concept that had thread its way to some attention with Robert Wyatt's *Shipbuilding*. In his wheelchair, Robert was the very picture of the Rough Trade pop star, with a hit song that had cloistered nuns the world over tapping their habits. Certainly, there could be no shame attached to wheelchairs, but there aren't many in the Top 40. Ever after, Rough Trade became the Smiths label, and mostly – but not strictly – the label joined the Smiths' world into the 1990s and beyond. Because of the Smiths, Rough Trade became known in Woolworths warehouses and Croydon kitchens, and the

label's tubercular image of the 1970s – hand-crafted on a spinning jenny by Geoff Travis – was scorched off the face of the earth. Once the Smiths had ended, Rough Trade became hopeful ever after of similar groups – and found them, without ever creating a group that was free of the Smiths mold. But the brutally drab initial imprint of Rough Trade died of chest complaints at the King's Head pub in Islington – face down on a beer-stained copy of *Spare Rib* magazine, and never again would a band resembling the Raincoats be entertained by Rough Trade. The Smiths provided Geoff Travis with a surprise ending, and showed him the way to a more playful world where – for the very first time – the music papers suddenly saw Geoff Travis as the uncrowned king of musical taste, and Geoff thus joined the immortal worthies – amoral wealth here, a Brit Award there, reliant no more on fly-posting the sacred word at Compendium Books in Camden. Suddenly, post-Smiths, Rough Trade belonged to the world of publicity rather than poetry, and, without any sense of texture whatsoever, Geoff's over-cautious admiration for Morrissey and Marr meant that his label would never die. He, of course, has no choice but to tell you otherwise. With owl-like wisdom, Geoff would dispense with the older custom-made RT retainers and replace them with workers who looked like Smiths followers. *Because they were.*

A born trick-cyclist, Geoff would even climb back into the 1990s ring with a new sense of sartorial style – a physical impossibility during his John Dowie days, when matching the sales of Virgin's *Kew Rhone* was the ultimate strike. Rough Trade became an industry of shops and bags and hip-kid accessories – none of which featured the face of Robert Wyatt. Once knitting for the troops, Geoff suddenly looked like someone who had inherited a shipping fortune, and Rough Trade were magically up there with Melrose Avenue, James Dean and *In Cold Blood*. However, when 'the Smiths' signed to Rough Trade, the British music papers laughed at the mis-step, or expressed sympathetic doubt that the move would not stifle the band. The vinegary spinster face of Rough Trade was no place for anyone seeking public attention, but it worked because the Smiths worked, and for the first time in his life Geoff was overmatched. Haunted, he could never praise the Smiths. When *The South Bank Show* pieced together a Smiths documentary, Geoff said to me, *'I'm glad I wasn't interviewed because I wouldn't be able to think of anything good to say.'*

'Did they ask you to take part?' I said.

'Well ... no,' he said, softly.

Geoff would instead maintain that the Smiths were just one of many who tumbled in and out of his office, even though, prior to the Smiths, what tangible experience had he of success? He still wore his old school jumper, as the very pleasant music of Peter Blegvad rang through the bunkers and lumber rooms of Rough Trade until the Smiths shook the bats out of the hayloft. It seemed that Geoff's excitement was held back by his unwillingness to share public attention. He works and wins alone. But he must surely be aware that, without the Smiths, he would have found himself wandering from kaftan to kaftan; the Westway above slamming out the Who or the Clash, but not the recalcitrant Smiths – who saved his life and made it count in the long run.

Johnny and I signed to Rough Trade as 'the Smiths', witnessed by Andy and Mike, with Mike signing the document as a reliable witness. (Years later, in a distant courtroom, he will say that he did not have sight of such a document, and the *most* honorable judge will believe him – even though his signature is there on the contract for the world and the *most* honorable judge to see – should their eyes ever open.) £3,000 is handed over by the label, followed by a further £3,000 on July 29th 1983 – the lives of Morrissey and Marr fully purchased, our skinny white bodies lowered into the Rough Trade cauldron. From this windfall, I pay a lavish domestic telephone bill of £80, and the rest is put into a bank account named Smithdom that will fill our tank up and down and across the M1. Geoff shuttles the band to New York (in row 62, cattle class), where Seymour Stein awaits with a deal to sign the Smiths (ostensibly) to Sire Records. The deal, though, is not quite what it seems (are they ever?), and Seymour is in fact signing Rough Trade for licensing access to the Smiths. As thick as two short planks, Johnny and I sign – once again witnessed by Andy and Mike. We have no idea what we're signing, in an act of legendary mental deficiency.

The champagne does not flow, and indeed there will never be one instance in the Smiths' history with Rough Trade when Geoff would treat the band to a lavish none-too-cheap dinner or salutary clink of earthenware. Celebratory toasts never befell the Smiths, and it was a mark of our quaint drowsiness that we hardly noticed. Johnny and I continued to live on a strict diet of chocolate, crisps, chips and Coca-Cola, and with such an a la carte menu board we undertook lengthy tours. Both the Rough

Trade contract and the Sire contract were signed by Johnny and I as the Smiths because the name and the project, with all of its ideas and concerns and worries, were ours alone, and no one else's. Although Andy and Mike would soon 'rally round the flag', they hadn't yet, and both still looked askance at this funny little Smithy gamble, with their eyes agape for better opportunities.

The release of *Hand in glove* told me, at least, that I existed. Every night for months the record is played on Radio One, either by David Jensen or John Peel, and I stand by the radio listening – a disfigured beast finally unchained from the ocean floor. The song rises out of the radio, and there is immediate support from music writers of integrity. The initial 6,000 pressing sells quickly, and the land is ours. The rush of success surged with certainty, and the press began stories of the Smiths turning down six-figure offers from CBS and Virgin, preferring instead Rough Trade – which was untrue. The only label that had offered the Smiths a deal was Rough Trade. Suddenly, *Number One* magazine lists *Hand in glove* at number 70 on their official Top 100, and our unrelenting self-financed touring attracts John Walters, who is producer and acting scout for the John Peel radio show. Our timetable then erupts with a series of radio sessions for both David Jensen and John Peel, and our reputation swells a hundredfold. It is a great feeling. John Peel, though, did not ever come to see the Smiths play live, and he did not attend any of the radio sessions. He is cited as instrumental in the Smiths' success, but if not for the continual exuberance of John Walters, John Peel could never have encountered the Smiths. When I accidentally meet John Peel over the years (two times, and both in motorway service stations), he shyly has nothing to say on both occasions.

All of the new motion and commotion shakes the thought-patterns of Rough Trade Records, who are repeatedly reminded by the press that they are in possession of their first commercial venture – an unthinkable prospect for Rough Trade thus far. But how on earth could Rough Trade ever prosper – out there against brutally crass commercialism – unless the profiteer strangles the artistic elite? By the late summer of 1983 we are in Elephant Studios in Wapping recording our first LP. Wapping was still dankly post-war ruined dockland, and occupied exclusively by the east London poor. It is still the Wapping of *To Sir, with Love* (1967), and taxi drivers give a confused laugh once you state it as your destination. Apart from Peabody Trust flats, empty warehouses, rats that talk, and the left-behind doggerel of deep regret, there is nothing at all in Wapping. The elderly poor still shuffle about, out of time and quietly insane.

An overstuffed confectioner's shop stands alone on a flattened street awaiting the council chop, and the part-eaten retainer behind the counter looks relieved to finally be on his way out of the new depersonalized world. I walk to the shop every day to buy things that I don't need, because I want the owner to still feel relied upon, rain or shine. Production is in the hands of Troy Tate, who comes from Yorkshire and who has been appointed producer by Rough Trade. Mysteriously, we don't object because we all quite like Troy, but his presence indicates a lack of concentration on our part, because we don't actually know him, and this unfortunately reveals itself in the rash rumble coming from the speakers. It is not Troy's fault, but recording does not go well, and we all feel that we must have another shot at it in view of the goggle-eyed interest from the weekly music papers. Geoff agrees that the LP must be right and must be improved upon from the Troy sessions. We do not, in fact, know anyone at all who could or should produce the Smiths' first album. We cannot produce it ourselves because we – and especially I – have minimal studio experience. I actually have no idea what anything does or where anything goes. I am as useless as someone who has been left only as a head following a horrific road accident. John Porter had played for Roxy Music on their second (and magnificent) album, *For Your Pleasure*, and John had also produced one of our radio sessions for David Jensen, and Johnny thought him a logical choice to produce the album. I agreed.

John was very gentle and understanding, and our radio session had been a good indication of how things could be. We re-arranged ourselves and we began again. I look back on the album that became *The Smiths* and I see nothing at all that had anything to do with me. Although the songs were very strong, the recording of those songs – in my view – failed everyone. The Smiths sound had already developed with a bullish fortification that doesn't remotely suggest itself on *The Smiths* album. Live, Mike's drumming had an incredible thunderbolt quality, and Andy's bass had a pealing swagger – neither sound vaguely evident on *The Smiths* album. In fact, the album sounds exactly how the Smiths were *not*: pasty and thin. As genial as John Porter was, both Joe Moss and I could see that John didn't quite know what to do with the Smiths sound.

The yearning thirst of *Reel around the fountain* was dropped in pitch, and John brought in his friend Paul Carrick to add frisky piano. The result is more caper than lamentation. Our live firebrand *Miserable lie* is choked to death and boxed in, when it had always up to this point detonated as a step-by-step incline crowned by a yowling falsetto – all of this lost in John's production, which pulls the song back to a plod and makes the falsetto sound breathless and futile. *I don't owe you anything* is sanitized into a squashy and spongy Spandau Ballet cuddle-up, and John's remix of our glorious *Hand in glove* finally proves that he does not vaguely understand the rival gang spirit of the original recorded track. The mass of constraints that are evident in the final mix are really and ultimately the fault of the band themselves – for failing to press STOP. The album ought to have been a dangerous blow from the buckle-end of a belt, but instead it is a peck on the cheek – correctly reviewed by the press who accurately assess all of the Smiths' qualities without any claims of debut-album perfection. It is generally accepted that the songs are very strong, but unresolved on *The Smiths*. It enters the UK chart at a staggering number 2, held off by the Thompson Twins.

Richard Boon, now on the Rough Trade payroll, whispers to me: *'You know, it would've came in at number 1 but we couldn't manufacture the cassettes in time.'*

My life sinks. It is a noisy bell to a quizzy mind, and one that sounds and sounds for five years to come, and it tells me that Rough Trade cannot quite produce enough testosterone in matters of big business, and they will hold the Smiths back. Nonetheless, in the market-driven viciousness of triple-platinum Queen and Phil Collins mega-ness, *The Smiths* is right there, insubordinates of an accidental

moment in days when there is no sign anywhere of in-
dependent artists or a disconnected view. The chilblained
mainstream would not comment on the arrival of the
Smiths, and then (as now) there would be no Radio One
airplay irrespective of how high the records climbed. Highest entry? Radio One had no interest except the ploy of
avoidance.

It is forgotten now, but the Smiths' success was held
firmly at bay by the music industry, who instead exercised
their *if-we-ignore-them-they'll-go-away* Punk banishment. We
are tellingly billed in the *Sun* for our first appearance on
Top of the Pops as Dismiss, and *This charming man* garnishes
triumphant reviews and begins a twelve-week chart dance.
But something is wrong. The single leaps up and then
glides down, then rockets then dives, and it becomes evident that Rough Trade cannot keep pace with the demand
for stock, for suddenly they have a single that people want
to buy, and they are caught cat-napping by the radiator.
This charming man spends its entire life hedging and hover-
ing outside of the Top 20, Rough Trade unable to supply
sufficient quantities when the Top 10 called out with arms
wide open.

I stumble into my first television interview, which is for
breakfast TV. At 7 AM I sit quietly in the Green Room with
George Best. It is too early in the day to smile, so we both
avoid each other's tired eyes. I am rolled out to face an icy
grilling from Henry Kelly — a little, pinched Irish madam
who has no time for me and who cuts me off mid-sentence,
with neither a 'thank you' or a 'good luck' as he minces
frostily into his next major superstardom moment. Some
people are just awful. Kelly was known as the voice and

unfortunate face of Irish Eurovision, wearing a suit that looked better on the hanger.

At Rough Trade's elegant Blenheim Crescent squat I arrive to find a mountain range of boxes bearing the words 'This charming man *remix*'.

'*What-is-THAT?*' I ask Geoff.

Geoff confesses that the remix is Rough Trade's first and necessary commercial speculation, and is needed in order to keep the original 7-inch disc alive. Self-exiled in the branches of his own tree, Geoff may not be joining the bureaucrats, but he is suddenly playing the game their way. I have no idea who has remixed the song, and I slide away.

A sudden flood of cash and Rough Trade abandon Blenheim Crescent wok, stock and barrel, for 61 Collier Street – a nineteenth-century workhouse where daylight is wise enough never to enter and where the dank air of Pentonville soups with the constantly lowering clouds of industrial north London. The building is a ringing hum of energy – the staff an encouraging ragbag of Oxbridge ganja dissidents side by side with wicker-basket protectionists, all itching to spar with do-er's delight. As *The Smiths* album putters about its 33-week chart stay, Charlotte Brontë's Mr Brocklehurst calls me into his office (which is now a real and proper room) and tells me that a writ has been served by Capitol Records in Los Angeles, who strongly object to the Rough Trade logotype on the paper label of *This charming man*, which replaced the old shattered-glass RT label and instead mimics the famous Capitol logo.

'*So? Why did you do it?*' asks Geoff – a paragon of unity

when wind fills the sails, but a rat up a drainpipe when it all goes pear-shaped. In a steady voice I tell him that the idea and execution was not mine, but Richard Boon's. But here is the true Geoff, desperate to distance himself at the first sign of trouble. Once he realizes that he can't dump the writ onto me, his face visibly collapses, and the Rough Trade Socialist Federation are nowhere in sight.

I nominate *Pretty girls make graves* as the third single, but a bastion of bearded Rough Trade battleaxes drop on me like a ton of beansprouts and argue against a song with a title that would have made Mary Wollstonecraft throw in the tea-towel. I am shouted down, and Rough Trade wheel out *What difference does it make?* as the next single. I had loved the song until its defilement on *The Smiths* album; the loose swain's saunter now sounded stiff and inflexible, the drums sounding too frightened to move, the voice sounding like something gone to its reward – or, at least, resting in peace. I use a photograph of Terence Stamp as the sleeve image partly because I am assured that clearance can be gained from Stamp through Geoff's mutual friendship with Sandie Shaw. Once the single is issued, Terence Stamp objects and will say (years later) that *'Morrissey did not ask for approval.'* A new shot is panicked together, wherein I imitate the Stamp shot, although I choose to hold a glass of milk in place of Stamp's strychnine-soaked muslin cloth. I am ugly against Stamp's glamor-handsomeness, but it will have to do, since the single has already risen to number 12. Evidently Rough Trade are quite pleased about the sudden censoring of the original sleeve, because it might mean that collectors buy the single with the new sleeve also, thus bumping up sales. I remind Geoff that there is still no sign of airplay (which secretly doesn't actually bother me that much since I don't like the song – but I don't tell him that).

'*Noooo,*' he offers, with that whooping-cough smile of his, '*but people like it and we have sales of 250,000.*'

Although Geoff is tediously teetotal, I assume he has recently hit the bottle, because sales of 250,000 for a single that is only number 12 strikes me as impossible.

Gallantly, Geoff introduced me to his friend Sandie Shaw by wheeling me around to her Harley Street flat. I had collected all of Sandie's slap-bang singles of the 1960s, and thought that they perfectly traversed the cheap and loud sound of east London skirty jailbait. I was delighted to meet her in her own London digs – a fascinating floppy padhouse of little and dark cubby-hole rooms, with Sandie still in her pyjamas making breakfast. She spoke excitedly (and often), eventually asking me if I'd like some toast – an offer I could never refuse. Sandie disappeared and then reappeared holding an eye-squintingly small Hovis-type slice in her left palm, which she did not offer to me until fifteen more minutes of conversation had elapsed, when she suddenly reminded herself with an '*Oh – here,*' handing me the cold toast, minus a plate or a napkin.

From this meeting Sandie agreed to cover the song *Hand in glove* as a single, which pleased me greatly. In doing so Sandie utilized Johnny, Andy and Mike as her flattered band – free of any studio or session costs. The single jumped to number 27, giving Sandie her first chart hit in fifteen years, and there she was – back on *Top of the Pops*, with Johnny, Andy and Mike behind her (unpaid), and with television throughout Europe calling.

She telephones me: *'We're going to Germany to do some TV for* Hand in glove, *but Rough Trade won't pay for you to go 'cos they say you're not necessary,'* says the Duchess of Cumberland Place.

'I had no intention of going to Germany, because, as thousands of nice people have rushed to point out, I am not necessary,' I say, in my best not-necessary voice.

'Also,' adds the Dagenham doll, *'27 in the charts might be great for you, but it's not good enough for me.'*

Ugh. I can hardly believe my ears. And yet, *I can.* The transparency rose as Geoff took me aside to advise: *'The percentage cut on Sandie's single is 30–30–40 … that's 40 per cent for Sandie.'*

'… because … ?' I attempt to complete his sentence. I am confused, since I understand that the track had cost Sandie nothing. (In fact, I do not ever witness one moment when Sandie treats the band to dinner, or even a bottle of stale ale.)

'Well,' says Geoff, suddenly transmuting into Dr Finlay, *'she needs it.'* His head is now softly to one side, as if a beloved family pet must be gassed for its own good.

To his credit, Geoff had found a flat for me at Hornton Court on Campden Hill Road in Kensington. It was to be a very happy time for me, and Geoff was becoming attentive without foolishly attempting friendship. The flat is haunted – as everyone who calls by testifies (even if the chilled atmosphere is initially assumed to be me). Air of leaden fatigue hangs outside of the bathroom, as if something is standing right there in the hallway. There is also a heavy sense of sadness in the bedroom where I sleep, an atmosphere I am used to leaving behind – but not finding as I arrive.

My social status leaps after decades of disqualification on grounds of radiation.

The doorbell rings and there stands Vanessa Redgrave.

'*Marcie,*' she begins, and then goes on about social injustice in Namibia, and how we must all build a raft by late afternoon – preferably out of coconut matting.

The doorbell rings and there stands musician Dave Wakeling, whom I've never met, but who asks me if I'd like to go swimming.

The doorbell rings and there stands singer Billy MacKenzie, whom I've never met, asking if he can come inside to sit by the window.

The doorbell rings and in swoops Elton John's manager, who would like to talk about Morrissey having personal management.

When the doorbell rings and I decide not to answer, Sandie Shaw edges out inch by inch onto a perilously small ledge, from which the drop to Kensington High Street would instantly turn her into packing material, but there she is – shuffling into view with hands and body flat against the kitchen window, as I sit watching her, cradling tea at the kitchen table. It is one of those moments. I open the window:

'*WHAT are you doing?*' I gasp.

'*Well, you wouldn't answer the door, so I'm coming through the window,*' she says, legs and arms sprawling through the gap like a giant millipede.

Ann West also calls at Hornton Court, and we sit and talk of her tireless campaign to keep Myra Hindley and Ian Brady incarcerated (both had sexually tortured and then murdered Ann's daughter Lesley Ann in 1964). Ann is Chorlton working class, now living at Grindley Avenue, just across the road from Southern Cemetery, where Lesley Ann is buried. Ann is frequently interviewed on current affairs programmes, where the depths of her feelings are often constricted by her cross-examiners (who of course have never been in her position), and this is curious treatment for a woman who has endured so much but who has never once shrunk back from her duty to her daughter. Ann riles with fury at Lord Longford, who repeatedly speaks up in defense of parole for Myra Hindley, and Ann tells me of the writer Emlyn Williams, once a famous stage actor but now more associated with his fleshy and painful account of the Brady–Hindley murders in his book *Beyond Belief*. At the time of his research Williams had pestered Ann and her family unremittingly, even appearing at the family home requesting a pair of Lesley Ann's knickers – the moral intent of which was lost on Ann, who would go to her grave shouting out that Hindley should also go to hers without ever knowing a free day. I am contacted by Winifred Johnson, whose son Keith was buried on Saddleworth Moor by Brady and Hindley. Keith's body was never found, and Mrs Johnson asks me for support with her struggle to persuade the police to resume the search for Keith's body. Of course, had Keith been a child of privileged or moneyed background the search would never have been called off. But he was a poor, gawky boy from Manchester's forgotten side streets, and minus the blonde fantasy-fetish of a cutesy Madeleine McCann.

Amanda Malone is an American bubble-child with a Lady Penelope voice and a Herman's Hermits obsession.

Probably mad, she is yet another visitor to Hornton Court. She has recorded her version of *This charming man* over the original Smiths backing track, which is remixed sufficiently to take the sound a step away from the original. I am convinced that the version is mischievous enough to be a hit single in its modishly kinky-boots mode. I am gagged on this issue by Geoff, and the master-tapes are buried under heavy stone in the Rough Trade graveyard. It is up to me, though, to tell Amanda that Rough Trade aren't interested. *'Oh, just give it to me straight,'* she says, all pinks and yellows and last train to Clarksville.

At Rough Trade the galvanized gang of Smiths aides were Scott Piering (now deceased), Pat Bellis (now deceased), Gill Smith (now deceased), Jo Slee, Martha DeFoe and Richard Boon. The mobilized strength of all six attempted the very best for the Smiths, and often beyond their call of duty. All six dealt only with me, very rarely with Johnny, and never with Andy or Mike. The team were very witty and full of heart, presenting a very powerful center with a genuine thirst for success. It was their punch that turned the musty wheels of the RT moped. Live booking agent was Mike Hinc, operating All Trade Booking, and he dug in deeply on behalf of the Smiths to frame a careful rise.

'You are one of the hottest tickets in London,' he explains to all four of us, adding, in quieter tone, *'for now . . . ',* a mumble I would never allow him to forget as the years passed with no sign of a popularity dip.

Gill Smith warns me that she is a REAL Smith, in a spill of East End idiomatic warnings and spiritual sensations. Gill is full of loud tension; Hermione Baddeley in *Brighton*

Rock, forewarning *'right's right and wrong's wrong'* – expensive heels and swirling 1950s smock-coats.

Gill never ceases with hysterical *'and then she said this, and then I said that'* accounts, without a single gesture lost. Two years my senior, she has all the Chinese wisdom of the ages, yet she cannot tell left from right. *'But since you write with your right hand can't you just think in terms of writing each time you need to turn right, and ...'* suddenly I'm beginning to sound disedged. Gill has a full and open heart, and a turn of phrase so quick-witted that it almost hurts to listen. A master of the Tarot and extrasensory slapdash perception, Gill arrives at Hornton Court and freezes on the threshold. A mute minute passes as she wanders down the hallway only to stop outside the bathroom.

'Morrissey,' she begins, in a voice softer than usual (which, for Gill, is still very loud), *'there's something in here.'* Stalking her prey, her heels dig in ... *'and ... it's here.'* She stands squarely on the spot where whateveritwas has stopped me in my tracks every single day, a look of mariner's discovery on her face. I say nothing to my mother and sister as they settle down for a night in the guest bedroom – both watching a small light travel through the center of the room. I am relieved, at last, to not be quite so alone, as the walls hum unpleasantly.

Balancing on the same deadly spot as Sandie Shaw once had – outside of the kitchen window, and just an inch away from a messy Kensington High Street splatter – I discover Scott Piering similarly risking death simply because of an unanswered doorbell. I swing open the huge window and Scott falls into the sink.

'Scott, WHAT are you doing?'

'I rang the doorbell but you didn't answer.'
'Yes, I know. I heard it.'
'One slip and I'd be horsemeat.'
'Yes, I know. Would you like some beans on toast?'
'OK.'

No matter what we thought we knew, Johnny and I were Tipsy and Topsy from the village when it came to the cackling jaws of business. We signed virtually anything without looking. We didn't ever make money from touring, and we had no idea where our worldwide royalties ended up. In time-honored tradition, we were just two more pop artists thrilled to death with the spinning discs that bore our names. The specifics of finance and the gluttonous snakes-and-ladders legalities were deliberately complicated snares that all pop artists are expected to understand immediately. The act of creating music and songs and live presentations are relied upon to sufficiently distract the artist so that labels and lawyers and accountants – so crucial to groups in matters of law – might thrive. It is nothing new. The basic rule, though, is to keep the musician in the dark at all costs, so that the musician might call upon the lawyer repeatedly. In fact, pop artists live in a world that is a dramatic distance from the world of commerce, and they are usually exclusively consumed by their gift or drive at the expense of everything else. A vast industry of music lawyers and managers and accountants therefore flourish unchecked due to the musician's lack of business grasp. Thus, any standard recording contract deliberately reads like ancient Egyptian script – surely in order to trick the musician. Rather than hide your face under the bedcovers, you are thus forced to do business with those *whom you least mind* ripping you off – chiefly because you have no choice, and also because the law insists upon a documented trail of every penny that you earn – mainly so that someone might take it from you. The artist is the enemy. Solicitors are trained to squeeze as much money out of their own client as possible, and accountants might deliberately steer their client into tax troubles so that those very same accountants are further needed to unravel the mess that they created in the first place. Damaging managers merely manage *their own* position in relation to the artist, and a knowing code of conduct sweeps the cohesive circle of lawyer/accountant/manager into an all-crooks-together sect, and all are enjoined by whatever double-dealings they have on one another – all at the artist's expense. Never do we hear of an artist who rips off a firm of accountants; never do we hear of the artist who embezzles the record company; never do we hear of the artist who defrauds the lawyer; never do we hear of the artist who fleeces the management – but the ferocity of such situations reversed is characteristic of how the music industry works, and why it works. Since pop stars come and go with lightning speed, while the fraternity of managers and lawyers remain in place forevermore, it is with unspoken admiration that the industry admires the impulses of their colleagues who get away with the pop heist. After all, the pop artist who complains about anything at all is universally damned as petty.

From the perspective of the tomb, all of this gives no heart to the musician, which is usually why most of them conspicuously drop out of the racket, or end up catacombed in a drugged death that is always assumed to be their own weakness. It is a paralyzing truth that once you enter the bullring of fame there is no one to help you. Most fall. Some don't. If you manage to get hold of your own money then you are left with the equally difficult task of actually clinging on to it. Claims on artist income flood in like begging letters, and *'Oh, you might as well pay them just to get rid of them'* is the frequent chant of legal spiritual masters, who would never do the same were they in your shoes. Betrayal takes many forms, and the money that you make somehow never belongs to you. With great music to produce, Johnny and I signed and smiled – always politely – but we lacked the cleverness to interrupt at the right time. The net of limited companies lowered its noose around our necks. Geoff Travis looked on, writing everything down in what appeared to be unreadable shorthand so that only a goblin from hell could possibly turn the scrawl into sense. The international licensing deals made in the Smiths' name reaped nothing monetary for the Smiths themselves. The cog on which Rough Trade spun was the principle that their concerns were not motivated by money. In fact, their air was more pure than that of major labels, but the Rough Trade trick was to juggle unseen. And they did.

'Well, you're the highest new entry, at 19,' announces Gill Smith one cautious afternoon at Collier Street, in the days when such a high chart entry was very unusual. *Heaven knows I'm miserable now* eventually rose to number 10, and *William, it was really nothing* came tumbling after at number 17, and suddenly the Smiths were pop pantheon regulars. These chart positions were historic only in view of the cottage-industry party pranks of Rough Trade and this

made each chart victory remarkable given the blinding and pulverizing expenditure and outlay of our payrolled competition. Spandau Ballet called the Smiths 'the scruffs', and, I expect, we were. My own name is by now synonymous with the word 'miserable' in the press, so Johnny putters with 'misery' and playfully arrives at '*misery mozzery*', which truncates to Moz, and I am classified ever after. I had originally decided to use only my surname because I couldn't think of anyone else in music that had done so – although, of course, many had been known by just one name, but it hadn't been their surname. Only classical composers were known by just their surnames, and this suited my mudlark temperament quite nicely.

Although *The Smiths* had done well all around the world, I am stubbornly certain that if not for the unusual artwork and the hint of what could be it would not have dented the public forehead quite so much. I vomit profusely when I discover that the album has been pressed in Japan with Sandie Shaw's version of *Hand in glove* included. I am so disgusted by this that I beg people to kill me. Many rush forward. Furthermore, the group's name is barely readable on the finished artwork, but I am aware of my cranky precision pressing too firmly on the Rough Trade stable-hands.

I am so troubled by the flatness of the debut that I present to Geoff the idea of *Hatful of Hollow* as an interim collection that might hopefully detain those scared off by the blunted thud of *The Smiths*. Geoff fully agrees, and the project works well – charting at number 7, and holding on for forty-six weeks, tipping the platinum sales point that *The Smiths* had missed.

Our touring unit is constant and strong, blotted only by clangers from Mike who, in a busy dressing room after a Manchester show blurts out (loudly) how his family do not like me. *'They think you're just trying to be Jim Morrison ...'* he rasps, and as everyone in the room turns away in embarrassment I sit in resolute stillness.

Generally though, the Smiths as a working unit are assured and agreeable, their main misfortune so far being the way in which they had been sold like a cow at a market to Sire Records. Like Allen Ginsberg perched on the top of your mother's wardrobe, Geoff Travis had looked down smiling his whooping-cough smile as the Smiths lumbered along, hopelessly unaware of their global financial worth. We had made our American debut at the Danceteria in New York, and had planned to continue to Boston and New Jersey. We were booked into New York's famous Algonquin hotel – so beloved of James Dean in the 1950s and a place of rest for Oscar Wilde many Decembers ago. But there was no glamor to drink in now, and I sat alone in an enormous room lit only by a bedside light. I call downstairs.

'There appears to be no lighting in this room,' I say.

'Uuh, you'll find a reading light by the bed,' I am told.

'Yes, but I don't want to read. I want to unpack, but I can't see anything.'

'Uuh, that's the only room available.'

I open the curtains and cracks of city light throw slits of hope into the room as I hear a loud fritter behind me. I turn to witness a line of hamster-sized cockroaches race across the wonky thrift-store dresser. To my right three more roaches fish about beneath the television stand, and the scurry of horses' hooves is heard coming from the bathroom. I lean in, click on the light switch, and five large roaches trammel the sharp corners of the washstand. I telephone Geoff, who is staying on the Upper East Side and concluding dinner at a friend's apartment, having coaxed Morrissey and Marr – with child-like ease – to sign a deal with Sire Records that will land several platinum discs bearing Rough Trade's otherwise unsellable logo on the Billboard charts.

'Geoff, there are cockroaches ON the bed,' my voice cracks.

'Well, it's only for a few nights,' he says, signing off.

I attempt to find the other Smiths, but there are no replies at each door. I walk outside, not yet in possession of a credit card, and I have no hard cash, so I walk around darkening Manhattan – delaying a return to the hotel for as long as possible. When I finally return I find that my unpacked suitcase has disappeared. I race down to reception, half-tearful, half-manic.

'Uuh, we moved you to 'nutha room.'

I sleep fully clothed in the new room – all lights burning. I walk onstage the following night at the Danceteria, and as I do so, my blindness and bewilderment lead me directly off the lip of the stage, and I crash at the feet of the assembled human spillage. Unaided, I scramble back up and onto the stage, and I limp directly off – past three blank musicians who are unable to cope with such embarrassment. My right leg is bruised from top to bottom. I step out of the toilet to a cold-blooded stare from Geoff Travis.

'You know you're going to have to go back on, don't you?' he says, my well-being mattering less and less as the seconds pass. The other three Smiths say nothing, but Andy is

laughing. For me, words fitting enough to describe the gloom have yet to be invented. As I walk back out, a shrill female voice from the audience screeches '*WHAT is WROOOOOOOOONG with yew?*'

Hello, America.

The following day we are set to move on to New Jersey (although, offhand, I have no idea why). Geoff tells me that he will not be coming the rest of the way with us – as if this might make any difference. His investment secured by the signatures on the contract, Geoff is not quite interested enough to endure a second American gig. I am then led across the hallway to where Mike has his room, and there he sits upright in bed – a mass of large red sores covering his face and upper body. It is explained to me that Mike had shared his bed last night and that the unlucky dalliance left him with an outbreak of Lebanese warts. This now means that our trips to New Jersey and Boston must be scrapped, yet we cannot leave the country until the infected body is able to travel. I pass several more days in New York by myself. Johnny is nowhere to be seen, and I do not lay eyes on him once during my entire stay at the Algonquin. I am baffled, or mentally deficient, or both, but certainly I am deliberately cut off from everyone, as a prearranged plot kicks into full gear. I am being frozen out. It is a difficult week of rigid iceberg weather, as I dig despairingly at the Strand Bookshop and cough my way through the cheap eateries of Times Square slime, and I now fully realize that the other three Smiths are taking great steps to oust me. Why, I do not know. New York has not yet been daubed with New World flash and brightness

– no sign, as yet, of the computer age, and here in the wrong section of Fifth Avenue it is still a quagmire of midnight cowboys and sterile cuckoos. Perhaps it is the best of times for New York City. I am never troubled or approached as I sit alone in Washington Square. Smells abound unique to this city, and a warring settlement moves too fast, and the lonely traveler is engulfed. When we all finally meet at the airport there is enough silence to indicate the end. As we separate in Manchester, fatality shrieks. Behind my back, Joe Moss has coerced Johnny, Andy and Mike into axing the singer, and Joe carts all three buffos off to a legal firm in order to sharpen the blade against the Morrissey monolith. Since Joe himself has written himself out of the picture, he has no wish to see the little tugboat sail on, and the Morrissey monsoon must go. For a while, the other three agree with him.

It takes Johnny a few weeks to lance the views of others out of his system, and he then calls me. Hanging by a thread, we resume – deloused of Joe Moss. May 5th 1984 is departure date for a European tour, and at the airport in Manchester I see DIANA DORS DEAD shrieking from the front page of the *Sun* newspaper. OH MY DIANA headlines the *Daily Star*, and the *Daily Mirror* keeps alliteration alive with DIANA DORS DIES. Although the press had always raced to name Diana Dors as a nationally corrupting influence (because she was happy and a free spirit), by her death she has won them over. Death evidently has its uses.

The European tour is a success, although there are no band wages to be had at its close. We are 'we' again. Evidently Joe Moss as lead singer wasn't something that

Johnny, Andy or Mike thought helpful. On a flight to Finland I plonk a headset onto Martha DeFoe's ears so that she will hear *Death* by Klaus Nomi, and whilst listening intently she bursts into tears. As Martha sobs, I do too, and I run into the toilet to avoid the embarrassment of appearing too human.

Engineer Stephen Street had worked on the unkillable *Heaven knows I'm miserable now*, and admirably so. He was shy and receptive and three thoughts ahead of every situation – technically masterful and very patient. I suggest that we make the second album not with John Porter but with Stephen alone, and that we fill in all the artistic bits ourselves. At once, all band members disagreed, and only I give the Stephen Street vote.

Johnny's affectionate closeness to John Porter had finally clicked beyond price with *How soon is now?*, and so dazed had I been that I ran from the studio with a final mix and jumped into a black cab, piling out at Collier Street, where I took the stairs five at a time and powered into Geoff's office. Geoff swivels in a large chair and I balance on a footstool as the song plays. *How soon is now?* struck me as a new landmark, but once the track had ended, Geoff broke the silence:

'*WHAT is Johnny doing?*' he said, '*THAT is just NOISE.*'

The Collier Street clouds lowered, and *How soon is now?* resigned itself to B-side status. With further return, Geoff removes his glasses. This means he is about to tell me something unpalatable and he'd rather do it in darkness.

'*Now, you realize that everyone is saying that every Smiths song sounds the same?*' Geoff had an impressive knack of implying in his question the answer that he'd prefer. But the curtain fell with a clank. I am a puzzled child on the St Anne's sands, shouting to sea-sounds of wave and gull. I am that stretch of sand that the sea never reaches. Like dumpy relatives, the Smiths were stuck with Geoff, and he with us, until term's end (a term which he – not we – would take steps to extend).

Undernourished and growing out of the wrong soil, I knew at this time that a lot of people found me hard to take, and for the most part I understood why. Although a passably human creature on the outside, the swirling soul within seemed to speak up for the most awkward people on the planet. Somewhere deep within, my only pleasure was to out-endure people's patience. Against sane judgment, I risked unpopularity with my adrift physicality; but there it was, and how could the world possibly be in need of yet another Phil Collins? The subject of sex remained theoretical, and no one expressed any interest in me, which I didn't mind as long as I could create.

Gill Smith suddenly wound her way in as a hottie of blouse-ripping biological urge, but I take too long as I measure chemistry against meaning and she moves on like a hot-blooded goat in search of a rutting ram. *Shakespeare's sister* bursts out one night in a snowbound studio in Surrey. I felt that we had out-stripped ourselves once again, and I loved Andy's cello denouement. To his credit, Geoff jumped into his battered Astra and chugged his way through a blizzard to hear the song at the studio, but he is not impressed with it. He lays out his compromise: '*I'll release this as a single if you give your approval for* How soon is now? *to come out first – as an A-side.*'

This was quite rich considering how Geoff had dismissed

How soon is now? as 'just noise' a few months previously. The gabbing tongue gabs, and having gabbed, gabs on.

In the event, neither *Shakespeare's sister* nor *How soon is now?* troubles the Top 20, and even worse is the fate of *That joke isn't funny anymore* – dead in the water at number 49. The Smiths are repeatedly pointed to as the hottest band in the country, yet we cannot respond with a visible hit single.

Recording what would become the *Meat is Murder* album in a predictably cheap studio in Liverpool, I saw relief in everyone to be away from John Porter. Mike, at last, was free to play his drums his own way – rock-steady, yet with horse-race pace. Andy's brilliance flourished without the schoolmasterly ear of John Porter. The key to everything, Johnny finally made his first album. I could see John's worth on *How soon is now?*, but Johnny, Andy or Mike were not musicians who needed to be told what to play. When they allowed this to happen – with *The Smiths* – the results were flat. I share the shame of being led. John had asked me to record *Reel around the fountain* line by line – that is, singing one line and then stopping the tape, singing the second line and then stopping the tape. I found this to be a horrific idea, but I bowed to someone who I assumed had something pictorial up his sleeve. He didn't.

With *Meat is Murder* we thrashed through all of the new songs back-to-back in order to see – just for the hell of it – where everything would land. Out poured the signature Smiths' powerhouse full-tilt that had been lost on the debut. Straight away the hard Ardwick aria spits out as *The headmaster ritual*; a live-wire spitfire guitar sound that takes on all-comers; bass domination instant on *Rusholme ruffians*; weighty and bruiser drums on *I want the one I can't have*. The

Smiths began to stand upright. The aspirant moment is the title track, each musical notation an image, the subject dropped into the pop arena for the first time, and I relish to the point of tears this chance to give voice to the millions of beings that are butchered every single day in order to provide money for agriculturalist butchers. *Meat is Murder* enters the UK album chart at number 1, kicking Bruce Springsteen's *Born in the USA* off the top spot. Although the title track of Springsteen's album continues to blast from radio stations on constant rotation, no radio station ever plays *Meat is Murder*. In the year of 1985, abuse and torture of animals is protected under various British laws, and if you therefore want to act in defense of animals then you are forced to break the law. To publicly make the observation that meat is murder is, in fact, to claim that the law is wrong. It is also to suggest that all British judges who enjoy hunting and shooting and fishing, and who have personal investments in animal industries, are themselves terrorists, which, when viewed from any perspective, is undeniable. The horror of animal abuse is now common knowledge due to such famous cases as Huntington Life Sciences, and the global conspiracy of animal abuse is so financially profitable to the highborn and the upscale that the judiciary reserve their most aggressive and severely exaggerated prison sentences for anyone who selflessly attempts to rescue animals from unimaginable conditions of torture. The debate has opened up considerably in recent years, and it is no longer denied by anyone that eating animals and fish are cruel things to do. You either approve of violence or you don't, and nothing on earth is more violent or extreme than the meat industry. Generally, the media still believe that animals deserve all that they get – after all, they are not human, so how could their feelings matter? In return, the meat industry offers the human race a menu of colon cancer, heart disease, swine flu, E. coli, salmonella, osteoporosis, obesity, diabetes, Crohn's disease, mad cow disease, listeriosis, shellfish poisoning, bird flu, tongue cancer, and so on. Either slowly or quickly, all of the above kill carnivores, none of which matters much as long as money rolls in for the farming fatcats. Mad cow disease is, of course, mad farmer's disease – since it is the madness of the farmer that destroys the cow. The cow itself does nothing to make itself mad. In the US, the homeland meat industry causes more deaths to Americans than any other known entity, and its array of contaminations place the heaviest burden on medical care. In the UK, the NHS has expressed anger towards people who smoke because such an avoidable habit ultimately saps NHS resources. Yet the same can be said of people who eat pigs and sheep. Environmentally, the meat industry damages the earth's resources more than any other known threat, and 80 per cent of global warming has been attributed to meat production. Yet people are still encouraged to eat death, and to have death inside their bodies – long after tobacco warnings have cautioned people into fits of fear. Although many people are certain that the planet is for human use only, and that sea life should be called seafood, the British judiciary continues to label animal protectionists as 'extremists', whilst being unable to consider the Holocaust carnage inside every abattoir to be extreme. If the RSPCA were a credible organization they would not allow abattoirs to exist.

'*Ohhh … I absolutely HATE the Smiths!*' I hear Slade singer

Noddy Holder say in a daytime radio interview, as in the same week Cockney Rebel singer Steve Harley tells the *Daily Mail*, '*I cannot STAND the Smiths.*' In Manchester, the famous *Manchester Evening News* desperately attempts to portray the Smiths as 'fans' of Hindley and Brady, and finally relent with the almost-invisible BAD BOYS ARE TOPS when *Meat is Murder* hits number 1. How delightful to be thought 'bad', I muse, as I sit by a reading-light, pawing George Eliot's *Scenes of Clerical Life*. Life is clearly so much better when you can get straight to the point.

Discounting *The Hollies Greatest Hits* (1968), *Meat is Murder* is the first studio album from a Manchester band ever to reach number 1 in England, and although rife with singles-to-be, we are already further at odds with Gentleman Geoff, who is insisting that *Hatful of Hollow* (Rough Trade's biggest ever earner) does not count as a contractual album (being what, then? A bountiful gift from the land of the fairies? Random sweepings from the flagged floor of the Rough Trade workshop?), and an unfriendly deadlock digs in. In the US, Sire release *How soon is now?* as a single, but they cannot get it onto the Billboard 100 even though the song is receiving national airplay and garnishing fantastic attention from coast to coast. Sire then paste together a predictably vomit-inducing promotional video to accompany the single, and my heavy heart sinks further as I witness the cold-blooded mess on VHS. The Smiths will encircle the US twice – to quite outstanding success in large arenas – yet Sire cannot get a television spot for the band. We have no publicist, and we have no support from the label. At a chaotically sold-out Universal Amphitheater in Los Angeles I announce:

'I would like to thank those who made all of this possible ... the Smiths' – it is petulant, of course, but it's the only way to get the point across.

Seymour Stein smiles: *'We have no idea how you're selling so many tickets!'* to which smiles and shrugs are meant to follow.

What he is really saying is that Sire have done nothing at all to pitch the Smiths in the US. In Los Angeles, our first visit to the city comprises two sold-out shows at the Palladium, and business elsewhere is even stronger – from Boston Great Woods to 12,000 tickets sold in Toronto. There is no media or press interest. It is unfortunate, and sad. I point Seymour Stein towards our support band James, whom he then signs, and who manage a hit single on the Billboard 100. Even our support band in the UK (Easterhouse) edge onto the Billboard 100, yet Sire cannot manage a hit single for the Smiths themselves – not even after two voluminous tours of screaming hysteria and stage invasions. There is no one in the wings to document or organize, and not even an American photo-session is suggested. Still travelling economy, the Smiths conclude each tour penniless – the funny and the lonely side of it all. Our mouths taped shut, we had no idea that the young audiences of America and Canada would be so feverish. *Rolling Stone* magazine repeatedly said *'No, thanks,'* and have kept their word for thirty years, yet they will applaud any sub-Smiths progeny who taps on their bunker. But that's life. Go first and be sure of a hard time.

Pain continues as a source of inspiration. Back in darkness, we begin recording *The Queen is Dead*. Geoff had interestingly suggested George Martin as a producer

– which is one of Geoff's very rare magnanimous proposals. George Martin declines, saying that he only wants to be known for his work with the Beatles. Johnny and I then have tea with Tony Visconti, most famously associated with the supremely noble works of T. Rex and David Bowie, but after our meeting Tony also declines. Free to howl again, I do so, and we record *The Queen is Dead* as we had recorded *Meat is Murder* – with Stephen Street making sense of it all. Johnny is in the full vigor of his greatness. He is a deluge of ideas and motion, and it streams from his every touch on *The Queen is Dead*. The chords are biteable and studlike, and it is Johnny's soaring attitude that leads Andy and Mike. Although I am now out-stripped by the Smiths success (I had no idea that it would jump to such proportions), the lesson deep in my soul remains the same: the music always comes first – before lawyers and accountants – and I am suddenly bolder in demeanor. I am now living at 66 Cadogan Square in Chelsea, as the Smiths zoom empirically, with the press always within ear-shot, complicating every question and inventing meddlesome Morrissey quotes. It is mostly amusing, and often deadly.

Once *The Queen is Dead* has been recorded, Geoff serves a writ upon me at Cadogan Square which states that the album will not be released until a court hearing decides whether or not *Hatful of Hollow* counts as a contractual album. There would of course be no need for a court hearing if contractually there were no grey areas on the matter. But there were, and so it was now merely a question of bully-tactics in a public courtroom ... *see the luck I've had* ... The writ is served upon me, but not on Johnny, Andy or Mike. However, Johnny very bravely attends the court hearing by himself – so certain that the law can't fault the truth. He is, of course, butchered and ridiculed by Geoff's uncivil barristers, and the common ownership kibbutz of Rough Trade kicks the shit out of the Smiths. *The artist is the enemy.*

Geoff had approached me after *Meat is Murder* had entered at number 1, and he leaked a little touch of sentiment that almost verged on the human as he said, *'I've dreamt of this happening all of my life,'* which seemed to me to be unlikely, since Rough Trade had never even remotely been in the running for a number 1 album, and with this gush of acknowledgement Geoff handed me a bag of biscuits bearing a 2 pounds and 75 pence sticker still affixed. I gave no answer. How could there *be* one? I assumed and hoped I was mid-dream.

Such sentiment had long since died away as I stood in the telephone box across from Peter Jones department store on the Kings Road at 9:15 one Tuesday morning, calling Rough Trade to find out whether or not *The Queen is Dead* had made its projected number 1 chart position. Although sales and press fervor are strong enough to ensure a number 1 position, my body sinks to hear Geoff briskly say, *'It's number 2. Phil Collins kept us off,'* and feet of clay carry me back to 66 Cadogan Square – somehow certain that the album had been disallowed number 1 status because of its title. I lit the fire and sat hunched and contorted for the rest of the day. *The Queen is Dead* is the album of the moment in England, but there remains zero airplay and it seems impossible to get all cylinders working at the same time. Radio One continues to ignore the Smiths, as does Capital Radio, and there appears to be nothing at all that anyone can do about it.

'The success of the Smiths is down to however many magazines you can get your face on,' says Geoff, wrongly. I push for Johnny to take on half of the press requests, but Pat Bellis says that magazine covers are only on offer if the interviewee is me. *Uh.* The creak of Morrissey attacking Thatcher is what the press would prefer, even though her name is annoyingly printed as 'Maggie' whenever I refer to her as 'Thatcher'.

I ask Pat Bellis, *'If I repeatedly say Thatcher, why do they print Maggie?'*

'We-ee-ll,' says Pat, *'people are getting a bit fed up with your list of complaints.'*

'And who do I complain to about THAT?' I ask.

In Scott Piering's office I ask the same question. *'I'd never call her Maggie, so why do they print what I didn't say? Thatcher is her name. I didn't invent that.'* But the press is in a world of its own, and you might add to it but you can't disturb it.

The daily tabloids fabricate bare-teeth stories with utterly stupid headlines – MORRISSEY: ROYAL ROW, MORRISSEY SAYS SORRY TO THE QUEEN, MORRISSEY APOLOGIZES ... as my spirit is stoked and tended like a downstairs furnace. I smash into Pat Bellis's office: *'Morrissey says sorry to the Queen? When? For what? Who has the right to print such lies??!'*

'We-ee-ll,' says Pat, her lipstick stuck to her teeth, as Scott Piering juts in with the untrue *'all publicity is good publicity'.*

'Me apologizing to the Queen isn't good publicity!!!!' I explode. A great wash of humiliating and penalizing editorials flutter through the daily newspapers, all superficial, and all stupid. SICK MORRISSEY alerts the *Daily Mail,* who write how the sick Morrissey has claimed that it's OK for boys to like boys as well as girls. With the tabloid press, nothing appears

to work, and I examine what appears to be an increasing sense of my own lunacy – as if I should only be dealt with through a small door kept locked. Chewing my way out of the psychiatric wing, I evidently sputter out apologies to the Queen's horses, and it all overflows beyond ridiculousness. In the *NME*, a writer opens a major piece by claiming that he rang my doorbell and I appeared at the door wearing a tutu, and no effort is made to assure readers that the writer is jesting, and I am shocked to discover that people assumed it to be true. Morrissey quotes shoot out from the press like darts, distorted and exaggerated, and something sniggers to me that my life is no longer my own. What registers is that I appear to be playing the naughtiness game, when, really, I am consumed with a question that is more difficult than it seems: *what can I salvage from all of this?* A *Melody Maker* interview is written by a failed Manchester musician under an assumed name, and becomes one of the first major hatchet jobs, wherein the writer's own questions are impressively printed as loquacious eloquence, and my own replies are printed as stunted fumblings. In truth, the writer's questions bore none of the intellectual swoop that his own typewriter later bestowed, and my real-time replies contained none of the stumble and fidget squirminess that journalistic license later decided they should have. Added to this the writer invents *as fact* the idea that I had spent my youth hanging around public toilets in Manchester. I protest about all of this to Rough Trade, and Pat once again rounds her shoulders with, '*We-ee-ll, it's a front cover ...*' and the new face of the Independents is interchangeable with that of the old Majors. '*But this is slander, or libel, whichever way you look at it ... and ...*'

'*Defamation,*' whispers one of the many now gathered.

'*Yes, defamation, and I don't consider a* Melody Maker *cover a good enough treat for the reputation of hanging around public toilets* ...' I am now hysterical.

'*We-ee-ll,*' says Pat, saying nothing.

But Johnny finds the right words: '*We're gonna get him,*' and he bangs a fist into an open palm, like Burt Ward as Robin the Boy Wonder. Because of the public-toilet disparagement, there are of course legal grounds to take action against *Melody Maker*, but Rough Trade are now making useful inroads with the press because of the Smiths, and they don't want to cause a fuss, and I am still too green around the gills to ignore their reluctance. I could attempt to tackle *Melody Maker* myself, but without the label behind me, I am at sea.

The meeting for the *Melody Maker* piece had taken place in Cleveland, Ohio, and after the face-to-face interview had concluded I had retired to the joy of pure cotton sheets. In the middle of the night the telephone rings and it is the journalist. I say nothing, confused, and I put the phone down and return to sleep. Whatever was it that the writer thought he might learn or access by dialing my number? Didn't the peevish printed article boom of enraged loss? Isn't it the case that wildly vitriolic reviews of hate usually have their waterlogged roots in personal rebuff — now and forever, *Amen.*

The summer of 1986 brought Anthony Wilson's Festival of the Tenth Summer, which took place at Manchester's G-Mex with a roundabout intent to salute Anthony Wilson as Manchester's occupying power. At first I said no to the event, because I thought the ticket prices were too high, when in shuffles a typed letter from Anthony H. Wilson:

This isn't about Factory, this isn't about Tony Wilson or Steven Patrick Morrissey; it's about Manchester, and Manchester only. I know you're worried about a Smiths fan having to pay thirteen pounds to see the Smiths. But this isn't a Smiths concert. It is designed as an event which reflects the achievement of the youth of this city, and the ticket price merely reflects our achievements. Our only reference in pricing was to go as we all do in our concerts for the lower end of the norm, but with regard to that norm.

It would have needed a fifteen pound ticket to have financed properly but we felt that thirteen pounds ... was as far as we could go. I felt rather in the mood to call the whole thing off. I have summoned up my energies one more time because I think the young people of this area deserve to know themselves, to under-stand how important they are. I think City Fun's greatest hits and Shy Talk and Out There should be reprinted, and have Cummins pic of the Electric Circus hanging on the wall; I think the works of Garrett and Saville and Mulvey and Boone should be displayed and ...

Yakkety-yak, **thud.**

In fact, the G-Mex event is a great day, and theatrician Wilson is at his best master of ceremonies scarf-flowing staginess. He calls everyone *'darling'*, but it's all a part of the public relations aspect of his showboat routine and not at all disingenuous. Before the Smiths go onstage, film-maker Derek Jarman is brought into the dressing room and is introduced. Johnny says *'Hello,'* and then turns

sideways to vomit. It is certainly a moment, but unfortunately it wasn't caught on film.

Onstage, the Smiths are received as a life-giving source,
and this begins to enrage Wilson so much that he flutters
and fumes backstage, demanding to technicians that the
Smiths' power be cut off. No backline crew will comply
with Wilson, who is effectively gagged at his own festival. At the base of it all, general opinion assessed Wilson's
rage to be the blustering fury in realizing that the Smiths
had meant more to the crowd than his nurtured protégés
New Order. Suddenly Wilson's divine right to be Mr Manchester is scuppered, and he spends the remainder of his
life with a Morrissey-Smiths wasting disease of the lower
limbs, whilst oddly admitting that his big mistake in life
was that he didn't sign the Smiths to Factory.

Yes, well, there we go.

Departing for a tour of Ireland, Johnny turns up at my
mother's house, wobbles, and collapses. Everyone waits
outside in the tour bus. It is perhaps 11 AM. There is much
fussing, and I retreat. Johnny is carried upstairs and placed
on a bed. Half an hour later my mother comes downstairs
and walks over to where I am standing by the window.

'*Well, he's OK,*' she says, '*but he owes me an eiderdown.*'

On arriving in Dublin, Johnny is whisked away by ambu-
lance. I am concerned, but I have no idea what is happening,
and I am told nothing. Bossy nurses take over and shove
everyone else out of earshot, as if none of us count. The
shows take place, and wherever we play in Ireland – Waterford, Dundalk, Letterkenny, Cork, Limerick – crowds
scream and rush the stage with fantastically warped mania.

Second by second it is thrilling. At Waterford, the audience hangs from any particle of stage-surround that they can grasp, and the operatic framework of this hoary old theater is ripped apart as – suddenly, the stage itself wobbles, having stood untroubled for more than one hundred years. In Letterkenny, the screams and squeals are of Bay City Rollers damp-knickered shrieks, and the Smiths are bundled in and out in a screwball frenzy. Geoff Travis had delayed the release of *The Queen is Dead* by nine months because of his court action against Morrissey and Marr (but not, let someone note, against Rourke and Joyce), and the bewildering excitement of touring ran alongside the legal demands of our lives being sealed up as the usual heel-dragging, fleshed-out, money-making and deliberately distracting court action takes place, and Johnny and I are fleeced from all directions. The Smiths may have saved Rough Trade from extinction, and may have allowed Geoff to lumber up to the spotlight, but all is fair in love and war as his legal eagles shatter the Morrissey–Marr defense. Johnny Marr, having never once deprived Rough Trade of a second of his outstanding and liberating talent, had been turned into a woeful joke by Geoff and his legal muggers. But life, *somehow*, goes on.

A letter arrives at Cadogan Square from Geoff. It states that he's terribly worried about me and wonders what has caused my current depression.

> *If I can be of any help please let me know. If I am the cause of this plight, and I can't imagine what I've done, please let me know also.*
>
> *Yours,*
> *Geoff*

Absurdly, Geoff had turned up at Johnny and Angie's marriage earlier that year in San Francisco – sitting and nodding whilst plotting court action. The ceremony went very well – I, with the infinite privilege of passing the wedding ring, yet, as ever I am too dazed to fail to notice the zero contribution to the day's events by the head of the label. My future conversations with Geoff become of necessity, whereas Johnny was never again seen in Geoff's company.

I am thrilled to receive a letter from the French actor Alain Delon approving his image for use on the sleeve of *The Queen is Dead* – this coming after a run of refusals from Alan Bates, Albert Finney and George Best. But the album title worries Johnny. His parents are upset to think that anyone would call an album *The Queen is Dead*, and Johnny asks me if I would consider switching the title to *Bigmouth Strikes Again*. I stand my ground and, knowing nothing of the kind, I assure him that all will be well.

Reviews had been very supportive apart from Ireland's *Hot Press*, whose title warned THE CROWN SLIPS. *Well, it hadn't*. It stayed on more firmly fixed than ever before, so thank you, *Hot Press*. Another review in an American newspaper commented: *'The first three tracks on this album are probably the worst three songs I have ever heard in my life.'* Ah, platitudes.

Geoff scratches out another spine-chilling letter:

Dear Morrissey,

I just didn't expect something so accomplished ... something so wonderful, musical and virtuous ... the strength of your delivery is majestic. On The queen *you bed down with the language of rock 'n roll and pour scorn on its conventions ... Without doubt the Smiths finest work and a personal triumph ... a new phase of command and vocal power. I love it madly.*

All the best,
Geoff.

This atmosphere of respect from Geoff would only ever appear in private letter, and seemed never generously shown for public ear or eye, where silence is taken to mean whatever you wish it to mean.

Meekly, I had missed the value of *There is a light that never goes out*, and I suggested to Johnny that it shouldn't be included on the album. He laughs a *you-silly-thing* warranty, and I drop the protest. The humiliation I live with, because this suggestion is everlasting since the song became – and continues to be – greatly loved as one of the most powerful components of the Smiths canon. It is often a relief to be wrong.

Pathetically, *The Queen is Dead* – like *Meat is Murder* – fails to cough up a Top 20 single. Something wrong remains wrong.

Whilst in Denver, Colorado, Johnny and I attend a concert by A-ha, whom we have met previously and whom we quite like. The hall is rammed with very small females who squeal at an intolerable volume throughout the concert, drowning out all of the songs. Because of this, the night is a mess. While it's true that girls screamed at Sparks, there was something utterly pointless about the high-pitched mass squeal that blanketed the hall for A-ha. There was hardly any necessity for the band to actually play. Backstage, A-ha are gracious. They are healthy and athletic and inherently decent, with their rosebud Norwegian propriety, and this is interesting to me because it shows me how the mission to sing isn't always a result of pain.

In Denver city center a plump girl bangs on the window of the car shouting: *'Ooh, I always wanted to meet you!'* which strikes me as odd since we have only existed for three years – 'always' surely not amounting to that much time at all. Johnny sits back and shouts: *'Ta'ra, fatty,'* as the car pulls away. I am shocked, but I then fold into convulsive laughter. Some terrible moments *are* funny.

At an airport in Toronto, Eartha Kitt is standing by herself – she who once famously shared a bed with both James Dean and Paul Newman at the same time (or so plain speaking has it). Full of sensuality, she pulled herself out of southern swampland to float insubordinate gestures across the map of American entertainment, and she succeeded very well. Amusingly, her daughter is called Kitt, which surely makes her Kitt Kitt. There are moments when you must give in, so I blandly stick my bland neck out.

'Do you mind if I say hello?' I ask Eartha Kitt. She laughs a head-thrown-back laugh. *'We're a group from England called the Smiths,'* throws in Johnny. Eartha gives a second laugh – possibly imagining a large family rather than a musical group.

At Heathrow Airport I sit next to Sir Richard Attenborough – once a fresh young Pinkie in the 1947 film of *Brighton Rock.*

'Does it all seem like a hundred years ago?' I ask him.

'Oh much more than that,' he smiles, but he then looks

understandably dumbfounded as I ask him about James Hayter.

Nerve deserts me in 1986 as I spot the American writer and social reformer James Baldwin sitting alone in the lobby of a grandiose Barcelona hotel. He is weathered and intense, absorbed in his own thoughts, with a face there could never be enough time to describe. I drink him in, but can do no more. I pin so much prestige to James Baldwin that to risk approach places my life on the line; I'd hang myself at any glimmer of rejection. History books overlook James Baldwin because he presented an unvarnished view of the American essence – as blunt and rousing as print would allow. His public speeches were intoxicating, his motivational palette of words so full of fireworks that you smile as you listen – not because of humor, but because he was so good at voicing the general truth, with which most struggled. His liking for male flesh gave the world a perfect excuse to brush him aside as a social danger, and he was erased away as someone who used his blackness as an excuse for everything. In fact, his purity scared them off, and his honesty ignited irrational fear in an America where men were draped with medals for killing other men yet imprisoned for loving one another. Pitifully, on this Barcelona day, I do not have the steel to approach James Baldwin, because I know very well that I will jabber rubbish, and that his large, soulful eyes will lower at someone ruefully new to the game. Shortly thereafter, he is dead.

The essence of Smiths Art (*MozArt*) was the will to have every Smiths sleeve as well turned out as possible, and it came from an idea I had to take images that were the opposite of glamor and to pump enough heart and desire into them to show ordinariness as an instrument of power – or, possibly, glamor. Bits of neo-realism, bits of brutality, with the task being to present cheerless and cluttered bed-sitter art in a beautiful and proudly frank way (note: *The World Won't Listen*). Rules, in all things, are simply laid down so that someone might break them. I had learned to guard my secrets carefully, and I had stored boxes of clippings over the years that would all now alight as Smithsonian sleeves. It would be the ache of love sought, but not found; buttoning your overcoat as you stand before an ash-slag fire as you ponder years of wasted devotion amid the endless complaint of boredom. It is, I suppose, the north of England. Of course it must be monochromatic, since the dreary past always was, and a loved but lost son is lifted into a stately frame. The realities of each northern day at the turn of the 1980s played out against a hardened background in late repentance, because the north is a separate country – one of wild night landscapes of affectionate affliction. There are no known technological links apart from the telephone box on the corner, and this can always be relied upon to be out of order. The north is important partly because of London's distance, and also because of the disregard London pays to the north – a north where the tongue is thought to be too free, and where we are said to show more warmth (although I most sincerely doubt it). In the north of the 1970s everyone had just gone to bed – or is about to go, that lengthy going-to-bed process being such a great relief and escape, for isn't sleep the brother of death? It snows harder up north, and we rarely see or hear of our hare-

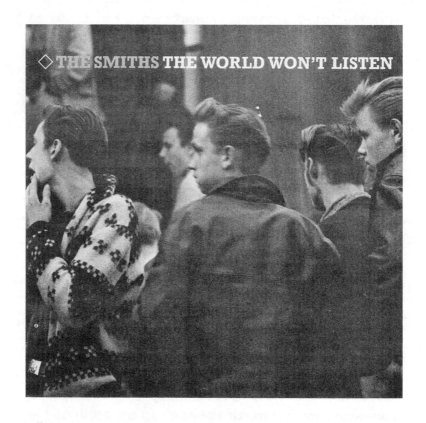

The Smiths: look at the past and see how much you've changed. The imperishable Smiths' sound remains too vigorous to be doubted, even if the Smiths themselves hasten to vanish

brained Westminster politicians or their messy private dabblings. In this pre-internet age, we can't even second-guess the slanted and skewed double-dealings of 10 Downing Street. We are in the dark at all times. The north, you see, is thought to be 'away from it all' (and 'it' is 'everything'), and a friendly street greeting is a morose nod of recognition with all personal names chopped in half for familiarity's sake. Television still emits only the King's English, which Manchester naturally dismembers by dropping any G that might be at the end of a word. As the British were raised to gaze adoringly towards America, we in the north were taught to cast a hopeful eye to London, where you might catch sight of people who mattered. Shut-out hopes struggle aboard trains at Piccadilly Station, having wrenched themselves away or explained themselves to death. *No mamma, let me go.*

Leaving Manchester always meant the train to London – giddy yet sad on a journey all alone. No matter how high-speed the train, the frozen reflection in the window is the collapsed countenance of your own face staring back at you, unchanged with the fast-track passing of miles, questioning, questioning, questioning, like a second you – an inner you, representing the superiority of reason, reminding you that there is nowhere to run. I am a child by a moldering wall; front-entry bus into town, train to London, alight from Euston, rear-entrance bus to confusing habitation. The ungovernable life is here in Manchester, all dark and unloving, with scaffolding and building work everywhere. Manchester's architectural heritage is demolition. Empty mid-century warehouses have cellars that are now converted into restaurants or nightclubs, neither of which welcome penniless me. February 1971 had divided locals into two distinct groups, one of which still spoke in old currency, the other of which grappled with the new. Unlike the world in which we now live, not many people were interested in music, and very few knew anything about this mysterious life-sucking machine.

The ever-moving world of music would lead me chin-to-chin with the unexpected, people whom I'd be unlikely to bump into at Stretford's DHSS inferno. There stands Shelley Winters, alone and dowdy at a carwash on La Cienega; there looms Anthony Perkins, walking alone around the Beverly Center; there is Eve Arden, erecting her own makeshift table at a bookshop where she will hopefully sign copies of her autobiography; there is Paul Newman, sitting quietly at the door of his Sunset Marquis villa; there is Patricia Neal, frail but smiling at La Luna restaurant on Larchmont; there is Paul Simon, sitting with Whoopi Goldberg, to whom the unemployable Stretford canal-bank cleaner is introduced. This all could be a dream, yet it is not sad enough to be a dream.

In New York, Mick Jagger arrives backstage and extends the hand of friendship. It is a big moment for Johnny, but I, of course, am a nightmare of judgment, and it takes me years to understand the genius secret of the Rolling Stones. Dismissal can be a secret form of arrogance, and I held this proudly against the Stones until the light shifted and I caught myself being utterly wrong. The in-built censorship can also often be a substitute for not actually knowing any better, and I now agonize over my criticisms of the Stones – with blather that was anything but a true reflection of the facts. In any case, Mick Jagger only stayed for four songs into the Smiths' set, but I felt no hurt at his departure because I could, even then, understand how my general being (which we dare not term a persona) was difficult for a lot of people to take. As the Smiths' singer I consigned all of my best efforts to conviction, and all of my being went into each song. This can be embarrassing for onlookers – an embarrassment that makes us turn away whenever someone bares their soul in public. But for me there could be no other way, because otherwise there would simply be no point and the Smiths would be eminently average. The ideas were rigid and the laws were as unique as one could expect, and I felt burdened only because I took things as hard as I did, so that whenever I'd overhear how people found me to be 'a bit much' (which is a gentle way of saying the word 'unbearable'), I understood why. To myself I would say: *Well, yes, of course I'm a bit much – if I weren't, I would not be lit up by so many lights.* However, at the hour of the Smiths' birth I had felt at the physical and emotional end of life. I had lost the ability to communicate and had been claimed by emotional oblivion. I had no doubt that my life was ending, as much as I had no notion at all that it was just beginning. Nothing fortified me, and simple loneliness all but destroyed me, yet I felt swamped by the belief that life must mean something – otherwise why was it there? Why was anything *anything*? I had become a stretcher-case to my family, yet this made it easier for me to put them aside at those moments when the wretched either die or go mad. The water was now too muddy, and, being nowhere in view, I am not even known enough to be disliked. The wits had diminished, and I am sexually disinterested in either the male or the feel-male – yet I make

this claim on knowing almost nothing about either. Horror
lurked beneath horror, and I could only tolerate an afternoon if I took a triple amount of the stated dose of valium
prescribed by my GP (who would soon take his own life).
Life became a strange hallucination, and I would talk
myself through each day as one would nurse a dying friend.
The diminishment could go no further, and the face can
only be slapped so many times before the slaps cannot be
felt. I became too despondent for anyone to cope with, and
only my mother would talk to me in understanding tones.
Yet there comes the point where the suicidalist must shut it
down if only in order to save face, otherwise you accidentally
become a nightclub act minus the actual nightclub. This,
then, was my true nature as the Smiths began: the corpse
swinging wildly at the microphone was every bit as complicated as the narrow circumstances under which he had lived,
devoid of the knack of thigh-slapping laughter. Accustomed
to people criticizing me, I am unruffled when the barrage
comes. By contrast, the other three Smiths were straightforward and had found fun, and they were not to blame for
inspecting me as if pinned and mounted under glass.

At New York's Beacon Theater Andy Warhol is present,
and I am frozen in a disconnected moment. After the
show, Johnny and I find ourselves in the Bowery district
with the poet John Giorno, who takes us both to the
quietly famous William Burroughs 'Bunker'. Through clattering warehouse elevators we are in ice-cold lock-up
depositories of vast storehouses and stockrooms, where
philosophical art-bits are scattered elegantly around mismatched sofas for those who might care to sink. The chill

drizzle of New York's 1890s is here, now, with the chill drizzle of the 1980s. It is here where the art set have suffered with relish, in rooms where turn-of-the-century migrant workers would have been fired for smiling. My infantile reactions do not match Johnny's; he is bored. His boredom suddenly alerts me to the realization that, yes, I am bored, too. I am introduced to Gregory Corso, which doesn't make sense since I am certain he is dead, but this is not something to raise when the subject stands before you. I may not necessarily have been wrong – such being the wonders of Warhol who could possibly achieve anything at all with the right stuffing.

John Giorno begins the process of explanation, and I begin to long for my own bed with clean sheets. John has an odd way of offering a slight giggle before speaking, because he obviously knows what he's about to say and he somehow can't wait to hear it, yet as he talks nothing becomes clear. It matters little. These accidental yet under-your-skin brushes spread blood through the tissue, and you are excited to at last be out and about.

The Smiths at the London Palladium raises emotion beyond the heart. The band's name is omitted from the actual ticket, and, as usual, those who should know why this has happened voice only bewilderment. We are warned that the audience will not be allowed to stand up during what is erroneously termed a 'performance', but the audience immediately stand, and the gang-show Red Coats give me a disapproving glare. Iggy Pop is present and makes his way backstage, but not to wherever it is I am. Opening on this tour are Raymonde, who are fronted by James Maker. Raymonde are an arresting four-piece from south London, whose first single had done well on radio, after which Geoff Travis had made haste towards them in search of a debut album.

'*The thing is,*' says Geoff, as if addressing a Transport and General Workers' strike, '*James can't sing,*' which is palpably untrue. But Johnny isn't keen when James elects to join the Smiths onstage during their set at Cornwall Coliseum, eager to be a part of the fireworks; he is instead led offstage and placed in a chair. The Raymonde album turns out to be excellent, dogged only by its somewhat awkward sleeve-art, wherein the song-titles are printed in scriptio continua, which effectively means that no one can read them.

Geoff had also interviewed Ludus (fronted by Linder Sterling) as a possible Rough Trade signing, but he told me that he had been put off when guitarist Ian had asked him, '*What kind of music would you like us to play?*' which Geoff rightly thought an undignified question. These are the days when almost any unsigned artist that I favor instantly awakes to find Geoff Travis sitting at the foot of their bed, a short-form agreement between his teeth. It's a compliment, of sorts.

In America, *The Smiths* album had stalled at number 150, and *Meat is Murder* spent thirty-two weeks meandering around the 110 position, whereas *The Queen is Dead* finally clipped into the 100 at number 70, and managed to cling on for thirty-seven weeks. Sire attempted appeasement by assuring me that neither the Sex Pistols' album nor David Bowie's *The Rise and Fall of Ziggy Stardust* had entered the Billboard 100 – as if this should be our eternal blueprint. Smiths' reviews throughout America remain uncharitable, and Sire is eternally absent, and the liberating hysteria at each Smiths concert does nothing to stoke Sire's interest. Even selling 40,000 tickets in California doesn't budge Sire's constipation, and the label remains clueless as to what exactly the Smiths are. At Irving Meadows, the audience rushes the stage so uncontrollably that the show is stopped by security, who point to me as the ringleader of the tormentors. Essential to any form of American business is the blame game. It is never one's own fault – but always the fault of others.

The frenzied panic at Smiths shows goes largely unreported. Berserk and wildly funny, the shows outstrip anything else that we are told is hysteria. Backstage in Los Angeles, the actor Richard Davalos walks towards me, and, saying nothing, places a square-faced silver ring on the third finger of my left hand. Looking not an hour older than when he famously played James Dean's screen brother in *East of Eden* in 1955, Davalos now lives in Echo Park and tends to his garden. A series of beautifully printed letters from Richard arrive at Cadogan Square:

> *by way of thanks for your magnetic performance here in Los Angeles. It was a truly remarkable evening. You are so very special. RICHARD.*

Richard's ring fastened itself to my finger for the next few years, until I suddenly wondered what it was doing there.

Back in London, John Porter surprisingly springs out of the bushes to mix a new Smiths track. I arrive much too early at the studio in Chalk Farm, and I find shrewd John huddled with both Johnny and, surprisingly, Bryan Ferry.

I walk into the room and all three freeze with Colonel Mustard unease. Ferry, the bogus man, immediately rises and grabs his belongings, and John Porter turns away, unable to look into the eyes of Mozzer-a-Becket. Johnny splutters a few surprised compliments, but minus any deftness. Saying nothing at all, Ferry smiles an unhappy smile and leaves. As if jealously guarding a can of sardines, Billy Bunter and his playmates are rumbled, and the Smiths battleship springs its first mutinous leak, with John Porter as sly Captain Bligh, and Johnny as the always-innocent young cabin-boy, hoping old Moby Dick will use his tune. And, to everyone's disadvantage, *he does*. Of course, I wasn't expected to burst in ahead of schedule, and Mary, Mungo and Midge were caught at it. I could almost hear John Porter as the monster in the middle cannily edging Johnny on with a *'Well, you know you don't need this Morrissey silliness ...'* and a crisis of spirits kicks in. When the Bryan Ferry single finally emerges, Johnny is there in the video looking lost, minus only a pair of slaves' sandals, and he is evidently only important for the gifts that he brings to the sherry-fed Ferry, who stumbles up to the spotlight as if direct from a pink-gin all-nighter at Redcliffe Square. *Johnny, I hardly knew ye.*

As *Shoplifters of the world unite* is released, the Smiths' dramatizations are finally of national significance. The graveyard school of poetry mixes well with incongruously striking guitar melodies, and such mixed metaphors are suddenly pointed to as a new 'type', and a generation of similarly styled cognoscenti appear behind us. The Morrissey Thing is lampooned on television, and music writers collectively sigh as 'more Smiths copyists' turn up worldwide. It is the success of self-culture and defiant self-government, and art is used as a weapon. When the *Old Grey Whistle Test* includes a Smiths 'video' in their phone-in popularity contest, the Smiths shrink against the titanic bands of the day.

'Of course you won't win,' smiles Geoff, ever hopeful. When it is eventually announced that the Smiths have won, Geoff climbs back into his pen, saying nothing.

I foolishly looked to Geoff for an explanation when the single *Panic* stalled for two weeks at number 11, inching no higher even though it is generally accepted that here is the Smiths' first unstoppable number 1. Johnny sends me a postcard yelling *'PANIC: NUMBER ONE !!!!!!!!'*, a common sentiment, yet once again, here we are, derailed by non-existent competition.

Geoff leans forward and removes his glasses. *'Do you know why Smiths singles don't go any higher?'*

I say nothing because the question is horribly rhetorical.

'Because they're not good enough.' He puts his glasses back on and shrugs his shoulders. I glance around his office searching for an axe.

Some murders are well worth their prison term.

Preparing to sing *Shoplifters of the world unite* on television's *The Tube*, I am ushered into an urgent Rough Trade meeting, where I am pressed to make a public statement about the upcoming *Tube* slot. The statement must clarify the true meaning of the song, and must dissociate it from the obvious tricky business of shop-theft, which, quite obviously, is the song's true essence.

Pat Bellis speaks up at the meeting. *'Look, if you don't say this then we can't appear on* The Tube, *and we won't be played on radio and there'll be no* Top of the Pops.' Around the table, everybody looks at me as if I'd just eaten a small child, and the Rough Trade faces seem newly traditionalist in the mid-afternoon light. Like a bull in a Spanish bullring, I look both left and right for clarity. *'But the song IS about shoplifting!'* I wheeze out.

'Ye-ee-ee-s, we KNOW that!' came forty-eight voices, *'but if you could just tweak the meaning then we're in the clear … just say something oblique.'*

Jo Slee has a face of granite, and Pat Bellis is now playing the near-to-tears card, whereas Geoff is the consummate fiddling parson wondering how he can possibly shift all that stock in the cellar.

'This is a great single and if you don't make this statement then we're all in a mess and you'll never be trusted on radio again,' says Pat – her lipstick under no doubts whatsoever. I am already formulating semi-acceptable dribble in my head, wondering how I can squeeze in the term 'conscious borrowing' in an effort to ease the entire nation and rid the world forever-more of emphysema. I feel slightly queasy. I have been done over by an aggressive tribe from Palestine and I don't know what to do. In the event, Paula Yates introduces me on *The Tube* as *'some prat'*, and Rough Trade sinks at the horror of it all, yet amazingly they manage to force her to apologize on the following week's show. *'So you get me to lie on a television programme that introduces me as "some prat" …'* I lobby outside Collier Street, partly delighted that Rough Trade's plan to commingle with *The Tube* went asswards because of Paula Yates. My smile stretches for miles.

Despite lowbrow persuasions from people who should

dress better, *Shoplifters of the world unite* is once again ignored by radio, and two weeks at the number 12 position does nothing to assuage DJs' playlists. As we leave for Dublin to play the song on a television show called *MegaMix*, Nannie dies. At 71, the undignified months leading up to her death had been a form of torture for a woman so shy, and we all bear witness to the usual redundant words of hope. Nannie is the central idea and notion of family, and as she loses hold so too does the meaning of family unity. It is all over.

Constantly on the watch and suspicious without reservation, Nannie's life had modest happiness, but was largely one of struggle and self-punishment; tragic importance given to gas bills and bus fares and begging God's pardon. Nannie pays a high price for virtue, and I always suspected that she sits in the dark of true reflection night after night at Milton Close, full of prayer that all will right itself, but not daring to make futile plans for days without hardship, yet hopeful that she might find someone to help wallpaper the hall for her. Of all of life's luxuries, Nannie had only ever been allowed to watch. Her duties prevent her from thinking about her feelings, and the bed-like warmth of ironing and the tea caddy now used to collect spare change for her TV license make up her winter musings. The phone rings unanswered during *Crossroads*, and Thatcher is spat out as the name of madness. Nannie is an overly civilized entity, having mastered the art of minding her own business. Peace is reserved for the time beyond the moment of death. I have never kissed Nannie, and only on her deathbed do I hug her because our mutual hope is a heap of dirt. Death is alive in life. I cry at the fixity of Nannie lowered alone into her grave; her very first time alone. She needs us still. The soul is not everything. Her face, her arms, her hands, they need us still, and they are what we know of someone, and all of these have gone. The soul is said to be somewhere, but the soul has only ever been visible through the eyes. It is the body that we know of someone, yet the body is the husk lowered into the earth of tatty Southern Cemetery when we are told that the body is 'not really' or 'no longer' Nannie. *But it is.* In some ways Nannie had always remained a child. She never knew Paris and she never sat behind the steering wheel, although she laughed with friends and managed many sunlit jaunts to America. The Queen Mother dies with debts of six million pounds, whereas my own grandmother would not be allowed to run up a debt of six solitary pounds without the threat of public dishonor. Nannie only ever received when someone placed a child in her arms, and the drudgery of moral codes clouded Dublin like a thousand zeppelins. Nursing destroys the body, ends the freedom, and no one gives any thought to the tenth month beyond the impregnated ninth. But, what about the sixteenth month – or the maternal madness beyond? Nannie's final request was that she be buried with her dentures in, but at the final open-coffin inspection, her request had not been followed through, and she looks in death as she had never looked in life.

The righteous heckles of the *Manchester Evening News* are still, in 1987, unable to offer a line of support to the Smiths as they gleefully report how *Shoplifters of the world unite* has 'been denounced', but been denounced by whom or why is not mentioned. It is not until the years pass and until local success is redefined by Oasis that the *Evening News* finally understands that they must support local musicians or face the humiliation of antiquity.

I pass away as *The World Won't Listen* compilation is released, and the artwork of which I am most proud is repulsively reduced for the CD format to an absurd fraction of the larger photograph. The side view of a blow-fish face in black and white looks stingy and paltry – a cheapened impression of the album sleeve, and I storm the gates of Rough Trade in a now familiar maniacal furore. In a state of homicidal seizure I demand to know why the CD image does not repeat the LP image.

'But we couldn't fit the entire LP image on the CD because a CD is too small,' says Richard Boon, unhelpfully.

'But they managed quite well with Sergeant Pepper's Lonely Hearts Club Band!' I stomp, suddenly wondering why I continued to bother. I could, instead, be skiing in St Moritz. As the years go by, and *The World Won't Listen* changes labels, the CD image remains heart-sinkingly abysmal compared to the majesty of the LP sleeve. These things count.

Johnny and I conduct another of our despondent and demoralized business meetings at Johnny's sw7 flat at Roland Gardens. We have been secretly approached by David Munns from EMI Records, who adopts a new tune:

Look, enough is enough. You both should be enormous artists and you're wasting your talents with Rough Trade, who don't appreciate you and don't even send you a Christmas hamper even though you've finally put them on the map. The Smiths belong at EMI. The Beatles, the Smiths. This is England. The Smiths are the new Beatles. Now, stop wasting time.

It suddenly felt like a case of writing yourself a leading part in your own play, or else remaining in a spear-carrying role in the bearded background. It's all very dignified to down-play popularity as an artistic goal, but if you love your songs as much as we did then there seemed to be no further point in avoiding accessibility. The aim was to keep listeners occupied for years and years and years, yet it was Johnny and I who struggled with the moral intent of Rough Trade even though the label themselves did nothing to celebrate the popularity of the band. Behind closed doors it was I alone who had been asked by Rough Trade to replace artistic intent with an all-round entertainer's fez. Very accidentally, I had become the most famous face of the Rough Trade enterprise, and like a Rank Charm School starlet I had an arranged marriage with the press, whose *NME* was now known as the New Morrissey Express. As long as the arresting quotes took flight there was no need for Rough Trade to invest in advertising. The press had also tagged the Smiths 'Mozzer's men', a docket that enraged Johnny and which hacked at our umbilical cord. In the complete pop context, a picture of my face would be printed with the Smiths name beneath it, and on the pictorial rundown for *Top of the Pops*, the single *Bigmouth strikes again* features my face only in the slot for the Smiths. Johnny fumes and makes steps to have the picture rectified by the following week, by which time the single has fallen off the chart anyway. This Blondie sphere rattled Johnny's chains, yet it has never been the case that someone other than the lead singer becomes the public face of a group (David Johansen was the *last* member to join the New York Dolls), yet the agitation can throw musicians into such a hissy fit that the group could weaken and snap. It must have been at this time that Johnny believed that *'If ... well, ummm ... if I just step from stage left to, ummm, center stage, then I, too, could gather lilacs.'* This, I think, causes many lead guitarists to incline towards the berko and quit a successful band with the hope of being the camera's desired one. Well, Johnny was not quite so addled, although the Smiths' apocalypse in this year of 1987 would seem to nail the assumption that stage left to center stage is not a desperately giant leap, after all. It is, in fiddling fact, so *very* far that it might span all your born days. Johnny and I had signed to EMI Records as 'the Smiths' for an advance of £60,000 each. The signing took place in secret, since there would be one more contractual album for Rough Trade. The secret lasted approximately two days. Leaping into black-widowed cat-suit action, Geoff Travis elbowed his way into a *Guardian* newspaper blast that quoted him as saying, *'The Smiths have signed to EMI for reasons of greed.'* Always ready to splice, I found Geoff had zero appreciation for the songs that had saved him from life's lavatory, and he had no warmth for the songwriting duo whose allure would ensure his own success for the rest of his life.

In the year that preceded the final album, the Smiths had become a quintet, for reasons that furrowed my brow. It was Johnny's will, and that seemed good enough on face value, but the reality of Craig Gannon was a fascinating bungle. Ripe from a Salford two-up two-down, Craig had a sullen expression, and said nothing. He lumbered onto the payroll and the Smiths were no longer a foursome. I understood Johnny's need to be released of basic rhythm parts and to then be free for more complicated lead riffs, but I struggled to notice any specific assistance to the sound. It seemed to me that Johnny was still playing everything. Craig undertook a lengthy US tour, and the continual difficulty was in trying to arouse him from bed. He would sleep for what seemed like fifteen hours a night and would pay no regard to call-times and departure times. Before going to bed Craig would feel duty-bound to either cause damage in the hotel or cause chaos in his hotel room – disorders for which the Smiths had no previous reputation. Suddenly there were bills for Craig's madcap habit of upturning large potted plants in hotel foyers, or generally being the behavior crackpot. Having played in Atlanta we were then set to fly to Florida for the next show, but Craig refused to get out of bed and we were forced to fly without him. One night our security, Jim Connolly, is showering when Craig pounds wildly on the door of his hotel room shouting Jim's name. Jim races into Craig's room, where Craig has positioned all items of hotel furniture onto his bed in a teetering pile. Word quickly circulates that Craig is probably unhinged at this point and – worse – that he has little interest in being a Smith. Once the US tour has ended, Johnny suggests that we do not make contact with Craig, in order to test whether he would actually bother to contact any of us. Unsurprisingly, Craig does not contact anyone, and it becomes evident that nothing useful vibrates in Craig's upper storey. The lift doesn't quite reach the top floor. Johnny's experiment sees Craig sealing his own fate as a Smith because Craig makes no effort to call either Johnny, Andy or Mike, and thus Craig silently fades away.

'*What does he want me to do? INSIST that he be a Smith?*' says Johnny reasonably. It is not announced that Craig has departed and this is largely because his name is never again mentioned, and the press make no comment on Craig's disappearance. Like mist he evaporates, and it is confusing to think that he had ever been present.

Instantly, Craig sues for 'loss of earnings' (*how? where?*), and also claims co-authorship with Johnny of certain Smiths songs (*how? where?*). Although Craig's claims are whimsical frolic, the court leaps to his favor and the case is settled for *almost* whatever he wants.

I have no tears left. *The law is a ass.*

And. *Yet.*

The only thing we can possibly control is ourselves. Under shocking circumstances the Smiths assemble in the city of Bath to record our final album for Rough Trade. Stephen Street is once again the link between our writing systems and technical language. Stern-faced, he detangles all parts. He is still very shy, but it is the Smiths that have made him grow, and he finds his confidence with each scholastic session. These days and these days alone will begin his extensive career as a recording producer, and will procure for him a stylish reputation that, to his credit, he will always measure up to. Every combination of chords has been done, but Johnny somehow manages the most imaginative bursts of sound on these final sessions, and the three other Smiths follow. I talk about the sad lilt in Johnny's chord structures, but as usual everyone offers iffy squints my way, as if I am being far too sappy. *Strangeways, Here We Come* is the most joyful and relaxed Smiths studio session, with crates of beer wheeled in at the close of each day and no war in sight. Andy's playing is exalted, and Mike registers St

George's explosion blissfully. I begin the vocal for *Stop me if you think you've heard this one before*, when Stephen stops me, even though he *hasn't* heard this one before.

'*Er, Morrissey, I think there's a grammatical error here – "who said I lied because I never" ...*' he aids, helpfully.

'*Yesssssssssssssss,*' I hiss, like an adder on heat, '*it's meant to be there,*' and *now* I know how Joan of Arc felt.

'*Ooh,*' he sinks, and allows me to proceed. I am an instrument.

A window-ledge in a forgotten corner of the Wool Hall Studios showcases a peculiar stringed instrument from 1777, which Johnny instantly grabs – '*Oh, let's see how this sounds*' – and, by second run-through, he can play the oddly stringed lyre that has no sound hole. The strings are possibly horsehair, and there is a barely usable tuning bar, but the sound Johnny finds is mesmerizing, and the song *I won't share you* is alive. It is a fascinating moment when Johnny's inner ear leads the way to somewhere unknown – somewhere mistrusted by all until the final depth of thought strikes. The technical term is *bling*.

The vocal room houses an old Red Lion piano that I decide to bang during a run-through of *Death of a disco dancer*. More Lieutenant Pigeon than pianoforte, the Donnybrook punch-up pianner nonetheless remains in the track, and for the first (and last) time I am loosely listed as a musician.

'*Do you mind if I re-do it and make it better?*' asks Johnny.

'*Yes, I do,*' replies Mrs Mills.

My leap into multi-instrumentalism equals Johnny's sky-dive into song, as he tackles his first ever vocalism. His tremulous quaver on *Death at one's elbow* is a honeyed flow, although he insists that he cannot sing.

At the close of the *Strangeways* sessions there took place a glut of meetings with accountants and lawyers at the Wool Hall Studio, and in the context of such, the Smiths breathed a last exhausted sigh, and folded. It happened as quickly and as unemotionally as this sentence took to describe it. No high-octane squabbles, no screams at midnight, no flying furniture, no one dragged head first into the snake-pit, no animated yelps from unused outbuildings (these would, of course, come eight years later, eight years too late, at the Smiths High Court trial). In 1987, at Roland Gardens, Johnny and I stood – he smiling, I not master but servant. *Sing me to sleep | I'm tired, and I | I want to go to bed.*

Strangeways, Here We Come was, we both knew, the Smiths' masterpiece, with everything in its perfect place. The search for wisdom had ended, from womb to tomb, and here we are – wanting to live yet longing for sleep. Johnny and I were both drained beyond belief, and there was no one around us to suggest that we disappear somewhere to rest, and apart. We do not telephone each other for two weeks, and then suddenly the press is rife with Smiths split stories. To obviate doubt, we hold off with communications, and I sit, watching the situation as if behind glass. An unnamable insider tells all, and the press launches stories of bitter feuds during catty sessions for *Strangeways, Here We Come*. These, we are all assured, are the facts, and professional fusspot Anthony Wilson jumps in with *'The Smiths have broken up because Johnny has had enough of Morrissey.'* Of unmerited renown, Wilson was never too busy to stick the boot in. His career had not lasted, yet he quite luckily managed a lengthy and slow decline which some thought was actually an ongoing career. The rumor is more important than the truth, and as soon as the rumor is half-uttered it gains strength. It is all too much, too sickening, and press reports tell us confidently that Johnny has left the country to work with Talking Heads; monogamous I, polygamous he. What erupts from such situations, when there are so many harmful and hurtful opinions darting about, is that we wind in on ourselves in a squalid effort to put up a defense against the noise, to save our reputations from the hoodoo chants who want you snuffed out; and no story is complete without blame, blame, fatal blame.

Everyone suddenly has an expert eye, and you just might find yourself contemptibly savaged or disadvantaged by scientific studies of what went wrong, even though those who announce *something rotten in the state of Denmark* cannot possibly have any way or means to account for their misinformation.

'Well,' smiles Geoff Travis ruefully, 'the general opinion is that side 1 of *Strangeways* is terrific, and side 2 is very weak.' By 'general opinion' Geoff means solely his own opinion. Geoff makes this statement knowing that side 2 tucks away *Paint a vulgar picture*, which vibrates negative electrons at someone in Geoff's humanitarian position. *'I've played* Coma *to the Jesus and Mary Chain and they think it's very funny,'* he goes on, as if such a red seal might finally give me the will to pick up the pieces.

As I stand up to leave Geoff calls to me, *'I can get Roddy Frame to replace Johnny,'* and before I have time to burst into tears (for I don't quite know what Roddy Frame's name is expected to mean), Geoff is up and out and gone. As quick as lightning, Frame proudly issues a *'Morrissey asked me to join the Smiths, but I refused'* badge of honor to the press – as if the mere request alone from Geoff had lit up his lunchtime.

Could things get any worse?

Why, yes, little one. *Be patient.*

The split is our final loss of innocence, and Johnny suddenly appears on television playing behind Bryan Ferry, as if this is what it had all been for, all along. Geoff brings in another guitarist to replace Johnny, and a session takes place in west London with Andy and Mike suddenly pledging allegiance, aware of the impending precipice. The session is de trop, and I have awoken to writs from both Sire and EMI telling me that I am, in legal piffle, their artist, and that I am legally bound to fulfill what are known as 'the Smiths contracts'. Dim and confused, I meekly obey without fuss, certain that no other ex-Smith had found themselves quite so entrapped. Equal partnerships, anyone? Oh no, not at this stage, when there is nothing to gain but burdens! Leave that all to Morrissey. We other three Smiths are as free as coaltits darting from hedge to hedge, but we'll be back later on, when the rough seas settle and there's a financial surplus. Sire and EMI both threaten me with legal action should I refuse to supply an album in order to mop up the Smiths' liabilities. There is no one I can turn to for sane judgment. In willowy isolation, I reflect on how Johnny and I had signed to Rough Trade, and then, by extension, to Sire Records, with no legal representation. The term 'sitting ducks' seemed far too mild – we were without doubt prize sapheads of the most embarrassingly gullible type. My doctor had prescribed a 'mood' tablet known as Pastalin, with which I scum-wrestle for a few dreadful months, and I begin not to recognize myself – saying things that I would never usually say – and my recalcitrant behavior is noted with concern by passers-by. I clamber back to Harley Street to complain to the doctor who prescribed this hideous mood pill, but I am told he is dead, and I am hardly surprised.

'*If you want the singles from* Strangeways *to succeed, then you should quickly take part in these promo videos,*' says Geoff, as he encircles the open grave. '*We have a budget of twelve thousand pounds.*'

Director Tim Broad steps in to make sense of it all, hotch-potching two videos for both *Girlfriend in a coma* and *Stop me if you think you've heard this one before.* The results for both are frustratingly unwatchable, although Tim did his best with such a mealy-mouthed budget. In the event, Rough Trade decide against releasing *Stop me if you think you've heard this one before* due to the lyric's reference to 'mass murder', and I argue that it is surely a bit late in the day to worry about offending anybody. '*Yes, but radio won't play it,*' offers Geoff, his cadaverous smile as colorless as an Islington sky.

'*But they don't ever play ANYTHING anyway!*' I choke, finally ready for the taxidermist.

Progress is made in the US, where *Strangeways* zaps to number 55 – Sire finally slapped from mummification now that the Smiths are stuffed. On a late-night talk show, Lorna Luft (daughter of Judy Garland) is asked about modern music. '*Well, I've heard* Girlfriend in a coma,' she laughs (for, would one not laugh?), and the Smiths finally enter having exited. The *Collins English Dictionary* furnishes its 1987 edition with *Smiths: a Manchester pop group*, an entry I read and reread until my eyes weaken. I tear the page out and I post it to Johnny. He does not reply because he is now far away and bleached free of emotional attachment – no solo commitment demanded from Johnny by either Sire or EMI, clever, clever boy.

The brain speculates but the heart knows. *Strangeways* becomes the fourth Smiths album to enter the UK chart at number 2, and the following year Rough Trade will gasp out a live *Rank* that will become the fifth chart entry at number 2 for a band of habit-forming sadness, now cold in its grave. It may close as a mournful experience, but at least I had known and felt the possible.

'*If five Smiths albums enter the chart at number 2, what is stopping them from entering at number 1?*' I ask Geoff (although, at this stage, with Rough Trade looking more like an old soldiers' retirement home, I wonder why I bother to fire the question).

'*Because when the majors see that we're coming in at number 1 they up their mid-week promo and they keep us at bay,*' says Geoff, delighted with his prognosis.

'*So why don't WE therefore up our promo in order to keep THEM at bay?*' I go on, like a jockey in search of a bolted horse. To this, Geoff laughs weakly, as if I'd suggested immediate space travel.

In flies a handwritten letter from honored British music writer Nick Kent, writing to ask that he be auditioned as 'guitarist/tunesmith' if the Smiths continue without Johnny. He is deadly serious.

Dear Morrissey,

... I am not a good self-salesman but I can confidently boast an encyclopaedic knowledge of the chord structures, dynamics etc. of Johnny's contributions to date ... My ardour is strictly from aesthetic dictates, not financial, vainglorious etc. ad infinitum.

Being musically associated with your very good self would signify the very apex of my crusade for immortality ...

Please keep me in mind.

Nick Kent

It is a methodical scrawl on yellowed paper, but I am still in shaky-split twilight zone and I cannot reply, for I scarcely know what to say. Nick Kent's parting shot appears in *The Face* magazine's March 1990 issue, a mediated slap-and-swipe Morrissey burial. I look suitably deathbound on the cover, and the piece within falls midway between tyranny and envy, as Kent outlines the ridiculousness of Morrissey, in unanswerable print. Ah, revenge!

When a Nick Kent book seeps out, its jacket bears a shambling quote attributed to me as I warn how the contents within will *'take the curls out of your afro'*. I contact the publishers, explaining that this quote is not mine – quite apart from the fact that there are no curls in an afro. The publishers reply with a *'We will remove the quote in the event of a reprint,'* which is meant to send me skipping off in delight.

Two years later, in Paris, Nick Kent is visible in the crowd as my new band launch into our comic-opera version of the New York Dolls' *Trash* (although comic opera was never the intent). I am confused by Kent's presence since his repulsion had made itself clear throughout his Morrissey assassination for *The Face*. Unfortunately for me, during this rendition of *Trash*, drummer Spencer plays an entirely different song throughout. Looking all Dostoevsky in a caped coat, Nick Kent lets loose a cold-blooded smile as the song blunders on and on and on with nothing to save it from death. Backstage my rage is soaked in sorrow, but Spencer displays only scorn. Weeks later, having heard a bootleg of the Paris night, Spencer now has no choice but to confess. *'Yes, I was playing a completely different song,'* he laughs.

Abandon all hope ye who sing here.

The Smiths fallout continues in Denver, where someone has held an entire radio station at gunpoint until DJs make the promise to play Smiths music. Unwittingly, this gunman is providing the very first active radio promotion on behalf of the Smiths, and evidently a loaded gun is what it takes to get a Smiths song on the airwaves. David Bowie, who feeds on the blood of living mammals, rises like Christopher Lee to present a bouquet of flowers to Johnny. But Johnny is not taken in. If I had felt that the Smiths' demise had left me on the scaffold, then Johnny surely felt the same. He quickly joins the Pretenders, and he just as quickly is 'asked to leave'. Chrissie Hynde explains to me that Johnny's perpetual lateness made progress impossible. For me, rationale comes from James Maker and Kirsty MacColl, both abiding friends, both level and impartial. Meanwhile, Stephen Street drops off a cassette at my flat of his own compositions – an action timed as if on cue, since EMI are muttering how the hour for a Morrissey disc has arrived. Ever helpful, the

Manchester Evening News yelp a two-page spread entitled MORRISSEY WAS HELL TO WORK WITH SAYS JOHNNY MARR. If the quote is fictitious, Johnny does nothing to correct it. *Ping-pong.*

I am approached with an offer of management by Gail Colson, a forthright Londoner who manages Peter Gabriel, and who is unlikely to take anything on the chin. Although she has never been further north than Watford, I quite like her combination of gruffness and Emma Hornett agitation. I tell Gail that I will sign a management contract if she also agrees to manage Stephen Street.

'I don't want Stephen fuckin' Street!' she rattles. But with a bellowing sigh she took him on, and twenty-two years later she smiles: *'I was offered a job lot.'*

Recording *Viva Hate* (the first solo album) was very difficult owing to the enslaved echo, coming from virtually everywhere, that told me I could never possibly be as good as the Smiths.

'Well, I think it's over now, anyway,' says Gill Smith, expertly folding me away like a winter bedspread.

Winding in like a serpent, Geoff Travis asks: *'Do you actually have money?'*

'Money?' I ask, confused.

'Well, it really is over now. Will you be alright, do you think?' He smiles, his face lit up with formaldehyde.

Suedehead, the first solo single, glides into the chart at number 6, selling 75,000 copies in its first week. There are no congratulations from either Geoff Travis or Gill Smith – both eager pallbearers two months previously.

A surprise letter from Linda McCartney:

Good one number 6!!!!!! If you ever want to do a song for the animals, get in touch.
Love, Linda

James Maker calls down from his observation tower. *'You've done it exactly right. This is the right single to launch the new you with.'*

As *Suedehead* climbs to number 5, *Viva Hate* jabs in at number 1, in the same week that Johnny's collaboration with Talking Heads enters at number 4. In America, *Viva Hate* springs to number 48, higher than any Smiths album, but Sire cannot get *Suedehead* onto the Billboard 100 despite surging and impressive radio play. I debut my solo being on *Top of the Pops*, standing alone for the first time, a *Queen is Dead* t-shirt beneath a neat blazer, and I sing *Everyday is like Sunday*, which has entered at number 9.

The wind, if nothing else, is in my sails, and all is in my favor until Gail Colson telephones me the day after my *Top of the Pops* debut. *'That was fucking awful,'* she says, and I drop the receiver on our relationship. Little wheel spin and spin.

Although Rourke and Joyce had gamefully participated in the 1989 singles *The last of the famous international playboys* (number 6) and *Interesting drug* (number 9), the unhappy past descends upon me each time I hear their voices and I decide not to invite them to any further recording sessions. Lawyers for Joyce then write to me, clearly stating that Joyce might take legal action in search of Smiths royalties, but will not do so if I agree to make him a permanent member of the Morrissey Band (a band which, in any case, doesn't even exist). I ignore the threat, unaware of any legal gripe that Joyce could possibly have against me, but the heavy-handed approach of his lawyers helped me to resolve to leave Joyce to his cleverness. Another page must resolutely be turned once more.

Because of a song on *Viva Hate* entitled *Margaret on the guillotine*, I am then compelled by law to attend a cross-examination by Special Branch Task Force so that they might gauge whether or not I pose a security threat to Margaret Thatcher. For the hearer's joy, I am drilled and recorded on tape for one hour under the penetrating glare of Special Branch.

'*Why exactly are you here?*' I ask them, and they explain that they are following up on an article in the *Star* newspaper that claimed that I would welcome the assassination of Margaret Thatcher. Following a very civil meeting, the men of Special Branch then request that I sign a photograph 'for a neighbor', and no more was heard or said on the Thatcher matter.

It was undeniable that I found Thatcher's egocentricity to be intolerable, but her leaking insanity would eventually force her own cabinet to boot her out, and if this would be the action of people who had never actually suffered at Thatcher's whims, how on earth were the rest of us expected to feel? I was cross-examined for allegedly welcoming the assassination of Thatcher, but when her own cabinet effectively assassinated her *they* were not subjected to a Special Branch investigation, or even arrested for a hate crime. Of course, politicians have their own laws for themselves (none, specifically), and tend to uphold laws against the public which politicians themselves can skirt in and out of because they have friends in low places. When Thatcher's daughter-in-law gives birth, Thatcher zooms her face into awaiting cameras. *'We are a grandmother,'* she announces, embodying Dame Anna Neagle, and now a comic figure. Disconnected and dispassionate, Thatcher's torrent of hate (for she has no other emotion) drains the young people of England, who see the Thatcher regime as militant and blinkered, and a dangerous tyranny clouds little Britain.

Life plops me at 2 Caroline Place, an odd little house in Bayswater that will be home (of sorts) for 1989, a disturbingly dry summer when the heat, mixed with the pollution of the Bayswater Road, brings on the panic attacks that I'd thought long-since gone. I sleep with the bedroom windows open, but the air feels defiled and contaminated. Months and months pass without rain. A local cat is a non-stop hunter, and I spend most of my time rescuing damaged birds that will never fly again. I carry them into Hyde Park and leave them within the enclosed and protected birds' nesting area, so that at least they have a remote chance of composure even if they will never again be on the wing. Cats will be cats.

I telephone photographer Juergen Teller to thank him for the excellent shots recently taken for the new *Bona Drag* compilation album, but after an assisting male voice tells me to hold on, I hear Juergen's voice whisper *'Oh, tell him I'm not here,'* and I quickly lower the receiver before the lackey has time to return to me.

Michael Stipe appears at Caroline Place, and we have tea

in the back garden as the dunghill wafts of Queensway restaurants foul the air.

'*I don't like this area,*' I tell Michael.

'*Then why do you live here?*' he asks.

'*I have no idea,*' I reply.

'*When I first heard* Everyday is like Sunday *I felt very jealous,*' he goes on, and he explains how he, too, would like to go solo.

'*I didn't ever want to go solo,*' I say, '*I thought the Smiths would run for at least thirty albums.*'

We walk through Hyde Park and then slowly across to Hammersmith. We enter the Hammersmith Odeon through the stage door, and six minutes later Michael walks onstage with REM. He is wearing the same clothes that he has worn all day, and he hasn't brushed his teeth.

The Smiths and REM had come to light at roughly the same time, and, as a Sire Records executive had remarked, '*It's just a question of which of the two will explode in America first.*' As the Smiths choked to death on a chip, the REM rocket accelerated. Michael's voice is a very cornfed John Denver sound, and in fact his real name *is* John.

Linder appears at Caroline Place to tell me that she is pregnant. As the full-stop locks the T in 'pregnant', the legs of my bent-wood chair give way and I splat onto the floor. We are both bagged. There can be no composure. Reason is lost for ten full minutes, as Linder and I are unable to look at each other, each fit dying down only to start up again with a further convulsion, and out peals laughter and tears combined.

'*Well,*' I begin, with postgraduate's calm, and suddenly we are both deranged all over again, painful laughter now causing concern, leakage imminent, sealed-up frenzy running loose.

Murray Chalmers arrives at Caroline Place to find me blocking traffic with waving arms, as an injured starling hops to the center of the road. Having shaken the bird from a cat's mouth, the bird is now further endangered by oncoming traffic. Murray is not sympathetic, and looks embarrassed as I scramble to get to the bird, who naturally does not want my help. The bird spends the night in my living room in a large, open box. Morning, predictably, brings death. It is always this way. Murray is head of press at EMI, and he tells me that the *NME* would like to know where I am, having asked Murray: *'Just tell us if he's north or south — we'll make a story out of it.'* Quite remarkable.

Although the summer of 1989 is traffic-fume toxic and unbearably hot, the year had begun in typically British gloom. In the 6 PM darkness of a January day, Tim Broad's resourceful Mercedes carried James O'Brien, Linder and I nervously up to the wild spirit of Saddleworth Moor. We skirt Ashton-under-Lyne, and as we enter the moor we are all silently expectant. The landscape is waterlogged, and the foursome is anxious. In the back seat, I make repeated glances over my shoulder and out into the blackness of the moor, reassured that nothing is visible yet also feeling nervous for the same reason. Next to me, Linder alights with tales of suicide specters — excited, then cutting short. These moors have another life, and that life is very much apart from the one you may have just left in Manchester, Bradford or Huddersfield. We are greeted by a dancing sheet of impenetrable fog waving above and around us;

no visible skyline, no tail lights to follow, no toasty pub lights in the distance, no comforting white noise, no sign of life – just this place of trepidation, with us in it. We are drawn to the moors with some shame, because some would have preferred to have left but could not. This 6 PM could be the darkest hour before dawn, as the temperature drops severely. At the wheel, Tim attempts to explain the vulnerability of the moors and our powerless straggling as we trespass. In the passenger seat James hands out torches *'because you never know'* – and we are absolutely certain that we indeed never know.

We are now where none could offer prompt rescue, as an even thicker blanket of fog comes rushing to meet us, weaving through beams of fog lights that are our only vision. Beyond that short stretch of light we see only blackness, and we wonder what the blackness hides. We have left behind the evenness of the A65 3 and have found ourselves at Black Hill, which looks across to Holme – which is anything but. We do not realize it, but we turn north again, without even a solitary remote cottage in the heights that might throw out a porch or landing light to dispel the loneliness. Who would live here? We are relieved at a small gathering of shaggy sheep, huddled together and everwatchful, eyes upon us in silent knowledge.

'Up so late?' says Linder. Surely there could be no one to call them home? Are there such things as 'wild' (as in 'free') sheep? Impossible to believe that no greedy landowners would see this sturdy family of sheep and not want to butcher them, as it is impossible to believe that any moorland animal would be left alone to live as it must. Yet, there they stood – with no whistle to herd them, and looking far

too robust to be felled by foxes. These sheep know more than we do about this barren moor. They can survive it, but we are trapped by it, for this is nature – of which humans know so little. Metal and stones and slabs are all that we know. Nature would kill us – as we are killing it. Gripped we are by the fear of being lost – lost, lost, lost – the right-sounding word for the meaning it gives. Drive further than intended to where the tips of imagination touch the tip of reality, and there will be no turn-off for nine miles. The biting wind tells you that nothing can save you against the unforeseen; these inner twists and turns are as unreadable as the Australian Outback. Unwise to have a heart attack here, or to choke on your favorite fatso's food. Now you know how animals feel when they are trapped in a city, and now you know how it feels to be the forever-hunted fox or deer.

This moorland remains unchanged for centuries and it extends no kindness, for why should it? It grinds on in its secrecy regardless of whatever changes sweep through Halifax town center. These moors you will not control, and something about the chilling darkness makes the motorist lean inwards – away from the window, where you thoughtfully check your own reflection to make sure that it is indeed yours. Historically, the moors have thrown up unanswered questions, and fueled by foggy footpaths and lowland crag the Brontës' imagination appeared to understand all workings of the heart even though such short lives rarely left Haworth Parsonage. The poor, trapped Brontës; myth unmatched and growing with each century – did they ever enjoy their own bodies? Did they ever even *see* their own bodies?

I start to sing, which doesn't help, and James jabbers on about some unfolding plot in *Brookside*. Linder, proudly, has no knowledge of *Brookside*. It is at this point that we decide to stop the car and get out. The private spot is a small graveled summit allowing some three vehicles (at most) enough space to pull off from the main road. The wildest views stretch to the western side of the moor, across hill and valley, peat and heather. The view is treeless, and beyond there are miles upon miles of black peat-bog, and we can now spot an array of tiny flickering lights, which Tim estimates to be about six miles away. What they are, we do not know. To the left, right, and rear of us there is nothing – not even sinking remains of stoneworkers' cottages. Sunken footpaths have nowhere to lead you. In mid-day brightness tedious people in hiking shorts will delight at the sight of shy grouse, and will ponder the secret world of ley-lines. They will make rough sketches of local stone and will calmly leave the moor without carelessly clashing with nightfall. We, on the other hand, are worthy game. There are moments in life to be foolish, brief though they may be. But what harm?

Tim switches off all power in the Mercedes and we are plunged into subjugating darkness, with no reaching trees to throw shadows. My thumb strokes the plastic pattern of an unlit flashlight. Anything to keep the conversation up, we all comment upon the stirring stillness that only has the soft high-pitch of a vicious wind to break it. What being could thrive and survive here – at the end of everything? A summit so bleak and deadly that surely all life has given in? Unthinkably, Tim suggests that we all step outside to reap the wild wind with its sweep to infinity, this 1989 landscape no different from that of 1777. We each force the car doors open, but they are pushed back on us by a sharply ear-splitting gale. Our faces disfigured, our bodies bent against the punishing wind, we huddle by the side of the Mercedes – hunched shoulders against the evil iciness that surely could not be endured by any other living creature.

Our searching flashlights scan the immediate area, lighting upon nothing but a pathetically vandalized public waste bin – a monument to what is oddly known as civilization. Not vandals as such, but more than likely to be those blandly smiling families, out for the day, restless and careless, the earth belonging only to them and their smelly children as they advance decay wherever they go. Here, the bleak moor has seen them all out: the determined fell-walker, the pot-holers – eager to fall in and call for rescue and, more importantly, to appear on the nightly news announcing how they will certainly be back on the moors as soon as their leg heals and their dentures are found – the revolting students, the wild and the visionary, the restless minds, the child-killers who murder and smile, the black hounds of literature, the girls who would be Jane Eyre, the spirits of centuries, the cowardly hunters who must shoot and kill in order to soothe the wretched agonies of their own souls, the cattle and deer who live their lives out in persecution; with no God to save them, the moor has seen them all out.

Urbanized society has yet to encroach upon Saddleworth Moor, and maybe it has tried, but a harsher energy has beaten it back. There are distinct atmospherics walking ahead and behind you on the moor, wrapped in the insidious fog of anonymity. Nothing metaphorical here – the threats are literal. I can scarcely imagine more terrible things as I stand here, as we are all silenced by the rising inferno of the wind. Do the wails of the gales drown out pitiful sobs? Might a roadside sack contain the remains of the sister of the murdered boy? Is it here where your lover might cut your throat and leave you, and where underground cavities lead to a box containing human bones? We are so gripped by how a life is brought to its end, enticed to this remote spot, the ideal locale for dark crimes and miseries. The fog is now black mist. James and Linder pile back into the car.

'Tim,' I begin, '*if you drive off and leave me I'll be dead before you've had time to change gear.*'

'*I didn't bring my cabaret clothes with me, anyway,*' he says. It's a joke, of course, but one that I couldn't grasp for at least a minute.

Once we are all re-seated amongst soft radio sounds and the reassurance of heat and light, and as the security locks all slip into place we realize that we have seen enough. We are soft creatures of habit, and we must return to enclosed surrounds of locks and bolts and alarms. Tim is unsure of the road back, but we can all recall passing a turn-off about a mile away, a road that looked wide enough to lead somewhere. The hardened darkness has lowered our spirits, and the dreary grief of moorland is surely safest in its own company. Our dreamscapes have had their fill. We back onto what we see as the main road, and it is barely broad enough for one vehicle, but we crawl along it in search of the turning that we had all remembered. Once again we are silenced by the expanse of blackness, and Tim drives more cautiously than ever. In the midst of this hostile landscape the Mercedes bobs gently like a small ship lost at sea, our silent engine heaving through, and we safe within. We all murmur a soft sigh of recognition as the entrance to the turn-off finally appears.

'I don't think there's any point in me indicating,' says Tim, as the wheels turn us on to the awaiting road. And it is here that it happens.

As the Mercedes made its measured maneuver to the right, throwing two strong arms of light onto the new road, rising up from the black of the earth came a figure – standing upright and then throwing his arms towards our lights in a terrifying and unspeakably forlorn plea for our attention. United in shock, we all gave a low cry at the sight of this specter. Within a split second of a hair's breadth, Linder shouts, *'Stop the car!'* and Tim jerks a fast brake.

'Nooooo!' I bang on the back of Tim's seat, and then Tim just as quickly lifts his foot from the brake and accelerates. James recoils from the passenger door where, just beyond, stood this wretched vision of sallow cheeks and matted shoulder-length hair, a boy of roughly 18 years wearing only a humiliatingly short anorak coat that was open to expose the white of his chest and the nakedness of the rest of his body. The vision chilled our blood as the boy threw out his arms in a forsaken Christ-like appeal. Zooming away, and with him now lost in the dark, our talk is a clutter of *'What WAS it?'* and *'Jesus, what … ?'* and *'How could ANY being be alive out here?'*

We had all seen the same thing, so there was no misunderstanding the form that the vision took. The worn face had pleaded for us to stop, or to notice him. His body rose to full height as if he had been crouched in wait, hidden in the browny purples, or else he had climbed the hillside to reach the road in order to flag us down. But something was amiss. He was very thin and quite tall, and apart from his nakedness there would be one curious factor that struck all of us at once, and this was how all the components of his body – face, hair, skin, crumpled little jacket – stood out as one sheet of grey.

We were given heart by an old-fashioned telephone box at the entrance to the village of Marsden. Here, too, a sign told us that we were on the Wessenden Road. Only 8 PM now, and the village is closed, its inhabitants pulling their chairs closer to the glow of a low fire – by hearth near heath, safely locked in from any creatures of endurance that may in their troubles find themselves wandering. There are such people, aren't there, so low in human spirit and so insignificant in their being that they can only gain your attention by frightening you.

We squeeze into the phone box, where we call the local police. Quaintly, all the necessary information is provided before us – emergency details listed clearly, and surprisingly free of modern-world graffiti. Tim explains everything to the police, but they cut him short. Tim pushes on. *'But the point is – he was naked, and I'm sure you realize it's below freezing point out here, and …'*

It is no good. Tim hangs up, and we look to him for an explanation.

'He said a lot of strange things have been reported on the Wessenden Road and that we should keep an open mind.'

'Keep an open mind about someone in distress?' I baulk.

'He is telling us that what we have just seen is commonly known as a ghost.'

Back in the car, we are all somewhat numb.

'You do realize what's just happened?' says James. *'We've all seen a ghost.'*

We know this to be true, and our hearts sink. In fact, we knew this to be true as soon as the vision hit our eyeline, and this was why we were all so instantly overcome with grief. We consider the possibilities, and Linder suggests that – if real and alive – the boy had possibly broken free and fled from a nearby farmhouse where he had been subjected to either violence or rape – or the violence *of* rape – and in a fit of exhaustion he had reached the road and saw our Mercedes as his only hope. James agreed, adding that the boy was obviously being hunted. Somehow I disagreed. My instincts told me that he had been placed as bait at a scene of ambush where cars are flagged down by a distressed figure, only then to be surrounded by marauders once the car had stopped. Tim held another view, saying that the boy was obviously a lunatic who had parked his car in darkness and who enjoyed the triumph of terrifying people. But it just wasn't enough. We sat up through the night and could not avoid the inevitable decision to drive back to the Wessenden Road in daylight, and by 9 AM the next morning we were there, stepping from the car onto a verge of flattened heather where our specter had stood, and we recalled his rise as if from some underground tunnel.

Saddleworth Moor at 9 AM was merely a slightly brighter version of its hellish nighttime, and our bodies still shook with the snapping cold. It was all we could do to stand upright. This spot, at the corner of the Wessenden Road, offered no clues as to the origin of the visitation, all points in full circumference revealing nothing to the eye – neither barn nor broken gate, nor falling coach-house – just miles and miles of friendless moorland, its craggy wet earth a living death that no soul could plough through, with no shell of a feeding shed from which a frightened boy might flee during a drugged liaison gone wrong. A weight fell as we noticed a pair of y-front underpants discarded in the wet grass, discolored with dirt, but certainly of the type which an 18-year-old might wear. We shook our heads and we shivered. The surrounding grassland and the roadside with its absence of any public footpath (for who would be using them? from where, to where?) indicated nothing at all of what this boy's experience could possibly have been in the immediate moments prior to our fog-lights landing upon him. He, or his cohorts, could not have parked a vehicle just off the road, for this deep wet earth would have pulled it in for good. If our specter had been here last night, would he not also be here now – watching us? In a desperate bid for survival he had called to us with the full of his lungs. Being mortal, we could not help – except with the discipline of prayer, which may have been all he required. How many unfortunates have Saddleworth Moor as their final resting place? Or are there still people so disfigured that they cannot live at society's lack of mercy, and can only find solace in dark places? There may very well be spirits of 1780 who still roam, begging for release by prayer – buried without ceremony, out of the way, beyond gaze, blotted out of creation just for knowing too much, or for saying too much, or for being witness to some dark crime;

rent boys and runaways, troubled teens and latchkey kids, motherless druggies and hastily pregnant Carol Annes, now silenced good and proper, deliberately dumped so far from their homes that even a most determined spirit could not find its way back.

Scattered singles flit through 1990, rounded off by the puzzle of *Piccadilly palare* (number 18), a student work of novelty that wears off before noon. I am so confused by the song that I turn down *Top of the Pops*. EMI would not speculate on a video, and there is – as always – no airplay, but for once I am not especially surprised. With the fluster of *Piccadilly palare* I am confused by a song that I do not overly care for – mainly because of the rinky-dink Kinks sound spurting from the pale and pasty *Kill Uncle* sessions. Recording something for the sake of recording delivered *Kill Uncle* unto the world, and I am finally up against the limits of my abilities, whilst surely not fooling anybody. Having been so right, it is suddenly shocking to be so wrong, yet *Kill Uncle* is number 8 in England and number 52 in the US. It will always be the orphaned imp that nobody wants, and even I – its father and mother – find it difficult to feed. But *Kill Uncle* shocks me into solid action, and in 1991 I brush aside my finicky ways and I undertake an extensive American tour. For this, nature compels the formation of a band, and north London will provide four musicians as, at last, the solo years begin. Friendship prospered with Chas Smash from Holloway, and for a while we are a loosely matching pair in Camden taverns and racquet-club steam rooms.

Of *Kill Uncle* Chas confirms: '*You've lost it, but you'll re-find it.'* I seem to be eternally cased in by friends who give me bad news *because they care.* Yet Chas introduces me to Boz Boorer, a known face on the British rockabilly scene, and Boz collects guitarist Alain Whyte, who works for Camden Council, Spencer Cobrin, who has a drum kit somewhere and who helps his father out in the family antique shop, and Gary Day, who plays bass and lives with his father in Neasden. They all know each other and they manage a certain harmony together, although Alain nurses an aversion to Boz that creates frequent difficulties. Generally, it works, and all four are essential to me after the session-musician embalming fluid of *Kill Uncle.*

Neatly typed letters from Nigel Thomas arrive, and he is certain that he knows the managerial way. He has the Nigel Patrick touch of British raffish elegance, being six parts Etienne Dumont champagne, the rest a checkered career in rock management (which is not the management of rocks, as such). Nigel is ten years my senior, yet he seems much more than that having lived fully and well as an intellectualist whose mind, in the words of Camus, 'watches itself'. He walks with mastermind determination and has no time for non-thinkers. He is always Brioni besuited, and he has no plans to lower his style. Jason King tobacco follows him everywhere, and *'Morrissey must live in Paris!'* becomes his catchphrase, and I feel disinclined to argue. Minutes later I am in Paris, where Nigel drags me through a host of rentable high-ceiling mansion-flats overlooking everything worth overlooking. It is only a question of the lift of an eyebrow, and Nigel presents to me a precision and colossus of knowledge with not a hint of amateur trifler. I am on my way. *But where to?*

Alain Whyte is introduced to me as a street-sweeper from Camden, which may or may not be a joke – I never could tell. He looks a bit like 'Kookie' actor Edd Byrnes from *77 Sunset Strip*, and he talks in a similarly bonkers 1950s backslang, which may or may not be a speech impediment. The jargon is baffling until he hits on something riotously funny – which, thankfully, is often. I like him. He is a skilfull style-guide and always looks spiffed up. The four musicians are instantly on a $1,000 per show payroll, and although Spencer and Gary complain ceaselessly (by nature), Boz and Alain are ready to launch and fire. However, none of us are prepared for the American concerts throughout the *Kill Uncle* and *Your Arsenal* tours of 1991/92, when enormity explodes as *Your Arsenal* enters the Billboard 100 at number 21. The outbreak of hysteria in every American city is so incredible that memory almost files it as improbable. I am forever trapped in a car on which young people lie across the hood; roads persistently blocked by a thousand Morrissey lookalikes; hotel security guards positioned outside my hotel room night and day, as entire floors are cordoned off to prevent fanatical do-or-die enthusiasts stopping at nothing to get to me. I am secretly bundled out of venues via underground passageways, and each day repeats itself with scenes of unthinkable madness.

'*Ohh, it's just like James Brown . . .*' says Gail Colson, a tone of regret in her voice.

'*You have made alternative music mainstream,*' says the President of Sire Records, '*and you have done it without the help of MTV – which is incredible.*'

Yes, I thought, and I've also done it without the help of Sire Records.

Airports have extra security on alert as check-in areas are swamped with 'Mozophiles'; Madison Square Garden sells out in a flurry of panic. The actor Tom Hanks comes backstage to say hello, but I don't know who he is and neither does anyone around me. He stands before me yet doesn't complete a sentence. The singer Ricki Lee Jones comes backstage, and I flutter out a few compliments – one of which strikes a sore note and she leaves the room in an inexplicable huff. Humans are certainly oddities. I am introduced to *'the most famous football player in America – who loves you.'*

'Does he have a name?' I ask, but suddenly this jockstrap hunk of studhorse has me in a crushed manful hug, into which I disappear like a pressed flower. Where, I wonder, am I?

'Oh, I think Morrissey summed it all up perfectly when he said...' and at this point prime-time television's Denis Leary bursts into mock tears – which is of course the punchline, and the loud audience laughter indicates understanding.

'So, my niece told me all about Morrissey,' says comic genius Roseanne Barr on morning TV.

'Oh, I LOVE Morrissey!' says Ricki Lake on her noon TV show, and the Johnny Carson Show is overthrown by Mozophiles who scream and shout their way through my first-ever appearance on US television, whilst main guest Bill Cosby mentions my name thirty times during his interview in order to elicit Beatlemania screams from the audience. *How can all of this possibly be?*

Two nights at the Hollywood Bowl sell out in a finger-click – breaking the Beatles' long-held record for speed. Wherever I walk, I am filmed by people I do not know – discreetly, or otherwise. I am locked inside every hotel I enter, leaving only to sign arms, legs, backs, necks – any physical part in need of a tattoo. It is T. Rexstacy gone mad – a Beatlemania that dare not speak its name. My face yellows with the news that Elizabeth Taylor – one of the greatest monuments of our age – will attend the Hollywood Bowl show. Has she confused me for someone else?

At Pauley Pavilion at UCLA – with only the varsity students acting as venue security – we are confidently assured by the know-all Fire Marshal, *'Look, we've had the Doors here. I am telling you that nothing will go wrong.'* The crowd of 11,500 unreservedly makes its way onto the stage and the show is stopped mid-riot. My face lights up breaking-news television reports for the next 24 hours.

I am leg-ironed in my villa at the Sunset Marquis and I watch it all unfold on the nightly news. I watch in disbelief as the UCLA is surrounded by police in their hundreds; the midnight streets are blocked by fire trucks that criss-cross and block Sunset Boulevard – all security officials shouting loudly as if a major building were about to fall. A mad axeman on the loose would cause less alarm. As if behind glass, I watch in amazement: *'The riot ensued when Morrissey instructed the crowd to "come party",'* says a reliable newshound to the on-the-spot camera, and the very idea of me ever sinking so low as to use the expression 'come party' makes me spray tonight's toddy across the television screen. In fact, the riot broke as I had been singing Y*ou're the one for me, fatty* – hardly an Altamont rallying call to the social underbelly.

Three days later, at Santa Monica Civic on November 4th,

a sold-out 4,250 people are on the streets awaiting sight of my car as it inches towards the venue with no idea of how to get inside. I am thunderstruck by the hundreds of police cars closing off each street that has access to the venue. Fire trucks are in full force even though there is no sign or likelihood of fire, yet their dazzling lights whirl at full speed as cool air rolls off the darkened beach front. The streets blaze with police and Mozophiles, who circle and clank in a confused fascination at something stirring – as if awaiting a public declaration to rouse the throng into civil action. Many were the young girls dressed in black; Hispanic boys elegantly be-quiffed, with chains dangling from the back pockets of their Big E's. I had never witnessed anything like this in my life – either for myself, or for others. *What do they think is about to occur?*

Bundled into the venue, I momentarily pass by a special room set aside for press reporters, and I see one very stately black man in an impressive suit speaking directly to a news camera.

'Morrissey conveys all the worst elements of homosexuality and bestiality,' and I wonder if he could possibly mean me. It is not enough, I note, to represent homosexuality fused with bestiality, but indeed I apparently convey *all the very worst* elements of both.

Certainly, this is already out of control. The concert itself is a storm of good intentions wildly received, and it is evident that it is only the media who are out for trouble. Once it becomes clear that I am neither Alice Cooper nor the Sex Pistols, the media backs off in search of gore else-where. How can we have a debauched rock report that is minus either sex or drugs? What exactly is being written about? A skinny singer who does not indulge in either sex or drugs? What badness therefore lurks?

I meet David Bowie for breakfast at a discreet restaurant at the foot of the Hollywood Hills. Both standing at the buffet with our empty plates, David hovers over what are horrifically called 'cold cuts'. I nestle up beside him.

'David, you're not actually going to eat that stuff, are you?'

Rumbled, he snaps: *'Oh, you must be HELL to live with.'*

'Yes, I am,' I say proudly, as David changes course and sidles off towards the fruit salad, and another soul is saved from the burning fires of self-imposed eternal damnation.

David quietly tells me, *'You know, I've had so much sex and drugs that I can't believe I'm still alive,'* and I loudly tell him, *'You know, I've had SO LITTLE sex and drugs that I can't believe I'm still alive.'*

1992 would bring a Grammy nomination for *Your Arsenal*, and the phenomenon of the prize system enters my life for the first time. The document from Grammy head-quarters quite naturally misspells my name, and I sniff a lack of serious intent. At Sire-Reprise, Howie Klein forewarns me: *'You won't win the Grammy,'* and full of dare-devil I ask, *'How do you know?'* and Howie says, *'Because they whisper the winner beforehand, and they haven't whispered to us, so you won't win.'*

Indeed I do not win. After all, what music mogul living in Brentwood splendor would vote for a scruffbag like me? The award goes to Tom Waits who, twenty years later, passes a message to me saying that I'm welcome to have the Grammy if I still want it.

A fax message splutters through to the Sunset Marquis

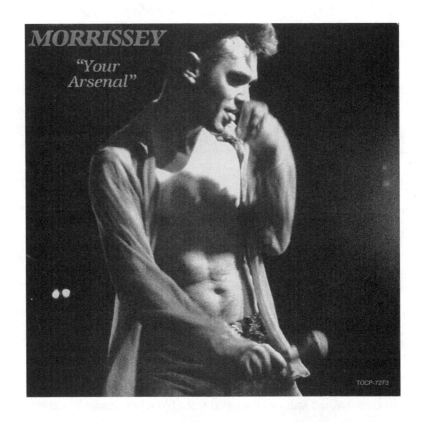

Your Arsenal, *1992, nothing to hide and nothing to lose*

(where I now live) from Chrissie Hynde, on Air Studios London paper:

> 25th Tuesday
> Johnny Thunders,
> Mr Genzale,
> died in New Orleans on Tuesday.
> Chrissie

Ahead is Madison Square Garden, which has sold all of its 22,000 tickets. I discreetly ask if David Johansen would open the night, but my live agent tells me, *'David said no because he plans to headline Madison Square himself shortly'* – an event which, as far as I know, has yet to happen. As an alternative, I ask around to see if anyone can track down Jobriath, who has entirely fallen off the human map.

'Are you saying you'd like him to do those old songs in makeup, and so forth?' asks my agent, Marsha Vallasic.

'Yes!' I reply in a half-giggle of excitement. A few days later my agent tells me that Jobriath won't be available. *'Why not?'* I ask, indignantly hard-pressed to think of whatever else he might be distracted by.

'Because he's dead, that's why not,' my agent says. In fact, Jobriath has already spent ten years in his grave. Such were the moods of the 80s and 90s music press that Jobriath's death would not be considered worth mentioning, and even I, as a dedicated listener, had no idea that ill-health had snuffed him out. Jobriath had gone alongside Klaus Nomi in an 'AIDS related' illness that usually quite specifically means AIDS.

Meanwhile, somehow alive, I am New York's 'hottest

ticket', as a stinky and steamy July brings me to the Garden's vast and lavish dressing rooms. I sit by a grand piano awaiting the evening's call-time, and I ponder on how the band aren't really as good as they ought to be, but nonetheless the march of time takes control and I am overwhelmed with all of the understanding of rags-to-riches monologues. I am afforded all of the luxuries and attention and private bathrooms where Elvis Presley had soaked before me, and as I lower myself onto the very toilet where Elvis had no doubt whistled away the call of nature, I wonder how all of this could possibly be, yet at the same time I am confused by its naturalness and its *right* to be. From Stretford stress – with those miserable miscreants running the Jobcenter ... those richer-than-thou troglodytes ordering files from me in the Inland Revenue cellar – and now, here I am, the glamor and clamor of Madison Square Garden, where people much older than me call me 'Sir', and where the Smiths are *tellingly* ... nowhere in sight. Teams of young people slip and slide through New York streets with my face on their t-shirts, and the proper and elitist Garden staff welcome me with a congenial half-bow. It is exactly like a Broadway born-in-a-trunk music hall tale where the rail tracks whiz across the screen indicating a speedy ride up life's ladder. Now there were no Smiths, and all of the Smiths' live crew had also gone. The name on the ticket is now mine, but with the continuing absence of Sire Records I couldn't point to anything that had eased the journey. The long corridors lead me to the stage, where the roar of 22,000 people makes the skin on my face shiver and peel back. The only way I can cope with the drama is to pretend I am elsewhere. It is a night to remember, and the final reply to a lengthy question.

Michael Stipe slips a note under my hotel door: *'You were very funny last night. New York gasped. MS/SM.'*

At The Forum in Los Angeles a royal David Bowie walks onstage to join me for the encore; he is stately against my last-gasp exhaustion. The 12-year-old within me – unable to leave for school unless I'd soothed my sickness with at least one spin of *Starman* – bathes in the moment with disbelief. But there it is.

The night clouds as television news announce the disappearance of 23-year-old Denise Anette Huber, who had left her Newport Beach home on June 2nd 1991, by herself, to 'attend Morrissey at the Los Angeles Forum'. Denise was never seen again, and a plea for information ran over and over and over on the California nightly news for several years until her nude body was found in 1994 in a freezer in Arizona. Reports were certain that, on driving home from the concert, Denise had stopped to assist someone in trouble, and had herself been bludgeoned to death in response to her act of kindness.

There are, of course, no UK press reviews of the incredible pandemonium at the US shows. Nothing, nothing, nothing. *Let it be.*

We head-butt our way through streets of bumper-to-bumper traffic in order to reach the University Hall in Las Vegas. The audience completely trashes the seated venue, and newspapers of the following morning report a savage riot with rows and rows of mangled and piled-up seats shown on the front pages. It is quite fantastic. We plough on to Chicago (The World), Detroit (Meadowbrook),

Cincinnati (Riverbend), Cleveland (Nautica), Boston (Great Woods), and everyone is mystified at the sheer size of the crowds, as what seems like small continents of people swarm in. The parking areas alone seem to go on for miles. I struggle to realize how all of these people have come along to see me. Toronto's Kingswood is a giant mass of screaming and swirling people – all very young, some demented, many hanging off the stage, others climbing across the heads of others in order to reach the lip of the stage, and I look into the audience at a mass of legs – not arms – in the air. The vision is an endless roll, roll, roll, of people being tipped off the stage, with coats, shoes, bags, posters all flying across the stage; highschool girls of long blonde hair projected ten feet into the air; tearaways in brothel creepers punch their way through in order to touch the tips of my fingers and yelp with joy. I laugh, I am horrified, I can't believe it, I'm tearful, it's dreadful, it's beautiful, it's dangerous, and all the young and vital reach to me – as I had never reached to anyone. By the time we reach Washington's Merriweather, local security has been given the nod, and the fat yellow jackets stand three deep between the stage and the front row, so that I am, in effect, singing to security alone. I walk off frustrated, and I ask that their numbers be reduced, but they won't budge.

'*Don't let your ego hurt people,*' shouts one security guard as I pass, and the ugly turns uglier as one security guard grabs me around the neck, and as his throttle begins to burn into me I swing back my right fist which is then caught by Jim Connolly.

'*Don't,*' he says, '*that's just what he wants – he'll have you for assault.*'

In the midst of all the chaos and violence, the band freezes. It is beyond them. At New Jersey's Garden State I am told that the American national anthem is always played before the artist walks on. I find this absurd and slightly fascist, and although I can't stop it from happening I follow it with an even louder blast of Buffy Sainte-Marie's *My country 'tis of thy people you're dying* anti-American detonation.

'*Is it having any effect?*' I ask a crew member from behind the iron curtain.

'*No. Everyone just looks confused.*'

At the Shoreline Amphitheater in San Francisco so many people clamber onto the stage that I am immediately swallowed up in the rotating mass. I crawl offstage on my knees as if out of a rugby scrum, the night lost to sheer lunacy of stage-divers coming from every conceivable angle. The audience is suddenly a giant mass of piled-up flesh with death at their elbows. The house lights come on, go off, come on, go off, pitch darkness, everyone screams, the PA shuts down, amps are pushed over as everything on the stage is grabbed by souvenir hunters, and the looting goes on and on with no one able to control the crowd.

'*Where is Moz?!*' panics a crew member as I coil behind Alain's amp-stack and belly-slide off the back of the stage. Even if seen, it could not be believed. Yet Sire do nothing, and say nothing.

In Chicago Alain sets fire to his guitar onstage; Gary smashes his bass into dust particles; Spencer kicks his kit over; and the police line up in a side-stage loop looking for someone to arrest. An enormous backdrop of a laughing Harvey Keitel blocks out the sky as police sirens replace the music. It is all madness. From Sire, Howie Klein looks away. By now, the nightly intent of ticket-buyers is to mount the stage and then to rip my shirt off – I, who have nothing. On this first tour alone I go through 300 shirts. People grab everything and anything and run off with it, having managed the impossible climb over barriers and through security to arise onstage. It is mesmerizing to watch. By November 11th we reach Nassau Coliseum and we face our first blip; the arena is only half-sold. We had been on a roller-coaster since May, but now Howie Klein observes, *'Morrissey shows are too violent'* – and of course they are bound to be too *something* – no suggestion from Sire that we must capture all of this on film. Each night continues as a sinister and desperate torrent of Beatlemania bodies.

In Nashville the local police line up on the front of the stage! Behind them, I attempt to sing to their backs! But I can't see through the line of porky-pig slime-buckets, whose jelly-assed cossacks block me from audience view. It is vaudevillian in its crackpot silliness. A very effeminate boy slips under the flatfoot mountain and whacks his face against the stage, and he is side-kicked away by our badged guardians.

'Who does he thank he is? Elvis Presleh?' says a Smokey the Bear Keystone Cop, as he gives me the glare of death.

'We've nevah had anythung like thas be-fowah,' says a police-woman – confusingly standing between me and the drumkit.

The Nashville front row hosts a large gang of boys wearing heavy makeup, and as I am rolled into the backseat of a waiting car, a man in his late twenties stands with tear-stained face: *'Just let me touch you – just once,'* and his sobs reach breaking-point. However, we all snap, exhausted and spent in a mayhem unmanned, and we cancel the final run of dates at Worcester, Albany, Williamsburg, Chapel Hill, Birmingham and Lakeland. It is sad, but the bough breaks. At JFK Airport, skinny Mozophiles are pouring through barriers and checkpoints, banging on glass as I hide in the airport lounge.

'We'll haffta take him through the back-way,' say police, and I am whisked through fish-stenched kitchens. I am Fabian in 1960.

'Would they believe this back in England?' I ask Linder, agog with her camera.

'They would never WANT to believe this back in England,' she says.

And she is correct. The most extraordinary tours of my life are never made known back in England, and attempting to recount the details becomes almost pointless.

'People in England have no idea,' says Nigel Thomas of the American madness, *'and unfortunately you are on a record label who are as slow as a dead donkey. They can't even get* Everyday is like Sunday *to number 80, never mind number 1.'*

Nigel quickly arranges for a studio session in New Orleans with the revered Allen Toussaint. Worn out, the band arrives at the studio where Allen will record the song *The thoughts of Jack the Ripper*, a ludicrously lost gem in Nigel's view, yet not the catchiest of titles. I slip into the studio and watch the band warm up. I say hello to Allen, who looks at me and then looks away. The band are rough to the point of bad – having been pushed around America like a debilitated Bay City Rollers, and Allen Toussaint looks concerned. I am now embarrassed by the sound coming through the speakers, of which Allen says to his engineer

'*What have I let myself in for?*' I overhear the comment and I catch the engineer's reply to Allen, which is a silent *sssh* in my direction, as if to say to Allen, '*Steady, he can hear you.*' Without fuss or calamity I rise and exit into the balmy air of New Orleans. Boz follows me.

'*So, what do you want me to do?*' he says.

'*El-vest has left the building,*' I say, not remotely funny. It isn't a question of vanity or ego, but occasionally there is simply no point.

On returning to England I am told by Murray Chalmers at EMI that a certain journalist is now the editor of the *NME*. This journalist is known to us because he has reviewed five albums by either the Smiths or Morrissey, writing with unabashed hatred, without an avenue of offensiveness left unexplored. However, the significance of his promotion to *NME* editor is that he has allegedly called a staff meeting at which he has passed the command that his staff writers must now 'get Morrissey', and that the plan was now underway to dislodge me as an *NME* staple.

Soon after, at a Finsbury Park concert, where the main writers from the *NME* are seated at the back of the park at the mixing desk, and one particularly irritating writer is suckling her newborn, I begin to notice a flux of sharpened pound coins flying at me from sections of the crowd. It takes mission, I thought, to part with so many pound coins. What is happening? I am forced offstage mid-set, which doesn't worry me greatly since I am not dish of the day, but the backstage view is that the coterie of trouble makers are an organized group.

However, the *NME* manslaughter erupts with their next

issue, where my face grabs the cover with the blaring question 'Is Morrissey flirting with fascism?' and their head-shrinking hang-ups waffle on over several pages of burning execution. EMI back off nervously saying, *'If this* NME *thing begins to affect the Pet Shop Boys then we'll be forced to do something about it,'* with no thought whatsoever of me in the burning wreckage of it all. Branded a racist by the *NME* (who apply just enough question marks alongside their allegations to protect themselves from any specific accusation in a court of law), the finger-pointing goes unanswered from me, but my refusal to feed the *NME* story causes a bushfire of speculation that forms a part of my biography forevermore. No one comes to my defense, and the ex-Smiths are noticeable in their all-lads-together silence. *''e'll get 'is hair cut reg'lar now,'* one can almost hear. It is a time, though, when Marr, Rourke and Joyce will only raise their heads in order to say something damning, which, ahhh, with maturity one is meant to shrug off.

Although all 36,000 tickets for the Hollywood Bowl have sold out within minutes, the *NME* is in full Morrissey concentration mode, and they milk and foster their racist allegations – full of high moral code and judicial thuggery. A picture of me holding a Union Jack is infallible proof for the *NME* that I do not like people whose skin is darker than my own. *'I wear black on the outside | because black is how I feel on the inside,'* I had sung in 1985.

Suddenly a new generation of pop faces drape themselves in the Union Jack, and the *NME* celebrates them all as the emergence of 'Brit Pop'; the Union Jack becomes the *NME's* badge, leaving little doubt that the Morrissey fiasco was a personal vendetta by the *NME* to gain mass attention for the paper and to eke out a historical moment for its own archive. Had I actually been racist, the *NME* comments would reveal nothing and attract no one, but because the accusation was so unlikely it would naturally have enough impact to stop traffic – which was surely the *NME*'s aim. Setting itself up as our moral guardian and jailer, the *NME* is suddenly our parental safeguard and an ever-vigilant arm of the law. In order to mesmerize the public you must accuse someone of being the opposite of what you have believed them to be, otherwise there's no story and there's no plot. Surely if any pop artist were, in fact, racist, it would be wrong of the *NME* to grant them so much suffocating publicity? The deathblow for anyone with a racist message could only surely be exclusion and neglect? Yet, instead, the *NME* smothered its readers week after week with the liquidation of 'racist' Morrissey, which, had the story any truth, would have placed the *NME* itself in the foreground for promoting the issue of race hatred so obsessively. The *NME* editor had written a damning review of my concert at Wembley, in which he assures readers that I had done '*an appalling version*' of the T. Rex song *Cosmic dancer* – a song that was not actually played on the night of the review! And *then* people say you are becoming neurotic about the press, when all one asks for is the truth.

I am called to a board meeting at Warner Records in Burbank where, in an enormously lavish office of pure glass, the revered head of the label examines me as one would a mummified relic.

'*Heaven will seem very dull after a lifetime in this office,*' I tell him, to which he does not smile, but I was simply trying to lighten the atmosphere – which admittedly is not one of my strong points. I am asked a few impersonal questions, the sub-text well hidden. I am being studied like something accidentally dug up.

'I don't exactly know why I'm here,' I say softly, *'on ... the planet ...'* My voice trails sideways. *'No, I'm sorry, I mean in your office.'* I try to straighten myself up. I have attempted a second joke, which must be like trying to strangle two people at once.

Seconds later, I am not in his office. I am politely ushered out. I ask key faces at Reprise what on earth it was all about, and I am reliably informed how Warner need a massively successful 'act' who is 'alternative', and I was indeed being auditioned for the star part since I had thus far been the most successful 'alternative' artist in America.

'Alternative to what?' I foolishly ask.

I hear nothing more, but I note the immediate meteoric Warner rise of Alanis Morrissette – the incongruous promotional manifesto enveloping her first album that shifts 27 million copies worldwide. Evidently Alanis had all that I lacked in order to gain a saturated global push.

'Is THAT why I was interviewed?' I later ask Howie Klein.

'YES!' he half-shouts, as if I ought to know everything.

Forever the bridesmaid, I have failed yet another interview, and I shall evermore only exist in French inverted commas, dreaming of how *Vauxhall and I* could have sold 27 million copies had the head of Warner warmed to the weave of my sleeve. But he didn't. Still, I was close to that ever-elusive upgrade in the promo stakes.

Mick Ronson had produced *Your Arsenal* as he struggled

on his cancer medication. I first met him at Hasker Street in Chelsea, where he had a neat terraced house on loan from a friend. The house is awash with dive-bombing bluebottles, and Mick casually swats them between his palms as we speak. I cannot think of anything to say on the subject of bluebottle protectionism, so I watch Mick splat, splat, splat. The house is just behind my flat at Cadogan Square, and here we are, together living the leisured London life. In his battered motor Mick and I drive to Bath in readiness to record *Your Arsenal*. We are good companions, and much of his life floods out on these journeys. Mick has a very attractive face – everything neatly in proportion, and I can still see the Hull school cherub whistling at the girls (and surely getting them without any fuss). Mick is always optimistic and is easy to be around. He takes me to a masseur who, oddly, works on both of our backs at the same time, and then the daily trip to the turf accountant fixes a firmer smile to his face. On our first recording session, Mick pushes drummer Spencer (whom Mick tags 'Nelson'), but Spencer is affronted and walks out of the session – his manhood bent. We reconvene the following day and all is well. Linder stands by urging more cut and thrust on the vocal for *The National Front disco*. Ian Hunter walks in and joins Linder's iron-hearted rallying – egging me on as if this were school sports day in Stevenage.

When I've finished the vocal, Ian says, '*Good God, you won't be going there again!*' and I'm not sure whether he means the National Front disco or, more likely, back into a vocal booth. For the sweeping coda on *I know it's gonna happen someday* Mick utilizes a heavily orchestrated pattern which we are certain echoes the falling moments of David Bowie's *Rock 'n roll suicide*. I am slightly troubled by this resemblance, and I point out to Mick that the envelope has been pushed too far.

'*Yes, well,*' says Mick, '*I wrote that original piece for* Rock 'n roll suicide, *so there won't be any legal comeback.*' Mick goes on to say how he wrote the guitar parts for *Starman* and *The man who sold the world.* Mick had been naive in the past, but it was not for me to comment since I continued to be naive in the present.

Suddenly David Bowie telephones the studio and asks to speak to me. I am thrilled, but he tells me that he would like me to do a cover of one of his recent songs, and he stresses that if I don't do the cover, '*I will never speak to you again, haha,*' which is hardly much of a loss since David *doesn't ever* speak to me. The song he'd like me to cover is called *Mr Ed,* and although I listen to the tape that he sends to the studio, nothing within the song shouts out to me. A few months later I am at my mother's house when the telephone rings. My mother hands me the 1940s shellac antique.

'*It's for you – it's David Bowie,*' and boyhood's fire is all aglow again, although I cannot understand how David found my mother's number. He explains that he would like to send me something through the post.

'*Do you have an address?*' I ask.

'*Oh, just write to me care of the management,*' he replies.

'*No, I meant do YOU have an address for ME?*' I say.

Dear Morrissey,

Came by to see if you were OK. Called a couple of times but no

answer. If I don't hear from you or don't see you, have a right
smashin' time in the States, and I will see you in the NY area.
Take care of yourself. I'll look forward to seeing you soon, OK.
Mick

A letter arrives from Spencer, who encloses a book of
Elizabeth Barrett Browning's poetry:

Dear Monsieur Moz,

I do apologize for making a mess at the Wool Hall. It was stupid
and immature, no excuses. I know we don't talk much which is a
great shame (well, to me anyway). Even though there is a lack of
communication, that doesn't mean lack of feeling, understanding,
and above all, respect.

All my best,
Spencer

The time with Mick in New York is brief. We play the
Paramount Theater, which is a great success, but Mick
chips in with, *'I don't know why you don't do any Smiths songs.*
People want to hear them.' I know this is true, but the imp in
me wants to establish a solo footing lest I be intellectually
battered for leaning too readily on the past.

Mick's health is in speedy decline, so I am surprised
when he telephones me to let me know that he is in great
shape. It is not a steady voice, and these will be our parting
words, since Mick will soon be dead. He tells me that he
has exhausted funding for his medical care, and my imagination contaminates itself with the despairing notion that
Mick's life might end in struggle. But the end comes sooner

than he, or I, dared anticipate. The order of the universe calls upon Mick in April 1993, the year still so young, but already it has taken three close friends from my dishearteningly slim roster. The telephone rang and it was Suzi Fussey – once the girl of a Beckenham High Street hair salon who had created David Bowie's 'Ziggy' cut, and then married Mick. Twenty-three years on from that day, Suzi says '*My baby has gone,*' and I knew Mick was no more. I am asked to write about Mick in the *Guardian* newspaper, and talk about him on Radio One, but indecent haste forbids.

Mick certainly saved *Your Arsenal,* and by extension he saved me. Mid-week of release, EMI tell me that the album is going in at number 1, but as I prepare myself for glory it lands at number 4. An old Manchester rear gunner, Paul Morley, reviews the album's opening single (*We hate it when our friends become successful*), which he explains is a title taken from Oscar Wilde, which, of course, it isn't. At *Top of the Pops,* 50s singer Marty Wilde approaches to shake my hand. Singing live, I fluff the words – *oh my dear God.* DJ Tony Blackburn would later say, '*I am not a Morrissey fan, but he was right when he said we hate it when our friends become successful.*'

There, now!

The solid basis of *Your Arsenal* threw the line back after the confusion of *Kill Uncle,* which could wrest nothing from the spirit. It didn't seem to matter now. In the US Reprise issue the track *Tomorrow* as a single, and stylish chief Steven Baker writes to me: '*If we can't make this a hit then we can't do anything.*'

Needless to say, they didn't make *Tomorrow* a hit. It emerges in a sleeve on which I languish by a swimming pool reading *Variety* magazine. In the background is bassist Gary Day, whom I most certainly have nothing against, but I ask that he be chopped off because he looks like a prop. I am told that no one knows how to take him out of the proofs (this is, after all, 1066), and so Gary remains on the sleeve and I feel slightly silly. Art must wait.

In the *Sun* newspaper in England a headline rings out, $5,700 FOR GIRL FAN SCARRED BY MORRISSEY, and I am utterly perplexed. The writer is Piers Morgan, who details how a tambourine 'thrown into the crowd by Morrissey' at a show in Texas ripped into the face of 21-year-old Shirley, who then 'failed to receive a personal apology from the singer'. The singer in question, I hastily assume, is me. Until the moment of this article I had never heard of Shirley or the incident, and I had always anticipated possible accidents by throwing tambourines *minus* their loose metallic discs. However, tambourines were constantly ripped from my hands, or grabbed off the drum-riser by someone who would then dive head first into the crowd, and we suspect that this is how 21-year-old Shirley managed to get whacked. However, from the Piers Morgan headline, the world would be forgiven for assuming that I had stalked Houston side streets at midnight wrapped in a black cloak concealing a sabre, ripe to slash to ribbons the next available plump face.

'*It's a shame he hasn't written to me,*' commented Shirley, now evidently fully recovered and giving international press conferences. Her slip shows as she concludes, '*I've got the money,*' which one assumes is far more useful than an unscarred face. Ah, the greasy grind of the press – the scribblers and scratchers, the slingers and spillers.

A note arrives at the Mark Hotel on Madison Avenue in New York. It is addressed to my pseudonym Vince Eager, and is from David Bowie. That evening I am called over to David's recording studio, where he guides me into a favored chair at the control desk – central to the speakers. David flicks on the tape and the mammoth waft of his version of my own *I know it's gonna happen someday* attacks the room with tsunami turbulence. Seated beside me in spiritual quietude, Linder is pale with emotional under-standing. David's beautiful wife, Iman, folds herself away in a corner seat. Iman had been plucked from the streets of Kenya to illuminate catwalks all over the world, and had become one of the first women of color to grace the covers of style magazines that had not previously given space to women who were non-Caucasian. Iman has a gentle patience and a friendly perception. She does not edge into the conversation until invited, yet her comments are always thoughtful and precise. I like her a great deal. Now launch-ing her own skin-care range, I ask her what products other than her own does she use on her skin. *'Oh, I just mix bits of everything,'* she says.

The sound coming from the speakers is the gift of life, and nothing will keep me level after David's bestowal. Here is the unimaginable culmination of a mad process that began for me sometime in 1970, as *On the Buses* chirped annoyingly in the background. Jets of steam rise in the New York streets as Linder and I walk slowly back to the hotel, scrutinizing events. David had been an infallible guide, and these are the years when he still developed his ideas with pride, and always at considerable distance from the sparkl-ing modernities of pop. I am all parts gratitude.

With no movement on the Smiths chessboard since the almighty crack of 1987, I decide to write to Johnny – hacking into mountains of ice. His handwritten reply instantly follows.

Dear Moz,

Sincere thanks for your letter last week and for your concern. I do realize that it must have taken a lot of brainache/heartache to have gotten in touch. The main thing that I want you to know is that I really regret us not being friends. I've only recently come to realize that you genuinely don't know all the reasons for my leaving. To get into it would be horrible, but I will say that I honestly hated the sort of people we became. I have no ambitions to be a solo guitar player. I will never point the finger at anyone but myself, and I am glad I took a step towards making my life sane.

After getting your postcard I felt that the only way to explain things would be to come round and see you personally. I also felt bad that you were so unhappy and it's only circumstances that made it possible.

I hope I see you soon.
Love, Johnny

A week later his Mercedes pulls up outside my mother's house and we are both briefly united. Behind the wheel, he makes for Saddleworth Moor, and the social unit slots back together again.

'*You really don't know the full story of what happened at the end, do you?*' Johnny asks me as rain whacks the window screen. If anyone has a right to raise their voice, it is me. So I do.

'I know NOTHING!!!' I shout.
Does anyone go to war and win?
No.

Everything I had said at the Smiths' demise had led me
directly towards trouble, chiefly because I could not
explain to anyone exactly why the roof had fallen in. I
couldn't even manage eloquent evasion. You begin to
imagine facts where originally there were none. A hurt
sensation rises like dough every time your own name is
mentioned. People who have been close do not need to
say very much in order to wound each other. The Smiths
were my first life's pleasure, and were turned into incomprehensible sorrow. Groups disband because they dry
up; the Smiths broke up as their powers increased. Even
amidst whirlwind success you might ask yourself if you
actually have a life. The seething rot that had shot the
Smiths down remained undisclosed by Johnny on this
drive to Saddleworth Moor (oh, Saddleworth Moor, so
much to answer for), and instead we let our minds run on
the joy of the songs created – songs that were still growing
in stature, working wonders for the strangled spirit. I
wanted a day without blame, since I had carried so much
of it like an unfed donkey on the streets of Delhi. It is a
simple truth that everything in life ends badly – few people
die in a fit of hysterics, so why should the Smiths be
exempt. In months to come, Johnny will appear on television several times under scorching lights. He struggles
with the truth, half-forgetting, he says he split the Smiths
up, and then in a later television spot he says he did no
such thing. Johnny spits out my name, changing his story

as he shifts from foot to foot; he says he had no idea, and then he says he fully intended to 'move on'. Always saying too much, something has happened to Johnny once again, and each appearance gives an entirely different account. He no longer listens to the Smiths' music and he criticizes it. Morrissey is a bad smell in the attic. Morrissey is a death-machine. Morrissey is evil and should be stuffed. But as Johnny spouts he looks all wrong. His clothes are crooked and the eyes are in torment. What had happened since the serenity of our drive to Saddleworth Moor, when the coffin-lid shifted and the old spark rose like a small miracle? Someone, by now, is preparing to save Johnny's soul as the nightmare of the Joyce Case flexes itself in readiness. The petty guidance of advisors are grooming Johnny for his upcoming role as sacrificial lamb – always a hit with judges who demand subservience above truth. Darting schizophrenically in the pursuit of self-interest, Johnny now looks pale on the scaffold – the opportunism of wolves giving him a notably punished look. Revenge is calling, and I am the quarry.

In the first few days of 1993 my manager Nigel Thomas sat up in bed and spoke a few pleasantries to his wife. At ease, his head lowered and he softly died a strange and gentle death. A month later, Tim Broad, who had directed all of my promotional films, lost his life to what the good folk of WeHo termed 'the Headache'. Ebbing away in the parlor of his terraced house on Clapham Manor Street, he looked up to ask an attending James O'Brien, *'Do you think I'll be remembered?'* as he faded away. A paragon of practical-ity in so many ways, he was unable to monitor his own urgings. And why should he? The church demands too much. There is no self-discovery in a safe life. Instead, Tim lived whilst alive – such a rarity. But there's a price for everything. Always full of fun, with the illusion of immunity, Tim had no idea how to moan. At his funeral at Mortlake, we are all hunched in an unbearable sadness. Like Jon Daley, Tim has gone at the age of 38. I am close to breakdown at life's inevitably disgusting final summons, as Tim is flushed away.

By April Mick Ronson's death forces me to accept the worst all over again, and I recall twelve months previously when four people sat in the same room discussing exciting plans for the year ahead. Since three of those four people were Mick Ronson, Tim Broad and Nigel Thomas, only I remain alive one year on. As we outlined our world-crushing grand-slam circuit clout for *Your Arsenal*, only I would live to tell the tale. In the midst of substantial sorrow a deadly writ is issued from a merchandising company called Giant. The final act of Nigel's wizardry was an impressive deal with Giant who handed over $1 million in return for use of my never-ready smile. After Nigel died, Giant sued for return of the outstanding sum, and I was dragged without resistance to the Supreme Court in Los Angeles where the money paid over was restored. The lead waggler was a famous Los Angeles entrepreneur named Irving Handsoff, who peeped over the head of the table and called for my head on a plate. Any plate would do. It fell to me to return the entire amount, even though $250,000 had gone to Nigel for management commission, and $58,000 had been paid to my London lawyer Tony

English in fees. I fought the action on the grounds that there was no need for any of the advance to be returned since, with time, Giant would recoup the cash from upcoming tours. But I felt the unfelicitous ferocity of Irving Handsoff call upon all of his fellow morticians to flatten me like a squashed pug, and as an out-of-towner against the swagmen of Los Strangle-us, I fell to the syndicate of goombahs and goodfellas before I'd even had time to toy with my rosary. Dimly I am pushed along the plank and dimly I oblige. For this joy, I am presented with legal bills of over 200,000 euro, and the joke is everlastingly on me. I suggest to my accountant that Nigel's family be asked to return the 250,000 allotted to Nigel, who, now dead, had no time to earn his slice.

'*You wouldn't take money from a grieving family!*' my accountant gasped.

'*But I'M grieving,*' I reply, and wherever I turn the trap widens. It was true that the art of getting money and acknowledging no superior was the rock on which the black hands of Handsoff had built his empire, and I was gooey putty against his Israelites. His was a mediocre way to spend a life, but it provided yachts a-plenty for his big-eyed militia.

I do not know Siouxsie, but I ask around to see if she would have any interest in dueting with me. Her manager responds, and I send her four covers to choose from, being *Happy* (Nancy Sinatra), *Loneliness remembers what happiness forgets* (Dionne Warwick), *Interlude* (Timi Yuro) and *Morning starship* (Jobriath). I call Siouxsie at her home in Condom in France, and each time she recognizes my voice there comes a small, impatient sigh as if I'd just interrupted her evening prayer. *'Can't we do something off* Ziggy Stardust, *like* The prettiest star*?'* she suggests.

'The prettiest star *wasn't on* Ziggy Stardust,*'* Mr Know-all returns. Siouxsie stiffens, and we shall never be friends. She is very much as I had expected – a physical blancmange that is six parts Kate O'Mara, two parts Myra Hindley and two parts Fenella Fielding. She had replaced Croydon for the Black Forest, and she appears to hate even the people that she likes. She looks at everyone and everything only with a sense of what is due to her, and she might stare you out as you lay dying on a zebra crossing. She is certain that her historical value outstrips Queen Victoria's (which, in my meager opinion, it actually does), and she has a duty to no one. Not for a moment will she forget that she is Siouxsie, who might pick fights with people whom her male friends would then beat up. Your mind's eye can see her in 1972, outside the pubs of Shirley, lines of cruelty already set in stone, full of sexless decorative art, plying very strange cargo – you're the pride of our street; black magic spun out and on the march – an Eve cigarette held aloft. The overground train to Victoria leaves behind the Oak Crescents and Acacia Avenues of *Bless This House* and *Terry and June*, where a better edition of Susan could never be constructed. It was never a question of becoming a pop singer, more a matter of entering the field of argument; a Nico iceberg who hates blasé dolls, and who will be very careful about whom she is photographed with. There are no penetrating opinions forthcoming, but Siouxsie the star is embarrassed by women, and possibly angry because she is one. What slips out is cultivated offensiveness and, thankfully, a stabbing trail of quite outstanding recordings as Siouxsie stomps through with zero emotional involvement and maintains this indifference for twenty very successful years. Siouxsie doesn't mind if she poisons the world, and here lies the appeal of the one who had said *No* as the millions of *Yes* girls smiled their way into the *Top of the Pops* cameras. The music she makes is a strict ice-bath of nightmare and caution, the hanging valleys of Bern – a black-eyed shopgirl hidden somewhere in the whistling cathedral towers of Notre Dame, refusing to be dragged back to Boots the Chemist, where both her shift and her insurance stamps remain.

Siouxsie chooses Timi Yuro's *Interlude*, and she pulls up at Hook End Manor recording studio in a black Mercedes. She is carrying her own microphone and she wants to get on with it minus any familiar chit-chat. In the event, she is a seasoned professional of exact run-throughs and topnotch precision. There is only one crack in the alabaster as she listens to her final take and softly asks me, *'Are you sure it's OK?'* It is the solitary moment when the Soviet Statue breathes. One can suddenly imagine real blood in Siouxsie's veins – and yet, perhaps not.

Siouxsie's manager calls me a few days later. *'Sioux says I'm too soft on you,'* he begins – inexplicably.

'S-soft?' I stutter, *'but you don't know me, and I don't know you, and she doesn't know me, and I don't ...'* and on I go, trailing away boring myself rigid.

EMI are delighted with *Interlude*, and there are torturous mutterings of 'a number 1 cert'. It certainly achieves its aim as a husky Bond theme, with the slipping-away wheeze of dentist-gas.

Suddenly a legal letter arrives at EMI from Siouxsie's label, Polydor, who insist that 'at very least this is a Siouxsie recording', and they would like 100 per cent ownership, which should be released with Siouxsie's name only. *Am I to be spared nothing?* Although I had paid for the recording, Polydor do not insist on covering any costs! It is all so typically, typically, typically convoluted crap.

I am now living at 18 Regent's Park Terrace, half-Camden, half-Regent's Park, and Siouxsie appears to discuss a video treatment for *Interlude.* We are gathered with a video director and her assistants, whilst Murray Chalmers makes tea. Siouxsie is wearing reflective sunglasses so that her eyes are not visible to anyone, and instantly her demands are barked out with a voice of punished ferocity. Within eight seconds she seems to have alienated everyone in the room, and as Murray fiddles about with cups and saucers his eyes roll ceilingwards each time Godzilla snaps out her stipulations.

'*Look,*' she says to no one in particular, '*I haven't got time for this, I've got to be writing some B-sides,*' and we all wonder what on earth she is talking about. The video crew visibly sink as Siouxsie outlines her suggestion for the video – a treatment which sees me walking through a park only for Siouxsie to emerge throwing stones at me, to which I evidently accept. The move is a crafty pecking-order trample that would emphasize Siouxsie's natural superiority to the world, whereas I, quite clearly, would be seen as a spectacle of misfortune. The suggestion is met by a terrified silence, not least of all because it is delivered with a look of advanced misery from Eve white/Eve black. Aware that she is coming across as a slightly glitzy version of sheer misery, Siouxsie advances to leave – too soon, unresolved, yet getting the drift. On the doorstep she asks me whether right or left would be the best direction to find a taxi, and although her best bet would be left, I suggest she turns right. It is churlish of me, but it is she who has set the pace. I return to the room where everyone sits in a circle, their jaws agape and their eyes sore at the attack of the beast from fifty thousand fathoms. It is disheartening, but there it is.

I piece together the artwork for *Interlude*, but the ongoing ownership tussle with Polydor means that the release date moves back, and is then shifted again when no agreement can be reached. In the event, EMI unsurprisingly become bored with the battle of the sea goats and *Interlude* finally escapes amid cloud and heartache, and success is impossible. Reaching number 25 in the chart, it is supported by one solitary radio play – but nothing else, and not even a photograph of Siouxsie and I together exists to rouse a nation.

In the US *Interlude* receives excitable airplay, but Reprise decides against a domestic release for reasons known only to the silent gods. Sleeve notes for a new Timi Yuro compilation gratefully point out how *Interlude* had recently become a UK hit *'as recorded by some miscreant'*. I expect they meant me.

Some years later a Siouxsie biography hits the shelves of Waterstones, and alarmingly she gives a highly divergent account of our video meeting at 18 Regent's Park Terrace, an account which naturally bombasts me with gobbledygook and ignites her own leniency. I am very surprised, and then saddened.

Gill Smith and I drive up to Cambridge to see Echobelly, whom I love. Gill's banger dates back to the Apostles so the journey takes at least five days. *'I don't like Sonya's voice,'* she says, *'she sounds like a posh bird trying to sound tough.'*

'It would be nice if YOU could occasionally manage to sound like a posh bird instead of Rita Webb,' I flick back.

The following week Gill writes in her weekly pop column how she *'went out with Morrissey and no one recognized him – a crisp packet would have caused more attention'*, and for this I scrub Gill's name off my *In Sympathy At the Loss of Your Pet Goat* list.

Laughed off by lawyers and accountants, pounder Joyce is now digging his heels in with his sudden claim for 25 per cent of Smiths earnings, swelling disfavor wherever he goes. I am legally advised to let him ramble on, skipping as he does from law firm to law firm – most of whom abandon his plea after a customary threatening introduction. *'It is what we fear that happens to us,'* said Oscar Wilde, which is true, but gives me no heart in 1994. Well, why should it?

I had jumped from a squatty terrace at Chelsea's Markham Street and had invested in something far better at Regent's Park Terrace, with the noise of Camden bubbling over the way, and I am illuminated by an accidental introduction to Jake Owen Walters. Seated at dinner in a badly lit restaurant in Notting Hill, Jake's face is one amongst many, and as his food order arrives I stare intently at what appears to be a sloppy dish of dog food on his plate. Jake and I have scarcely spoken to one another, so he can't possibly know that I have long-since passed the stage of attending any table where dead animals are served up as food. I therefore automatically stand up and walk out of the restaurant. I walk all the way back to Regent's Park Terrace. Suddenly, you come to a certain situation and you are unable to live with it, and the only protest you can make on behalf of the butchered animal is to depart the scene. Whether this be considered irritating or rude by the gluttonous carnivore is of no interest to me. Nobody can possibly be so hungry that they need to take a life in order to feel satisfied – they don't after all, take a human life, so why take the life of an animal? Both are conscious beings with the same determination to survive. It is habit, and laziness and nothing else. Once inside the house, the doorbell rings. It is Jake. He obviously understood my sudden exit, and he had been curious enough to follow me home.

'*Why did you mention Battersea in that song?*' is his opening gambit.

'*Because it rhymed with Fatty,*' I reply with magnanimous Philip Larkin *don't-trouble-me-now-child* eminence. Jake pulls down his lower lip with two fingers and the word BATTERSEA is tattooed into the painfully fragile skin inside the mouth. Suddenly life becomes a world without hours. Jake is stubbornly macho and has lived a colorful twenty-nine years as no stranger to fearlessness. He has no interest in being nice, therefore his leap towards me is as new and uncharted as mine to him. An ex-schoolboy sadist with a flair for complicity, Jake is the perfect buffer, lacking only what I have in abundance – and vice versa. He lived where he had been born, in the only detached house on Battersea High Street, where his sculptor father remained. Non-surrendering, Jake is a profiteer with a certain confidence of wit.

It's horse-hockey claptrap, and every minute has the high drama of first love, only far more exhilarating, and at last I have someone to answer the telephone.

Masculinity is marked out by a million intolerably exhaustive guidelines – defined by a sea of should-nots, must-nots, do-nots – and male friendships are bogged down by a welter of touch-me-not rules. With this it is assumed that the world is saved. Yet Jake and I fell together in deep collusion whereby the thorough and personal could be the only possible way, and we ate up each minute of the day. Socially, we harmonize with the intuitive intimacy that fully communicates across the crowd by a series of secretive blinks and winks and raised eyebrows; a concurrent widening of the eyes and Jake would suddenly be outside with the engine running whilst I delicately take leave. There will be no secrets of flesh or fantasy, and we managed to parrot on non-stop for two years in a jocular fourth-form stew of genius and silliness. The knowing grin was a bolt of lightning in ancient walks through pulpy woods, or amid the annoying white noise of Los Angeles.

On Delresto Drive, a small and shaded hamlet above Sunset Boulevard, I unwisely invest in a monstrosity where ten hours of fried-alive sun burns daily into each room. The road has just a few houses, one of which briefly belonged to Marc Bolan during his ill-fated attempt at Americanization in the 70s. It is this inescapable fire that makes me ill after just one week, and since I cannot breathe my doctor prescribes an inhaler. I walk around the inferno from kitchen to hallway, my breathing heavy and my eyes permanently crossed.

So instead I spend as much time as decency allows at Arnold Stiefel's home on Beaumont Drive, encircled by Arnold's rescue dogs and by his attentive maid. Arnold waves me off each night with beloved jars of exotic nuts, and cake-tins full of luxuriously moist cre-ations. But the lonely season must return, for that is what it does. No matter how your new circumstances pad themselves out, the roots of your behavior patterns have already marked you out for slaughter. The realistic essence of the true you made its mold back in the Queen's Square and Trafalgar Square of years lost. My days at Delresto with Arnold, free of the monastery – full of child-like forgetfulness – all come to a sudden end as night returns at last. Back, instead, to the slowness of days and London's grey noons, where I pack up my new life and, *why bless my heart alive*, how unusual to find myself alone and perishing once again.

Arnold had taken me for lunch at The Grill in Beverly Hills, where he had casually ordered a bowl of frog's legs.

'Er, no, Arnold, please don't order frog's legs in front of me ...'

'I will! I'm sick of you holistic vegetarian busy-bodies telling me what I can and cannot eat!' shouts Arnold, suddenly a 9-year-old demanding three extra scoops.

'You don't need to eat the little legs of little frogs!! Surely you can find something else!' I rise on the pulpit.

'I want frog's legs!!!' stamps Arnold – with both feet, which, like the frogs themselves, he would probably like to hold

on to. *'How would you like it if someone ordered YOUR legs for lunch?'*

'I want frog's legs!!!' and with that, a bowl is placed on the table with some thirty dainty little legs decoratively hanging over the edge of the bowl. I do my now familiar vanishing act and my brief days under Arnold's wing end – sadly, for me, but far worse for the frogs entwined around Arnold's teeth.

His frog's legs aside, the otherwise cheerful countenance of Arnold had given me great hope of continued American success. He was a man of strong imagination and unmatchable wit – affectionate but competitive, frivolous yet deadly – and an hour spent in his company would never be an hour lost. Forever testing how much he could get away with, his wit was the source of his art, and his generosity matched his astounding memory. With Arnold at the pump, *The more you ignore me, the closer I get* becomes my first (and last) hit single on the Billboard 100, having a fifteen-week run and rising to number 46. Miraculously, it is aided by a video in which I finally look healthy and almost attractive. As Arnold wields his personality with all the thoroughness of a cement mixer, the US label takes me aside to complain of his methods. In London, EMI also complain about Arnold's demands, and suddenly I hear that he plans to sell me to MCA for $8 million. *Vauxhall and I* jumps onto the US chart at number 18, which is my biggest success so far, but Arnold hates the title. *'Why couldn't you call it* The World Won't Listen, *or something?'*

Arnold badgering the labels was not a problem because he was surely doing the right thing, as *Vauxhall and I* entered the UK chart at number 1. He was more savior than sinner, and his power-maniac drive was easily misunderstood. In a gale of criss-crossed wires, the relationship murdered itself on that afternoon at The Grill.

Peace came at last with *Vauxhall and I*, streaming out in a lavish flow and leaving me stupid with smiles. A last sun warms, as if it had always been awaiting its chance. The album became the first start-to-finish emotional journey, each track as warm as the last, noise and poetry turned loose in one of those visionary sessions that your future returns will constantly search for. Faulty emotional development can ripple like the sea, and only by the creation of art can your inner isolation seem insanely worthwhile. *Vauxhall and I* is an arm held out, ushering others to join, even though its singer has feelings impossible to satisfy. When the escapist spirit hits tape in a moment of failure, it weakens; but when the last heave is full of honor, it vitalizes, and here is the tightrope that I can never escape. The choked words become silly when there is neither point nor purpose, but *Vauxhall and I* restored everything beyond price, and I had just cause to be happy. Some shyly, some boldly, but all reviews for *Vauxhall and I* glowed with restored fortunes as the *NME* continued to do its utmost to pump life into their *Morrissey-is-racist* pantomime. Although detractors would forever gleefully remind the world how the *NME* racist allegations damaged my position, they overlook the fact that, in the heat of it all, *Vauxhall and I* swooped in at number 1, indicating surely that very few had swallowed the *NME*'s fatuous farrago.

Although *The more you ignore me, the closer I get* reached number 8 in the UK, the follow-up, *Hold on to your friends*, was dismissed with a wave of the hand, struggling to touch

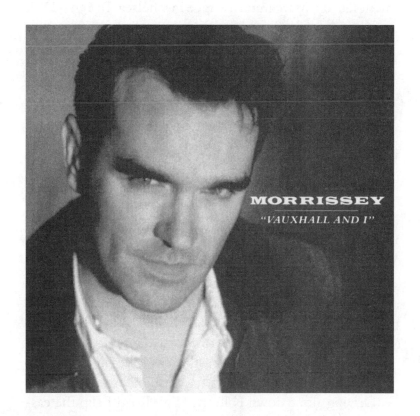

Wanting everyone, needing no one – Vauxhall and I, *1994*

number 47. I had hatched an interesting video made up of segments of the film *The Blue Lamp* featuring Dirk Bogarde, Patric Doonan and Peggy Evans. It is Doonan, not Bogarde, who flags down my interest. Born in Derby, he didn't rise higher than fourth on the bill, and he took his life at the age of 33 – gassed by an unlit stove in his basement flat at 4 Margaretta Terrace in Chelsea. In 1994, Dirk Bogarde was now living just off Cadogan Square after many years in France. He had, it seemed, returned home to die. We briefly correspond, and initially he is willing to approve the video for *Hold on to your friends*, but having given him a copy of V*auxhall and I* he recoils and withdraws his approval. Unaccustomed to backing down, I make my way to his Chelsea flat, but before I can reach the doorway I am met by his spindle-shanked figure groping along a Chelsea side street. Drenched in self-exile and secrets, his eyes are wide with elderly shock. It is a moment of panic, and I turn away as he struggles by, letting it all go. A few months later he is dead.

In any event, EMI refuse to use the video for fear that Dirk will arise from the grave and lash out with his walking stick. No radio station will play *Hold on to your friends*. *'I'm sorry, but you look cross-eyed on the cover,'* says James Todd, who is touting for management (but before I have time to say *'Thank you, but no,'* he is dead, as the cast of casualties in Morrisseyland piles up like bodies in Lady Worthington's library).

Driving alone down Kilburn High Road I slip the cassette on and boom *Hold on to your friends* at loudly coarse volume. I pull over to the side of the road, stop the car, and break down into a torrent of tears.

At the British Flag pub (somewhere around Battersea) I sit with Chrissie Hynde and pass a dull Monday nursing a Tennent's Extra. Chrissie could make people laugh at the funeral of triplets. She has the ability to throw a rip-roaring punch line without altering one single facial muscle. Her deadpan feed lines are effortless, and the rich intellect eats up everyone around her. Even a nod from Chrissie can challenge the attention, and she is by far the funniest person I have ever met, whereas I can't attempt humor without a host of giveaway facial tics and squirms. This is not to suggest that Chrissie *has* a sense of humor, because she doesn't appear to. Pestered by a disheveled drunk at the bar, Chrissie swings around: *'Look. You don't know me. I don't know you. Let's leave it at that.'* And sure enough he leaves it at that.

In another bar, a screech-owl female frump begins a beer-sodden tire-slashing attack on Chrissie with, *'You used to mean SO MUCH to me,'* to which Chrissie breaks in with, *'Yes. But I don't now — so fuck off.'*

Such responses are difficult to follow. This night at the British Flag finds the pub empty apart from the dying bar staff and an elderly gentleman standing at the bar – his little loyal terrier standing by his master's feet. *'Do you know what dogs love?'* Chrissie asks me, *'they LOVE this,'* and she calls the shaky terrier over to her, and then lifts it up onto her lap where she quickly sinks her teeth into its neck. The little dog clicks into a freeze-spasm like a kitten in its mother's mouth. The dog's owner and the dying bar staff watch stricken with horror. *Life with Chrissie.* I wouldn't miss it for the world.

'Dirk Bogarde was here once,' says my neighbor Alan Bennett, *'but he didn't say anything.'*

'How interesting to have a visitor who doesn't actually say anything,' I chirp, thinking I'm Jack Kerouac to Alan's William Burroughs.

Alan lives on Gloucester Crescent, directly to the back of my house on Regent's Park Terrace. The post box is across from the wide front window where Alan seems always to be sitting like a tawny owl – busy with his busyness, looking out yet not looking out, writing something down yet not. Alan will usually knock at Regent's Park Terrace at around 7 PM, when, I think, he finds himself at odds with himself. He will sit in the kitchen and say very little, and no conversation will be forced upon him.

Jake and I fiddle about with our own tinkering pursuits.

'Now, now. What's going on? Something's happened, hasn't it?' says Alan.

'Umm ... what?' Jake looks at him, puzzled.

'You haven't spoken a word to one another since I arrived,' detects Alan.

Alan isn't entirely fumbling in the dark, as I had already made plans to lower myself into my new flat on Fitzwilliam Place in Dublin. My Irish social security card and my tax-exemption documents drop through the letter box and the new life wipes out the old as 1995 kick-starts.

I dart about Dublin in the Saab, which I park nightly in a lock-up on Lad Lane, and I feel certain I will forget London and Los Angeles for eternity. Dublin life is a steady focus on pub culture and simple pleasures. The streets are safe and it is difficult not to make friends. Instantly I find my own stray cat, who is white somewhere beneath the blackness of dirt. He patiently awaits me every morning, but disowns me once he is fed. There will be less suffering in his eyes as the weeks pass, yet his business down Dublin's back alleys is of more concern to him than the variety of cat-basket enticements that I lay out for him should he want to edge in permanently. But he doesn't. I never fail to supply daily sustenance, and he equally doesn't fail to be at his appointed spot, full of simple devotion. The inevitable morning draws me to the large Georgian windows from which I see his pathetic, half-flattened body in the middle of a deserted street. I race outside and I lift his body up into two large bath towels, the body now lifeless, yet softly in my arms for the first time. His short life now over, as death always wins.

I rely heavily on the iron-column kindness of Martin McCann, who is the lead singer of the band Sack, and his friendship always makes the day better. Martin seems to know everyone in Dublin, and he can always find something to do. He introduces me to the Thrills and the Pony Club, and I invite both to open for me at the Royal Albert Hall in London. From this, the Thrills will secure a deal with Virgin, whereas the Pony Club will mysteriously remain in Kimmage, lost in space. Ten years on, I drive slowly through Los Angeles and the Pony Club are played on mid-day radio, as their magnificent song called *Single* makes my mind halt, a gamut of sad moods imposed upon me, all dragged away by lifetimes gone.

In March 1995 we all gather at Hook End Manor in Oxfordshire to record *Southpaw Grammar*, and the news comes through that Ronnie Kray has died.

'*Oooh, good!*' shouts producer Steve Lilywhite as I freeze with confusion, '*the world doesn't need people like that.*' The abiding distinction of the Kray Brothers, for me, had nothing to do with their circle of violence, because that is nothing new or unusual: the wheels of the world spin entirely on violence – military science, whaling, nuclear weapons, armed combat, the abattoir, holy war, jailing key members of the Earth Liberation or the Earth First emergency groups, terrorist police using Taser stun-guns, the killing of Jean Charles de Menezes, the punishment block, the bailiffs, the predawn rampage, riot police assaulting innocent civilians with plastic bullets and pepper-sprays – all in the name of controlled force. Violence is the ruling word in most persuasive human action. The history of the judicial system is the history of torture, from the ducking stool to hanging, to the death of Bobby Sands. Brute force and cruelty are entirely the point of the halls of justice, and fear is forever the key. The Krays were criticized because they knew how to use their fists – as if this were a terribly unusual thing. However, since they were also working class and far too formidable, this was the spur for the contorted well-bred to bring them down. The Krays had been too strong, and more importantly, their empire promised no financial gain for the government. Something had to be done because no one can be seen to thrive unappointed outside of the law. Imprisoned, the Krays were unfairly locked away for the rest of their lives, and they died quietly.

I was surprised to receive a handwritten letter from Charles Richardson in 1995 from his home in Kent. The Richardson brothers had power in south London similar to the Krays' power in east London, and their gory glory days ran parallel. In his letter, Charles explained that a feature film was to be made of his life, and he asked if I would consider playing him on screen. I was astonished at the invitation, but I hadn't the nerve to entertain it since I couldn't act naturally at all – not even whilst sleeping. From Charlie Richardson to Julie Christie to Alan Bennett to Richard Davalos to Anthony Newley, I stood back from it all and wondered how all of these people had come into my life, and what a strange jigsaw they all made. How could I have ever imagined Anthony Newley as a weekly correspondent?

We had started the *Southpaw Grammar* album in the south of France, but the deserted farmhouse atmosphere seemed all wrong, and we returned to England where everything clicked with a killing. The band is now in impressive strike: Spencer's drumming winning out magnificently and Alain delivering a showstopping slam of inventive guitar and crowning backing vocals. Boz remained the star in the firmament, orchestrating and pointing the way, although I heavily felt the strain of the emotional clash between Boz and Alain. My deal with EMI had run its course, and it felt like the right time to move on – or sideways, or away. EMI would send a new offer, but it had neither heart nor promise, and you can usually tell a record label's intent by their financial investment. I had watched with blank astonishment at how EMI had actively and generously promoted younger bands who seemed likely to appeal to a Morrissey audience, whilst my compilation *World of Morrissey* had full-page ads in all the major music magazines with a printed release date that was in fact a week later than the actual release date. I bang my head against a thousand walls. It seemed to me that EMI were itching to possess an artist that was its own discovery (and not, like me, inherited from another label), yet who is similar in artistic temperament to me – but who is preferably *not* me. They succeed in this very well in the immediate years to come. Disheartened also by Reprise, I reject their contractual extension, but alas they already had *Southpaw Grammar.* Knowing that I have already left the label, Reprise kick *Southpaw Grammar* down the slipway to obscurity, and it enters the chart at a very unlikely number 66. On a flight to Chicago I bump into a Reprise executive who doesn't surprise me in the least by revealing: *'You know the label deliberately crippled* Southpaw Grammar, *don't you? Because you wouldn't re-sign?'*

At the record company meeting | on their hands a dead star | and oh the plans they weave …

I thought at that moment of Howie Klein's *'You know, every time you tour the States the Smiths catalogue jumps?'* and I feel a grinding gut-sensation.

In Europe, I hastily sign a one-album deal with BMG/ RCA, bemusing the label at the conference table by overseeing the deal with no legal intervention. My smartness backfires on me, though, because I would never earn any royalties from *Southpaw Grammar,* which enters the UK chart at number 4, and the £200,000 placed upfront by the label disappears into recording and producer fees. Tuesday August 8th 1995 is the launch of *Southpaw Grammar* at Terry Venables' club Scribes West on Kensington High Street. I prepare to leave but then quickly turn back. I just can't face it – there is too much clattering about inside my head. I stay home and I put the kettle on, talking aloud to myself and pondering on how even Billie Holiday had sex. *'Oh that's so Morrissey – he doesn't even turn up for his own album launch,'* says someone with scurvy and rickets. Suddenly I am unremunerated, having relied on EMI royalties, which had ceased in 1992, never again to be. But still, we were young and we could die tomorrow.

Warner UK had bought the Smiths catalogue from Johnny and I in 1992. Rough Trade had heaved and collapsed under a sea of bankruptcy and courtroom humiliations, but would later resurface with a slight alteration to their trading name. Rough Trade of old had wheezed its last, and their Smiths-days staff were packed off to the slaughterhouse.

'I suppose you're enormous in Cleveland?' asks David Bowie.
'No,' I reply, utterly baffled.
'Oh.' He slumps.

Because Johnny and I were not in communication with each other, it was deemed wise (by my lawyer, who also represented Warner! *Oh, the maze, the maze ... the quagmired maze*) that I accept an offer of £734,000 to let the Smiths catalogue go. So I did, and I assumed that Johnny received the same amount, to naturally be whittled down by those ever-helpful wire-pullers who logroll such negotiations. Warner immediately reissued the Smiths' entire album catalogue with considerable success as seven Smiths albums lodged in the top 75 for a few weeks, the stars of which were *Singles*, reaching number 5, and yet another compilation, called *Best*, which reached number 1. Although I had no personal involvement in the reissue project, I found myself heavily criticized in the press for the quality of the Warner artwork. When asked to do a voice-over for a television commercial to promote *Singles*, populist John Peel refused due to what he termed *'the Morrissey racism question'*. Himself a sermonizing pillar of wisdom, Peel quite interestingly wasted no time on moral prevarication when the Queen called him to Buckingham Palace for the bureaucratic OBE badge. Oh, at last he is fully plumbed with the stamp of approval from those who count.

For the sleeve of *Singles* Warner had used a bleakly soothing shot of Diana Dors that I had housed at Rough Trade many years ago in readiness for the next block of Smiths dynamite. It should be noted that at this stage neither Andy nor Mike were involved in the Smiths catalogue sale, and they had no involvement with Warner as catalogue buyers, since neither Andy nor Mike had a contractual position with Rough Trade or Sire Records.

Back in New York, David Bowie asks me, *'Do you, er, still have the same band?'*

'Yes,' I say, and he looks downwards.

The word is well established that the Morrissey band is not as good as the Smiths, or even up to much in their own right. It is an accusation that I must live with for the rest of my life, irrespective of how often the line-up changes. It is true that Spencer's drumming was initially not earth-shattering, but he became greatly impressive, and his gypsy profile earned him a few screams. Insanely, he elected to abandon the drums precisely at the moment when he had polished and refined his craft. His temperament forever remained a puzzle, and in San Francisco he unwisely elected to throw a microphone stand off the stage. It bounced off the head of a security guard who was then rushed to hospital as his head gushed blood. This act by Spencer immediately placed my neck on the guillotine, since the security guard obviously had grounds to sue – that is, to sue me, but not Spencer. Quite incredibly, the guard asked only for an apology from Spencer, and equally amazingly he managed to get one. But by this time Avalon venue security have blacklisted Morrissey shows as being too violent, and they would keep me blacklisted until 2005.

Shamefully my interest in video as promotional tool had never exactly been pentathlon in endurance. The twitching brain could never connect, and the feet felt glued at the call of 'action'. The ideas for almost everything from *Girl-friend in a coma* onwards rolled off Tim Broad's pen. I stood and watched like a prized lemon. Mildly wicked storyboards drowned in their own sources, and I found myself plonked in there somewhere, matter-of-factly. It was Tim's idea to travel to Fairmount, Indiana, for the *Suedehead* video, even though the song itself assumed an Openshaw expression of life-as-a-waste-of-time. The surviving members of James Dean's family were happy to allow us to use the Winslow farmhouse where Dean grew up, and where many now-famous photographs caught Dean half-boyhood, half-Hollywood. Summers in baggy western jeanwear, confidently fooling around, barnyards and animals, before literary pretensions kicked in and lost the bespectacled boy to fame's barbarity.

We arrived at Fairmount after passing through Marion, where Dean was born. There is nothing to see, and there is nothing to say about what is not seen. You can only wonder how those who live in the sheltered white wooden houses pass their time, never changing, always the same, off-center if not immersed in family and reproduction and just getting through. All aspects of the outside world must be deemed negative in order to justify your reason for not joining it.

February of 1988 was blanketed by snow and sealed in by frost. The camera crew had glassy strips of ice in their facial hair. It would be impossible to stand on Main Street for more than three minutes; the bones rattle, the face sags, the cold is unmerciful. Layers of restorative thermal under-wear and a pair of boots that would otherwise be beneath my dignity just barely save my life. To these locals, I must seem like a bit of nonsense from Montague Square. A diner on Main Street remains where the young Jim slipped away his days, and he is remembered politely by the owners as I plough into French fries with white bread, for there is noth-ing else on the menu that I can eat. The Citizens State Bank remains, as does an intoxicating record store of spellbind-ing LPs and 45s, preciously presented, yet too voluminous to flick through, and the mind races at the wonderland of stacked shelves. As irritating as ever, I request: *'Do you have anything by the New York Dolls?'* and I am met with what seems like an hour of silence. James Dean's old high school stands abandoned. Four of us break the ever-choking laws of the land as we approach the school just before nightfall.

Tim Broad pulls at heavy boards that block the windows and we soon find a way in. An abandoned school is an eerie place – a worn-out husk of sadness that throws the mind in several directions. Walk through the cold corridors and all sorts of things test the memory. I stand on the school stage where James Dean attempted his first recitals, my mental vision revolving, banging as it goes. I sit in the old classrooms where desks and chairs remain since the 1940s prime of Fairmount High. I fold two chairs away with their Fairmount School badges still attached, and I will later ship them back to England. This can hardly be considered theft since nobody wants this junk anyway, and the poet within sighs at the likelihood that Dean himself once occupied these chairs with a wide sprawl of the legs – the stuck pupil awaiting the final bell so that he might be free to become eternal. I am standing in the school shower room where toilet cubicles are without doors – surely an army notion? But ... *for children?* No privacy to sit and lighten life's load? I wondered if the girls' section also had toilet cubicles without doors, for part-strangers to walk by and peer in? Probably not. The boys' open cubicles face a frontline of shower heads, and it must have been here on noisy after-noons as the hardy annuals stripped off that Dean met his undiscovered nature. No hiding place for the hefty lads of the mid-west.

The Winslow farmhouse is unchanged since the 1950s, and I recall a thousand photographs as I look around the kitchen where Dean and cousin Markie allowed the camera to click. Of those now ancient photographs I had been caught by how casual Dean and Markie had always been – no primly proper smiling into the lens, or embarrassed expressions, as were my own memories of childhood photographs. Whereas we stood to attention and gave the world a smiling face, both Dean and Markie allowed the camera to observe them whilst offering it no thought. The record retained is alarmingly convincing – as if Dean already had no doubts about his inner bearing. I sit in the old barnyard where Dean once sat reading his beloved *The Little Prince*, and then the adult Markie takes me aside to show me something that few have ever seen. At the rear of the barn there is a large slab of cement covered by oilcloth. Whooshing back the cover, Markie reveals the handwriting of the juvenile James – signature and hand-patterns pressed into soft cement one exuberant 1940s summer, making his mark for such as I to trace decades later. I shake like a ship in a storm. It is a fact that even warming moments overwhelm me with despair, and this is why I am I.

I am filmed sitting by Dean's grave, but the ground is a block of ice. Tim provides a square platform to spare me the icy discomfort, since every set-up seems to take hours. The platform is hopefully to be hidden by a flowing overcoat, but alas, the edge of the block is visible on the final film.

I am approached by an elderly farmhand who speaks in a whisper. He has James Dean's signature from 1949, and he is prepared to sell it to me for $3,000. I ask to see it, and out comes a school yearbook with the Dean signature written mid-page in pencil. The man runs off when Markie appears, waving something at me.

'*Did you write this?*' he asks me sternly.

He is holding what unfortunately became of an essay written by me in the late 1970s entitled *James Dead is Not Dean* yet irritatingly printed by a Manchester workshop as *James Dean is Not Dead.* A dreadful heap of 70s juvenilia, the essay brought me 40 useful pounds when nothing else could, and I had no idea that it would turn into a bookish presentation that would haunt me till death's sigh. My head shamefully tilts, and Markie storms off, and minutes later we are off the premises. Thankfully, we had all of the filming that we needed, but there were no friendly mid-western waves as we chugged away from the farm.

It was also Tim's idea to contact the embalmed comic actor Charles Hawtrey to hopefully take part in the video for *Everyday is like Sunday.* Now in elderly exile in Kent, Hawtrey had always been media-shy and reportedly high acid. Rumors of vodka-soaked loneliness and intolerable eccentricity signaled the end for a British comedy actor whose aura of greatness always lit up his secondary roles. Even without dialogue he could steal any scene. I am given Hawtrey's telephone number and I dial nervously, linking myself to the lost world of the British comedy film. A cadaverous component lifts the receiver with a hushed '*Hulloh?*' and here is the voice of Charles Hawtrey – ripped from the palms of the dying, never to know how great he was. Our conversation inches along as I explain myself very badly, and I hear Hawtrey wheezing weariness. He is merely considering the point at which to drop the receiver, and sure enough, down it goes as I stutter mid-splutter. He has, I suppose, earned the right to be cantankerously rude. I shrug weakly, but I don't blame Charles Hawtrey for finding me dull, since I, too, find me dull. Later in that year of 1988, Hawtrey dies, outstripped by horror multiplied as surgeons advise him to have both legs amputated or to face certain death. But Hawtrey is drenched in death anyway, and so the little man urges death to put its dukes up.

The mule-cart media make a feast of his distorted life – a notable failure, a lonely death for a man whose last wish was that no stone or plaque be in evidence to mark his resting place – if, indeed, rest is to be found in death.

'You are obsessed with dead people,' my father tells me, *'you ought to get interested in the living.'* He is right of course. Yet off I go to Charles Hawtrey's house on Middle Street in Deal, which is now listed for sale, and a macabre wind sucks me in to inspect. As a lumbering nonentity, I enter Hawtrey's pasty smuggler's cottage on a depressing narrow street – the type of street that would remain shadowed and cold even during a heatwave. I inspect the solemn 1930s kitchen, and the rough coconut matting by the grim plastic bath. There is heavy rope in place of a banister rail alongside the stairs, up which Hawtrey surely inched himself night after night having thrashed the Gordon's. The main bedroom carpet is a patchwork of noxious stains, and a small corner sink is clogged with pubic hair. In the cellar, three ugly settees are positioned to face each other in an occultish triangle as a central red light bulb hangs down between. A mock-Moroccan bar tilts in the corner of the cellar, as if this had been Hawtrey's afterhours den – a playground for those lucky nights when he could manage to persuade a sailor back for a nightcap, and, God willing, the sailor would be prepared to stand upright and then look away and bless Hawtrey with a momentary flash of human kindness. I leave the house feeling dreadful, but it really is my own fault.

I am amazed when Tim's video for *Interesting drug* (number 9, 1989) is shown on *Top of the Pops*, with its inclusion of a skinned baby seal; surely a first for *Top of the Pops*, who then cut to smiling DJ Peter Powell, and the Middle Ages are back with us once more. Tim had unraveled the cinebeast of the *Ouija board* video in Oxfordshire woodland, where Dadaism was stretched too far. In the muddle of Kathy Burke as idiomatic clippie, there is Joan Sims as mediocre medium, plus tragic singer led through woodlands by pantomime children. The movable stage is Joan Sims, now of old-school comedy, who could tell an entire joke without saying a word. Joan is yet another of the Carry On regulars who has lived forever unattached, whose face is known to millions, but whose comedic talents are not thought to be of great value. She lives alone in Kensington Square at the back of Barkers department store on Kensington High Street. The day before the shoot, Tim climbs the stairs to Joan's intimate flat only to find the front door open and Joan sitting by the fire in tears. Around the walls are lines of framed photographs charting a lifetime of backstage moments, beaming smiles with people met that one time only, yet testament to a successful career now sealed up. On this day, Joan explains that her tears are for Hattie Jacques – another Carry On matron – and there is a curse on behalf of all the theater individuals who save their best moments for their time on a stage, and not for their private selves, for there are no private selves. *'Do you know Nicholas Parsons?'* asks Joan, possibly tipsy. *'He is a c**t,'* she says, and that's that.

I do not blame Tim for the silliness of the *Ouija board* video, but it doesn't help the footing of a record already far too ornate and *burlesco* to interest critics of the first rank. We would travel in April to Death Valley in California, where at last I had Sire's good grace for a proper video with a grown-up budget. The single is *November spawned a monster*, a pivotal allegro of agitation whose sumptuousness frees me from the recent past. Like it or not, I remain the opposition – regardless of how the rules shift. The dissonant heart appears on *Top of the Pops*, where no sooner does *November spawned a monster* begin than I am drowned away by fake applause and I kindly leave the stage.

The coterie wonder why I bother to wiggle onto the program at all, and the press point to a didactic dirge. The *Sun* newspaper lists the record at number 12 and also at number 15 in the same chart! How one record can occupy two positions must surely bend science sideways. I am criticized by singer Tracey Thorn for *'singing about people in wheelchairs'*, and John Peel opens his radio show by playing the song in full, and once it dies away he breaks the silence with: *'Well, what do you think of that, then?'* as if a roasting on an open fire is all that will cure me.

In Death Valley the roadsides were lined with abandoned donkeys that walk and walk in soaring heat, destination nowhere with ribs protruding. Even in the dead of night they continue to walk, the oncoming traffic of no interest to them, and humans of no help. Disowned, they must walk and walk until their legs give way to earth's final pull – a feast for rats and buzzards. Tim had asked me to do the entire *November spawned a monster* video naked. I explained to him that this would be impossible since my entire lower body had been destroyed by fire in 1965. His expression remained wide-eyed with belief as he replied, *'Oh.'* After watching the video, my father commented, *'Shirley Bassey will be furious,'* which left me momentarily puzzled.

Tim had directed the *Sing your life* video at Camden Workers Social Club, an undisturbed private world behind Kentish Town Road. The first time I had visited the club I almost cried with relief at its 1950s mix of High School dancehall and ruthless elitism warding off the trendy-bender copyists. Camden Workers was the real thing, more church than social club, and in a room full of rightly righteous purist rockers, it was not a place where you'd want to be unwanted. The dancefloor is Wigan's Casino for the sharply chiseled pale profiles stomping a Cajun-reel in Depression-era American workwear; Appalachian spit-curl stomps of Nathan Abshire or Dennis McGee. Every record booms to distortion, and the smell of machismo threatens to bosh a roving eye. It is all inside you. How incredibly these boys dance – and where do they practice? And why does each boy dance alone? Ah, the great unsaid. The sharp duck-tails and the lemon stitching of vintage denim leave me trying to attach the image to the thing seen. Because of Camden Workers, and my new ally Debbie Dannell, I will make an effort with my hair and my clothes to look better for the future. Debbie reveals all the coded details of selvage ('self edge') signals on vintage denim, from back pocket rivets to belt loops; red tabs on 506 jackets, and how to spot a genuine chambray shirt. In a beer-fed gallop, the dancefloor shakes with the thunder of unfolding pleasure. Naturally, I can't join in because someone would laugh at me, but I emerge from it all slightly bolder in demeanor, and Lord may a hand stretch out to greet me.

We had traveled with Tim to Berlin to make the girly-gush *Pregnant for the last time* video, and then to Arizona for the self-damned *My love life*, where I am seen driving through the streets of suburban Phoenix. In fact, local police will not allow the process of driving whilst being filmed, or filming whilst driving, or breathing whilst living, because the economy turns on permits and taxes and unimaginable local county charges, with the revolving lie that all laws exist only in order to protect someone. The world is not ours. The earth is not ours. The car in the video is therefore hoisted onto an automated platform whereon the camera also sits. With all sense behind me, I grab the wheel and attempt to look natural as I drive at 10 mph on a deserted side street (as one quite naturally would).

May 1992 found us in a very sunny Wapping, filming *We hate it when our friends become successful*, an almost delightful video capturing one of those lost British afternoons of timelessness, and Tim's *You're the one for me, fatty* catches the same spirit the following month, with sunlight late in the day at Battersea Park. Much later, Tim confided to me that the title of the song was undisclosed to the girl who played the part of 'fatty', and I thought this very uncivil of Tim, even if quite funny. In December we shoot *Certain people I know* in Chicago. Gary and Alain were very late for the shoot, and without apology, which enraged me and made it difficult for me to give a convincing account of the song.

By January 1995, Tim is in his grave, and James O'Brien directs the *Boxers* video at York Hall in Bethnal Green. A boy actor from an insurance commercial on television is tracked down to oppose professional Cornelius Carr in the ring. It doesn't occur to anyone that the second boxer ought to be me, and when I mention this to James he looks unusually blank.

In September of 1995 we film *Dagenham Dave* in a council house in Dagenham, with Jenny Jay (who had starred in an excellent television play called *Two of Us*) and Mark Savage (who had been famous in his role as Gripper Stebson in the telly teen drama *Grange Hill*). James also directed the *Sunny* video in east London's Victoria Park in November of the same year. In the midst of such filming, with each video generally brushed aside as twiddling footlings, the grand drapes had been pulled back and the stage has been set for a comic-opera production of *The Night of the Long Knives*, and something resembling a giant rat is crawling up the stage curtain.

Off in the wings, Michael Joyce had gone through his Smiths years in a smoky dream. Now, many years after the split, he had been shaken into consciousness. His finances frittered away, Joyce decided to turn to those who had served him generously in the past and he decided that they should continue to provide him with cash – now, in the uncertain present – and off he went, a flea in search of a dog. Excused from all adult obligations in his Smiths past, Joyce and his legal practitioners wondered what they could scavenge from all that had gone. With devious cunning, Joyce instructs an array of legal firms (most of whom disappear after a few months of feigned interest) to hound me at addresses that I had long since left, hoping to establish evasion on my part and lawful stealth on his. It worked. With other people's money (as always), Joyce ran his case on Legal Aid despite sporadic months of employment. This, too, worked to great effect. Certainly, in the years running up to what would become 'the Smiths trial' – years during which Joyce ran out of the legal time allotted to file a plea – everyone who knew of Joyce's meddling was confident of his eventual failure given the wealth of evidence stacked against him. This reasonable assumption was made on the logical but apparently wrong understanding that the trial would force Joyce to prove his claim to be an equal partner. Joyce wanted his moment of confused respectability, even if the road to such fame was a sorry sequence of events. If he had been in possession of any documentation indicating that his royalty split had ever been 25 per cent, then there would never have been any need for a court case. But he had nothing and sadly needed nothing.

If you undo someone, you make history. It is the type of move that will impress only the simple mind, but it is history nonetheless. Here in 1996, Joyce wanted to do what he had never previously done: he wanted to finally look at his life and be responsible for it. With sweet-faced confusion the middle-aged boy said his appropriate Yesses and eventually hit upon a legal firm who would no doubt welcome the publicity, and thus the piggies went to market with their star well-drilled in *I-do-not-think-or-remember* formulations.

I am lumbered with the additional weight of bad representation. They, too, would like the financial flush of a major court case. Lights, camera, action. In preparation, Joyce makes so many glaring mistakes that his Witness Statement is withdrawn and re-chiseled four times prior to the hearing – not because he hasn't had enough time since 1987 to get his facts straight, but because he doesn't know what his facts *are*. A plea for publishing royalties to be split and shared with Johnny Marr is thought an unwise move, and is dropped from the final Joyce Witness Statement, as is a plea for a financial share of whatever I had been paid for designing Smiths sleeves. This latter is rethought and dropped when it is discovered that I had never been paid for Smiths artwork, yet one sees the mechanics of Joyce's counsellors trying to squeeze money from anywhere they can. Here was Joyce in his early Witness Statements placing his songwriting contribution equal to Marr's, and his contribution to Smiths Art unquestionably equal to that of Morrissey. What mind drove such a challenge, when Joyce had not once contributed to Smiths compositions, and had not once expressed the smallest interest in Smiths Art? Such is the certainty of his early facts that he quakes and then annuls his statements *without* any pressure from the opposition, who are nonetheless aware that he is also conducting a similar case for royalties against another group with whom he has worked briefly. He is running in his own circle. The plea for co-designer of Smiths Art had obviously been removed once Joyce had been advised that no payments had ever existed. Had there been, no doubt the plea would have remained. Joyce maintained his plea for 25 per cent of Smiths merchandising advances, even though any such advances in their entirety served to set up each tour as it came along, and absolutely never fell into the hands of Morrissey and Marr. Joyce maintained and forced this plea even though there would be no evidence that either Morrissey or Marr had benefited on a personal level from such advances, yet Joyce was now happy for both parties to pay him 25 per cent of large sums of money never seen nor received by the very two people who had given him fame. Joyce retained his demand for a 25 per cent cut of all Smiths live earnings on the unproven and insane assumption that 100 per cent of such earnings somehow and magically swept themselves into the personal bank accounts of Morrissey and Marr, and although there were no records indicating that all live fees had ever reached Morrissey and Marr, and although the vast expense of launching each tour would not be considered, Joyce nonetheless wanted money from Morrissey and Marr right now and without question. In essence, Joyce demanded 25 per cent of absolutely everything (excluding publishing) that had ever been created in the Smiths' name, assuming – without proof – that all sums were handed to Morrissey and Marr as clear profit.

Joyce was making these demands now, in 1996, but had never made such demands during the Smiths' existence. Never in his wildest dreams could Joyce have believed that fate would combine to present him with an antiquated deputy designed to force success on the plaintiff, a judge who would unleash a torrent of invectives against me and never be required to explain why. John Weeks was the name of the Circuit Judge wheeled in from Bristol to preside over the Smiths case. Appointed to circuit judge under Margaret Thatcher, John Weeks lived in the richly ornate Brympton d'Evercy mansion house in Yeovil, a Grade 1 listed building hidden behind 33 acres of parkland. With its coats of arms and tracery and its Henry VIII wing, Brympton was considered to be England's most beautiful showpiece manor house. A home for the highest echelons of British aristocracy, its rooms also had connections with royal blood, having been built in 1220. Lavish television dramas such as *Middlemarch* and *Mansfield Park* had been filmed at the home of John Weeks. From this, John Weeks presents his elderly, small and shriveled frame as the ideal, unsmiling Lord of the Hunt, with an immutable understanding of the world of the Smiths. It seemed to me a less qualified judge could scarcely have existed. This was an 'entertainment case', but John Weeks appeared to operate with the sense that an enormous criminal trial was about to take place, and considering his own background and connections, I wondered how much he or any judge would know of the Morrissey in the dock, not only anti-royal and anti-Thatcher, but also an animal protectionist – all of which could provide grounds for hanging even before a single word of this case is uttered in camera. How on earth did Joyce manage to get his case to the High Court? Why has this case been accepted? Like an old, weathered tree-trunk, John Weeks made his entrance as a famous star – wig trimmed by Edith Head. He is a bent little man with big eyes in a small face, an unfortunate vision that even his personal wealth cannot save. All he lacks is a gun over his shoulder. His first task is to watch the assembled gathering during the customary judicial bow. Whereas the head of Joyce touches his toes, my own head remains motionless, and for this, I would imagine, deputy Weeks marks my card. The prosecutor of defenseless people opens his miserable mouth, and gives a wave to his jesters to begin. So *this* is what hell looks like.

Two days prior to the trial, my solicitor sends a fax to me explaining that she cannot attend court due to illness, but she promises the robust surety of her junior as an adequate stand-in. I have never met the junior, and I would never again see my solicitor who, as far as I am able to tell, has simply run off. Furthermore, the barrister chosen to guard my human rights also steps down, and his replacement is appointed just a few hours before the first hearing. My head spins at the sudden shambles – now of unimaginable proportions – and I walk into court with a small set of complete strangers. There, though, is Johnny, who walks directly up to me with a wink.

'Don't worry, Moz, we're gonna win this. He hasn't got a leg to stand on.' Minutes later Johnny is leaning in to a seated Joyce, and they are both in unified grin.

Although Joyce, Rourke and Marr are all seated in the first two rows, I am alloted a seat way at the back, yet central to the eyeline of Weeks – who will watch my reaction to everything that is said. You are of course directed to sit in specific seating, and I wonder who determines such positioning and with what aim. Like a stillborn play, the dismal proceedings begin. For everyone, I am the center of interest. As the opening pleas are made, it feels like deputy Weeks is fixed entirely upon my face to read my reactions to each statement, but he hardly seems to cast an eye towards Marr, Rourke or Joyce. The muddy black pools of legal precision are insufferably overdone, and even at these opening stages I feel as though the outcome has been strategized in backrooms of closed curtains where my epoch has been cut short. The protagonists of punishment determine that the only function of the unfolding court drama is to force each peg into an unsuitable hole, and make the cold-blooded destruction of one unfortunate party seem fair – and how dare you feel contemptuous of this court, and how dare you raise your voice to the level of the cross-examining barrister, and why exactly would you feel moral indignation towards a regime that cannot succeed in balance, but only in the punishment of one party against the other (never both, and never neither). My heart shrivels up at the black despair of it all.

First into the witness box, Joyce cannot at any stage find the right words with which to explain his position. A blubbering mass of blubbering mess, Joyce cannot even recall the date of his own marriage, as he mispronounces simple words. With feet glued and voice dying, Joyce finds that his mouth doesn't work properly, and the half-asleep replies chime out a sonata of false notes which leaves him groping in the dark for the light switch. With the drooping sag of bloodlust, John Weeks listens to the humiliated plaintiff. Joyce is nothing and knows nothing, and, small and lost as he is, I feel sorrow for him as he struggles hopelessly by repeating over and over again – in a voice getting smaller by the second – *'I just assumed I'd get 25 per cent,'* a comment that would close any case if this were a case of fair judicial outline. The voice of Joyce disappears into a pained whisper, as victims must always whine. In order to get into the High Court, one might assume, a plaintiff should have some documentation to wave about. Joyce had nothing. Yet, there he was, explaining to everyone that he was here in court because 'a friend' (who is not herself present at the High Court) had told him he should be getting 25 per cent. An individual with no forensic powers would need only take a quick glance at Joyce in order to see an aggressor posing as a victim. His tatty *'I just assumed'* gabble, after several hours, had told us nothing at all – except that he had 'just assumed'. Luckily for Joyce, almost anything that he says during these hearings proves to be immaterial. He is not the quarry. He is not even qualified enough to be a nonentity. What he is best at is confusion. You can spin as many theories as you like, but the ardent zest to finally topple and silence an outspoken pop artist took its place firmly and unashamedly as this trial began.

Like a well-fed Roman emperor, Andy Rourke took to the witness stand complaining of financial starvation. Too funny to be taken seriously, his evidence blew about in a thousand directions, his throat sounding tighter and tighter, each sentence abandoned halfway through as though he realized the silliness of his own words. Heavy-hearted, Rourke himself could not explain how things either were or are. As he tried to defend a 25 per cent cut for Joyce there were moments in his replies when his brain collapsed, and this shut-down swept the room with an intense and terrible hopelessness, and I imagined that we were all suddenly wondering: what sort of lives are we now leading? Whose deeds bring us here?

'It is not about money,' Joyce had said – but far too quickly, and with a seemingly over-rehearsed child-like openness. What, then, was it all about? Cookery? Science?

Johnny, too, was a bad witness, crumbling neatly from the top down. Although he and I were ostensibly on trial together as business partners, we were not actually business partners, and we had not even met once over recent years to discuss the Joyce claim, or the protocol of trial. I got the impression that Johnny's verbal disclosures jumped about willy-nilly and concluded with his exhausted inclination to accept anything at all that was said against me — in what I assumed was the hope that he might be separated from the one target who did not beg for sympathy. Financially, if Morrissey shouldered the blame, then Marr could be seen as a victim, too, and could run off and play. In the tiredness of stale and over-long cross-examinations, Johnny finally caves in and appears suddenly agreeable to any discredit lobbed my way, just as long as he can be let out of that damned witness box. He will, by now, apparently say almost anything at all in order to stay free, and seems willing to push anyone into the water in order to save himself. Collapsed, he attempts to answer a thousand questions about my behavior, and notably fewer questions about his own behavior. Divide and rule. If we can squeeze in between Morrissey and Marr then any cracks in their relationship will beam and glare like incorrectly described flying objects. It is Johnny, not I, who allows this to happen, and over he trots to the other side, having emptied his bucket. The walls hummed with silence, and yesterday is long ago.

At the close of each day, we are told that we must not make contact with one another overnight (lest, no doubt, we resolve the issues between ourselves and rob the judiciary of its prey). John Weeks, like everyone else, appears to want his day on stage, and somehow the conclusion must be his alone to make, and most certainly not tied up in a friendly fashion by Marr and Joyce and Morrissey in a Wapping pub whilst the squeezers and benders of an oh-so-civil courtroom sleep their cognac sleep.

Johnny telephones me at my squatty room in the nearby Tower Thistle Hotel where I sit alone, wondering how

Hand in glove led to this. Oddly, the hotel is inches away from where the very first Smiths album was recorded. Things were different now. Johnny asks me if I would meet his legal team tomorrow evening, and I agree, for it was difficult at this stage to see what the court itself was actually doing for me. Something I say to Johnny makes him laugh loudly, and I hear the Johnny that was once an air of adventure, and because this is now such an unusual recollection I therefore realize how we have moved too far away from one another to ever again have corresponding interests, yet justice had already fouled by listing Morrissey and Marr as a one-and-the-same unit without any conflicting interests, which was blatantly incorrect to anyone who would want to notice such a thing. If anything at all, since Morrissey and Marr were not a working partnership there was no obvious reason why they ought to have stood trial as one, and there were a thousand reasons why they ought to have been tried separately, which was a critical point that was raised by no one. Read one way, the Joyce case should never have reached civil proceedings. Read another way, any case against Morrissey or against Marr should have been declined by the courts since in the eyes of everyone the partnership of the two had ceased eight years earlier, yet the legal process would grind along as if Morrissey and Marr remained an active and unified business, and a judgment would be made on that very basis, which in itself seemed unfair when one considered the truth of the situation. Johnny promised to call me back with a time and place where I would – for the first time ever – sit down with his legal team for an off-the-legal-record meeting, but the call did not come, and in the courtroom the next day, neither Johnny nor his set of vultures will look my way. Someone must have changed Johnny's mind, and any notion of camaraderie disappeared, and so much for walking in a pack.

Daily newspaper reports of the ongoing case are plentiful, the lyric *'Beware! I bear more grudges than lonely high court judges'* appears as a headline, and as John Weeks quite possibly noticed, the reports feature my name and no one else's in their captions; a photograph of my face, but never of Johnny's. In a case already seeped in eternity, Wobbly Weeks hasn't the right to hang anyone, but he will get someone as close to the rope as allowable.

As I take to the witness stand I feel a communal intake of breath, as if now is the absolute point of the entire circus. Joyce's legal team suddenly sits upright, having spent the last few days dozing like overfed apes. I am now close enough to Weeks to smell the moth-balls. I am asked, unfairly in my view, to give my home address – with no apparent understanding (or, perhaps, with *every* understanding) of how endangered this places me. It is the first humiliating step in reducing the spirit of the witness.

Absurdly, I am asked to swear on the Holy Bible, an action that had not stabilized the evidence of either Joyce or Rourke, but which is trotted out as yet another court procedure aimed to humble and shrink the witness, and to falsely imply that none but the honorable shall succeed in these rooms. Acting for Joyce, the cross-examining barrister is one Nigel Davis, with a face I could never be cruel enough to describe. His task (for which he is paid money) is to impugn the evidence of the witness, therefore whatever I say to Davis by way of reply must be ridiculed by Davis in front of this gathered gaggle. Nigel Davis must only possess patience above wisdom in order to weaken his witness.

Throughout my cross-examination I notice John Weeks repeatedly nodding to Davis. A small nod always seemingly pleased Davis. By return, Davis smiled meekly at the judge. Crucified by his own enormous teeth, Davis is further weighed down by a colony of purple boils decorating the back of his neck. His most irritating quirk is to repeatedly and repeatedly go over old ground in an effort to wear out the witness or to force the witness to say the wrong thing, or – as had seemed to work with Marr – simply force the witness to agree so that we might all go home and shower this wretchedness off us. The task for Davis is to make confusion seem like a strength for Joyce but a weakness for Morrissey, and to persistently convince the witness that anything they might say by way of reply has no value. When we think we are guilty we can then be easily controlled, and by complicating every question Nigel Davis can first demoralize and then make inferior. Everything is expressed by Davis with a tone of intolerance, as if his presence in court encroaches greatly upon his precious flower-bedding time. Davis insists that a solicitor whom Johnny and I met only once (but whom we did not engage) was, in legal fact, our acting representative. Joyce's case involved Davis arguing that this solicitor fully and absolutely represented the wishes of Morrissey and Marr, a falsehood upheld throughout the trial with dismal imperfection by Davis and then Weeks.

Verbal flights from a flurry of defendant witnesses were supplied. Firstly, by Patrick Savage (the Smiths' accountant), who spoke directly to the judge and said, *'Andy Rourke told me "We get 10 per cent".'* Judge Weeks decided that such a conversation between Savage and Rourke *'never took place,'* thereby dismissing the evidence of the Smiths' accountant. Further evidence from Scott Piering, Geoff Travis, Joe Moss and Andrew Bennet-Smith all maintained that Joyce and Rourke were not equal partners to Morrissey and Marr, and that the division was palpable no matter which way the circumstances were viewed.

With his venomous face game for controversy, it seemed deputy Weeks would dismiss all witness evidence against Joyce – from all of the above key witnesses, not allowing this healthy gathering of plausible sources to have the most remote effect upon the will of Weeks. In effect, John Weeks quite impossibly deemed the evidence of Savage, Travis, Bennet-Smith, Piering and Moss to be 'unreliable'. By contrast, Joyce had no witnesses and nor did he need them. Neither his wife nor his accountant (who both held great importance in his written testament) is called upon to give witness testimony. For Joyce, the less that anyone spoke for him the better. A sane voice would ask why Joyce's accountant – who had apparently stirred the action in the first place – was not called to court. Yet sanity was not required as one painfully unjust day bled into another.

Why was Weeks disinclined to accept anything at all that was said against Joyce by a slew of enlighteners; by, in effect, those who were witness to the truth of these affairs? Their presence in court was due only to their profession, and not due to any obliging friendship that they may have with Morrissey or, less importantly, Marr. On the other hand, any evidence spoken in my favor was somehow very skilfully turned against me – as if the witness had been misled or mistaken in thinking anything positive of me. When Joyce himself admitted that he found me to be *'too honest'* a person, the crumpled Weeks assumed that Joyce meant 'artistically honest' but not personally honest, and Weeks settled for this assessment without finding out whether Joyce's meaning differed to the one chosen by him. At this point, with Weeks insisting that Joyce meant 'artistically honest' (even though Joyce had made no reference to art), it is interesting to wonder what John Weeks had known of my 'art', and why it seemed safe for Weeks to attribute honesty to my art, but not to my character. For a deputy judge who admitted that he hadn't heard of *Top of the Pops*, it seemed unlikely that he would know anything about Morrissey – unless privately enlightened by his friends. It is also interesting to wonder why Weeks found it impossible to link honesty in art to honesty within the person who had created the art, or that he could not see how one automatically led to the other.

For John Weeks, nothing spoken under cross-examination had provided anything at all in my favor, yet the constant inaccuracies and assumptions vomited out with leaden fatigue by Joyce had said so much to the judge. The extraordinary zeal with which Weeks battered out his final judgment raised questions on how far judges should be allowed to go in their assassination of a defendant. Certainly, a witness such as I, with no criminal record, and one who believed that he had always acted with kindness and generosity towards the plaintiff, could not possibly have deserved the skewed and vile attack as spewed forth from John Weeks. If such actions as mine are ultimately not thought to be correct it is only because they are ultimately not thought to be, but this does not show that they were originally designed to be incorrect, and certainly, nothing I had ever done had broken any existing laws. So why did John Weeks use words so violent and apparently preferential in his final judgment? Why did Weeks not simply admonish Joyce for failing to sort his own personal business out all those years ago when the time was right? Why was the failure of Joyce to organize his own personal life deemed to be the responsibility of Morrissey and Marr in 1996 – even though the judge also said that he had no doubt that Joyce had always been equal to Morrissey and Marr? If, as the judge insisted, Joyce had always been equal to Morrissey and Marr, why would that same judge also deem Morrissey and Marr accountable for the supervision of Joyce? How could this ever be the case if all three were of equal partnership liabilities? And if indeed they were, why did the judge not take Joyce, as an 'equal partner', to task for any alleged business failings made by Morrissey and Marr? If all three were 'equal', how could there ever be a point when that equality separates? Weeks wanted it both ways: he mysteriously sees unquestionable equality from the very start of the Smiths, yet all supervision and responsibility were the duties only of Morrissey and Marr, and not Joyce.

If anything, this ought to have lowered Joyce further into the mud in the mind of John Weeks, because it underlines how Joyce had 'failed' to uphold his business partnership duties. Instead, it appeared that all failures on the part of Joyce were shifted over to Morrissey and Marr, without even a suggestion from Weeks that Joyce had ever been careless. Emerging from all of this, I came to the very

basic realization that any personal wish from Joyce was
going to be granted by Weeks. This was a civil case, not a
criminal case. Placing the evidence of Morrissey and Marr
aside for one moment, and assessing the case on the opening pleas of Joyce alone, surely it could not be possible for
any judge to listen to the stumbling and incomprehensible
Joyce and correspond those blunders with truth? A
demented child of six years old would see the circuitous
deviancy in the Joyce pleadings. So why couldn't Weeks
see this? Stuck in blame thirteen years after the event, it
was hard to comprehend how anyone could believe anything at all that Joyce had said in relation to the events of
1983. Without any understanding of knowing when not
to speak, Joyce had prattled on, trying to make the notion
of sacrifice work to his advantage. Did John Weeks really
not see how confusion and guilt are often the same thing?

Comically, Weeks sought to emphasize a considerable
disparity in age between myself and the other three Smiths,
referring to Morrissey as 'an older man', which would of
course set the stage for decisive corruption. That the other
three each had grammar school education compared to my
secondary, and that they all held bank accounts at the
Smiths' formation whereas I had lived without such security, were points given no weight by Weeks. In actual fact,
of the four, I was the least worldly, and it was only because
I was the oldest of the four that Weeks could labor this
fact as if it should have an obviously dark meaning. Several
days in, it is generally acknowledged that the case is Joyce
versus Morrissey, and those present will know that any
defeat I may suffer within these walls shall be as important
to onlookers as any triumph I may have had elsewhere.

There is not one friendly face, nor one shrug of sympathy towards me from the lines of predators seated with such propriety on the benches. I am entirely and utterly alone. Marr has neatly edged his way over the dividing line, and is safely tucked away as everyone's friend – yet no one's. Even as Davis points out my personal sense of pride, Weeks later ridicules such an idea as if not one word in my support must be allowed air. It is crystal clear to me that this case must go against me even if I am right. Joyce is indecisive; I am fully decisive. My clarity annoys the judge, whereas the fog offered by Joyce only seems to help him. Joyce cannot remember, and says so three hundred times, yet his self-willed lack of recall does not annoy the judge at any stage, whereas my clarity aggravates. I can vividly remember, and I say so three hundred times.

DAVIS: *You are very careful with your words, Mr Morrissey.*
ME: *Well, I'm in court.*

Being careful with words is sneered out by Davis – as if it were in itself an anarchic act, as darkness descends all afternoon, and Davis attempts to divide me from Marr – which I am determined will not work. I have already been set adrift from everyone else. I have nothing to hide, and I have nothing to reveal that is not already as plain as day. Cross-examination is really only badgering, and it only takes place because the barking barrister is paid good money to badger. It is unlikely that he even believes the words that he speaks, yet his vocation is to badger in return for money – as with a common bailiff – and this is what Nigel Davis does for a respectable living. Surely unable to fist-fight, he feels safe in the world of words where his cross-examination slaps the face of another over and over again, until they tire and give in. It is an unchristian way of grinding people down, but this is how the legal system makes its money – and a colossal amount of it. Perhaps the wrong verdict is reached, perhaps injustice wins the day, but barristers and judges have little concern for the cruelty of their sport as long as they have the boyish joy of concluding it on their own terms, even if law clashes with truth. Their time in the courtroom is a grand performance, whilst outside is the world they rarely inhabit, and which they more than likely know nothing about. Cross-examination by a barrister is a game whereby the first one to blink is the loser. It really is *that* silly.

Weeks decides that he 'prefers' the 'evidence' of Joyce, yet Joyce's evidence is that he can't remember anything. My vivid recollections do not fit in with how John Weeks wants to wind up the case, and so I therefore receive derision. Back in the witness stand, Joyce still cannot remember, cannot remember, cannot remember. Why force a case into the High Court if you cannot remember anything about it? Joyce 'just presumed', and then 'can't remember', and then 'just assumed'. Quite apart from turning up at the High Court with neither evidence nor witnesses, Joyce's presumptions and assumptions are tolerated by the presiding adjudicator, even though Joyce has nothing in writing, has no evidence to support his claim, and does not appear on any Smiths recording contracts! At what point does the absurd become psychoneurotic? Surely the law should not entertain presumptions and assumptions under any circumstances because they are not evidence, they are meaningless, and they are a waste of the court's time?

Yet deputy Weeks, applying the Partnership Act, 'prefers' the assumptions and presumptions of Joyce, and what a great moral task it must have been to bark out laws from 1890 at a time, now, when nothing else from 1890 applies to modern life. Why is such silliness allowed, when usually a court of law requires written evidence? When faced with the evidence of a host of professional functionaries, John Weeks will consider accountant Patrick Savage to be imaginative, and Weeks 'prefers' Joyce's inability to recall. The Smiths are brutalized not by Joyce, but by Weeks, whose judgment marks me out for prolonged and eternal milking by Joyce. As if not enough, Weeks will also make me an easy target for lifelong jokes in the press by carefully shaping and delivering his own description of me as being 'devious, truculent and unreliable', which amounts to a very deadly first-degree assassination of anyone's character.

Three words were used that had never previously described me, thus their weight as a catchphrase for eternity. Had Weeks described me in words befitting my character, no one would care or give any attention. The meaning of 'devious, truculent and unreliable' is to present a description so patently unlikely that ears prick up. We all know that, if repeated often enough in print, words are bound to eventually be believed, and it seemed obvious his quote would indeed be printed often enough. In the event of any future court action shading my life (fame = money = lawsuits), the 'devious, truculent and unreliable' stinger alone need only be used once by any opposing party and my defense would come unstuck, because 'devious, truculent and unreliable' in judicial parlance means 'evil, aggressive and a liar'. What was the reason for this attack on me, so aggressively fueled and so overdone that it appears to want to bring a life to an end? Surely judges have no need to unleash thoughts that are actually more violent than anything done or expressed by either plaintiff or defendant. What, then, was John Weeks thinking of? In the quiet room of his final years he will be delighted that his potential was realized by a famously recurring quote. It is a quote powerful enough to poison everything. Weeks could have merely said that someone was right and someone was wrong – or, indeed, that both parties were wrong. Instead he leaves a quote that might be rancid and powerful enough to cause one subject to be unable to ever again conduct business; to never again be trusted, or – even better – to kill himself with the brandishing shock of it all. It doesn't take much to force someone over the edge, but Weeks' judgment in itself could have constituted manslaughter.

I had done no harm. I was decisive. Joyce was indecisive. Would the judge not accept one solitary word of my exhaustive evidence? The pounder-drummer will become up to £3 million richer because he said *'I just assumed it was 25 per cent'* – and that's all it took. By 'just assuming' it was 25 per cent, he was now awarded 25 per cent. Having accepted a 10 per cent cut throughout his entire career – and beyond – it was only when the Smiths broke up that Joyce decided upon a 25 per cent gamble – after all, what is there to lose when the case is funded for Joyce by other people?

Joyce may not thank God, but he has much to thank John Weeks for, since it was Weeks who postmortemed the cobwebbed crates of the nineteenth century to give meaning to a case that was not won by Joyce himself, but that was made easy for Joyce. Without this anachronous act, the case should have collapsed seconds after Joyce first opened his mouth. In puerile rambling the hearings had dragged on and on. Like an irritable child on a hot day, Johnny took to the witness box for a second time, his newly primed approach resembling a sea-dog with news of a sinking ship: *'Well, Morrissey's mother, and Morrissey's mother, and yes, Morrissey should've sorted it out,'* and with this the hounds are now fully snapping at my heels, my mind's eye wandering to late August of 1983 when I inch back the curtains to see my mother and Johnny's mother driving off together in order to get to know one another. I think of my mother helping Johnny on the day he turned up at her house in a terrible state, and now here he was dragging her into this vile scenario as if it were all she deserved. By now, Marr, Rourke and Joyce have magically transformed into the Beverley Sisters, each chanting how that awful Morrissey had destroyed their lives – and just when they were all doing so well with their musical careers. It is an inferno of betrayal that I can bear no more, and I walk out of the court, the human mess of it all now so overcooked and grotesque – as if the subject all along had been dis-covery of human remains in someone's potting-shed, and not simply a chubby drummer chancing his arm. What would they say at Salford Lads' Club if they caught the stench within these walls – Johnny Marr crying off for being held accountable for his own actions, and all Mancunian camaraderie shafted. It was true that Johnny may have run a little wild, but people who were angry with him always forgave him, and here he was in late repentance – folding for Nigel Davis, his head to one side, seemingly imploring credit for at least being friendly. The shapeless Weeks brought his eyes to bear on Marr as if to question why Marr had made him wait so long. Johnny tunneled his way towards Weeks, a child again, wanting anything at all except the disapproval of complete strangers. Now, like Joyce, he too speaks with the voice of a child begging forgiveness, and the hunchbacked Weeks now looks as if he has his catch.

It takes courage to make yourself unpopular with your legal bully-boys for the sake of mere loyalty, and Johnny did not have that courage. A virtuoso of to-ing and fro-ing, you might swear that you are in the company of identical triplets as Johnny stands before you. I think of the happy months recording *Strangeways, Here We Come*, and I think that at least we had those times. Now, in this sunless and seditious High Court I had endured enough insults from people who had only ever profited from knowing me. Like royalty at the opera, the suffering face of John Weeks increases the web of sorrow as his deferential orderlies and his tide of little helpers are sworn to silence around him. Behind a bundle of oh-so-terribly-important papers, the huge teeth of Nigel Davis appear to expand at signs of fatigue and collapse in Marr – as if the only point of the exercise was to wear the witness down and to make him say what wasn't true. I imagine barristers and connoisseurs of honor and civil scurvy roaring with laughter in their civic backrooms as they think of the clownish playthings that gather before them in search of justice in the godly Great Halls.

Alone, I left the court's moldering walls. I left behind its odious gasses and I stepped out into new air, leaving the gabbling gargoyles stewing in their pitiful little warren; barristers soaked in fake humility, Johnny goaded by his little clan, Weeks wringing his creased little hangman's hands whilst resembling a pile of untouched sandwiches, Joyce telling the world over and over again how he spent his Smiths years in a state of assuming and mis-hearing and mistaking and presuming, playing the daft-as-a-brush card up and out to the balcony, announcing *'It's not about money,'* and *'I just a-shoe-mmmd,'* and *'I just want my money,'* as if his personal wishes were in themselves law. Leaving the court's yard, a squirrel of a solicitor who is representing my lawyer (who did not appear at the hearing) tugs my arm.

'Mr, ummmm, Morrissey, ummmm, what about our fees?'
Bleak House, indeed.

Although the trial was originally set to run for several more days, the second that I left the courtroom the trial ended abruptly, everyone was sent home and the door closed upon all of us. It was as though, without my presence, the taunt was no fun, and darker shadows rolled in as Weeks shuffled away to construct his literary masterpiece known as the Final Judgment – a judgment that made the entire Smiths case much worse than it had ever been, and also placed me in unimaginable peril, as it effectively served as an open invitation to others to take action against me. A final judgment must dwarf everything that has already been said, and with his death-rattle voice the fossilized Weeks left untouched the vital question of why Joyce had waited so long.

Weeks seems adamant that after five years of constant recording I had done nothing at all to earn the respect of Marr, Rourke or Joyce: no one present owed me a grain of consideration, yet the welfare of Joyce is underlined as everyone's concern. With this, nothing in the final judgment strikes me as fair, final, or justice. But the judgment did not move Marr to action – not even in the name of *Last night I dreamt that somebody loved me* or *Please, please, please let me get what I want*. How could Joyce – even in thought – allow what I felt to be a gangland elimination of me by Weeks, with *Hatful of Hollow, Louder than Bombs* and *The World Won't Listen* effortlessly pushed aside?

Rourke was not a fighter, and did his poor best, but everyone who had spoken in court had torn the evidence of Joyce to pieces. So how could the results ever be what they became? Nigel Davis had made so many mistakes – repeatedly referring to Joyce as 'Johnny' – but like twin pugs with matching flea collars, Rourke and Joyce were poor company even to each other, yet they allowed the savagely lashing Weeks to know us all much better than we knew ourselves.

Joyce Iscariot raced to the press caped in victory: *'It's not about money,'* he kept saying, which told everyone that it had purely and absolutely been about nothing but money. For someone who supposedly ran a case that was not about money, the self-unmade Joyce grabbed as much of it as his tenure on earth might allow, and none of it found its way to charities for the socially displaced. *'I just want what's mine,'* said Joyce, reaching out for that which clearly wasn't.

Finding nothing in the 1980s to assist the Joyce claim, Weeks instead delves back to the 1890s because, although

Weeks is adamant that the partnership was a four-way equal split, he cannot produce anything throughout the history of the band to support this insistence. Joyce was thrown a lifeline, yet the worn-out husk of Joyce looked bewildered, as if he couldn't quite believe his fortune, like a wobbly Lotto winner. Going easy on Joyce, Weeks tore into me with a thunder reserved for rapists and murderers. In the Smiths case, there had been no proof of intent to break the law, and therefore a charge of intending to break the law could not be made. But! Weeks! How do we rap these outspoken pop stars on the knuckles? How do we put them out of action? Here's how. Or, at most, we can try. Without a knighthood to shut them up, the vocal pop artist must be nabbed, because otherwise their platform is their freedom. Allied to the peerage, judges keenly relish judicial law because they themselves have probably never been victimized by it, and their knowledge of how the police work in reality is zero. In what might be called the public gallery I had recognized only two faces in the courtroom. The biographer Johnny Rogan (whom Johnny had amusingly re-named Johnny Rodent) had climbed in amongst the small gathering. He wore dark glasses as the tools of his trade so that he could examine others intimately without them catching the dart of his eyes. As self-appointed Smiths historian, Rogan had gained attention as an Albert Grossman cannibal-disguised-as-Christ squealer – presenting every word as factual record and whose prize findings are incriminating evidence. Rejection motivates many biographies because the writers (being ennobling moral exemplars in themselves) gain public fascination due to their betrayal. Popular biography must demystify and destroy in order to have any practical value. I approach him and I speak gently, to which he seems taken aback – as if he half expected me to spring at his throat.

Angie Marr was also present, and as we walk into each other I touch her on the arm, and she looked at me with a shake of the head as if to say *'and what a sorry ending it all is'*. I recall months of driving around in Angie's sky-blue Beetle, with Angie at the wheel and Johnny in the passenger seat, wondering how we could persuade this drummer Joyce to have enough faith in us to join our band – never imagining he would launch us into such heavy waters by way of thanks. But whatever begins must end.

Finally, here in the mid-90s, Joyce had a new career. Having been rescued by the Smiths in 1983, he was again rescued in 1996 by the ensuing fame of the court case, beginning once more to be known, and beginning once more to profit by latching onto Morrissey and Marr. Yet the tatty particulars of the case caused a worried constern-ation, and press photographs scan a *what-HAVE-I-done* countenance across the money-hungry Joyce face. His wife may very well bask in victorious Third Party Orders for the rest of her life, calling instructions to her highwayman from beneath a blistering sunbed, but Joyce has lost his Smiths – now, today, tomorrow and always, and his own sentence begins on the day of his confusing victory, and it would run longer and harder than the sentence bestowed upon me by Weeks. I am as I always was. No future band came to the aid of Joyce, presumably in fear that he might do to them what he had done to the Smiths.

Collecting his enormous winnings, Joyce is a little boy of 45, a friendly heart only wanting what's fair and due, and it is with Nigel Davis that Joyce systematically and dutifully stands, steeped in eternity, as money changes everything. But in the years to come, when Joyce shouts out for a Smiths reunion (and why would he want one if his experience the first time around had supposedly been so bad?), it will not be to either Nigel Davis or John Weeks that Joyce calls.

The role of Joyce had always been so elementary that it never needed to be explained. With the face of a philosophical horse, Nigel Davis was the newly appointed Smiths patron. It was he who knew how things were and how things must be: Morrissey was inherently evil at all times, and Marr was given credit for untiring gibberish. Rourke and Joyce were the sensible of the four, and so fastidiously united that they lacked only matching nose-rings. Yet Joyce spoke in generalities so vague that he obviously could not convince even himself about his own powers of contribution. Surely Weeks knew that Joyce needed several attempts at his own Witness Statement – such was the certainty of his facts? As the limited mumble of words tumbled from mumbo jumbo Joyce, his theory of always being a 25 per cent partner had never actually been tested at any point in his Smiths career, and on this howling fact alone surely the law would somewhere, somehow, find in favor of Morrissey and Marr and not Joyce, if Weeks had felt open to such reasoning? Shouldn't Joyce be punished for never taking his own business matters into his own hands? As an equal partner, why leave your tax issues to Johnny Marr?

However, Joyce was not the point and the outcome was the opposite of how things were and how things had always been. Throughout the trial I had been tested and tested every single minute – leaving me wondering if the end had already been drawn up. Each time any statement was made by others, Weeks seemed to dart his eyes towards me, in order to weigh the effect. Unable to get his way with his mother, Nigel Davis is alive in his courtroom, with the mouth of an excluded three-year-old, thrilled to be our executioner, and delighted at his own ability to recite interminable passages of law – done with a lap-dog smile, longing to be taken up and placed on the judge's knee. On two occasions it is all so ridiculous that I laugh, and commandant Weeks catches this (since his obsessive glare never seems to leave me), and his return tells me that the commandant is annoyed, and if all of this sounds silly – that's because it was.

Amid trumpets, the judgment of Weeks announces my funeral. *I, I, I,* – the droning climax. *I, I, I.* The deathly component is probably all the more enraged because I do not attend the handing down of judgment, yet there sat Marr, Rourke and Joyce in their web of sorrow and cheap suits, Joyce still no doubt drumming his mantra through his head: *I do not think or see or remember, I just assume.* One trial closes, but another far longer trial begins. The Smiths are underaged children, and here the comedy plays out. How can someone who is not creative pass judgment on someone who is?

The pride of the pipsqueakery, John Weeks begins his judgment by falling flat on his fat face: he brilliantly announces to the world how the Smiths formed in 1992 – his judicial accuracy not to be questioned!

'In 1992 Mr Marr was playing guitar with the help and encouragement from an older man, Mr Joseph Moss.'

The year, of course, was 1982, but John Weeks is apparently unable to recall this most basic fact.

Weeks further insists that the January 1984 *Top of the Pops* for *What difference does it make?* was the Smiths' first appearance on the show, which was hopelessly incorrect. Stranger still, the notion that *What difference does it make?* had been the first ever appearance on *Top of the Pops* by the Smiths had not even been suggested by anyone in the case! Based on these errors, by now it seemed that Weeks was in a perilous dreamland of his own making.

Weeks refers to a document drawn up by myself and Johnny in 1982 claiming copyright of our work recorded under the name of the Smiths, and holding the rights to extinguish involvement of additional group members. Weeks said this document had no value 'because it was not shown to the other members of the band' even though at the time there *were no other members of the band.* If there had been other members, and if those members had seen the document, Weeks did not say what difference this would have made.

Weeks describes me as being 'more assertive' than Johnny, which is a description that no one now or then would say is true, yet it is not contested by the one person who ought to have spoken up – Johnny himself.

Weeks claimed: *'Morrissey liked to make decisions but lacked the courage or the will to communicate them to others.'*

Since my entire personality covered almost every speck of the Smiths' presentation and lifespan, how did Weeks consider all of this to have been conveyed – via a medium? If what Weeks had claimed was right, how could there ever have been the Smiths? What would the band even be *called?*

His next verdict is on page 2 of his judgment:

'Morrissey first decided that he wanted to control the finances with Mr Marr.'

This appalling statement seemed to me to reveal what I would argue in the Court of Appeal was the bias of John Weeks. Weeks had never been told that such a thing were true, and Weeks seemed to disregard the fact that Joe Moss had initially acted as quasi-manager in the early stages and had opened a company called Glad Hips, the finances of which Joe controlled. Yet, here, Weeks decides of his own fantastic volition: *'Mr Morrissey decided that he wanted to control the finances with Mr Marr'* – of course, allowing Marr to 'tag on' and not to be circled as a decision-maker himself. It had been made plain to Weeks that neither Morrissey nor Marr could implement any business decisions without joint cooperation from one another, but already we see a judge dispensing verdicts that, to my mind, didn't fit the evidence he had been provided with, as he rewrites the whole script.

On page 3 of the judgment Weeks supplies a further half dozen factual errors, as he introduces Rourke and Joyce as *'the other two'*. If the concrete basis of this judgment is to establish proof of equal partnership, why would the judge introduce Rourke and Joyce as *'the other two'*? Why are they 'other' – which means different, unrelated or additional?

'Mr Morrissey decided that he wanted himself and Mr Marr to have a larger share of the group's income than the other two,' is the next verdict made by Judge Weeks, along with, *'Mr Morrissey wanted a larger slice of the group's recording and other income.'*

This seemingly ignores the Morrissey–Marr partnership wherein no decision could be made by one without the other, and ignores the fact that a 40:40:10:10 split had remained in place for the following fourteen years – unprotested by Marr. Weeks did not explain what he meant by 'other income', and since he has the last judicial word, no one is allowed to ask him to be clear about whatever he is trying to say.

Weeks claimed that the 40:40:10:10 split made Marr unhappy: *'and he considered leaving the group,'* yet Weeks does not explain that Marr, in fact, did NOT leave the group, and instead continued with the 40:40:10:10 split for the coming fourteen years. By this statement, Weeks is confident that a person's actions are far less important than their thoughts. One might assume that whatever anyone CONSIDERED doing would be of no interest to a judge. All proof of conduct is in action. The vulgar picture being painted may be of blurred vision, but its result is to crack apart the Morrissey–Marr partnership in order to punish one and to pity the other. Johnny allowed this finagling to be announced by Weeks, even though he, like me, must have felt it was blatantly unfair and fallacious.

By page 4, John Weeks states that everyone in the band was 'unhappy' with Morrissey, but that 'they continued playing together'. Of course, if everyone had been unhappy, they would not continue to play together. The reality suggests that they were not unhappy at all.

Weeks refers to an 'initial meeting' with a solicitor named Bowen, the word 'initial' suggesting that consequent meetings took place. Weeks knew very well that there had only ever been one meeting with Bowen. *'Mr Morrissey did not take to Mr Bowen and he was not retained generally to act for the group.'* As Weeks knew, Mr Bowen was not retained *at all* – but the word 'generally' opens the notion that Mr Bowen might have been utilized for some matters, but not all. Weeks also knew that Bowen was equally disliked by both Morrissey and Marr, but Weeks does not include the name Marr, and Morrissey is hooked in as the bully.

Weeks points out that Bowen 'wrote two letters', but does not say on whose instructions, and he sidesteps the fact that both letters were unsolicited, and nor does Weeks mention how Bowen had misspelled my own name eight times – which is hardly something a solicitor would do if actively representing a client. *Lee | please | stand up and defend me.*

But let the bigger picture build. *'The second letter from Mr Bowen is written to Morrissey's mother, who took a keen interest in her son's career.'* Weeks does not mention that neither letter from Bowen received a reply, or that after the one and only meeting with Bowen, Morrissey and Marr neither spoke to, or even met, Bowen again, and no fees from Edmonds Bowen & Co were ever sought from Morrissey and Marr, yet Bowen is referred to as 'the band's solicitor' by Davis during the trial and then by Weeks, even though there was clear evidence that Mr Bowen was someone met only briefly by Morrissey and Marr. If Bowen had been 'the band's solicitor', as Weeks firmly planted, why had Bowen never once billed Morrissey or Marr – or 'the band' – for his work? Is any solicitor so blind with dedication that they work for free?

Apparently so!

On page 6, Weeks refers to Arthur Young accountants

being instructed to do the partnership and the company accounts, and highlights a meeting in the spring of 1984 at which Mr Morrissey was *'surprised'* to see Rourke and Joyce in attendance, and states that Arthur Young were also Marr's representatives. This all adds to the falsehood where I alone grasp the financial reins to the exclusion of all three other band members.

Although at the Arthur Young meeting the accountant suggested a future 'cut-off' point of royalty payments made to Rourke and Joyce – to which Rourke and Joyce unsurprisingly disagree – Weeks does not mention that this suggestion came from the accountants, thus leaving the court to wrongly assume that the cut-off period was put forth by Morrissey and Marr.

John Weeks inaccurately refers to the Arthur Young meeting as *'one with all four of their clients present'*, this statement building support for Joyce where there is none, since neither Joyce nor Rourke *were* clients of Arthur Young. There is nothing to even suggest that Rourke and Joyce were clients of Arthur Young – not one single piece of correspondence, no telephone calls, no billed payments to Rourke or Joyce, no indication that Rourke or Joyce had ever paid for the services of Arthur Young.

On page 7 Weeks states: *'On 8th May 1985, Arthur Young wrote to Morrissey, who effectively held the purse strings.'*

This is perhaps the most disconcerting of all the statements made by Weeks, for there is no evidence anywhere to suggest that I had 'held the purse strings'. But Weeks also makes this statement in order to suggest that Arthur Young would much rather have written to all four group members, but sadly could not do so for reasons unknown.

If any reputable accountancy firm acknowledged four group members as their clients then they would surely copy all four on crucial correspondence. If, as Weeks insisted, Simon Bowen had been 'the band's solicitor', why had he never met Rourke and Joyce, or even written to them?

It seems that I cannot be allowed to even receive one letter from my own accountant without it being further evidence against me. Weeks gives no weight to the Morrissey–Marr partnership and my name seems repeatedly set aside for special disapproval. Even though there is nothing essentially illegal in my receiving a letter from my own accountant, Weeks is distracted by the fact that the letter was not also addressed to Joyce when, in fact, there was no reason why it ought to have been.

On page 8, Weeks states that: *'In July 1985 Arthur Young were replaced by Ross Bennet-Smith. The decision to change accountants was taken by Morrissey and Marr without reference to Joyce or Rourke, and their letter of appointment is signed by Morrissey and Marr alone.'* What I can't understand, however, is that if all four were the indisputable partners that Weeks insisted they were, how could such an accountancy switch have ever taken place? It could not.

Weeks does not consider how Joyce or Rourke responded to their not being consulted, and he does not ask them why they allowed such a switch 'without their consultation', and Weeks does not consider how possible it would have been for Joyce and Rourke to initiate the switch from Arthur Young to Ross Bennet-Smith *without* the compliance of Morrissey and Marr!

It is evident here (as elsewhere) that Joyce and Rourke were *not* considered to be equal partners to Morrissey and

Marr by either set of reputable accountancy firms. If Joyce and Rourke had been recognized as equal partners to Morrissey and Marr, then surely neither Arthur Young nor Ross Bennet-Smith would accept such a critical move without the approval of Joyce and Rourke. Weeks flagrantly says nothing about correspondence from Arthur Young to Rourke and Joyce reminding both that their 10 per cent royalty would not continue once the band had broken up.

Joyce had said in court that he had never seen the original Rough Trade contract – yet his signature is on the contract as a witness to the signatures of both Morrissey and Marr! Could the lumpen lunacy possibly dive-bomb further?

At this stage, and at all stages, all evidence of Joyce and Rourke's junior position is dispelled by accusing Morrissey and Marr of secrecy. In doing so Weeks also calls into question the professionalism of both accountancy firms, and he also fails to ask Joyce and Rourke what on earth they were doing when such critical business transactions took place. Even more importantly, Weeks does not ask Joyce and Rourke what steps they took once they realized that 'their' accountant had been changed. Why won't Weeks ask such questions? Could it be because he knows the answer won't help Joyce?

On page 9, Weeks states of Ross Bennet-Smith: *'on behalf of their clients, the four partners'* and also states: *'Unlike Arthur Young, they did not meet all four partners in person.'* Before one asks the rudimentary 'why not?' it is fascinating to see Weeks hammer and hammer the notion of 'the four partners', knowing that he is the only person historically to have ever done so. Certainly, Ross Bennet-Smith and Arthur Young have never once referred to 'four partners'!

Furthermore, why would any professional accountancy firm accept the business of four partners if two of those partners had never been seen or heard? What was to prove that the missing two 'partners' even existed? The Judicial Judgment now enters the realm of the hallucinatory.

On page 10, Weeks states: *'On 12th November 1985 Mr Bennet-Smith sent Mr Morrissey only a copy of the 1983/1984 accounts asking him to arrange for all four band members to sign where indicated.'* No one, including Weeks, asked why Mr Bennet-Smith would write to only Morrissey if all four were recognized as equal partners. What was preventing Mr Bennet-Smith from writing to Joyce? And why would Mr Bennet-Smith not write to Joyce if Joyce were indeed an equal partner? Weeks is adamant that the partnership was a four-way equal split, though there is no documentation throughout the history of the band to support this insistence. Weeks relies excitedly upon the fact that Arthur Young had *'met all four members of the band'*, but he does not mention that this took place only once, and at a meeting to which Arthur Young had not invited Joyce or Rourke!

Overall, the point of interest is shifted in Weeks's judgment to one group member (Morrissey), who, according to Weeks, gained the attentions of accountants so that Joyce could not. Yes, the judgment of John Weeks was that silly. Weeks apparently didn't feel the need to ask why Andrew Bennet-Smith (and others) did NOT write to Joyce as well as – *or even instead of* – Morrissey. After all, why ask one person (Morrissey) to *'arrange for all four members to sign where indicated'*?

Surely if all four were equal partners, and surely if all four were seen as sensible adults, it would be the duty of any accountant to themselves obtain signatures, and not to give one the responsibility of chasing the others down? Further, Weeks will not consider the fortune of Joyce in *not* being burdened with the responsibility of either hunting down the signatures of others, or personally answering any accountant or lawyer.

If, as Weeks drummed and drummed in paradiddle echo, Rourke 'was always' an equal partner, why did Rourke eventually accept a financial settlement to drop the legal action that Joyce continued with? One might think that Rourke would only ever do such a thing if he knew deep down that he had never been appointed 25 per cent equality.

When Craig Gannon became the fifth Smith, how could there continue to be an equal 25 per cent split between the 'four partners'? It would be mathematically impossible. This fact does not serve Joyce and Weeks does not mention it in his final judgment – a judgment that lists no less than thirty devious, truculent and unreliable errors on behalf of its author. Weeks succeeded in depicting Morrissey and Marr as oil and water; Nigel Davis succeeded as the reason why all kings kept court jesters; Joyce succeeded as an adult impersonating a child; the tenure of the Smiths is desecrated into comic opera; Rourke succeeded as an overgrown houseplant – his brain battling with woodworm; the truth clashed with an outmoded law; I must account for everything I have ever done and everything I have not done, whilst Joyce need only cry tears of non-responsibility; Johnny's crime is that he watched it all and said nothing, hoping to avoid the noose already tight around my own neck; the three tough Manchester lads sat like nervous girls, as the Weeks of great title and wealth buried *How soon is now?* in a sorefooted farce of bewildered sorrow. *There is a light that now goes out,* and Joyce bows his head as the agent of disaster.

Nothing and no one can alter the artists' position. *'I do possess what none can take away,'* Oscar Wilde had said, but an appeal against the Weeks judgment will only succeed if fresh evidence is found. Hysterically, fresh evidence is provided by Joyce himself in January 1999 when he appears on a television documentary on the Smiths (principally the court case) where he addresses the camera with the statement:

'We didn't come to an agreement we were going to get 25 per cent.'

There it is. Why didn't he say that in court? And how exactly is perjury defined? Not that it would have made any difference, Weeks is so weighted in favor of Joyce that he expects me to prove the 10 per cent agreement, and allows Joyce to rely on the presumption.

Nevertheless, I rush a VHS copy of the Joyce interview to my acting barrister Murray Rosen. Here is Joyce, on camera, admitting that 25 per cent equality had never been proposed during all of those years when he readily accepted his 10 per cent (a 10 per cent which, it's worth adding, amounted to an enormous sum of money). I hear nothing from my barrister or my new solicitor as the appeal approaches. I am worried. I demanded acknowledgement of the VHS. It is not forthcoming. I demand that the VHS be presented at the appeal as new evidence. I warn my new solicitor that he must impose urgency upon Murray Rosen to utilize the VHS, and by reply, my solicitor resigns.

At the appeal the VHS is not submitted. Instead the appeal rests on documentation from Ross Bennet-Smith that was sent to Joyce during his Smiths term which clearly outlines to Joyce his 10 per cent cut of Smiths royalties, which Joyce admitted that he received and accepted, but added that he did not understand the implication of the 10 per cent figure next to his own name. Surely this was proof that Joyce knew and had no issue with being a 10 per cent member? Of the three elderly appeal judges, Lord Waller fell asleep unashamedly throughout the entire hearing – his chin resting on his chest. He awakes briefly and his right index finger lodges in his right nostril, as he fiddles about with the unseen. It would be comical if not so grotesque, and we can only despair at how lives and reputations rely so urgently on the thoughts of such puppetry. The more alert Lord Thorpe dismisses the acceptance by Joyce of the 10 per cent documentation with the appalling '*I accept that Mr Joyce received this documentation, but he put it away in a drawer and said he didn't understand it, and if Mr Morrissey claims that he didn't understand [aspects of accountancy] then I accept that Mr Joyce couldn't either.*'

What Lord Thorpe is saying is that Joyce hadn't the intelligence to detangle:

M. Joyce 10 per cent

and Lord Thorpe is also saying that Joyce can be forgiven for, instead, believing that he imagined he had read:

M. Joyce 25 per cent

With that, this crucial and indisputable piece of evidence is strangled, and Joyce once again has the luck of the Gods. Thus, my Appeal is thrown out on the basis that Joyce cannot possibly be expected to understand anything that I, the axis of all human endeavor, might not understand.

What on earth have the private actions of Joyce to do with me?

Plainly, my barrister, Murray Rosen, would not produce the VHS evidence of Joyce admitting that he was not an equal 25 per cent partner because Rosen wanted to protect John Weeks. Rosen was in line for judicial promotion, and in the halls of justice, solidarity amongst the adjudicators must never be jumbled by mere scruples.

The very final words of the appeal belonged to Lord Waller who, now awake, said, in May 1999:

> The Judge was right to conclude that the basis on which the Smiths commenced their partnership both as a fact and as presumed by law was never varied, and I would dismiss the appeal.

However, if the judge was as right as Lord Waller had no doubts that he was, why would Joyce announce on television in January 1999, 'We didn't come to an agreement we were going to get 25 per cent.' In the circle of Joyce, Lord Waller and deputy Weeks, someone is trifling with truth like a trooper.

The truth sleeps, and the moon above goes on and on saying nothing.

I cannot be robbed of anything that matters, but the Smiths are dead, and it's so lonely on a limb.

I emerge bolder. Everything inside me has suddenly changed. I arrive at full growth as the press titter the success of Joyce in crushing monster Morrissey – yet Marr is never mentioned even though the case was officially Joyce versus Morrissey and Marr, and, whilst the press manage to report the Weeks verdict, they cannot penetrate it. As always, Johnny slips out the backdoor unnoticed.

I am blessed with a lucrative deal from Mercury Records in New York and I begin recording the album *Maladjusted*, yet another collection of unpopular themes, and one which will largely pass unnoticed, although I swell with pride at *Trouble loves me, Ambitious outsiders, Alma matters* and *Wide to receive*. I suddenly find myself represented by Vicki Wickham, who had tripped up one night and found herself dancing with Marlon Brando (who probably mistakenly thought she was a woman), but *Maladjusted* slumps in at number 8 in the UK and number 61 in the US, with the usual barrage of vicious reviews.

  'I don't understand it,' says Vicki, *'it's not as if anyone ELSE is doing anything interesting.'* No, but this doesn't mean that I am, either. Although I love *Maladjusted*, the artwork is out of my hands and terrifies anyone who gazes upon it. Vicki is stumped and can't drum up any ideas. I pay her £80,000 and say goodbye to her. She takes the money and runs – the first time I see her in action.

  For the single *Alma matters*, on-the-beam Willie Garcia

takes me to Skid Row in downtown Los Angeles for a back-alley photo shoot where I lounge against a hep automobile that stands neglected and stranded in time. A sullen, idle posture is wasted as a seven-foot homeless blackface jumps in with: *'You show up on these streets one more time and I will have you killed.'* I am impressed by my own composure, and by how at least *some people* have the nerve to get straight to the point.

Having left the band for better things, Spencer sends a note:

> *Listen luvvy, I have decided to go to drama school. I am going to Chicago as I have a couple of interviews out there. How's your screenplay coming along?*
>
> *It would be great to see you again.*
> *Spencer*

This is a surprising communication from Spencer, because he had evidently left the band in a huff — he did most things in a huff — giving up the drums forever and cursing me for holding him back in his bid for stardom. I do not ever see Spencer again, but he joins the familiar cycle of musicians who walk away but somehow refuse to leave the building, and instead tag on with tatty tales as the years go by — unable to flap their own wings, after all. Morrissey is indeed the mother ship, from which every act of compassion must be followed by yet another act of compassion — *or else.*

Maladjusted had been recorded once again at my spiritual

home, Hook End Manor. Time at Hook End had always been a time to reflect on velvet lawns of dreaming spires where the quiet winds its way. The most bucolic spot of winsome British charm, the lithely blithe Hook End shelters specters dating back to the 1700s, and an underground tunnel from the 1200s. Unmarked by the injuries of time, the bosom of Hook End melted everybody's heart with its greenest of greens against the bluest of skies; a paradise of deafening birdsong around the red- and mellow-bricked splendor of jutting chimneys and latticed windows – all leftovers from the Jacobean era of liturgical dramas. Silence always, except for the occasional 747 waved off at Heathrow, or the caws of crows as they chase off a bird of prey.

There are lush lawns for games never played, and majestic trees blocking out the ugly outer world. To live this way forever, amid lavender and foxglove, cracked flagstones and fluted birdsong, jet-trails and giant snails, batty bats just missing your hats, show-off peacocks on outhouse sheds, where watching television seems like a sinful waste of life. The staff and their pets, the owners and vets, all change with time, yet I remain, a constant of three decades of waxed floors and soothing mid-day soup. The photographs for the original *Kill Uncle* are taken on the Hook End lawns; the smiling *Greatest Hits* cover taken in the White Room; the lounging *Piccadilly palare* cover taken in the same room; the *Our Frank* cover taken in the woods behind the house; the *Ouija board* video filmed in those same woods; the *Sing your life* photographs taken further into the same woods; an *NME* ad sees me emerging from the dining-room doors; the sleeve for *Interesting drug* taken in the Brown Room upstairs. Hardly a yard of Hook End stands without its Morrissey mark, a history full of senti-ment for me, if no one else, with tears always gathering at the final umbilical slash.

With *Maladjusted*, I attempt to get on with my life, but the seaweed of Joyce clings like a parasitic tagtail. Although John Weeks had allotted Joyce 25 per cent of all the Smiths' past earnings, no provision had been made by Weeks for how such money would be found, or collected, or if such money even existed almost ten years after the demise of the band. Therefore Weeks kindly yet clumsily left it to Joyce to find the money for himself, and Joyce was allowed to add on any penalty fees and legal fees as Joyce might see fit during his time of recovering. In essence, Joyce was suddenly free to bleed both Morrissey and Marr forever. Immediately Joyce sent his lawyers to close down my Lon-don bank account, and empty it of every last penny. With the words of Weeks behind them, they had no trouble. Joyce then took legal action to seize my mother's house – assuming it to be in my name. My mother steps into her garage one day to access her car, and is startled to notice one of Joyce's legal lice trespassing at the back of the garage, half shadowed by darkness. My mother threatens to call the police and the solicitor runs off in a fit of guilt.

The word TRUCULENT appears painted in six-foot-high letters across the wall at the front of my mother's house. My mother's cat crawls into the kitchen having been doused with deadly paint that almost kills her. Eggs are splattered across my mother's front door. When Joyce dis-covers that my mother's house is not in my name, he makes a further charge on the grounds that the ownership was switched to avoid paying the *'it's not about money'* drummer.

When further legal scrambling proves that the house had not been in my name for many years – long before the court action – Joyce withdraws his attack, leaving me with new legal bills of £200,000 for defending myself against his whims. Joyce then takes action to claim my sister's home, where she lives with her two children. The process begins again, and once again Joyce is thwarted since that house, also, is not registered to me.

Once again I must lay out up to £100,000 deflecting his harassment. Finally, he lays claim on all of my royalties from Smiths recordings, and as Warner comply with his wishes (although they quite interestingly *do not* contractually take him on as a recognized Smiths partner!) Joyce grabs all he can, and this continues unchecked and unmonitored for over a decade to come, thus I no longer have free possession of any royalties for Smiths sales. Insatiable, Joyce collects approximately £3 million – or thereabouts, since Warner don't clarify the situation with me. It is a farce of unimaginable proportions, with the dominion of Joyce enjoying eternal command because John Weeks, deliberately or accidentally, laid down no boundaries for the smash 'n grab.

In January 2001, Joyce utilized his own private website to disseminate defamatory statements by email that would foment contempt towards me. When asked (by 'fans' of the Smiths) about his latest musical venture, Joyce replied that both he and Rourke were part of a group called Aziz, but he said: *'We are not a part of the record contract, which technically makes us session musicians.'* Here was Joyce tripping himself up yet again. If Joyce had considered himself to be 'only' a session musician in his new group, why was he not considered to be so during this time with the Smiths, given that the contractual standing of both positions was identical? Also, if he had honestly thought himself to have a rightful claim of equality in the Smiths, why would he not make similar demands in ensuing ventures? Further still, if the axle upon which the relationship between Morrissey and Marr as the Smiths swiveled had been the main bearing of the written songs, and Joyce had no rights to publishing, how could equality ever exist if two group members are naturally excluded from the central pivot that maintains the group's success and existence? It couldn't. Publishing was not a minor Smiths facet (the songs are why the Smiths are remembered), but was, in fact, the essential center of the Morrissey–Marr partnership, without which nothing else existed. How can any judge see an equal partnership in any business where one entity (Joyce) is unconnected to the central work of the relationship that, in itself, gives existence to that relationship – and without the aid of Joyce? It cannot be argued that Joyce is equal in all things except publishing, because publishing (or song-writing) is 100 per cent of why the Smiths became the Smiths, and if someone is not a part of the publishing then they could never be found to be equal partners under any circumstances.

It is difficult to find legal professionals who will now represent me against Joyce, because to fight Joyce is to fight the judgment, and it feels like no lawyer or solicitor is allowed to question the word of a judge.

I ask one lawyer, *'Why not? Why can't the actions of Weeks be scrutinized?'*

She replies, *'Because he might lose his position.'*

At my appeal against the Weeks decision, Lord Justice Thorpe had said:

> There is one submission advanced on behalf of the appellant (Morrissey) that attracts a response of a family lawyer.
>
> Although not highlighted in the skeleton argument Mr Rosen (Morrissey's barrister) did in his oral submissions eloquently expressed his client's sense of injustice at what he in effect labelled a gratuitous and unwarranted character assassination of his client by the trial judge (John Weeks). Since this was a straightforward money dispute between two former partners the complaint, if substantiated, would deserve strong support and due remedy in an appellate court ... A distinction is to be drawn between an assessment of credibility, an assessment of demeanor and an assessment of personality. In my opinion the judge in the passages under review was stating his assessment of Mr Morrissey's credibility ... I am quite clear that the judge was expressing no more than an impression of the value of Mr Morrissey's oral evidence ... The circumstances in which a judge is entitled to make a personality assessment in civil litigation must, in my opinion, be much more limited.

Peter Gibson, LJ, then spoke:

> No dishonesty was imputed to Mr Morrissey by Mr Nigel Davis QC for Mr Joyce, nor do I read the judge's comments amounting to a finding of dishonesty.

However, John Weeks described me as 'devious', which, in any language, is understood as meaning 'dishonest'. What makes this attack harder to understand is that Weeks concluded the case based on the 1890 Partnership Act, yet he also went on to foul the air with personality assessments, the latter seemingly unnecessary once the 1890 Act had been presented as the final word. Rounding off the case with personality assessments would only be necessary if those very assessments were the reasons why the case must conclude as it had, but why is there a need for personality assessments if the wording of the 1890 Partnership Act supposedly said all that need be said?

Although the comments of the appeal judges in their own shy way cleared my character of dishonesty, this aspect of the events went unreported in the newspapers. Each man kills the thing he loves, and Joyce had murdered the Smiths.

In 1999, a case similar to the Smiths' circus reaches the High Court, but is swiftly booted out by the judge who examines the relationships within Spandau Ballet. Justice Park concludes: *'It is unconscionable for the [ex-members] to lay claim to large sums of money that they knew the group founder [Gary Kemp] had regarded as his own.'* The rationale and intelligence of Mr Justice Park further highlighted the wayward will of Weeks, and, at the same time, Michael Stipe is interviewed in *Q* Magazine where he describes John Weeks as 'a fuckhead'.

Years later, when fattened and bored and watching the clock, Joyce manages to get two letters to me, one of which begins *'I know you must hate me,'* (which reads as 'you have every reason to hate me'), and he continues with a plea for renewed friendship, whilst making public declarations in favor of a Smiths re-formation. Johnny, too, tells me that he is ready for a re-formation. But neither were ready for a re-formation during the trial or in the immediate years that followed, when neither felt any obligation to prevent the Smiths' ruin; when Joyce denies 10 per cent whilst accepting 10 per cent, when sad-eyed weakness is utilized as an instrument of power, when Joyce finally makes himself count only via disagreements, when Nigel Davis suggested that I had considered Rourke and Joyce to be as replaceable as parts of a lawnmower (a quote which the national press then gleefully attribute to me). Joyce, Rourke and possibly Marr were too simple to realize that the repercussions from these High Court days would be felt for the rest of their lives, and with Morrissey dishonored in a million ways – his ruin made certain from the start. In 1996 and 1997, Joyce and Marr set their own terms, allowing court events to justify their lives more than *The Queen is Dead* ever could. Self-confirmation was found only in the wobbly words of Weeks, the life of Joyce justified by hateful ingratitude to those who were his companions in pleasure and success. He spoke as if accompanied on harp, exclusively absorbed in self-pity, present in court because he had nothing else to do.

Yes, time can heal. But it can also disfigure. And surviving the Smiths is not something that should be attempted twice. If the Smiths split was designed to kill me off, then it failed. If the Smiths court case was a second attempt to kill me off, it too must fail. *There is another world, there is a better world; well, there must be,* and even if the passing of time might mellow you into forgiveness, it doesn't mean that you ever again want to be friends.

Sickened, I left England. The good life is out there somewhere. I found increasing strength as I purchased 1498 North Sweetzer Avenue in the West Hollywood zone of Los Angeles – the city of promises. Mercury Records had sacked its president and had also fired all of the artists that he had signed – one of which was I. I had no idea then that seven years would pass without a new label. But I have a real home with hardwood floors, and I am momentarily free from the petty wars of England. Palm trees range around each window of 1498, a house steeped in Hollywood history since 1931. I wake surrounded by weightlessness and a long-forgotten feeling of relaxation. I am alone, of course, but that is quite usual. My neighbor is the very famous Johnny Depp, who looks away should I ever appear. When my seven-year tenure at Sweetzer ends, Johnny Depp will buy the house for use as a guest annex.

In the third week of paradise found, my new car is stolen in the dead of night from my garage. Although both the car and the garage are fully alarmed, the sophisticates of robbery take moonlight possession with masterful silence. The insurance company is annoyed with me, but they pay in full as the car is found burned out on Figueroa. I buy a new car that is then dented by heavy kicks as it sits outside the house. *Yippee.* I am being watched, and every single day brings the oddest dilemma. The daily tedium of keeping house and garden acceptable becomes an enjoyment, and the pain of life slows down. Each evening raccoons cautiously totter down the hill at the back of the house and perch themselves on the water-fountain, where they lean in and wash their hands with human motion. If they spy me lurking by a window they will stand erect on their hind legs and stretch to their tallest position, as if to show me what a fearsome brute I might be dealing with. Grey squirrels begin their usual getting-to-know-you courtship, and it doesn't take very long for their tap-tap-tap on several windows to rush me into serving up today's menu.

However, the running feet bounding across the roof throughout the night I am certain belong to something other than squirrels. Since this house is built on sand, I am then told of desert rats that leap from tree to tree like monkeys, and my neighbors assure me that keeping the rats at bay is a non-stop occupation – a detail oddly left out of the realtor's brochure.

The weather is a continuously inspired moment, making everyone stretch, whereas the blackboard sky of London makes everyone shrivel and walk with a hump. In England, days bleed into each other without distinction, yet in Los Angeles every single day seems like what it is – a new day. My disciplined life is greatly aided by my close neighbor Charles Moniz, who is on 24-hour call to solve a floodtide of incomprehensible household problems. Uncomplaining, Charles will arrive with drill or ladder day or night with a duty of friendship that is first and last. Charles sells vintage autographs and stocks of famous Hollywood costumes in a shop called *Baby Jane* on Santa Monica Boulevard. His house on De Longpre was once owned by Charlie Chaplin but now shelters Charles and his two dogs, who are introduced to me as Jane and Blanche. Jigsaw, jigsaw, jigsaw. In the 1962 film *Whatever Happened to Baby Jane?* the sister known as Blanche is confined to a wheelchair, and, abstractly, Charles' dog named Blanche has lost the use of her back legs and drags them behind her as she moves – as if mimicking the screen character of Charles' most fondled film. Charles is a good friend, and we take several car journeys across the Mexican border.

England calls with an offer of a role on *EastEnders*, as the son (so far unmentioned) of the character Dot Cotton. I would arrive unexpectedly in Albert Square and cause births, deaths and factory fires every time I opened my mouth – numb to shame throughout. Funnier still, an offer slides in for a role in *Emmerdale*, and the most fascinating aspect of both offers is that somebody somewhere had thought it a good idea.

Since I dare not be myself, I would surely be even worse as an actor.

In July 1998 the *Guardian* ran a double-page damning assessment of my 'decline', and in the center of both pages their sole photograph is of singer Edwyn Collins, whom, such is the accuracy and expertise of the *Guardian*, they evidently assume is me. *Uncut* magazine also run an extensive *nine*-page account of my 'decline', while a *Mojo* headline asks: WHAT WENT WRONG? and the lid is slammed shut on my casket. The frenzy of attacks in the press becomes a fascinating study, with not a single line of defense to attribute balance. *It is done.* A plot is marked out and the hearse is hired.

> The thoughts of others
> Were light and fleeting,

Of lovers' meeting
Or luck or fame.
Mine were of trouble,
  And mine were steady;
  So I was ready
When trouble came.

A. E. Housman

Suddenly my life jumps, and the past is not me. The prevalent complaint of boredom subsides as whatever is sought is found. My forties flip and flash with Tina Dehghani, who becomes a lifetime constant. Iranian by birth, Tina's family were forced to Los Angeles when she was two years old, and had lived in Woodland Hills ever since. Her father had been a key figure in the overthrown Iranian government, and if a move to the US had not been made the family would all have been executed. Tina is a host of brown-eyed good intentions and patience and endurance, and it is only in the ninth year of knowing her that she lets slip her first and last complaint. Although tough and unperturbed, Tina's nature is to place others first and herself last at all times, and her spirit is never infected by gossip or betrayal. We take our place together almost without noticing, and all is said with such small gestures. We are a steely duo at our favorite restaurants and watering holes, and time never drags. The life I had always led is not the same as the life I now lead, and with Tina, all sorts of strangeness become less so. I have still, to this very day, never known her to be late, or to refuse, or to decline, or to grumble, or to umm or err. Tina is my first experience of uncluttered commitment, attached – quite inexplicably – to a woman of great independence and logic. Having been raised on scraps, this is daunting for me.

Tina's parents had married and then divorced, then re-married and then divorced, and then married for the third time and divorced for the third time. Sweetzer is giving me a matter-of-fact life, so softened that Tina and I discuss the unthinkable act of producing a mewling miniature monster. Had I ever previously known such a thought? Lounging with incomprehensible joy in my own bed I am now a symbol of rest instead of panic, as the swooning view of West Hollywood rooftops from my bedroom window ushers the sun in every morning without fail. The questioning and the discontent are left to brood else-where – with someone else. My mind is open and happy, inscrutably grown-up and running my own life. I wonder if I could ever take it as it is and just enjoy it? Well, *no*. I awake at 7:00 AM on September 11th 2001, aware that the downstairs answer-machine seems to be clogging itself with bleeps and blips and dying voices. Someone, I assume, is dead. I bolt down the stairs and my mother's voice is the latest booming message: *'Turn on your television – your country is being bombed!'*

My country? With a feeling of utter impotence I spend the entire day watching the television news reports of the Twin Towers horror, wondering whether any meaning could be left in the world. As the second plane glides into the tower I suddenly have no words to voice the hurt inside me. I do not know why what is happening is taking place, and my mind slows down, lagging behind the TV reports. The heavy-heartedness I feel for the people strapped into their seats – whose deaths I have just witnessed – joins that final roll of Concorde as the most appalling sight imaginable. This poor and pathetic human race. *Human?* Well, no, not even human. The scene is untranslatable.

Los Angeles becomes a ghost town for a full two weeks, as a deathly silence keeps everyone in their homes, so stunned and sickened are they, and nervous of further blasts. Everyone is frightened to breathe. The feeble newshounds quite naturally alert everyone to an anticipated immediate attack on Los Angeles, and urge investments in food stocks and rubber clothing lest giant ants mutate from small pods secretly buried in Bel Air gardens. Instantly, anyone with a Middle Eastern face is certain to eat you whole, and all of America overthinks itself into a stupor. Exactly how authorities are so certain of a second wave of attacks is peculiar since they claimed no knowledge of the first wave of attacks. How can they know now, if they didn't know then?

As life begins to formulate some fashion of normality, the events of 9/11 are nonetheless used forevermore as a reason for policing authorities to treat the public abysmally, and nowhere is this more apparent than the gratuitous rudeness of airport and airline staff. From this moment onwards I shall never again use a domestic American airline.

The horror also, of course, gives President George W. Bush something to do, and with no understanding of why people of foreign lands might dislike American policies, Bush does the manly thing by ordering more death and destruction, with American error being forever unthinkable. Claiming that his war is 'against terror', he can only fight such terror by exerting more terror, and, in doing so,

Bush himself becomes the world's most famous active terrorist, as he bizarrely bombs the innocent people of Iraq out of existence in the name of freedom and democracy. We are asked to accept that the bombs being dropped on the harmless people of Baghdad – so grinningly approved by the British Prime Minister – are not, in themselves terrorizing, as babies burn and America's problems are solved, rah, rah, rah.

The contracts to rebuild Baghdad are distributed amongst the fatted friends of George W. Bush – back yonder in the land of the free. This joint action to desecrate Iraq undertaken by both Bush and Tony Blair suddenly turned all of us into terrorist suspects – making air-travel security checks a migraine of harrowing proportions, while the resulting bombings in London that claimed more innocent lives were the answer to the ever-grinning Tony Blair's meddling in Iraq, thus rendering him guilty of war crimes that his honorable judicial friends would make sure would never land him in the cooler.

If not for Tony Blair's self-interests, the people who were blown to pieces on London's transport system that July morning would more than likely still be amongst the living. Although Bush and Blair collectively made the world a more dangerous place, neither of them, then or now, lead unprotected lives and neither is susceptible to the dangers that they have carelessly created for ordinary British and American citizens. In dippy downtown Beverly Hills – where trout-pout women push their be-ribboned poodles along in garnet-studded baby-carriages – graffiti appears yards from the sacred church of Needless Markup, as the empowered scrawl of *BUSHIT* remains for months and months for three-laned traffic to nod to. On such streets of famous gaga dizziness, it is remarkable that the fuddled fuzz had allowed such glaring graffiti to remain for so long. At a Beverly Hills theater I catch the latest show by comedian Joan Rivers, who comments on the US bombing of Baghdad, *'But ... come on,'* she says, *'who cares about a city that doesn't have Gucci?'*

I gulp as the audience roars.

I drive to Northridge to see a show by the incredible Al Martino. Time has not taken its toll, and his voice shatters glass and topples pillars. I sneak side-stage after the show and ask him to sign one of his CDs for me, and he does so, but as he bangs his signature onto the disc his eyes are fixed on a young female standing a few yards away. I thank him, and he offers me no eye contact or warmth, and he turns away saying nothing.

Channel 4 television burst into my life at Sweetzer, wanting to make a 90-minute film for television. Contractually, they give me total control to say and do whatever I wish, explaining: *'It's time the tale were told – your way, and nobody else's.'* It all seems too good to be true. *And indeed it is.* Once they have their footage securely under wraps, they are gone, gone, gone – to edit, chop, revise and delete in such a manner as to now give a 'balanced' view of Morrissey, bringing in anonymous sources who impart unflattering views. Yet again I am thrust into a legal battle to have the film removed of its blood-stained bitchery. Battered and bruised, I succeed, and the film emerges as an extremely modest success. Could life ever be sane again?

Kirsty MacColl had entered my life in 1985. She had arrived at RAK Studios in north London to sing backing vocals on *Bigmouth strikes again*. She walked towards me carrying a bulging Londis bag.

'*Today's laundry?*' are my first words to her.

She laughs and opens the bag to reveal a cluster clutter of canned beer. '*If I'm gonna sing with Morrissey I want us both to have a good time,*' she says, and chuckles that warm deep-in-the-chest giggle of hers. A friendship for life is born. There is no war between men and women as far as Kirsty is concerned – she who mused her youth in Acton pubs, almost unmanageable in her goodness, yet nobody's pushover. Lower Addison Gardens in Kensington is currently her cave, from which the Rolling Stones smoke her out to sing on their new album, and from which Bono smokes her out to organize the track-listing of a U2 album. *Cursed* is how she signs all letters and postcards, but *loved* is how she is. Her father, Ewan MacColl, had, of course, written *The first time ever I saw your face*, and had also recorded the somewhat lesser-known *Morrissey and the Russian sailor*. When the Smiths record Lynn Ripley's *Golden lights* Kirsty sings on that, also, and here and there come *Ask*, *Interesting drug* and *I'd love to*. '*I'd never refuse you ANYTHING,*' she vows, and I chug along in the Saab to her new Ealing pile, where she has asked me to listen to her new song, which is called *You know it's you*.

With the soft suburban life around us, and with Kirsty hunched over a cognac, and me in endless fidget, the 1990s are being sewn up. *You know it's you* is zealously magnificent, although Kirsty is neither artificial nor inflated enough to ever lower herself into the fat vat of stardom. In 2000,

Kirsty telephones me in Los Angeles to ask about Mexico, because she knows that every drab Thursday I excitedly flit over the border. Kirsty wants to know if Cancun would be worth the trek, and I urge her to go. Before she rings off she reminds me about *You know it's you* and how she'd love me to record it. Her voice trails away as Cancun calls, and it is there, a few weeks later, that she will be killed. On the first day of her holiday, Kirsty takes her two boys Louie and Jamie for a dash into the sea, when an out of control speedboat rages towards the boys. Kirsty throws her body into its path in order to shield her kids, and she is smashed to pieces as the boys look on. They had been splashing about in a spot that is forbidden to boats of any kind, yet all investigations into Kirsty's death are blocked, and whisper upon whisper reveals that the boat had been operated by an indestructible Mexican businessman, and inherently decent bureaucracy strikes again. Watching and waiting for a development on the story, we all have no reason ever again to have faith, as the hands behind the wheel are suddenly said to have belonged to a meager milksop Mexican minion, and a pitifully small fine is imposed for the life of one of Britain's greatest songwriters. Government officials in Britain fail Kirsty. Investigations into her death prove to be a long and thwarted battle for Kirsty's mother, Jean, and life is a pigsty.

Weeks after Kirsty's death I receive a card which she must have posted to me the second she arrived in Mexico. It reads:

You know it's you.
xxx Cursed xxx

It is an unusually overcast Sweetzer afternoon as I plough logs onto the open fire and crack open a bottle of vodka, and cradle Kirsty's card in my hands like a prayerbook, wondering if she would still be alive had I talked her out of traveling to Cancun. The vodka induces bewailing, and I cry myself blind for yet another lost friend.

Los Angeles is essentially the ever-youthful Promised Land, and although I have been offered several recording contracts it becomes impossible to pin anyone down the day after the promise, as numbers on cards no longer exist, as people are eternally unavailable in the revolving world of Ago lunches. For the first time in my professional life I am certain I look slightly desperate. I am tapped several times by Merck Mercuriadis, who appears to run the entire Sanctuary label.

Canadian, yet American, yet Greek, yet British, Merck makes genuinely impressive sidechatter and is as dedicated a watchdog of music as I have ever known. Now a responsible axis for a label in fast ascendancy, there are enough exciting signposts in Merck's roll of ideas to soften my heart. One more strained meeting with a gaggle of snarling industry panthers here in the city of dreams and I would drop dead. However, I tell Merck how much I hate the label name because it brings to mind pasture and refuge and soup kitchens and hiding places.

He says, '*Well, don't use it – rescue a credible imprint from the 70s and make it your own. We have Attack, Black Swan ... a host of unused labels from the late 60s ...*'

'You – have – *ATTACK?!*'

'*Yes.*'

My signature lands on a Sanctuary document within seconds.

In 2001 my cousin Matthew, who lived in Stockton, California, had his life cut short at 29. As the eldest child of my mother's sister Mary, the shock of his death concussed the entire family. I attend Matthew's funeral with my aunts Rita and Dorothy. Twelve months later, Rita herself has died at 48, a sudden assault of cancer making war on her entire body. Beautiful and loving, Rita shrugs at her doom.

'It's the luck of the draw,' she repeatedly says — as if it is she who is now protecting us with her calmness.

We attend to her during her final weeks at her home in Sale, still she smiles — losing the hair she had attended to so proudly, each good day inevitably leading back to a bad day, her two teenage sons knowing yet too shaken to fully grasp. Rita had been there every day of my life, and I had felt certain she would be there for the remainder of it.

Suddenly, her body is a hostile stranger, and all of us around her are talking gibberish, bumping into one another as we fuss — giving the attention that nobody wants — as Rita fades before our eyes, minute by minute, forty years ahead of schedule. You catch yourself lying, and you are choking on your own in-built censorship, and you are only able to watch as Rita becomes less and less present in the body that she had meticulously maintained all of her life. There are seconds of forgetfulness in her eyes, until a conversational pause forces her face back into the darkness of her pillow, unable to look at her sisters and her sons. Neither we, nor she, can do anything, and we all explode with rage. Days of Queen's Square and Trafalgar Square and Milton Close and Roebuck Lane, and now Rita closes down on Winchester Drive, facing what is just meant to be, sitting in the garden with a blanket across her knee – always a vision of an awaiting final journey for souls to be traded. So much life in Rita, her daily visits to the gym, her cycling, her salads, her garden, and now all to be sucked away – and, for what? Even now, one is asked to be patient as the final days are addressed and Rita's breathing becomes heavy. Why do we not all howl and rage? Rita wants to live, yet is longing for sleep, a solid fixity of positivity, *'but these are not my legs,'* she says, looking down at the swollen limbs – and it is true, they aren't, yet she is still the girl of Piccadilly, in a fixed image of vigorous fun, a listener of playful nature, the Supremes at full voltage, a room teeming with hair products. Now, I hold her hand, not wanting to let her go and she not wanting to go. Soon we are checking to see if she is still breathing, as the chest heaves in struggle, and Rita will wheeze out an apology as the physical limits are reached and the soul cries to be let go – not to be let go from life, but to be released from this state of departing, so grotesque in its sucking dry and wasting away. Rita's smile had become lifeless, and we all begin to snap at one another as we stand around feeling useless yet wanting to stop time. There is too much brain involved, and as Rita's will surrenders to erosion, we all feel a mixture of relief and repulsion. Death is one of many penalties of being human, but nothing will tidy up this situation for Rita, a finishing off that bleeds the body dry – as if anyone could possibly deserve such a slow execution.

It is not as if the death of Christ would prevent our own

deaths – we must also go the way of our own final muster, and always unresolved, always too soon. Suffer and accept, because here you are faced with something far stronger than yourself, and even your intuition leads you nowhere. How many billions donated to cancer research? How many billions of animals tortured in the name of research – and, to what progress? And what if progress were ever truly made? How many giant industries would fall – fully dependent, as they are, on cancer victims? Has a cure been found but blocked? Now is the time to dig down for questions, impossible to accept that your powers are so limited, and impossible to accept that your own body can't always behave and respond well. Life is a mesmerizing mess, but if you were a proper Christian you'd find a comforting answer for the finite and infinite, the temporal and spiritual, with no grasping insistence that tomorrow, after all, will *not* be just another day. Isn't it all too burdensome, this life, with so much loss taking its root in the heart, as the body goes spinning on towards a dreadful cessation. As Rita dies, I am a clenched fist, and we are soon in the church, where our intensity must be contained because you must accept that for a while you are here, and then one day you are not, because it's all part of living. *Accept, accept, accept.* Accept even the unacceptable. As the months pass, I drive along Washway Road near to the turn-off to Rita's house, and I cannot believe that she is not there, rattling about the house, busy with the small things of life, lost in cleaning duties and shopping lists, up and down the stairs, organizing the week to come, brushing her hair and answering the telephone. How could that heart ever stop? Oh Rita, I shall catch up with you in the afterlife, and if there is not to be one, then neither of us shall be alert enough to be disappointed.

Elaine Stritch cooks in the mid-day sun, long-necked and busy at her courtyard table at the Bel Air hotel. She eats chopped fruit from a large plastic Zip-lock bag. Stritch stretches back one hundred years, a true star of the American stage, and a hallowed prize on any of her rare television appearances. She is a cauldron of Lucille Ball, Tallulah Bankhead, Coral Browne, Estelle Getty and Beatrice Arthur – her creaky tough-nut croak of a voice is loud enough to fill the hotel foyer. She is a blasé broad of yesteryear – so funny that people hope that she will soon stop talking. She has the rare distinction of ducking commercial speculations unless they please her own infallible critical guide.

'*Y-y-y-yes?*' she looks up at me as I approach her table.

'*My name is Morrissey,*' I start off.

'*That's a funny name sit down,*' she orders – minus any commas.

Like the very best of them, the face of Elaine Stritch never twitches at her own lightning wit, and she remains stone-faced even whilst delivering the most rafter-quaking retort. All of her acting takes place around her mouth and eyes. The body doesn't do much. We sit and talk for an hour, and I explain that I had seen her on stage in New York in a play called *A Delicate Balance.*

'*Oh, yeh,*' she says, midway between gruff and boredom (but probably very interested), and I remind her of her harrowingly funny contributions to BBC Radio's *Just a Minute* with Kenneth Williams.

'*Oh yeh,*' she looks away, '*I remember him,*' she coughs, suddenly a commendable wreck.

I can imagine Elaine in the heat of disagreements to be savage and pitiless – '*calling 'em as she sees 'em*' – with useful enemies trampled to death. Elaine is here in Los Angeles to film an episode of the television comedy *Third Rock from the Sun*. '*Come along and watch what time shall I pick you up and what's your home address?*'

Elaine's studio car pulls up at Sweetzer the following day and off we go to the television studio in Burbank. Elaine is given a mobile-home dressing room, but as I step in she tells me to step out. '*No, you go and busy yourself leave me alone for awhile,*' and she grabs another Zip-lock bag of fruit and slams the door. I am not offended. I understand the tubercular theatrical typhus of one such as Elaine Stritch, who acts as if she had fought under the Sultan of Turkey (and probably had). The crushing replies to silly questions were all part of the ungovernable control, and the overreaching frenzy of rage is high altar in the depth and sweep of theater. It isn't friendly, it is a substitute for intimacy, and even if it seems overdone you will still accept it as a passionate experience of truth. The art of the put-down is in no hands more capable than those of Elaine Stritch.

'*Did you ever know Richard Conte?*' I ask, like a bouncing cheerleader.

'*Oh, STOP it,*' she says, a square of watermelon jumping into her mouth, '*how many thousands of years old do you think I am?*'

On set, Elaine introduces me to a host of people whom I do not know and who do not want to know me – because Elaine is in the room and her gift occupies space with volcanic power. A constant interrupter, Elaine wants it known that she has been there first – as she has, irrespective of where 'it' might be. The monumental face is a wretchedness that is great, and, because she has never learned how to be timid, she points the way for all assembled technicians and actors. She knows herself and she knows her worth, and we all spend our entire lives in search of such prizes.

'*Ah, the very best,*' says the star of *Third Rock from the Sun*, John Lithgow, as he extends his hand to mine but has already raced past before I have time to return a single word. A herd of bison encircles Elaine, and I back away as she is led to her mark on the set. The episode is called 'My Mother, My Dick', which I assume to be a pun on Nancy Friday's famous *My Mother, Myself* book. I watch the live taping from a secret spot side-stage, where French Stewart, who seems to act with his eyes closed, paces the room whilst running his lines through his head. Elaine is enviably brilliant, and gets a huge roar from the audience each time she belts out a contemptuous snap of dialogue. She is a great success. I slip away without saying goodbye because I feel like excess baggage. A week later a handwritten letter arrives from Elaine, and I reply, but she then doesn't.

I am back in the same studio some weeks later to watch a taping of *Friends*, having been invited by Reprise Records. *Friends* has become the most popular TV show in the world, showing life as it is commonly lived in America's carefully preserved unreality. The cast *is* friendly, and I am immediately taken aside by the scriptwriters and asked if I'd jump in on a newly jumbled plot-line where I appear with the character Phoebe in the Central Perk diner, where I am requested to sing *'in a really depressing voice'*. Within seconds of the proposal, I wind down the fire-escape like a serpent, and it's goodbye to Hollywood yet again.

Nancy Sinatra coils in a recliner at her Beverly Hills home. We have become good friends, and she is desperately generous and humble. She has recorded my song *Let me kiss you*, and it is to be released as a single, and I am dumb-struck with excitement at the fullness and strength of the final mix. There is a flickering sensuality to Nancy's voice that is unique, and with the restorative power of Sanctuary behind the release, I sense a huge hit. On this day Nancy points to a large upstairs room that houses all of her father's private belongings, and she tells me that she is struggling to store them properly due to lack of space, and she must therefore move on to an even larger house. I think Nancy is lonely, and a little lost, but given her biblical Beverly Hills upbringing she is uniquely sane and lacking in the fussy flash of the 90210 privilege. Unthinkably, *Let me kiss you* gains no airplay, and plonks onto the UK chart at 46. In the US the situation is even worse, and it is as if the recording didn't exist. I am aghast. What *does* it take?

Robbie Williams sticks two notes into my front door. His handwriting is so bad that I can only make out one central line that shouts *'Let's do something TOGETHER.'* And then another note shouts out *'I LIKE YOU!'* He fragments further with scattered lyrics from *You Are the Quarry*, adding, *'If we sing together it would really confuse them.'*

I am then invited to sing with Robbie at the upcoming Brit Awards, of which Robbie has somehow collected eighteen (it need hardly be said that my own award cabinet

Friendship without reservation, Nancy Sinatra has my head on the door

remained polished and empty). I politely refuse the request, but the ever diplomatic British tabloids jump in with MORRISSEY SNUBS ROBBIE. It is inconceivable to the press that a refusal could submit good terms and accord instead of sizzling spite.

Wherever I go I seem to see the Duchess of Nothing, Sarah Ferguson. A frantic gadfly at the Four Seasons in Chicago, there she is running a business breakfast, talking loudly with the intention of being overheard – hoping to make even more money out of a position freakishly acquired in the first place. A male member of the British 'royal' family wants to sleep with you and suddenly you are a Duchess, and because of this sexual fumbling the entire British population is assumed to be overtaken by a jittering interest in the nonentity now tinkeringly known as a Duchess. It's all so easy! There she is again in the bar of the Mandarin Oriental in Knightsbridge, looking around as if awaiting fireworks of recognition, and there she is again at the Dorchester. This time she stares me out. She is a little bundle of orange crawling out of a frothy dress, the drone of Sloane, blessed with two daughters of Queen Victoria pot-dog pudginess. A thousand embarrassing press exposés will not persuade her to back off, and although Diana Spencer, too, was stripped of her Potty Princess title, Sarah Ferguson remains lodged in the US talk show mind as a British 'royal' boil, or at least as some-one who has had the honor of hearing the Queen belch after a rousing luncheon of peppered horse. Diet shows, *Oprah*, business ventures, commercial ventures, Sarah Ferguson chases the limelight until it will kill her – *or you.* It is the unfortunate drive of the overly untalented.

The Tiffany Theater is a small cognac room on Sunset whose navel-high stage had historically drawn in Holly-wood's best late-night entertainers, from Phyllis Diller to Rusty Warren to Fabian to Rich Little to James Darren to Debbie Reynolds; sophisticated cocktail glamor for those too rich to go home. I am pulled in to see a show by Lypsinka, who is a living picture created by the man who hides within, John Epperson. This show is so fascinating that I return to see it eleven times, and each time I laugh louder. Although the entire show is lip-synch'd (naturally), there is never a single moment when it seems as if anyone other than Lypsinka is singing and talking with her own voice – which she isn't, of course, since the soundtrack is a high-speed montage of female voices from American entertainment history; Oscar acceptance speeches, crude recordings, vintage commercials, sitcom snippets, familiar splats of show tunes, all of which cease to be the property of *A Rage to Live* or *Valley of the Dolls* and instead become copyright Epperson to the watcher's eye.

Visually, Lypsinka is a fresco assemblage of Eileen Heckart, Lucille Ball and Barbara Billingsley mid-seizure. A sensual and sophisticated vision, Lypsinka's audience burn incense at the mention of her name; the imagination is insatiable, the vicious taste of unrestrained passion, the waist Mitzi Gaynor thin, the Rita Moreno dancers' legs agile and smooth. Does Lypsinka visit? Or is she dwelt in? It's so good that it's hard to describe, and the assembled audience – although laughing – don't seem to know what it is, yet cannot look away. Without reservation, the audi-ence dispenses gasps and applause at the Epperson skill; a star absolute, a star essential, but very, very clever – and far too intelligent for the clod-hop world of dopey drag. Pencil-thin Epperson has done something far more import-ant with mime and it increases throughout the 90-minute show, even if he himself is Lypsinka's alter-ego and not the other way around. With a lover's eye, he mimes the moves of others, but he is the last person who could be accused of doing nothing, since the physical stretch of his duty across the stage is athletic. In fact, he works harder onstage than those who delivered the dialogue in the first place. Is he bleeding to death? The erotic sensitivity of a Lypsinka show tests every paradox; the stage moves are Flamingo show dancer of 1958, the steps are Cyd Charisse perfect, the recall is genius – with so much wisdom behind each gesture, the pace is frantic, the body is a multifarious prop, slowly inching up noisy satin or savagely distorting the Martha Raye mouth. The facial expressions are too rapid to allow a second of slackened control, and the secret to Epperson's genius is his understanding of the under-statement; nothing is overdone – quite the reverse. I am a helpless target. The face replaces a real voice, yet moves like a washing-machine in overdrive. It is the most remark-able thing – yes, *thing* – I have ever seen, and no creative visualization comes close to this genius construction of a show fumed with fantasy and comedy. It is an art pose of a man as the woman of men's dreams, yet men are simply a diversion for Lypsinka, who would probably eat her lover's face. She hints at the sex act as either a service or a personal favor (but then, what else is it?), and all of life's relationships are simply contracts. The narcissism of John Epperson (who is only Lypsinka under stage lights) is, of course, artificial, and is more than likely a lonely flight since the stage show is a one-man presentation. John puts his entire life into the hands of another, and only resumes ordinary expression when not being Lypsinka. Does John exist for Lypsinka? Is Lypsinka to be gratified and considered above John? Is it John who is used as an instrument, after all? Is it a drag show? No. It is above and beyond; part Dalí, part Cocteau. I will never forget John's work – whatever it really is – as talent roaring above the wind, and I can see the Epperson childhood spent coiled in a sofa, laughing behind his hands at Jan Sterling or Paul Lynde or Gale Gordon or Gladys Cooper – the boy from the deep south swamps who knew that he shouldn't be knowing enough to guess the undertones.

You Are the Quarry is recorded in Los Angeles with producer Jerry Finn. Jerry was orphaned at birth, and his adoptive parents have now both died, but his brutally funny outlook helps the frenzied joy of this overdue recording session, which brings a massive presence of hope and newness into my life. The band is in excellent form, and the recording studio is suddenly a new place full of promise. The songs pour out magnificently, and here is the afterlife – full of excess mileage and sentimental climax. Every day is a hysterical hometown Saturday night – with Boz at full voltage, and Alain escaping himself into fantastic self-release. Our understanding of everything widens, and *You Are the Quarry* shapes itself as the most important step yet, blotting out anything else that had ever mattered.

   '*Do you ever get tired of singing "I, I, I, I, I, I, I"?*' Jerry asks me.

'*I?*' is the indignant reply.

Out on the open plain, *You Are the Quarry* spends its first five days of release at 'mid-week number 1' position, yet on the final day the group Keane have magically returned to the number 1 spot. *Quarry* has sold 72,000 in its first week, and although the reviews are predictably pasty, there is enough promotion to make it the album of the moment, and its first single, *Irish blood, English heart,* has entered the charts at number 3 – my highest ever single position. I argue to Sanctuary that, since *Quarry* had been released on a Monday it had had six days of sales assessed, whereas the Keane album had had seven days assessed, because it had been available on the Sunday prior to the *Quarry* Monday. '*Ah, yes,*' came the scientific reply. The obvious is usually impossible to spot. In the final event, Keane out-sold *Quarry* by just a few thousand, but if both albums had been given seven equal days of sales, *Quarry* would have been certain to be number 1. There's always something there to remind me. Keane, astonishingly, send apologetic well wishes, saying that they were hoping *Quarry* would be number 1. In the event, *Quarry* does very well, and hits platinum sales, and it is the only album of the year to spawn four Top 10 singles in England. The fourth of these singles is *I have forgiven Jesus,* which amusingly sits at number 10 during Christmas week, but thrives unmentioned by rock watchdogs. As radio vomits out its usual patchwork of puke-inducing Christmas songs, *I have forgiven Jesus* is heard only once – on the Steve Wright Show. I am ready to drive a nail through my head with frustration. In the US the Walmart outlet will not accept *You Are the Quarry* because I am holding a gun on the cover shot. Since Walmart

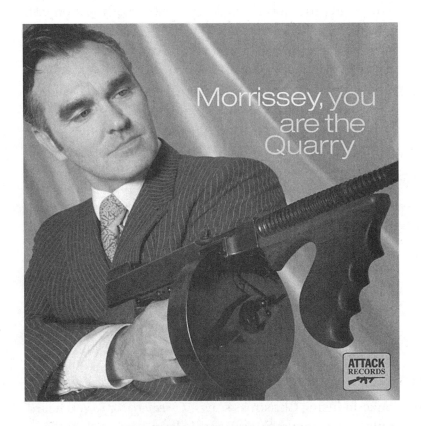

You Are the Quarry, *2004, the irreducible miracle,*
the machine-gun in the pulpit

surprisingly account for an enormous percentage of sales, a cut-down version of the CD photograph is pressed where only my bewildered face is shown, which isn't attractive in the least. Although this pressing is designed for Walmart only, it somehow seeps into the entire market and still survives today as the iTunes official artwork for *You Are the Quarry*. *Sigh times five thousand.*

The album enters at 11 in the US, and I can't help but notice how Walmart are stocking the new DVD by Brad Pitt on which he is holding a gun. *Sigh*. No rap on the knuckles for Brad.

In Korea, *You Are the Quarry* is presented in an entirely different sleeve using a gun-less photo; naturally my verbal flight falls on deaf ears.

I have proudly convinced Sanctuary to release a James Maker single on the Attack label, and *Born that way* is the astounding result – a song sung with a brilliantly elevated delivery, and I shiver at the richness. This is the voice of someone who does not intend to be elbowed offstage – a carnally realized nicotine fit, with a message to deliver, and in its first week it registers at number 92 in the UK Top 200. *Born that way* is an eternal absolute, sitting next to Patti Smith's *Because the night* as the triumph of the gift that nobody knew they wanted. Where had it been all these cruel, cruel years? And why did it make us wait? A previously unheard Jobriath single also honors a release on Attack, and it lodges at number 101 on the UK chart, which is surely the very first time any Jobriath composition had registered on any sales chart, and I am delighted. Of course, 101 is nowhere in the almighty's great schemes for civilization, but we must take into account how diametrically different a Jobriath disc is in relation to the easy, standard pap of pop.

As we begin the *You Are the Quarry* tour in 2004 we say goodbye to Alain, who shuts the door upon himself – taking himself off the road amid fears that he is suffering from exhaustion, which certainly seems to be true. Backstage at the final Alain show in Dublin, he takes me aside and whispers: *'I know who is planning your downfall. It is not me.'* I stand back and I let chance stirrings take their lead, but as Alain departs we are contractually bound to find an immediate replacement, and we eventually settle with the steely and stylish Jesse Tobias. We had all felt great concern for Alain, but, always knowing too much, I await personal criticism for Alain's departure – having had no part in it. Assuredly, criticism whistles through the poplar trees soon enough with accusatory emails from Alain, and my only surprise is that I'm surprised. By such gestures I now live, as if whatever you bestow has no value unless the flow is endless, and as soon as your life-giving generosity retires, you are human filth. That's just the way it goes. Having rescued Alain from the mad-death of his mind-crushing job at Camden Council, he would now cross continents rather than say a hello to me. When both Nancy Sinatra and Marianne Faithfull cover songs written by Alain and I, he has nothing to say, as if it had always been his due, and as if it could so easily have happened with any other co-writer from East Finchley.

'Where were the New York Dolls from?' asks Alain, as he trails away. I'm so confused by the question that I can't utter any sound by way of reply.

Soon, the decade is already beginning to pass, and you let it pass. *The South Bank Show* re-emerges, expressing further interest in filming The Morrissey Story, and I agree, with the proviso that they can arrange a face-to-face with the fudge of Judge John Weeks, so that he can explain the reasoning behind his judgment for the world to hear. But he refuses. Without his obsequious starched clerks around him, he is nothing.

A UK-based record label ask me to compile a list of treas-ured recordings for their *Under the Influence* series of CDs. One track, *Saturday night special* by the Sundown Playboys, had only ever been issued in England on the Apple label, who are contacted for permission. Although the team at *Under the Influence* had written to Apple, a reply comes addressed not to them – but to me:

Morrissey:

No, you cannot have permission to use Saturday night special, *and I won't change my mind so do not ask again.*
Neil Aspinall

Part of the reason why this is interesting is that I had not ever written to either Apple or Neil Aspinall, although I knew him to be a Beatles hanger-on from the 1960s. Mean-while, the boys from *Under the Influence* have discovered the true owners of *Saturday night special*, who are delighted for me to use the track and who explain how Apple have no rights whatsoever to the recording. When Neil Aspinall dies in 2008, I think to myself, *Well, that's what you get for being so nasty.*

Time leaps on. Merck's management motivation unleashes a torrent of touring that will run for several years. I leave the safe-cracking to Merck, and I rain as many releases onto the world as I possibly can. Despite the ghastly John Weeks, and his munchkin Michael, I now step into the most fruitful period of my life with a trio of full tilt, successful albums. All three are the recordings of my life, and never have I felt more pride, each adding love and ferocity in equal measure, and number 1 chart positions are logged here and there around the world. A *Greatest Hits* notches up another UK Top 10 as it glides in at number 5. Scandinavia erupts with a new and quite massive teenage audience – the crowd growing younger as the singer unfairly continues to resemble Jean Gabin after a good beating. The sentimental climax is 2004's Meltdown Festival where I am asked to curate two weeks of events in or around the Royal Festival Hall, gathering all those who had won me at varying intervals. Sacha Distel agrees to be master of ceremonies, but eight weeks later he is dead. Buffy Sainte-Marie agrees to play, but then decides that she cannot leave her ailing mother. Danny la Rue agrees to be mistress of ceremonies, but then later steps away in apology because he fears he could never again look convincing in the dynamic frocks that dragged him to international fame.

Amid trumpets, I stand in my backyard at Sweetzer Avenue and I cautiously telephone David Johansen at his Woodstock hideaway, and I put the idea of a Dolls reunion to him in as cheerful a voice as I can muster. With David Johansen, it pays to be exact since his responses are famously unpredictable, and, like the Smiths, the Dolls divide had been every bit as complicated as a Hollywood divorce. I gulped my third Grey Goose and prattled on. I told David how the world had hung on for too long, and that it was now time for David to reunite with Sylvain Sylvain and Arthur Kane as the last surviving members of the New York Dolls.

'*Well, would YOU get back with YOUR old band?*' his teeth snapped. It really wasn't necessary to muddy the waters with that topic. Three Dolls had already died, and the remaining three were by no mean ingénues, and the clock on the wall makes fun of us all. I went on about how the Dolls had exercised a wide influence, and that David was still in demand as a singer and social observer, and there was the slightly complicated matter of simply saying Yes instead of No.

'*Ummmm, I never thought of that,*' he says flatly, in his gruff Rémy Martin voice.

'*You've never considered a reunion?*'

'*It never once crossed my mind,*' he said.

The Dolls' reputation had never faded, whereas the host of American bands who had mimicked them had all died of cash poisoning. I paced around the garden of Sweetzer Avenue holding the phone to my ear as if awaiting the owl-screech of a slapped newborn. David slowly drawled me a '*Yes*', and that June night when the Dolls walked onstage to a full house at the Royal Festival Hall to an almost overdone roar of welcome from the crowd, a terrible case of neglect seemed set to be rectified. Johansen was back in the ring where he belonged, unbloodied, and Sylvain and Kane were almost embarrassed at their own joy at once again being Florence Ballard and Mary Wilson. On guitar, Steve Conte induced the proper spirit, and here was an edition of the New York Dolls that no one had thought possible. If not for heroin and slackened ambition, Johnny Thunders and Jerry Nolan would have been here, too, and, make no mistake, the New York Dolls in 2004 in their original line-up could have burst stadiums the world over. But the sordid actuality of fact is never quite that easy, and these new Dolls would never be freed from their kiboshed past. For now, though, the British press rushed to their side with posies and cigars, and after a variety of stop-start careers David Johansen was once again the captain of the ship – full steam ahead and blast the torpedoes. Could it be? Could it *really* be – now, in the future, when all's well? The Dolls once again opened up to an opened-up world, and could finally talk big. The surgical-curtain-raiser of the Dolls playing together for the first time in thirty years was the high spot of Meltdown, especially since Johansen, Sylvain and Kane had bitterly bickered about one another over the years as only musicians do. But, a month after Meltdown, Arthur Kane is dead, and here is the Dolls' tough luck that concludes each chapter of their career; the snakebite at the picnic. It could only be the New York Dolls – strangled by their own Karma beads, as if enough dues hadn't already been paid. The two breathing members suddenly had every cause to sleep with the lights on. Menace had stalked the Dolls like pestilence since their first UK tour, when drummer Billy died in a Kensington bath. Their story reads like

Agatha Christie's *And Then There Were None*, with all the cards of fate that mother nature sends holding no aces.

Accidentally, the Dolls story has shaped itself into a disturbingly touching motion picture for modern Hollywood to sink its shifting dentures into – it's all there: drowning, spectacle, adventure, and the gutter – a mutilated Ziegfeld Follies jacking up on Selma Avenue, starring Billy Crudup, Patrick Dempsey, Shawn Hatosy, Guillaume Canet and Andreas Wilson as, oh, you beautiful Dolls, you great big beautiful Dolls. But meanwhile, back at the Royal Festival Hall, their two nights of overdue glory throw them into the emotional black, and broke a spell for a time. Proudly, like a stage parent, I watched from the wings, moving through this strange hallucination and becoming an appendix to the Dolls story when I had once been too modest to live, and was now too screw loose to cry – *like they was my babies,* when once I had been theirs. It's a bit like finding yourself Headmaster to the teachers of your past, and fittingly, if David and Sylvain were ever capable of showing some love and support my way, *they didn't.*

In their defense, it must have been oddly unpalatable for them to watch their most club-footed zealot achieve the chart success that had always eluded them.

And now that it's over, what you gonna do?

For the release of a live Dolls CD/DVD from the Festival Hall, I glue together raw art for the front of each disc. I had found a photograph from the early 1960s of a female model with a freshly blown bubble passing her face. I tilt the picture sideways so that she looks as if possibly lying on the floor – a little tight and tipsy after four too many egg nogs during a night of Mickey Finished buffoonery on Hans Place. I love the final effect, and I whisk it off to David Johansen who … *doesn't* like it.

'*It's too gay!*' he complains (*this* from a man who had spent his entire life impersonating Simone Signoret). The artwork is reluctantly accepted, but the back and inner designs are slapdash Bleecker Bob's rock 'n roll, as if to redress the cloistered-nun aura of my front dabblings. I had first met David Johansen in New York during the summer of 1997. At that time, he was the only Doll I hadn't met, and a midday coffee shop marked the spot – the way kindly arrowed by Danny Goldberg at Mercury Records. I was taken aback by David's welcoming hug since he had never mentioned my name with fondness and for all I knew he couldn't stand the sight of me. Indeed, as we talked away an hour, I found that David wasn't entirely warm-blooded, and I seemed to irritate him with questions of what we had all now lived long enough to call the old days. Instead, David would break the thread with information about his current venture as Buster Poindexter.

'*Can you buy Poindexter CDs in London?*' he asked me.

'*Yes,*' I say, having never in my life seen a Buster Poindexter CD, but wanting David to feel wanted.

Such meetings reveal that which we all darkly suspect about those whose art we have loved: that they are unlikely to be whatever it is we imagine them to be.

'*You mentioned Diana Dors in the song* It's too late, *and I wondered if you were aware that Diana Dors herself released a song called* It's too late?' I ask, at full beam.

'*Noooooo,*' came his long sigh, '*that was so looooooong ago,*' the deep-chested soreness continued.

I fogged the window screen further with: '*Is it true that Roy Wood had agreed to produce the Dolls' third album?*'

By now, David is pained, yet I wasn't overly concerned since I thought it unwise of him to expect me to talk about anything other than his Dolls days. I wondered what he had *expected* me to talk about?

He was soon gone – driven away, possibly feeling like a museum piece.

I would befriend Arthur Kane, who lived just along the way from Sweetzer, and who, like David Johansen, would never once make any reference to my own music. Arthur and I sit one night at Mel's Diner on Sunset. He is not a sight for small children, looking oddly axe-wielding, yet speaking with the voice of a broken heart.

'*Do you drive?*' asks Arthur.

'*Yes, of course,*' I say.

'*Do you have a car?*' asks Arthur.

'*Yes, of course,*' I say.

'*Will you drive me around to a few job interviews this week?*' he jumps in.

'*No,*' I reply.

Arthur tells me that he has been asked to write the music for an upcoming film called *Josie and the Pussycats*. It's the kind of taradiddle you will hear non-stop in Los Angeles. If people only spoke of what they had done as opposed to what they were about to do, it would be the most silent city on the face of the earth.

Frequently I spot Arthur standing on the grass verge

in the middle of Santa Monica Boulevard, close to the Troubadour spot. I often wonder what he is doing as he watches oncoming traffic until, doodle-brained, the inevitable thumb calls to passing cars.

'Isn't that Arthur Kane thumbing a lift?' asks a friend one day – her mouth dropping open in muddle-headedness.

'Yes,' I say, turning up Indie 103.

Arthur would leave long messages on my answer-machine, deftly complaining of loss of earnings and speculating on how he could track down lost income. As a living Doll, Arthur had only ever received $200 per week, yet he would tell me that his Dolls tenure blurred itself out with a non-stop stream of alcohol and what he termed *'bad behavior'*, and I would leave him to make the connection himself. Arthur would never ask me how I was, and he would never make any reference to the fact that I made music. I therefore assumed that he didn't much care for it, which is not unreasonable, but there was a certain mad-eyed dithering to his countenance that suggested self-imposed brain-damage.

'You can buy New York Dolls t-shirts at Urban Outfitters for $45,' he would rage, *'but why would people do that when they could SLEEP with me for $45?'*

I wasn't cruel enough to explain to him that most people would much rather have the t-shirt.

Brigitte Bardot had respectfully turned down my offer to appear at Meltdown. I had asked her to come onstage each night to introduce 'a glamorous glut of jazzy talent', which was possibly not the most tactful way to urge someone out of retirement. Brigitte's video for her song *Bubblegum* which also starred Claude Brasseur, remains one of my favorite of many French pastimes. It later struck me that if Sacha Distel and Danny la Rue had appeared at Meltdown it would have been their final appearance as, along with Arthur Kane, they were closer than they realized to that final tap on the shoulder.

A beautiful handwritten letter of thanks from Sacha's wife is as close to him as I would ever get, until his son Laurent appears backstage in Paris smiling a smile of wonder, examining my face as I speak. Sparks agree to play the songs from their exhilarating *Kimono My House* album at Meltdown, but I am singing in Italy that night and I miss the light that still guides me. In a flurry Nancy Sinatra, Lypsinka, Alan Bennett, Ennio Marchetto, Ari Up, Gene, Linder Sterling, James Maker and Jane Birkin rush to my aide with their frenzied resources, and something hangs in the air and you want more.

Nothing can fortify you against the Glastonbury mud. It's an unwinnable struggle against nature's slop, and the whites of eyes peer back as a black Mercedes bumps me through the crowd. The view outside brings to mind Gdansk trenches of war-torn Poland, where hope would not do. Backstage is an open slum, and I am carried onstage in a humiliating rag doll position lest I slip beneath the sub-soil forever. I immediately address the crowd in the wrong way.

'Don't OD without me,' are my opening words, and somewhere in the crowd a boy ODs. Loosely reputed to be sane, I feel ashamed. Rhapsodical cheers greet the set, and I do my best to lay aside my awkwardness. How do they stand and stand and stand interlaced with so much mud?

As I walk offstage my timorous legs give way and I slide backwards into the waiting gooey glop, which is quite naturally caught on split-second camera. *It could only be me. Thank you, God.*

By July 3rd another festival awaits in Denmark. This time I headline and the crowd are magnificent, with not a plop of Glastonbury gunk to be seen. Drunk on sun, everyone's soul is fired up, and singing back to me the crowd is love itself, with eyes too blue to be true. Just landing my feet on Danish soil had always brought me peace, and I don't know what it is about this part of the world. The spritz of cyclists seems visionary, and the hotel breakfast is such that I disguise myself for three separate sittings. A dead mule might make up someone else's idea of a hearty Full English, but strawberries in muesli is all I have eyes for. And content I am. Denmark is sadly a hellish place if you happen to be a pig, but the brioche and fruits that tower on the table before me have me hastily attaching a feedbag.

Even when the squares of Copenhagen are rained on, the cyclists all remain joy-ride chipper. What, after all, is a bit of rain? Why curl up and die? By July we return to England and to the Move Festival. I can do no more than guess at the shocking irony of the chosen venue which is Old Trafford Cricket Ground in Stretford, where I had died several unspeakable deaths during the 1970s.

The stage in fact overlooked the Inland Revenue cellar where I had worked for a few weeks at 17, three steps lower than an abattoir, and hastening my plans for self-destruction. Yet the cost of such a life had led me to return in triumph, even if it would only be the sort of gift that

God would give to someone whom he knew had suffered. On Great Stone Road, 17,000 people charge in to hear me sing. David Johansen and Sylvain Sylvain are there, too, the final remnants of the New York Dolls, climbing onstage to tell us all that the oblivion that had claimed Arthur Kane had not yet claimed them – settling accounts being the dominant mood of the Dolls' entire history. They played a blistering set and made a mass of new friends. Inches from my old house at Kings Road, all those Doll-dreams ago, the Move Festival proved my point, and there I was, like a schoolboy in a tuck shop, unable to do anything unwitnessed.

Local police whisked me out of the ground and off to the safety of the Lowry Hotel, and the deep-set self-contradiction of life is all too much. You see, I *walked without ease | On these | The very streets where I was raised* ... and now ... a protective police escort! I'd laugh if I knew how. The Lowry is the sharpest of Manchester's hotels, many of which I stood outside for hours awaiting a squinted glimpse of Marc Bolan or David Bowie. And now it's my turn. The bar is cleared as my private party is ushered in to take over. A security guard stands outside the door of my suite all through the night (and *then* people say you've gone slightly egotistical).

December 18th pulls me into Earls Court in London – sold out at over 17,000 – and so much for devious, truculent and unreliable. John Weeks, may you turn in your urn. The concert leaps concurrently with an impressive poster and billboard campaign for *You Are the Quarry*, which has already become my biggest-selling album worldwide. The Earls Court night becomes a live album, but I hemorrhage rage when I hear a final shop-bought copy and discover that all of my between-song yatter has been cut out. *'It was for your own good,'* says a sanctimonious Sanctuary voice with all the gentle understanding of a village vicar snipping roses. My stack is blown. Censored by one's own record label!

The tailspin continues as the LP version of the same album features a world record number of printing errors, with *'The world is full of crashing bores'* printed as *'The world is full of crashing boars'*. Cain cannot be raised any higher, and every silver lining has a cloud. There are so many stupid errors on the artwork that it appears to fall to obvious sabotage since no human could possibly be quite so blasé. The errors of the artwork for *You Are the Quarry* were also hard to live with: lyrics muddled about, words invented, the gatefold absent of a group shot thus leaving an enormous and silly space of yellow nothingness. Yet nothing could equal the shoddy clanger of *Your Arsenal,* which had *'Track 1 taken from the forthcoming album* Your Arsenal' printed on the label! The dabbling duffers who proof-read such errors should be hung in public squares. The censorious moral guardians of EMI Australia had refused (!) to allow my first solo album to be called *Viva Hate,* and had decided instead upon *Education in Reverse.* As a result, civilization enjoyed a new birth having been spared the blackness of Hades.

It was enough to have made van Gogh chop off *both* ears.

Life blurs, like newspaper print held too close to the eye. Jesse Tobias, our Mexican panther-like style-baron, is the slick and sleek key to our new presentation. The marriage is perfect. Departed guitarist Alain had curdled somewhat prior to *You Are the Quarry* when a legal letter arrived demanding that Alain's face appear on the cover artwork of the new – and every future – Morrissey album. Well, *no*. Life doesn't quite work like that, especially not in the land of logic. His lawyers also demanded that Alain be given the right to publish his own book detailing his life with Morrissey. It wasn't for me to bestow or forbid such rights, but the request certainly made me nervous. I didn't quite relish the thought of Alain with a notepad watching me as I slept.

By April 1st we return to Göteborg, where we have sold 6,000 tickets at the Scandinavium. It is also Jesse's birthday, and we all gather backstage to fumble through the usual blundering presentation of makeshift gifts. It is a moment when everyone is always stuck for words, for it requires truth, and who can tackle such a thing? How can we ever tell others how we feel about them, unless we are dying? Certainly, people are as equally incapable of face-to-face praise. There is a large birthday cake for Jesse but he won't sample it because he doesn't eat either eggs or cream.

The following night we play the Hovet in Stockholm. The 7,500 attendees are the usual mix of teenage jailbait and superior Smiths scholars – they who are always further back in the arena where their taskmaster duties of taking notes are untroubled by the schizoid scramble at the front of the stage. By the 7th we are in Malmö at the Baltiska Hallen, and the 3,500 within are even younger than before, appearing to me, now, as hip kids of early teens. What is going on? The half-pints and whiz kids open their mouths wider than necessary to sing *First of the gang to die*, a song which, now, is a call to invade and raid, and the crowd sways like crashing waves shouting at one another.

Tuesday April 11th is the day of yet another appearance at the fiercely royal l'Olympia in Paris. Leaving the hotel for the soundcheck I catch the glare of the very famous Eric Cantona frozen for an age-long few seconds as I emerge from the lift. In the mid-90s Cantona had been asked during an interview the very lazy *'So, what have you been up to lately?'* question, and he had replied, *'Listening to Morrissey.'* With my usual tact I had been quoted in *Time Out* magazine during more or less the same period, saying, *'I'm very fond of Eric Cantona as long as he doesn't say anything.'* On this day in Paris, Cantona has clearly measured both quotes, and although I offer him a rarely used smile, he doesn't want it and he turns away coldly, and I am nixed like a fatty at the church steps. Eric takes his place in the hotel restaurant for the catch of the day, which is evidently not me.

Jean Gabin is everywhere on the streets of Paris. Like all other foreigners I walk around gasping and gawping, and then I feel useless for not having been born here. It is always mid-morning in Paris, and the sun always does its best.

On the drive through Yorkshire I wonder what goes on in all the houses that I pass. The house is a world in itself. Imagining how others live leaves me lost in great questions. Who rattles around these Halifax houses, or these friendly rooms in Leeds full of books and CDs.

The Morrissey gangs outside the pubs that face the venues do not appear, to me at least, to be in battle with life. They take it as it is and enjoy it. At the Victoria Hall in Halifax I make an unfunny joke about Victoria Wood

Hall, halfway towards an unnecessary smile. At the turn of the 1980s Victoria Wood had entered the television realm singing *Northerners*, looking like someone with no advantages, hurt transformed into useful fantasies. This was her first series for Granada Television, and it presented life as seen from behind a tea-tray – full of Alan Bennett inscrutability, it is cabbage-soup humor of genius, but you can sense fat-person pain behind each scream of a joke. Wood sings the words *'Fog, smog | sitting on the bog | cobbles in the morning mist | Park Drive | dead at 45 | from a back-street abortionist'* and whilst it ought not to pay to have great fantasies about television comedians, I cannot ever forget these lines or how they were delivered because of the relief of hearing self-analysis born out of despair. Victoria Wood is now very much the deserved mighty dome of establishment, but in 1981, with her very first weekly TV series, she moved as if running out of time – the flattened heart with no more cards to play. Her sketches were easy to read, and they all told of not a snowball in hell's chance, with the dimmest view held by Wood for her own Manchester self – as if derision were surely all that she had coming. Born in the Prestwich area of Manchester, she did not betray herself with self-pity, but each written line revealed a lifetime of having been passed over or refused. Consequently, a Genet-type genius bubbles to the surface, and the girl who sang *'Pretend to be northern | just smile and act dense | pretend to be northern | it doesn't have to make sense'* changed British comedy for both men and women whilst accidentally also saving herself. As with Alan Bennett's students, people who studied Victoria Wood became funnier people in themselves. With the first airing of her mythic *As Seen on TV* the mountain finally came to Mohamed, and rightly so.

Thursday May 11th at Blackburn and I am heckled. I can't quite make out the complaint, but I have now found that people will do this if they think you might answer them. The heckler is impossible to overlook, but the words jumble themselves. *'Ignore him!'* shouts someone else from the crowd. I had just announced how prison sentences of twelve years had been bestowed on animal protectionists relating to the famous Huntington Farm case, and I spluttered out how the murder of a child would only land you with six years in prison. Just ice.

The following night at Liverpool's Philharmonic Hall I search for clefts in the rocks where I might hide so that none may track me. In other words, I am dogged with flu. It is a mournful experience to walk onstage knowing that much of your vocal range has gone, but much emphasis is placed on the power of the crowd and the sudden medicinal purification of being out there where sore throats are forgotten as hidden strengths are called on. Sometimes it works, and sometimes it just cannot.

'Oh, you'll be alright once you get out there – the roar of the greasepaint, the smell of the crowd ...' say those who remain safely backstage. Often local promoters will send their doctors to examine you to gauge whether or not you are bluffing (and why on earth you'd want to bluff such a pointless prank is beyond me), and the doctor will always give you a clean bill of health so that you have no easy route to cancel the night and claim on insurance. This has happened

to me many times, and I have faced an audience having no choice but to prove that my voice has, in fact, shattered, at which I am usually asked, *'Well, why did you go on?'* Legally, no choice. Ancient boos from long ago at Dundee's Caird Hall and Aberdeen's Capitol Theater when it all went wrong – these memories still sting many years on, because all you want to give is your very best even when you feel your very worst.

Two nights after Liverpool, I am crawling back to health at the London Palladium.

I think of Kirsty and daylight leaves the room and I sink to my lowest.

Istanbul hums from all of the scenes that you might expect. There are notably very few females on the street, all of which empty as evening prayer calls in the loud Holy Joes (men only) whose murmured prayers can be heard across the city's rooftops. The preachers preach and the sinners sin sincerely. Pelicans gather by the bay. At the city's oldest hammam we cleanse and purge, Brillo-padded to vanilla squeakiness, swabbed down on ancient tiles where the men of Istanbul launder themselves slowly and twice-over lightly, buffed in the buff. Twelve thousand gather for the Morrissey concert, and the promoter smiles to me. *'You are very big here. I just hear* Roy's keen *on the radio.'*

My smile crashes. *Roy's keen?* A bubble-headed choice.

The young of Istanbul chant the words back at me with clerical address. I had no idea. They urge me on, their arms outstretched in entreating petition. *Why didn't anybody tell me? I like it here, can I stay?* I am at my happiest, and I have the smarts as each song begins and screams of recognition run aground at the touch of each opening chord. How soon could I return?

Eighty-five thousand people stand before me at Roskilde on Friday June 30th. The crowd sing so loudly that I struggle to hear my own voice above theirs. Bright and happy faces appear brighter and happier as the sun falls and *Irish blood, English heart* is thundered word-for-word across what seems like twenty miles of bobbing heads. As always, I am detached, swamped in love, wondering how I could possibly repay it. Once again, all is well in Denmark:

> I've been dreaming of a time when
> The English are sick to death of Labour and Tories
> And spit upon the name Oliver Cromwell
> And denounce this 'royal' line who still salute him

Oh, whirlpool 'round my heart, this is what they call creative power – when thousands upon thousands sing your words back to you in order to let you know. Two hours later we drive through the night to France. At the festival, Bob Dylan stands side-stage as my best endeavors rip out across an impossibly youthful crowd. Dylan watches in his crumpled, cramped way. As I leave the Belfort Festival I am asked if I would like my photograph taken with Bob. I say *'Yes, of course.'* Minutes later comes a new announcement: *'I'm sorry, Bob said he doesn't want to do it'* and my pecker rises since I didn't make the request in the first place. A similar scenario would happen a few years later with Paul McCartney, when a knock comes to my dressing room and someone drenched in backstage stickers asks if I would be in a photograph with Paul, to which I say yes, only to be later told that *'Paul doesn't want to do it,'* and I said, *'Well, neither did I until I was invited.'*

By July we are in Hungary, where I am surprised that the venue is half-empty. I am told that the tickets are £85 sterling, which is far too high for undernourished Budapest. *'Even I wouldn't pay that,'* I say.

The following day I am walking by the hotel swimming pool when I trip up and fall sideways into the water like someone directed by Billy Wilder. I resurface and naturally there are three hundred people watching wordlessly with stern Hungarian glares. I smile at no one in particular as I struggle to clamber on land.

On July 6th Zagreb is cloaked in huge color posters of my huge face busy licking an ice cream as taken on the back streets of Rome. The posters are everywhere, and every wish fulfilled. The hotel staff line up to greet me as a visiting dignitary, and at last I smell the august solemnity of VIP grandeur. Management talks to me as if they have always known me – gravity and courtliness mixed with decorum. I am led to the presidential suite, and from my balcony overlooking the square I see a bag lady surrounded by her treasured tat, squatting beneath the shrubbery with legs outstretched on the park lawn, having endured a lifetime of dying. I gather all of the hotel bathroom luxuries and I empty the mini bar and I drop them all at her feet in yet another bag. She peeps into the bag and smiles a floodtide of smiles.

'You shouldn't have done that,' says a band member, *'she might be a recovering alcoholic and you've just plonked six bottles of whiskey at her feet.'*

'*Yes, well,*' I say, defiantly wrong.

Croatia briefly becomes my new Italy. A razzle-dazzle wedding takes place in the hotel courtyard and I watch it all from a safe distance – like Richard Dreyfus at the end of *Close Encounters of the Third Kind.* I wonder why they even bother with the ceremony. It seems like such a great deal of trouble for everyone, and merely because two people have found themselves sexually compatible – but with no suspicion that their feelings might change with time. Hidden behind a huge plant, I cannot imagine giving any more to life than I have already given. I can see through the human heart, and I know that life's biggest prize is to have the day before you as yours alone to do with as you wish.

By Friday we are in Serbia, sold out at 50,000, and my tired face shoots out from interplanetary screens as soft rains do nothing to halt audience fervor. Two days later I am calm in my beloved Finland, where my entire body sighs and a day of sun makes problems matter less. The Dolls are also on this bill at Turku, and I wonder if they will shuffle by to say hello. But of course they don't.

Turku gives me a whole life again, and my Scandinavian bonds bind tighter.

By Tuesday we are at the Montreux Festival in Switzerland, where I can't relax because my hair is far too long. The show is our best ever in the one country that had always said '*No*'. In its first week of sales, *Vauxhall and I* had sold twenty-six copies in Switzerland, and probably none in its second week. Switzerland had forever been the uncrackable nut, with no way in, which seemed unsporting considering our great success in all the countries that bordered it. However, there are many comrades at the Montreux Festival, but possibly all tourists. Round and round and back to Sweden, where two nights in Karlstad have sold out quickly. The band are edgy and my voice sounds tired, but glances and gestures from the crowd remind you that your time and your life could not be better spent. In Sweden, the front row gets younger and younger, whereas I unfairly get older and older.

In Oslo two days later I sit by myself in a city center park. It is mid-day and Oslo is a-jitter with all of the usual Thursday mid-day jitters. There is never enough time. It is always too soon. I reflect on how I have reached the unthinkable stage of forgetting which musicians have played on what. At the Oslo show there are 20,000 in attendance, and I begin by singing a few A-ha lines, which was probably greatly irritating to everyone. Dropping into icy Reykjavik for the first time, I gaze out of my hotel at a noiseless city where everything has the appearance of a vacant slab. I give a brave laugh because even the cladding and panel plywood layers are oddly attractive, even though I can't lay my eyes on a single soul. I have sold 5,500 tickets – which is a great surprise, so I try to take possession of my usual exhausted self and forge gusto, and yes, the night is an Icelandic wow. There I am, too, in the record shops in the center of town, surrounded by Iceland's very own vocal dreamers – so far from Manchester.

Austria gives off a seductive smell. I am backstage at the Salzburg festival, beginning to lose track of where I've been. It is August 17th, yet another Thursday in a calendar seemingly made up entirely of Thursdays. The 50,000 throng are singing back at me their sonorous birdsong, all impossibly small and young and sinewy, and smartly attired in their rock-star chic of chains and mock-vintage denim, and I wonder exactly when it was that everyone around me suddenly became younger than me instead of older. I know that you are there somewhere. Forget me completely.

Wafting across a sun-drenched crowd I once again swallow everyone up in the sheer fright of contemplation, managing to avoid the monotonously clichéd rock festival yatter. I am an older person. It is fitting. I am ready, now, to be swallowed up by Mexico, a country that has occupied my dreams for too long. The Guadalajara VEG Arena is stuffed with 6,000 yelpers, and I swim in a web of giver-receiver mania. *Mania!* The close of the set jumps to a chaos so calamitous and insane that the building appears to be falling apart, and I am pulled and pushed and pulled and pushed. Sapped, I run off, and the stage is a street-scene of rubble and naked life. Two days later at Mexico City's Palacio de los Deportes I have sold 12,000 tickets. *'You have sold twice as many as Oasis,'* the local promoter tells me, yet it is Oasis who are all over Mexican television, whereas I am – as ever – nowhere to be seen. Outside the venue t-shirts bearing Elvis Presley's face are sold with *Morrissey* printed across, or down the side, or somewhere. An army of villagers sit outside the venue making anything at all on which they can sew or print the name *Morrissey*, so that these wooden dolls and kitchen towels might sell as souvenirs. There are children's dolls, candles, bags of toxic candies – all bearing my name. It is yet another Thursday, and once the intro music has blasted its way, the audience advance a cavalry charge towards and upon the stage, everyone calling out and standing on one another's heads as tears mount upon tears amid fights and punches. I have no idea where everyone is going. It's as if flames were blocking the exit doors. The air hangs like Mexico '70, streamers and unbearable heat, then smoke rising and liberating howls and calls of approval as each song is instantly recognized. This is my physical outlet. I must be explaining something well because here, now, 12,000 people understand. Fascinatingly, they refuse to leave the venue once the show has ended, and swarms of armed police crash in to order everyone home.

At a television studio I stand before the crowd like a political reformer, and then I catch sight of myself in an enormous camera lens and I look fat. But if I hadn't noticed fatness I would have noticed something far worse. The critical eye never fails to find a flaw. What I am saying to people is: *This is why I adapt poorly to the outside world, and by the way, let me kiss you.*

At the beloved Chicago Aragon Ballroom, compressed kilos once passed between 1930s racketeers; George Raft, fresh from the honey wagon, each hand in each side pocket, legs astride, rattleboned and full of vinegar. Nothing's changed since then. The Ballroom reeks of brawl and that which Chicagorillas would once call 'nigger heaven' – northsiders' monkey business with southsiders, dirty grandeur ornately down in the mouth. The Aragon lights up the cattle town, and song and dance calls to every never-wuz, and the downwardly mobile *phffffft* here in The Loop. Of course, I have always loved the Aragon Ballroom, with its gangster slop of menaced glop. When I first played here many lifetimes ago, I sneaked a peek at the queue –

confrontationally all over the street, disrupting traffic, shouting back, unctuous and effusive, and there stood an army of male blond quiffs, tattooed arms and *Hatful of Hollow* t-shirts. Nothing, now, could hurt me. By contrast, the life of a politician looks hopeless.

Saturday November 25th in Athens, Greece, brings on the same power, yet the audience are a different set of dream bait longing to be eaten with a spoon; unsmiling Adonis after unsmiling Adonis pile into the hall, spruced up and sweet on the songs. Two days later in Thessaloniki the suave crowd seem to be almost exclusively male. The head-crushing roar dies away and I return to my cell. The next day a young woman is standing in the hotel lobby looking like Arletty gone terribly wrong, nerves leaving only a chopped chatter of words. She talks to me as if I am a priest. She touches my hand with abnormal gentleness, as if stroking alabaster. I leave it alone. I couldn't bear it if my heart were made off with.

By December the roll is all too much, and although I do not like arena shows I am here at Newcastle Arena – walking on as if newly hatched and freshly plucked, wondering where I will find the 'more' that I must give. I find it in the response.

There it is again, the following night at Nottingham Arena as 8,500 pairs of eyes burn into my greyness, the dying swan all over again – ah, this list of inner displacements. By Sunday I fall into clean sheets after an incomprehensibly insane show in Luxembourg. I shall never use the same between-song patter twice. A week later I am back in Berlin, lifted way too high to ever come back, my life spared once again by the love of an arena crowd, and further saved at the Color Line Arena in Hamburg on the following night, and *'I have been true to you, upon my guilty soul I have'* (Charles Dickens).

December 22nd and 23rd are Manchester nights, here at G-Mex, where I am greeted as the foot soldier that saved the Empire. Each second is wrapped in eternity, my loud comrades happy to the last sip. I go my way yet leave something behind, for these are the good old days.

The *NME* generously issues a CD called *Songs to Save Your Life*, which they graciously allow me to compile with some of my favorite recordings by other artists. As the CD goes into production the *NME* adds four tracks by newer groups who are *NME* favorites – mainly because all of the songs I have chosen date back to the Roaring Twenties. These last four would never be my choice, but the *NME* argues (not unreasonably) that by adding the newer bands the CD has modern currency against my Bronze Age tastes.

A postcard arrives at Sweetzer from Ron Mael. He thanks me for being *'such an inspiration'*, and such praise from Caesar makes me collapse in a heap. A lengthy handwritten letter arrives from Julian who sings with the band the Strokes. He is angry and apologetic at a recent *NME* interview in which he is quoted as calling me *'a faggot'*. Julian writes that no such comment was ever made, and nor would it ever be made, and that the writer had simply faked an entire paragraph.

> You cannot hope
> To bribe or twist,

Thank god! the
British journalist.
But, seeing what
The man will do
Unbribed, there's
No occasion to.

Humbert Wolfe (1886–1940)

A very small, flightless bird is now living in the back yard. I feed it constantly, and at night I place it on a blanket and fence it in using large boxes so that it has freedom to move about but can't be pounced on by predators. Whenever I handle the bird I use gardening gloves because I have noticed its parents watching from the roof and they will not accept the bird if it has had contact with human flesh. For days and days both parents call down to the bird – encouraging it to fly up and join them. But it can't. Twice they swoop down to feed their baby, causing it to skip and flutter in drunken excitement at their contact, but as they move away they are still urging the bird to follow, and it freezes in fright. This scenario continues for two weeks, and I won't go to bed unless I've made sure that the fledgling is secure. One morning it is gone, and I am distraught, pulling apart every bush and outdoor plant in search, when suddenly I look up to the roof and there is the bird *finally* positioned between both parents. Not everything ends horrifically.

Last night at the State Theater in New Brunswick I sang to save my life, and I am overfed with varnished love from

400

an audience of all ages and shapes and colors. New Jersey throws back a desperate generosity – returned by the singer. The singer sings to the dreamer, and the dreamer confirms unfolding pleasure. The following night we are at Lowell Memorial Hall, where 2,862 tickets were grabbed with witch-trial madness. Lowell is there – somewhere, under great mounds of snow, and privileged suburbia twinkles its decorative lights and moneyed upscale tush from wooden antiquarian homes of welcoming porches alive with signs of megabuck kids and chipped pets. Surely Gordon MacRae is ready to charge out from a handsome doorway all beaver-coated and beau-hunk, part lover boy part pretty boy with a song on his manly lips – bored on the fourth of July, and nothing to do but 'be' in order to win it all. I spy the delights of wealthy American safety, so drummed into the popular mind since the troubled waters of the corny cornball 1940s. The lie of American film entranced the world and made everyone expect a handsome ransom from life, on which the economic arrangements of the western world seemed to settle themselves for good – which is all very well if you are William Reynolds in *All That Heaven Allows*, but not quite so if you are carrying a large pot on your head in Somalia. Here, Lowell life imitates art. And very well! Lowell is, in fact, a *Has Anybody Seen My Gal?* university town of ballgames and sleepovers and star-spangled tripe. The old glory oozes and the downright neighborly are as righteously swell as home-cooking. I am, of course, seduced. Would they let me stay? Could I begin a life without pain? Could I cast aside this dark lantern? Would I be allowed into the buddy club? Could I become so sweet that I, too, dripped diabetes? The Memorial Hall is utterly and sensibly organized, and in my cozy dressing room I mentally race through all of tonight's lyrics – an unexpected echo in these American legion rooms. I step onto the stage and the heave forwards from the crowd is like a mudslide as hockey tonsils roar back at me. It is an avalanche of heavy petting, and what discreet Lowellians might refer to as 'night baseball'. Jesus, I am loved. Having never found love from one, I instead find it from thousands – at the same time, in the same room. The inquisitives want a closer look, and the well-meaning want to know what this strange man is about, whereas the outstretched front legion are flirting a face-rape pass at me. The touch of their hands to mine ignites electricity, and I wonder how on earth I had ever become anyone's idea of a hot number. In the midst of it all I am expected to behave – usually with sympathetic understanding and moral balance – yet I can't for the life of me think why I should. *Morrissey?* Wasn't that the sneeringly caustic way by which those crude St Mary's schoolteachers had called to me – each bark full of shitheel slander?

Yes, it was.

Torn down, put down and shot down, it survives the skinned-alive ethics of the working-class secondary modern and becomes a word loved instead. Oh Manchester, so much *you can't* answer for.

Tonight at Lowell a young woman is present backstage. She is flanked by police officers, is British, and had been working locally as a Nanny when a baby in her charge had died. She is an ongoing news topic throughout the world as she awaits trial. She is nonetheless escorted here tonight to hear *November spawned a monster* on this November night as speculators assess whether or not she is, or isn't, a monster. The world still loves a good hanging. By Monday 24th we wind over to rough Buffalo where, again, all 2,699 tickets have been snapped up. It is not a high figure for most artists, but to me it sounds extraordinary, since I am flatly denied big-league entry onto page-one America. *Never mind.* You see, I do not sing about chicks or screws or eight-track studettes, so I am left adrift, too complicated to be taken on. I walk onto the stage at Kleinhans Music Hall and I witlessly shout *'Hello, Paris!'* (since Buffalo and Paris could not be more sharply dissimilar, you see), and the next day a review in the local newspaper says, *'What a shame he forgot which city he was in.'* I bang my head on cold concrete with frustration. Can one attempt to be witty in Buffalo? Is it allowed?

As we leave, a girl pulls at me. *'I can't believe you're here ... I can't believe you came to Buffalo,'* and the ice wind blows both of our spectacles off.

In the daytime the wide city streets are north-star miserable with the homeless constantly on the march (where to? where from? what for?), and the rain falls harder on the dark-skinned folk.

December 1st steers us into Sweden, which always feels like a reward. We are finally released from the American highway with its unending stream of identikit fast-diarrhea diners with their deathly menus offering only murder or sugar – not food at all, and it isn't half-baked to accuse such 'fast food' outlets as being responsible for the deaths of millions of Americans. Now, here in Sweden, food resembles food – and even looks edible, although I would never give in to herring. Fish are not food. Driving along Göteborg's motorways we persistently see lighted signs directing traffic to *'Morrissey concert, next left'* or *'Morrissey concert, this way'*, as if I am finally a landmarked grave. It is chilling.

Snow-blind motorists meet traffic police who are also guiding everyone to the Morrissey concert, and now I know how the Pope must feel in his little fancy shopping-mobile. It is warming to be a part of Göteborg life, and my heart swells to think of teenagers fastidiously checking their appearance in bedroom mirrors in preparation for tonight and whatever it may bring for them. Touching, too, are the vast car parks, some full, some almost full, their owners already inside the venue waiting for me, in each car a refreshers cassette of *You Are the Quarry* or *Hatful of Hollow* lodged in the receiver. In Sweden I appear to be known everywhere, in tones of tender gestures. In Göteborg I indulge myself with the child-like pleasure of taking photographs. I quite possibly will never look at them. With each Swedish concert my love for the country deepens. The crowds are young and they shriek like airplanes streaking down. Their sensuality is strong, and there is a subtle uniqueness in our relationship, because it leans not on the gullibility of the pop audience, but on its intelligence. I am surprised that my life has turned out like this. Nothing but promise erupts from everywhere in Sweden, and the life-giving enthusiasm of the audience feeds me. From the stage I see faces I shall never forget, in a wobblyscope hand-held array of quite beautiful eyes and mouths, clicking along with camera-shutter speed. Life is only now. I begin to worry that my humility can be seen as a part of an act, but then, to edify my natural feelings is to then *become* an act. What do you do? There must be truth in all of it otherwise you are no different than a door-to-door sales-man. To never feel guilt when you look into the eyes of your audience. I will border on silliness – anything at all to avoid self-indulgence replacing the old hunger, for that is the route they all go, and can't help but go. Why is the crowd at Lisebergshallen so young? Why are they looking at me, when all I ever read about myself is one of intoler-able egocentricity and dramatized depression? Each city responds with the same rhythm, and Scandinavian success seems automatic in that there is no struggle. Is this the 'accidental' life? Is this the first time when all I need to do is accept? Over in Helsinki the snow is so heavy that the audience is draped in overcoats and scarves and hats even whilst inside the venue (for surely no cloakroom could accept thousands and thousands of horse blankets?). Of course, this is the famous Ice Halle, where rubber sheeting covers the rink as, above, everything vibrates to the trans-mutation of pop nights. Three thousand five hundred heart-shaped faces beam back at me, withholding nothing in their excitement.

But my body is changing once again, and I now look avuncular, and it can't be helped, and I can't measure the love they transmit as being to the sexual or to the paternal. Either way, it cannot matter, but it is a point nonetheless. See the crushed rows of Helsinki yupsters and nearly-shavers; sonny boy teenies and bubble-gum girl rockers. How do they find their way to me? The young fry and the twixt-teens shout my words up to the ceiling knowing that my own time at their age was spent behind a small door kept locked. Pride and pity hit the blender at the same moment, and the band sound ruthlessly loud, kicking each second forward and faster and forward and faster.

I never wanted to kill, I am not naturally evil
Such things I do, are just to make myself more attractive to you
... have I failed?

and this audience roar a *'Noooooooooooooooo!'* creating their own part in a song written long ago, in silence, in tangled solitude, with two broken legs. The loving nature of Finland matches Sweden. Each move deeper into the country answers hesitant prayers for love and acceptance. Finland bore the unusual distinction of a Smiths appearance many years ago, and my mind wrestles with the memory of that festival billing and of audience disinterest and of harshly blowing rain. I recall standing at the lip of the stage as if dragged from a river, the microphone slipping out of my wet hand, and no one around to caution how rain and electricity are deadly components to the overheated flesh. We played on and on in the whirring rain as the audience disappeared, yet we clung on as if trying to prove something, yet proving only absolute stupidity and a childish inability to make sensible decisions. All those tears ago. This thought returns to me on the night of the Ice Halle. Post-show, I stand in a spirited hot barrack-style shower for all of thirty minutes, stone flags beneath my feet, snow piled up against fortress windows. Outside, the twitter-twitter of high voices leaving the venue – always in the corner of my ear, the young blood excitement of satisfaction and of things that must be said. A voice sings in the snow. Naked, I walk across the hard floor and my mind stalls and I lie down on Helsinki hardwood, and I am mine.

The following day I cross the market square with snow wrapped around my knees. The cheap lights of the market stalls contrast amusingly with the rampaging snowfall, but nobody minds, everyone is happy, and the snow hides the dirt. A cluttered record shop piles up Eastern Bloc rock – artificial pop-poop, fish music, or Death Metal. In the midst of the shuffled jumble the only name I recognize is mine – a privileged placing for a hankering catalogue.

'*I luff you,*' says a girl with a rosebud mouth, and away she sludges.

For December 10th we have taken over Battersea Power Station in London. It is a beloved monument clinging to life and surrounded by bits of forgotten land that no one seems to know what to do with. There are bent lamp-posts on cobbled streets where this happy breed surely lived out their lowly lives. It's all about to fall, yet doesn't quite. The Power Station is the pride of south London and fills the heart with love, yet nobody knows more about it than that. All 6,000 tickets have sold, and the night is full of trenches tension and the call to arms. Again, the cheer that greets me as I walk onstage is so loud that my hearing distorts and I momentarily lose balance. The roar is male, the crowd a manful facet, and every lyric is chanted loudly as if by sloshed Tibetan monks. The audience mosh – which is very funny to watch from the apparent safety of the stage. It is a helter-skelter free-for-all of dangerous dives (where to?) and blindsided charges. Bodies vault an impossibly high barrier and lunge at the edge of the stage – howling as they land into the holy mess of the front row. Some heads are squashed. Some aren't. The security struggles in the mix, but all I see is one great caress. Were Smiths concerts ever as wild? *Sometimes.* Must it all be intellectualized? *Yes.*

I will later be down on my knees beside a little white table. The audience understand even if the critics refuse to, and much rather this way than the other way around. As I am driven away from Battersea Power Station the main road is a long chain of Moz-posse walking home, happy (it seems) with emotional involvement. It could be a football crowd if not for the mass of t-shirts bearing the Morrissey mug. As I watch and study, I am mirrored by a handsome legion of the tough and the flash, and with this vision all of my efforts succeed.

It was all for this. It stares me in the face. I need not be told because I can see it for myself. This magnificent stream of humanity represents the power of accomplishment, and fifteen minutes later I am dropped at the hotel. Alone in my room, I am bewildered, yet more purified than mournful.

Soon, the pretty town of Eugene, Oregon, as the Morrissey trucks roll in like Andy Warhol's *Pork*, out to whip the insane and forever mark the young. Lusty lives queue to get into the McDonald Theater on this August evening of brilliant light, with just a flicker of subtle oppression pansying around us. Stepping off the bus and heading in through the stage door – watch, and be careful, for they can tell everything about you from your eyes. Like many a Bible-belter before me I was sent here to Eugene – but not to raise the Good Book, but to finally get under the skin with the power of song. It is the song of the un-resolved heart, and is so disconnected with sorrow that the sorrow turns in on itself and becomes triumph. Save the last dance for me. Backstage, I drum my fingers through the lyrics, like a stage actor memorizing *Macbeth*. I am simply waiting my turn.

This old theater smells of new paint, and my dressing room has that quaint American touch of an old stove and leaden pipes. Who on earth sat constipated on this anti-quated lavatory in 1923 or 1931, making up their mind as they sat? And then rose to join the world in emotional decline once again. The grand theaters of American Music Hall are now simply famous graveyards for that generation of trophy dancers and trombone jugglers, with Sophie Tucker and Julian Eltinge solidly under the sod, their place taken by such as I. This drops me into the dubious bracket of entertainer, and I will readily agree with anyone who argues against this observation. Yet no politician receives the love that greets me in Oregon, no court judge could ever possibly know what it is like, and no gee-whiz journal-ist should dare to understand it. Nowhere are there more natural smiles than those of a welcoming audience. In response, my heart sings and breaks.

Drawing into Fresno on September 10th, darker even-ings close in. Outside the Rainbow Ballroom, Fresno is Hollywood and Vine condensed into a single image of gangs, gangs, gangs everywhere. Gangs watching other gangs, smartly prepared in fastidious attire – bare arms of black and red tattoos on hard-bitten storytellers; big boys with small girls. The homies walk and talk it, their chicks click and clink with accessories, and no language heard but Spanish slang. The streets flood with Morrissey. I do not know what to do with all of this happiness. *Viva Hate*

emblems; art-hound T's, tank tops and bags graffitied in
Morrissey-code. Most of all, every arm, every neck, every
hand mobbered with a Morrissey tattoo. Fresno! Fresno!
Fresno! Here is the light! And never go out! Shaven-headed
buddies and lazy dykes, and all around that taste of fantastic
danger. Peeping from side streets, the police hide –
watching this crowd to see if they can possibly make any
money from it by way of tickets and taggings – every arrest
a potential notch and a sexual thrill for the cop crotch.
Could I disembark at Fresno and join the good-looking
stud-muffins? No. I am as cut off from the crowd as I was
in 1973, stressed in Stretford.

Inside the Rainbow Ballroom the walls drip with sweat
and *hi! hey! yo! sup? how's by you?* Fresno is Morrissey Central
and the good buddies are out in their mainman force, each
posse and tribe bonded by their busting fresh flyboy look.
Yet chuchala-muchala is all, as amigo and little brother
hamma squeeze together. Why do you come here? I face
my race. I wonder how they found me. All Mexican mellow, yet ready to put the chill on. Here in Fresno I find
it – with wall-to-wall Chicanos and Chicanas as my syndicate. I walk onstage and the roar that greets me nearly kills
me – would Italian godfathers find better respect? For
once I have my family. The songs halt at times as fights
break out in the room, and smoke rises amongst the rings.
Hairpins scream and suddenly it's a risky business, but the
more the red flag waves the more the steam box sweats.
Snazzy and spiffy boys point to me, sticky hands squeeze
any part of me, and my bluff is called. Dare I take one on?
The fire-eater within me leaps out, and I belong nowhere
except over the line. Sex is advertised yet withheld – go

on, make my day. It is gritty prison-cell sex, and I am shaking with courage. Outside, much later, no one is going home. Fresno streets are blocked by the spunky and the nervy Moz-posse, turned out in black and white or expertly battered denim. There are no Caucasian faces – which is a remarkable answer to those dap snappy London music editors, each boxed up in Bow, who would have me hanged as racist for daring to sing about racism.

The new Morrissey audience is not white — not here, at least – and they are the frenzied flipside of the Smiths' pale woolgatherers. These new V-men will go to the wall, or the mat, heavy sluggers with fat lips. Do you get the audience that you deserve? I sincerely hope so. Did you see the slugfest out front? Did you see the scrappers in the foyer? Yes, and love them I do, with noble heart. They were alight, too, at El Paso, where we had played on September 2nd and 3rd. Every runaway and throwaway crammed inside as if waiting for a call to war. El Paso's heavy artillery of players and beefed-up drifters amongst the Juarez boy-chicks and the butch bitch diesel dykes. The rug-munchers rule, and I'd lay down my life for the lost boys of El Paso – the sad shootists and pack-a-rods.

Meanwhile, back in England, they still write *Heaven Knows He's Miserable Now* and call me an ex-Smith (for who would know me otherwise?). My new Latino hearts are lost on the know-alls, those self-appointed fusspots and the pernickety chickenshits. I smile at the thought of a Smiths reunion, for I've got everything now.

At Santa Barbara Bowl on Tuesday 5th I am told that Peter Noone is watching from side-stage. Peter is from Manchester and attended Stretford Road School near my iron pile slammer, St Wilfrid's. Peter, of course, sang for Herman's Hermits, and I had covered their *East west*, which had probably piqued his curiosity. On a television show a few weeks later, he proudly name-checks me and I blush for a fortnight.

'You must call your next album Steven,*'* says Manchester luvvie Tony Wilson, and I stare back at him – wondering if he had ever actually had a good idea in his life.

Wilson repeatedly turns up at Morrissey concerts and then automatically lambasts me in print or on radio almost as if he enjoys his hatreds more than he enjoys his joys. *'Let's face it,'* he says on Australian radio, *'Morrissey really IS a horrible person.'* Weeks later I am behind the wheel of my sky-blue Jag in Los Angeles, stalled at traffic lights. I spot whom I think to be Jerry Springer walking across the street in front of me (Miller Drive, should you care), but of course it is Urmston's answer to nothing, and Wilson bows his head towards me and offers a smile – as three-faced as ever he was.

Stephen Street appears on British television: '... *which is why Morrissey is big in America'* – and then he catches himself floundering with a compliment – *'well, in certain pockets of America.'*

God forbid that Stephen would grant me the full map, especially if certain pockets might exist that are resistant! Oh, Stephen, waddle yourself to Morrissey nights in Fresno or El Paso or Chicago and you'd quake yourself spitless. People will not let you move on if it means that your progress shoves them further into the past.

As the tour bus hums and clips its way through the Bakersfield night, I remembered how Alain would apply hair-gel
in preparation for bed. I had never come across such an
over-developed sense of vanity – funny though it was.

'Why do people always say Rome wasn't built in a day?' Alain
once asked me.

*'It's just a silly expression because, in fact, Rome WAS actually
built in just one day,'* I lied, straight-faced and honest-
toned.

'Reeeeeally?' Alain gasped – the child alive in his eyes.

'Yes,' I confirm, and I wobbled down to my end of the
bus.

Hush, now.

Merck has arranged for *Ringleader of the Tormentors* to be
recorded in Rome, the city of vaults. An ancient church in
a Parioli square just north of the city center will be our
squat for several months. Outside, in Piazza Euclide the
stylish youth of Rome stand about stylishly doing nothing
– their scooters parked irresponsibly as the hunting teens
tear into alcohol and pastries, and freedom is 80 per cent
of what life is. No doleful sights here, no slum mums
defined by their murky children. The young people of
Rome know precisely what delights await them because of
their choking beauty, and this because of their global position of sun and wind combined to shade their skin a
smooth and healthy hew. It is that tone, and the pink lips
and slender frames and the heritage of natural style that is
the Italian soul. It is all a question of beat, and the kids of
Rome do not look elsewhere because what they feel is
acted out, and never do they watch television since they

are too busy living out their own storylines. And this they are free to do since street crime in Rome is rare, and police presence is never a threat. It is the only city I have ever traveled to where the police appear to want to help, and where they have a certain confidence in their public charges. In Rome, people appear not to hate the police at all, whereas in Los Angeles you must prepare yourself for trouble from any emerging police car. In Rome, people will even smile at police officers as they walk past, whereas attempt to smile at an LAPD officer and you would be pinned to the ground in the city where everyone is guilty until proven guilty.

It is a glorious relief to be away from all of that now, here in Rome, where the harshest sound is laughter, and from which American authority could learn so much – if ever it would allow itself to be taught anything. Italians are blunt, but this is because they are relaxed, whereas in Los Angeles a sickbed politeness permeates all conversation – rendering it not conversation at all. The very proximity of people happily walking so close to one another in Rome is in itself a revelation to most Americans, who live their lives at yardage distance from one another lest a slight brush instigate court action. Yet America demands world-wide respect for being the country that got it right – on all matters, even though fear remains the central key in everything that it does.

The reclusive cardinal of Italian music is Ennio Morricone. Although historical and royal, he has agreed to conduct his orchestra on the track *Dear God, please help me.* This is unusual, since the maestro of maestros has refused

U2 and David Bowie, but somehow says yes to porky me. The grandeur engulfs us, and my heart is pushed to the point of collapse as I watch Ennio in studio action. I find myself wishing for tears that don't come. Oddly, I introduce Ennio to Tony Visconti, to whom Ennio gives one very quick up-and-down disdainful look, says nothing, and turns away. Tony is not troubled by this, whereas I would slit my own throat at the shock of such a rebuff.

Rome has been my city for several years, with all of its soft sorrows of browns and reds. I live for almost one year at the Hotel de Russie, guided by the olive-dark face of Gelato, whom I had met at Dublin Airport. Gelato is classically Italian in appearance, peeled off the Pasolini screen with studied sloppiness, the Florentine face knowing very well what people see in him to like. He runs a wine shop and teaches youth soccer, and he is younger than me – as all people now are. His motorbike takes us around Rome – too fast, of course, too precarious, of course – and the battered graffiti walls are a red mass of haunting melancholy. After Los Angeles, the chattering enthusiasm of Rome is simply incredible; millions of teens at ease in dreams in the eternal nocturnal city. Temples and tombs rub against Prada, columns and arches look down on Gucci, and everywhere there are shadowy marks of the dead because every single step of the way is a grave.

Gelato had gone too far for me to spit him out, and the obligatory appointments are made to see Appian Way houses that are up for sale. I am told that this is the first, or the oldest, road in the world. I am fully prepared to believe anything. Kneeling beggars remain in the city squares, while

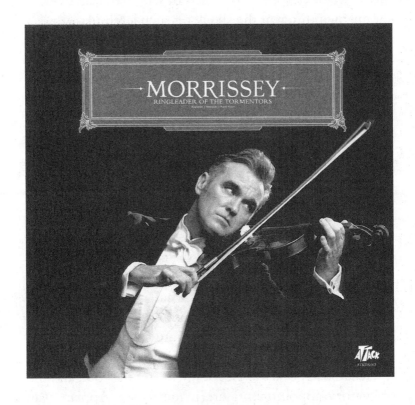

Left with whatever this journey had made me, Ringleader of the
Tormentors, *2006, chilling exposure with gains because of losses*

out here above the catacombs the fields are rife with cats, but the houses are mildewed in comparison to those of Los Angeles, and I am flooded with too much choice.

Alain's writing for *Ringleader of the Tormentors* had elegantly surpassed itself, with what would become *Life is a pigsty, I will see you in far-off places* and *The father who must be killed* defined for all time as the very best. Recording traffic noises for the song *The youngest was the most loved* we walk around late-night Piazza Euclide. A hardy shout comes from an open-top mini (which we later use on *At last I am born*), whilst Alain's impromptu *bop-a-bop-bom* loops itself into the opening confusion of the track. Tony Visconti shatters my gooey dreamland when he tells me, *'Mikey is actually a very average musician, you know.'* This is not true, and I won't be unsettled during such a picture-perfect session. Some debates are better left unvoiced.

I wake in the middle of the night and I have no idea where I am. Jesse is my main companion, of late-night walks and cellars full of wine, whereas my friendship with Alain had reached its natural term long ago. My nightly walks with Jesse would begin at the tip of Villa Borghese where Via Ulisse Aldrovandi lines up its glossy array of roadside prostitutes – mostly male, hard-bitten heroes fastidiously attired as sons of Eros. Their eyes are darts of desire, standing in the trees beyond, with legs wide apart. Every single night they are there, like a soccer team awaiting the club bus, and we are struck by how none of them are identifiably emasculated; they are just manly sons of mothers in search of others.

The blaze of the May sun falls on curtained doorways

and shuttered houses, and all of my questions paralyze action. Could I possibly, possibly just take it all as it is? The timeless chirp of distant children always seems to be somewhere, and on my daily walks I reflect on how my loneliness had cost enough. The sunniest pair of eyes are never mine. Only the grand completion of a recorded song allows my heart to laugh, and *Ringleader of the Tormentors* crowns a satisfying collection of songs, filling a final need in a lengthy search for perfection. But once you have said *Life is a pigsty*, where to go from there? Was it all the end of me?

One afternoon at the studio Tony shows me a film of a singer called Kristeen Young playing somewhere in New York. Everything about this singer is new. The solid fixity of her presentation is as striking as having a safe drop on your head from a tenth-floor window. She belongs to no other time or fad. Even her makeup is a mystery. The voice sails and then anchors at perfect pitch – ready to swallow up children and out-pace migrating herds. She is Maria Callas if not for the keyboard that she plays like a set of drums, talent as much a demand as a gift, and eyes lost in stark sadness. She does not plan to waste her life making tea for in-laws. A midwinter heart, her Julys are darker than her Decembers – carried away like a thing lost in the early stages of pregnancy. I am quite possibly in ... quite possibly in ... what's that compulsive, addictive, obsessive hairball mess thing called? ... um, yes, *love*. There, I've said it. Eternally caught in life's screen door, Kristeen will discard the dress and wear the hanger. Her voice soars to unimaginable heights – straining blood out of stray cats as it rises. This Pola Negri gives such a swirling chase of emotion to each song that I feel I am witnessing the mutual understanding of struggle. Be this, or die – cannon fodder for art, tears with accuracy. Whenever she speaks, I do not want to miss a single word. Weren't we made to be this way? Kristeen and I become great friends, and my life would have been emptier for not knowing her.

Mikey Farrell is an outstanding addition on keyboards – an infallible guide of new sounds and dry wit, of midwestern hardiness and team squad yardage. Interestingly, a vast knowledge of show tunes and an ability to play almost anything ten seconds after first hearing it. His opening words to me were, *'I'm a poor man's Roger Manning,'* in his shaggy-hangdog look that would soon sharpen itself into stylish *Pepe le Moko* aspect.

'My wife saw you at the Roxy when the Smiths first played in LA,' he went on.

'Oh, that must've been an interesting night since we'd never played the Roxy.' God forbid I just leave things as they are. From Cleveland, Mikey is of Irish grandparents and is stubbornly competitive, which I enjoy since it usually works to my favor. Proof of something is the sun-drenched day when we all play football at Hyde Park in London, and once I've scored the first goal I close down the match since *'it seems obvious where this is going.'* Mikey fumes since his chance to wrestle me into unconsciousness is thwarted.

ME: *Do you know what you haven't got?*
MIKEY: *A personality?*
ME: *Well, besides that. You don't actually have piano fingers.*

It is a noisy gathering at Pizza Express on Parkway in Camden.

MIKEY: The Queen is Dead *had a big influence on me in high school.*
ME: *A bad one, I trust?*
MIKEY: *Of course.*

I smell a new world of music with Mikey, but I also realize that he's the type who would jump ship should the royal wave come from Barbara Strident. If I was anything at all, I was sewage disposal. The mouth speaks first, and then thirty seconds later the brain catches up with whatever it is I've just said.

Whilst recording in Rome I meet Elton John, who is shockingly down-to-earth and gives me high praise for *You Are the Quarry.* He tells me how he loved the New York Dolls and Jobriath, but how he considered Bowie to be '*a vampire*'. A pleasant evening passes under a Rome sun which – even into late evening – seems not to go away.

2006 sweetens with the news that *Ringleader of the Tormentors* has entered the UK chart at number 1, which is my third number 1 in three different decades (and *still* Alain Whyte says nothing). Jed Weitzman and I dance around a Hamburg hotel room like childish imps once Jennifer Ivory had delivered the news. Jennifer, of course, remains of Griselda composure whereas I beg forgiveness for my insane happiness. Jennifer held the Sanctuary branding iron and had cut her industry teeth quite quickly once her native Lost Angeles had been abandoned for the drainpipes and black cabs of London's asphalt and the whateveritwas of Belsize Park. It was Jennifer's idea to issue *I have forgiven Jesus* as a single during the Christmas period, and although I laughed at the bleak absurdity of such a move, it proved to be a great success. *'But you can't expect radio to play it,'* Jennifer finger-wagged, *'even cutting-edge radio finds you too cutting-edge for their playlist.'* Although the record had reached number 10, there would be no *Top of the Pops* invitation, even though records that had yet to be released were included in the show as I lay languishing and neglected at 10, like a discarded lodging-house towel. What is everybody so afraid of? From *Ringleader of the Tormentors*, the lead single *You have killed me* had already bounced in at number 3, and these victories have so much meaning in the face of the now standard zero airplay and the usual knife-wielding reviews. Buying a Morrissey disc remains a political gesture, but the strain shows on the follow-up single *The youngest was the most loved*, which has a mid-week position of number 1, yet finally lodges in at number 14. A third single *In the future when all's well* rattles in at 17, and fourth single *I just want to see the boy happy* clips in at 16, but still, radio DJs in England will not play these songs, and the consternation is quite incredible, as if you just haven't earned it yet, baby.

But the final sting of 2007 is an interview with the ever-lurking *NME*. In fact, the interview is very pleasant, as the writer is very sensitive and courteous. The day after the interview he contacts my manager with sincere thanks, and he respectfully asks for tickets for the upcoming New York shows. The latest *NME* editor then offers me a special *NME* Award with the industry whisper that he is determined to get Morrissey and Marr in the same room together at an *NME* function. I politely decline the award because the glitzy grandiloquence of the prize system tends to present itself as the ultimate reason why artists do whatever it is they do, and once you've seen a thousand lightweight mediocrities flouncing offstage clutching their Brit Awards, you see the silliness of it all. I refuse the *NME* award, and then suddenly the editor elects to write the interview piece himself, booting his journalist sideways.

The piece emerges as the most offensively malodorous attack, reviving the *NME*'s groundless racist accusation, but the editor gives the story teeth by switching the wording of my replies, and by inventing questions that were never asked. It is catastrophically controversial.

The writer who conducted the interview fires very stressed emails to my manager explaining how *'this piece has nothing to do with me,'* and *'it has been taken out of my hands,'* and *'I just don't understand that magazine anymore,'* added to his *'Morrissey was so charming during the interview.'* However, the editor is stung. When I realize I have no choice but to legally challenge the *NME*, its editor tactlessly writes to the Love Music Hate Racism headquarters in London, and he warns them, *'If you support Morrissey in this dispute you can forget about any support from the* NME.*'* It is a fascinating explosion of frantic egotism. However, I fight the *NME* for over four years (quite naturally, even though all could have been resolved within one afternoon since the original interview recording was freely available to both legal teams). For me, there seemed to be nothing to debate, since we could all listen to the original interview – which began and ended on affably good-natured terms – and then we could read the final printed piece, the editor's damning fantasy bearing no relation whatsoever to the truth of the meeting. It was a stitch-up so severe, with the editor's misdeed so manifestly grave, that a court loss could kill off the *NME* for good, since its fortunes had slumped.

In the event, the *NME* ultimately apologized for the piece, although it would cost me several hundred thousand pounds for them to say what they could have said four years previously. I was satisfied with the apology, and I had never sought damages. *I've been stabbed in the back | so many, many times | I don't have any skin | but that's just the way it goes.*

Up here in Spokane on May 6th we are in bear-baiting country, which grants me dutiful attack. I suggest we hunt the hunters, and the crowd roar approval. By Friday we are in Omaha, America's bosom, city of sawdust and mockingbird houses. Daytime streets are dry and wide and always empty, but the audience at the Orpheum belies Nebraska's poverty of spirit as parents hold their small children up to the stage to be kissed or hugged by a baffled singer. The art of song lights the touch-paper in a way that nothing else can. The audience is confused, though, when I sing David Bowie's *Drive-in Saturday*, because evidently they don't know what it is. It is the only moment when I lose the crowd. By Wednesday I put on my little suit and sing to the Indianapolis joyous. The Murat Theater, once again, seems full of parents with their small children. The kids wear homemade Morrissey t-shirts and are so deep within the gnashing jaws of the front rows that my concern distracts me. Children effect a dramatic passionate mimic at my every move – so solemn and heavenwards, yet unborn even at the time of *Southpaw Grammar* – they go the way of their parents. There is so much meaning to success in Indianapolis or Nebraska because they are the parts of middle America where most fear to tread. If you can make it here, you'll make it anywhere. The Kansas City

Uptown Theater the following Wednesday is over-stuffed at 2,200, and everyone lets go with so much love that nothing I could say or do could fail to hit the right tone. On Saturday in Austin 5,000 witness such an appalling sound-system that I croak and twinge myself into further despair. A woodland setting, my agitation becomes tiresome and the night fails everyone. The audience are for the most part a robust and forgiving bunch of crunchies; crested hens with their daisies in army black, it is an exciting and perfect swarm of double-barreled broads. The sound at San Diego a week later is so abysmal that I give up halfway through the set – because there really is no point. We have sold 10,000 tickets but there is nothing I can do. Everyone looks to me for bravery, but at this open-air bayside concert the winds are so strong that the sound blows west as we direct our efforts south. It is unbearable and very embarrassing.

At Riverside Auditorium three days later Jesus is in his heaven and all is restored. A sky-scraping image of my face drapes the front of the building, and what good is it all without love?

'*Why, after all these years, are you so surprised?*' asks Mikey, '*why do you still question the love?*' I wave the question away, the heart stuck in an ice-cold morning of 1970. I am impossible. Inside the hall it is Osmondmania, but thankfully with the wasted corpse of Morrissey in place of the oily Osmonds. The madness makes local television news, with a reporter's shrug that is so familiar to me now for it tells us what is happening with a look and a tone that suggests it ought not to happen, as if vibrations of Satan follow wherever I go.

By Friday we play the Hollywood Bowl, and Mikey presents a personal guest list long enough to encircle the city, and I reject it since the eye-crossing cost of it is ultimately subtracted from my pension fund. Mikey sulks at the rejection and this creates backstage tension. Filmed as we walk on, we all look uncharacteristically unhappy. Mikey and I will not look at each other, and consequently the concert lacks form, although new-found drummer Matt Walker magnificently takes us all to a new standard, and this disciplined ship is suddenly the best military band in America.

'*I always wanted to live in Bakersfield,*' says Boz as we pull into a pile of dust.

'*But there's nothing here,*' says Jesse.

'*Precisely,*' says Boz.

A 2,800 sell-out in hazy *Hud* country brings on a clatter of audience scraps, but I am not at all concerned, and in fact I find it to be quite funny. If people want to fight, then let them. Who's to say they shouldn't? I'm not St Francis of Assisi. By the 25th we are in New York at the ice-cold chamber of David Letterman's television set. David always has the studio at Icelandic temperatures because he apparently sweats a great deal. Fish-eyed, we endure. The shuddering genius of Kristeen Young is with us to alarm David with her spirit-of-the-sea backing vocals, plus a few mid-ocean arm movements as we play *That's how people grow up*. Kristeen wears her self-made 'bubble' dress that is a sirenesque bubble-wrap of *Star Trek* in collision with *The Jetsons*. Kristeen is miffed when the same creation appears on Lady Gaga two years later.

In Birmingham, Alabama, I rush myself to a dentist for

the first time in 20 years. I insist upon codeine mixed with heroin and gin in order to settle my nerves, but this simple request is denied. The molar masher is a delightful woman who cures my fear of dental bashers, and my childhood memories of being savaged at a Stretford Road Clinic by a Third Reich dogcatcher had set off an endless mental bleep, and only now, in Birmingham, Alabama, did gentle kindness show me how. I would never again fear dentistry, and my visit makes the front page of the local newspapers the next day. How very odd. If only those hawks at Stretford Road Clinic knew – but surely they are all toast by now?

I walk onstage at Chastain Park in Atlanta and I am confused by the audience. In fact, I do not know who or what or where I am. The audience appears to be all families sitting at tables, ploughing into their homemade hampers of Jesus knows what. Evidently this is what happens at Chastain Park – everyone brings their lunch of skyscraper wedges with a sprinkle of rabbit neck and eagle shit. What a very strange sight it all is. I can't help wondering how much sow belly gets crunched each time I launch into another crowd-killer. Why am I here? 'Well,' manager Merck tells me, 'it's the salt pork American underbelly, and if you can crack it here then ... you've cracked it.'

Cracked what? The chili-dog fraternity? The po-boy submarine grinders' club? Get me out! I launch a box of Cheez-Its into the audience shouting, 'You've brought your lunch – here's mine,' which, as ever, just wasn't funny.

By September 20th we are in Tijuana, minus our marbles. The show is nuthouse insane, with plaster peeling onto the heads of a joy-popping crowd. Leaving the venue, we are driven by a local driver for a four-minute skip over the US border. Twenty minutes later we are on a darkened highway, and it naturally falls to me to speak up.

'The border was four minutes away, why are we still driving twenty minutes later?'

Sitting next to me, the tour manager says softly, *'Yes, I've noticed that.'* My personal security (who is from El Salvador) sits up front next to the driver and begins to tough it out, demanding an explanation. The driver shrugs and is sweating badly. He makes a sudden and dramatic swerve from the freeway exit and continues into highland darkness.

'STOP THIS CAR!' I shout, and bang my fists on the back of the driver's seat. My security orders a stop, and I jump out as the car drives on. Kidnapping in Mexico is almost an expected eventuality for anyone crossing the border with an entertainer's visa. Insignificant as I am, tonight's snatch was I, organized by those who obviously didn't realize that my market value wouldn't raise enough money to feed a family of five rug-rats. I sit on the ground in the dark, a disused gas station tipping over behind me. As far as the eye can squint, there is nothing.

'You realize that was a kidnapping attempt?' I say, looking up at my tour manager.

'Yes, that's what I thought,' he says as if ordering a Spanish omelette.

I hold my head in my hands, shrouded in darkness and miles from the nearest asylum. Two hours later we finally reach our destination – which had originally been four minutes away. All heads hang. All questions unanswered. Who was the driver? No one knows. Where were we going? No one knows.

Barely alive, we make it to Waukegan for October 17th.

The Genesee Theater is lit up like a giant roller-coaster, and someone remarks on a slayer serial-killer who had made Waukegan famous, and I am surprised there is only one. By Wednesday we are in Royal Oak at the Music Theater, and once again the crowd is hyper-charged. How exactly I came to represent a goulash of hardball punk force is a mystery, but Royal Oak plays out a gutsy night of bone-crushing peppiness. The following night in Merrillville at the Star Plaza is a Saturday atmosphere gathering the biggest frogs in the pond. The husky and hefty give whatever it takes, and again, as I pull away from the venue, Merrillville streets rain down Morrissey t-shirts and America IS the world, after all.

In January, six nights at the Roundhouse in London are attempted, but stuck in the stuckness of insufferable winter, my voice has gone as everyone around me coughs and splutters with a hot flash of the chills. In the midst of it all, I am expected to remain immune. Four songs in and I am dead meat. Done for, I walk off, and a harum-scarum crowd fast burn into a conniption fit. Who can calm them down? From the audience, up jump dapper television faces Jonathan Ross, Russell Brand and David Walliams, each so certain that slick Wood Lane telly-patter would extinguish the madly nettled crowd. It did not work. With gears grinding, the audience turns on Jonathan and Russell like hounds at a foxhunt, and each wondered how or if they'd get offstage alive. Russell's tap-dancing chatter stiffed with gasbag finesse, whilst Jonathan's gassy gobbledegook boomeranged back in his face. He would later tell me that he had never faced such a hard-shelled audience – to which, of course, my chest swells with pride. The intervention of

Jonathan, Russell and David touched me greatly and told me that I had friends. They saw a bad situation and tried to make it better. I am indebted. But it didn't work.

Tellingly, this kill-crazy flare-up that gathered Jonathan Ross, Russell Brand and David Walliams (three of the biggest names in British entertainment) onto a London stage in order to calm an audience ruckus, gathers no media attention whatsoever, and the Morrissey embargo rolls on. Had it been any other pop artist, the newspapers would blast their blast with excitable dribble. But what is the point of running a Morrissey story if neither HEAVEN KNOWS HE'S MISERABLE NOW or BIGMOUTH STRIKES AGAIN have any relevance as headlines? There could never be such a story.

June flames with an appearance at Dublin's Museum of Art. When a Dublin audience is in the right mood, anti-ballistic missiles can't stop them.

By July 4th we headline at Hyde Park on a Friday of 25,000 strong. The actor Lior Ashkenazi flies over from Israel just to see the concert. Standing next to him backstage, it is difficult for me to shine, for some people are too in-spot to be matched, and Lior is such a person. Chrissie Hynde is there, achingly funny in great flux. I need only catch sight of her in the distance and the great knot of my heart is untied. Irony is Chrissie's pattern, and though the word is rarely understood in its proper context, Chrissie manages to take people in so that she might ambush them with the truth. It is a play of the mind, or jeu d'esprit. She would pose nude on a ladder if it meant assisting the cause of animal rights – a hero in the modern sense, but not in the forgotten origin of the word (which, oddly, denotes neither virtue nor honor). Chrissie has been thrown in jails the world over for attempting to rescue animals from torture labs, but her unshakable conviction garnishes no humanitarian awards, and she stands her ground unappreciated with the grammarians of modern rock.

Arriving in Madrid I am cornered by Siouxsie, who is tonight's opener. She wants to know why she has been dropped from next week's bill in Tel Aviv. Being Siouxsie, she is ready to wrestle me to the ground and jab my eyes out for use as vestibule knickknacks. She had been listed as third on the bill to myself and the New York Dolls, but had been removed at the last minute because *'she won't stay in that hotel.'* What hotel, I have no idea, but I am told that she has pulled out and that the local promoter has filled her slot with someone unlikely to convulse. Siouxsie is on the warpath (well, *what else*), catsuit all a-wrinkle, having been booted off. I, too, am enraged since the third on the bill is now someone I've never heard of and who is, in the event, a roadhouse atrocity, yet who announces to the world that they were lovingly hand-picked 'by Morrissey' – I being forever the funmaking funster. *Oh, dear God.* Obviously someone paid cash to get this thumbs-down moose onto the Tel Aviv bill, and the story about Siouxsie refusing to come along unless her catsuit had its own en-suite was absolute tosh. The Tel Aviv day is further exacerbated when the old Dolls fail to turn up for their soundcheck. In fact, no one knows where they are, or if they'll even arrive. With minutes to go, they stumble in, ready to flash groove Israel.

There isn't a word of apology or explanation to the production crew, and once the Dolls are finished they dribble their way out of the venue as if this were 1973's Club 82. The Dolls were often said to have stonewalled their own career with a runaround attitude, and I had never believed such trash until this day in Tel Aviv. We all do our best to piece together a professionally buffed program, but the Dolls fell in and fell out like careless Great Kills itinerants.

My hotel balcony overlooks a beach, where most of the young crowd are naked but for the thinnest strips of soft flannel. They would like everyone to see – and to enjoy – whatever it is they have, and they would like to see you seeing them. Further along the beach a woman sitting with her three children is shot dead by a passing gang of young funsters, and the incident is reported with casual horror on television, but is not the lead news story. Towards the end of the day I sit fully clothed at the rooftop pool and I am submerged in an oh so familiar sadness.

Bahrain has been rebuilt in the center of Brussels, by people who moved in but didn't care too much for what they saw. The change from my first trip to Brussels some twenty-eight years ago is ungraspable. Our Saturday night show has 4,000 Belgians jumping sideways with apparent pleasure, and I am embarrassed by my own happiness. No dreamy reality could ever equal my first ever concert in São Paulo in Brazil, when the crowd lifted a girl over their heads towards me, and as she came closer I could see that she held a white stick, and closer still I could see that she was blind, and as the crowd placed her gently on the stage she handed me a note which read, *'I cannot see you, but I love you.'*

I am always in Berlin, and here, yet again, at the Tempodrom. I circle estate agents looking for a loft overlooking life, but I'm always distracted by onward travel. By Monday we are sitting in the bar of the Four Seasons Hotel in Dublin, where winsome Damien Dempsey is singing his Margaret Barry songs loudly, dispensing relief and joy to all except the duty manager – who tells him to shut up. He of sweet heart continues, and we inch our chairs closer into a tight circle. The duty manager's shoulders sag, but Damien captivates and enchants with all the love of one blessed and unselfish. I see myself crying at his funeral, missing him already. The road has no end and suddenly I stand bristling with romance (or, as good as I can muster) at the Pomona Fox in California, as the *iloveYouiloveYouiloveYou* audience rushes the stage ... Smiths re-formation? *What for?*

There is a loud boom in the hall as everyone stamps their feet, and firecrackered air fires up. The following night at San Diego's Symphony Hall is all too suspiciously perfect; love exchanged, do or die, and I pray words of thanks. Such nights are in place of whatever is absent, and whatever is absent would not mean as much. Our car tears through red traffic lights for fear of being clambered upon by those who must. Let me live before I die. By Wednesday we are on the George Lopez television show in Burbank.

'*You know Morrissey's here when you can't get into your own dressing room,*' he announces on air (and this is not because I am inside pulling at the door handle). I feel fat and ugly, but I pipe my way through *Don't make fun of Daddy's voice,* of the lost canon, an A-side hit in a drawn-out dream. The audience stand up, step up, scream forwards and start to mount the stage as blocked cameras withdraw like Daleks. Very young kissin' cousins touch the tips of my fingers, and they look at the touch, and shirttail kin move in, Echo Park homefolks, all Silver Lake blood. I am off-key, but I do my best. The band bites each line a knockout blow, and a loud audience roar concludes great television.

My Moz Angeles love affair is back on, Roman Spring it may be, your place or mine, but the following night at the Gibson Amphitheater is a black cloud of unworkable noise, and the word 'sabotage' jumps from conversation to conversation, as if someone may have been down in the basement disconnecting wires. In the city of Handsoff, no one is safe. *'You don't cross Handsoff,'* says one too fearful to cross a road. Oh, Handsoff! An empire built on spurious triumph! Whose knaves and cohorts spend their entire lives under tables and know as much about the sound of music as I know about black kids on the needle at the mouth of the Amazon.

Steel takes us up to Ventura for a dark December night's conclusion to a great touring ycar. The Ventura streets sway away with Morrissey tribes crossing at the lights (*this once was me, but now I'm a*), loading up at liquor stores – and what it must be to be 17 and leading the right life in the right skin. Always behind glass, I peer out, mental photography of the Morrissey subterraneans seeping out along Ventura streets; a laughing Pete Duel in a *Ringleader* t-shirt, a Kristeen Young lookunlike waiting for her best friend whom she cannot stand; a James Brolin from *Marcus Welby* full of healthy aggression in a *Smiths is dead* t-shirt, and all the lazy dykes commandeering the corner in a universe that denies their existence. The hall drips blood, full hearts sing, the humble guest kneels, the last night of the fair, and I thank our beloved crew, and one day goodbye will be farewell.

Peter Wyngarde writes:

> *It's becoming the Mad Hatters Tea Party for me … just phoned the number Samantha gave me [he means Sarah Yeoman, my PA] which I took down wrongly and got a complete stranger's voice! As I'd scribbled the number down during cooking I'd obviously …. Apologies, but as Vivien [Leigh] says in GWTW 'ca ira mieux demain'. Wondering if the mental dept would consider seeing me as soon as possible, before it's too late ….*

Peter is still living in Kensington, in the flat he shared for many years with Alan Bates. It's an Edwardian warren of clerical ferocity – a tornado of books and papers and swelling pyramids of typescripts, half-finished, half-begun. His voice is still of great clarity and sound, his eyes unchanged since that period known as his prime. But he is no longer on stage or television. Film generally tells us that people of Peter's age don't actually exist, or, if they do, they are hopelessly infirm and in the way of the main storyline. He sits before me as one who knew his duty and did it, beyond all praise, alive in the cinema of the mind. He takes the bus down Kensington High Street and jumps off at the Albert Hall, where I have loaded my latest machine-gun. After the concert he comes backstage, all a-buzz, genuinely excited. It is a relief to receive praise from someone who has a true perspective on all things, and who is not easily fooled – if ever fooled at all. Someone, also, who has downplayed accessibility. Out in the hallway people nervously approach him to ask questions.

'*I am sorry,*' he cuts across them, '*if I don't answer you, but I'm hard of hearing,*' which isn't true, but is the perfect way of telling people to get knotted, especially as the whispers of '*It's Jason King*' ripple loudly. Peter Wyngarde is what the world now calls 'the real thing' which, let's assume, means serious artist. He adapts to different listeners, and the magnified popularity of his most famous television role was never his goal. His favorite actor is Jean Gabin, and Peter's genius is such that all of his actions work on two levels. Jason King complexly became one of the most well-known names on worldwide television, but the meanness that England always shows to its home-grown talent was the reason why Peter gave up and left for Vienna, where he opened his own acting school. Invariably in search of ghosts, he came back, and he found Kensington still very much as it always had been, with Edwardes Square maintaining its true self in the new world of noise, noise, noise – computer noise, cell phones, pings of ringtones, alarm apathy, and the new mad craze for constant house renovation. The city moves on without you, and nostalgia becomes a problem, and the number of days spent in solitude and stillness suddenly increases tenfold and you realize that day after day you are actually beginning to barricade yourself in. You have lived long enough to finally be able to say that you have survived, but at the foot of the stairs to be climbed to bed, no one meets you. And if your heart should stop? It is only today in which we live – it is not as if we can live today and tomorrow as one. Finally aware of ourselves as forever being in opposition, the solution to all

predicaments is the goodness of privacy in a warm room
with books. I only know of life in the non-human world,
which never clashes with genial kindness. Fame can demand
upon you a sudden wish to get along unseen, after those
riddled years of wanting nothing at all but to be heard. It
is important not to make matters of business the final
word, and although eccentricity is now permissible – since
your art has paid its dues in the swamps of self-torment
and the scars of failures, even your mis-steps can suddenly
seem honorable. You are, in any case, disqualified from
what is known as 'normal' society (that is the society in
which none qualify as being 'normal' since 'normal' doesn't
actually exist) because you don't fit into anyone's drab
philosophy. You have cast yourself in the starring role of
an unfilmed *despised-while-living-acclaimed-when-dead* standard
melodrama, and you are only inclined to discuss the rumors
about yourself that you most like to have circulated. This
is considered egotistical to anyone of famous platform, yet
not to window cleaners and anonymous citizens to whom
it also applies in precisely the same measure.

On the issue of unqualified madness, I had been called
upon to visit the writer/diverter Julie Burchill at her mansion flat near Russell Square. The area had shrunk back
from its glory years as an imaginative space once warmed
by queues of prostitutes (and the word 'prostitute' does
not automatically mean 'female'). As bombs burst over-
head during World War 2, Russell Square registered its
value with explosive bursts of men and women who
wanted to buy or sell sex – and immediately. The spirit
under fire is no cause to forget the flesh. Now, in the age

436

of meaninglessness, the conversational tone of Julie Burchill soaks through these walls in an awakened state. She is both master and servant to all of her life's pleasures, yet she only evolves by confrontation. I knew of her, naturally, when I, too, was crying at the foot of the stairs, and her early writings for the *New Musical Express* (which is not at all the same thing as the *NME*) were always a performance worth catching even if her chosen subject held no interest to you. Her personality indicated unleashed enslavement, and she was always unhappy about something – which suited me very well. Like all bullies, she had never thought much of herself, and instead of changing the inner self she decided to complain to anyone who would sit still long enough to listen. It worked. Now, twenty-five years on, I sit before her, and I, now, am today's crab sandwich. Julie Burchill is, of course, not loveable, and has pitifully late-middle-aged legs, but her aim is to show the way for the rest of us, and this she does – biddy disease or no biddy disease. No Kit-kat cuddles ever take place in this flat that has a touch of Beryl Reid as loose-covers fall off armchairs, and a kitchen that bomb-disposal experts would refuse to enter. You see, she is a busy modern writer, so you can't expect less than eight chips around the rim of the British Rail mug that she hands to you as great slops of muddy black tea professionally spill into your groin. There is, quite naturally, no chance of a Rich Tea biscuit, so don't bother asking. When her questions fire, her head goes right back – as if she is squinting to read something that she once wrote on the ceiling, and we are asked to have confidence as we await a jolt of literary lightning. Her naked self probably kills off marine plankton in the North Sea. God stopped her body from being right. Unchained from the cellar, Burchill will make sure that you remember her. She leaves the room mid-flow, and I look around at the Loch Ness mess that could be thought to be the home of someone who couldn't walk properly. In fact, *it is*. Sweeping back in like a bundle of smells, Burchill has thought of another question, so here it is. She dresses like a spiritual advisor, one ready to accuse *'thou liest!'* should a need for truth be called upon.

It's the unfortunate period where the whale-bearing hips throw the woman out of shape and the only sensible diet involves barbed wire interlaced prosaically from top lip to lower lip. I imagine she crawls out onto the scaffold outside the living room window in order to sleep at night. She speaks as if her role on earth is to be God's mouth, and since she would now never be seen in a music venue, all of that life now relies on the lap of memory.

I ask her why she wrote 'Patti Doesn't Wash Here Any More', a dreadful executioner's piece on Patti Smith in 1979 when, after all, Patti Smith alone had saved Burchill from becoming under-manager's assistant at World of Leather in the Bristol of 1975. The old goat squirms in her seat (and *on* it, too), as if we aren't allowed to ask, as if one isn't allowed to know, as if writing is one thing but flesh-to-flesh debate is quite another, and never the strain shall meet. I tell her that Patti Smith read the piece backstage some-where just before going on to sing, and that she ached in every bone of her body as a result of Burchill's revenge. For that's what it is – *I want what you've got* revenge, with a hyena's code of conduct. It is Burchill who is punished though, feeling certain that she will soon be trapped by whomever she loves. Better to kill off Patti the Confessor with premature haste and with all the inky fingers of Margery Allingham than wait for Patti to ask *'Julie who?'*

When the article appears for this day's sizing-up, Julie Ocean has been as gentle as she would ever allow herself to be, yet she can't help but slip in: *'Morrissey lives with his boyfriend in Santa Monica.'* This is the headless-trunk aspect of Burchill that can't help but snap her choppers. It is also a great lie, since neither sexuality nor Santa Monica had been plumed during the interview. Oh, but *oh.* It is fascinating how writers such as Burchill can believe that what has not been said has somehow been said, and it evokes a gentle pity, because we suddenly have a picture before us of Burchill alone at midnight, a bottle of Gordon's gin resting against her typewriter (yes, typewriter), her small-girl urgings flapping to the fore like a cargo of dead piglets being offloaded at Dover, suddenly laughing at the inclusion of fingerlicking fantasy. Burchill will one day be found dead – probably in Bedford Square, a paragon of Cadbury's, having been burned and hanged and stuffed on the legitimate grounds of being an irritable woman, so loaded with secrets and folds and folds of H&M outer garments, having never been anybody, yet having understood the glacial power of the written word to its greatest disadvantage. I shall be honored to attend her funeral, and I might even jump into the grave.

Of the other great modern writers, they, too, have itched and scratched their way upwards via the world of spinning discs, and they are Michael Bracewell and Paul Morley, writers who make the readers see, and who do not allow themselves to be defined by other writers. Like a team of horses they canter through the 70s, 80s, 90s and beyond (for that is where we are now: in the beyond), always three years too young, always full of sensible condemnations – having robbed the modern Faber poets of any accidental meaning. There are, of course, no modern poets in the swill-bucket of British poetry where even the most savage denizen of the deep can become Poet Laureate – to loud yawns of national disinterest, and where all armpit media poets-on-standby ought to be stretched a foot longer than they presently are. It is Burchill who still leads the pack, like Barbara Stanwyck on horseback, restoring horror every time she picks up a pen, which, thankfully, is often. She may very well give genius a bad name, but she can still wow and slay like no other entertainer. Yes, *entertainer.*

Peter Wyngarde writes:

> *Forgive my vanity for not entertaining but I had an attack of psoriasis today which makes me look like a baboons arse. Have been writing a film script on Roger Casement.*

When you telephone Peter at his home he will lift the receiver and instantly say *'Ahh! THERE you are!'* even though he has no idea who's calling.

I am distraught when the tower of Mikey Farrell leaves the band with the usual and unlikely intention to 'move on' (he then accepts a job on *American, I, Dull*), and I am pensive because he is an incredible musician who can manage a ferociously huge sound for any song. But more than that,

I have begun to lean on him and his able-bodied barrel chest, his mid-western industrial strength and his parental soundness. When most musicians exit, it is a relief of sorts, since they have already begun to hover darkly, but Mikey complicated my thoughts for a long time to come, and I indulge myself in meditative regret. Once Mikey has left he then says terrible things about me – all of which are true.

Not that I would ever be lacking. The mid-west had also brought Matthew Ira Walker and Solomon Lee Walker into the frame – brothers drenched in distinction. Chicagoan rebels, really, but via heaven. With Matt on drums and Solomon on bass, the live sound was finally ready for any-thing, and they both played so magnificently that I momentarily fell off-balance. An indescribably strong core, they played as if trying to get out from behind bars, both stamped with a genius that neither seemed aware of, full of Chicago track-and-field force – Matt a big battalion of strong-arm tactics direct from the set of *Our Winning Season*, and Solomon the boot in the face of belt-tightening Spartanism, but with the type of blasé wit that even a hangover couldn't burn off. Luckily, both are also compel-lingly precise musicians, and, even better, they cannot be offended, which, given my over-reaching squeaks of tour-ette's, is useful. They brought with them the shipmate fellowship usually (and oddly) associated only with the Smiths period, and along with Jesse – who stalked the stage like a wolf encircling a lame Bison, fraternal Mikey – blood spurting from each finger – and main man Boz, the band were a hundred percenters hard-hat hellhounds at last.

Like bravo desperados we toured nihilistically – an

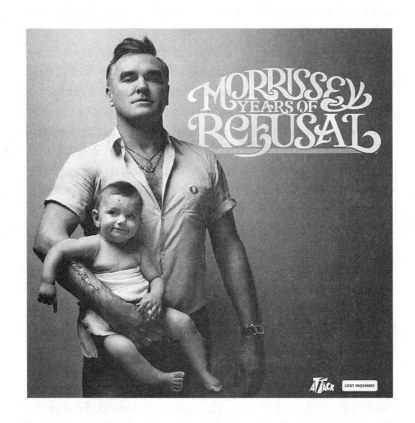

The refusal to be destroyed into irrelevance, Years of Refusal, *2009, strives*
mightily above the psychological toll

unstoppable destroyer, fearless in the face of press execution. Fasten a green beret on Solomon's head and he's ready
to clean up North Korea within an hour. With a sailor's
roll, Solomon is so schooled in humor that he is almost
unable to talk straight – like a professional comedian who
looks worried unless delivering a killer punchline. Matt is
the rear-gunner, a delivered message of hope who can even
manage a gung-ho gong solo. Onstage, I turn and watch
Matt's *have-come-am-here* earthquake determination and I
recover from a lost moment. Inspiration is everything, and
Matt is the trainer stirring the fat blob who dreams of pizza
with every sit-up count, and calling the team to the 50-yard
line. Sadness whispers, now forgotten, through the poplar
trees. There are now too many laughs, and the band is a
Yale water-polo team when not a musical unit. But outsiders will forever try to run it down, and none of these
musicians will gain a scant line of press attention in England. Elsewhere, yes. England, no. Our masterwork *Years
of Refusal* had been released in 2009, the final tour de force
for producer Jerry Finn, who died suddenly from a brain
hemorrhage, not living long enough to see the release of
such an accomplished hot rock. The refusal in question
was the refusal to be knocked out, but Jerry would be dead
at age 38 – the same age that both Tim Broad and Jon Daley
were when they heaved their last. I sit by Jerry in the last
two weeks of his life, propped up in his bed at Cedars Sinai,
he looking finished with it all, shriveled and ancient. Around
the bed everyone speaks loudly when quietly will do. I bear
witness as we all say to Jerry the things we would never say
were he standing before us in perfect health. Now, Jerry is
a child again, his eyes wide with horror, the voice silenced,

the mind locked in, unable to answer any question put to him. Touch says more, and I fiddle about with his bedsheets – straightening what doesn't need to be straightened, tucking in what isn't trailing out. It is the act of getting close, but without the ability to hug, for, even now, with the close of it all upon Jerry, we remain embarrassed to be human. The earth's pull has already kicked in, and Jerry is elsewhere. I will soon walk away into the late afternoon sun, with the task of filling up the rest of the day, as Jerry remains trapped and falling to one side, mouth wide open as if screaming at a pitch so high as to be beyond the range of human hearing. I recall the sessions at Conway Studios, amid joy and heat, none of us knowing that Jerry's body was calling out for its final halt. It will come if it should come. I recall the listening party at Jerry's house in the foothills, with Chrissie Hynde and Russell Brand looking bemused, and where for the last time I saw Jerry laughing, his health on the skids, scoreboard completed, life's job done.

Universal had signed me for *Years of Refusal* against their will, and lumpen new management densely release the album during the week of illicit industry cardsharping known as the Brit Awards – a fishy con game where the most powerful labels pay each other off with jiggery-pokery awards for the acts that have already been earmarked for calculated enlargement in the year to come. My name belongs nowhere on such a list, and although *Years of Refusal* is mid-week number 1, I am kicked off by the end of the week when Brit Award overkill enhances the chances of others and leaves me bloodied and bruised –

over before it began. My lumpen new management had rib-tickled with the news that the leading single *I'm throwing my arms around Paris* is gaining exceptional airplay, and *'We think you'll be very surprised by its chart entry.'*

With such a nod and wink, I am shook heartily, not unreasonably expecting a Top 5 position.

'You d-d-don't mean .... Number 1?' I ask my managers, for why would they bother with such excited whispers if not?

'Just you wait and see!' is the reply.

I'm throwing my arms around Paris flops in at number 21, and the child within is finally murdered. The single doesn't even chart in France, yet here I am with allegedly the most powerful management team in the world. They seem unable to do *anything*.

I retreat, alone, to Los Cabos, sitting on a deserted beach at dusk – a small boat rowing towards me as if to meet me. The waves crash quietly, then loudly, then quietly, then loudly, conversing amongst themselves. Another pelican is dying on the beach, folding its enormous wings around its head in order to bring the darkness sooner, and to screen out the watching gulls. Not for the first time I wrap a dying pelican in large bath towels and carry it to the hotel reception. They are not remotely interested, but they wryly entertain me when I tell them that I will pay whatever it takes to have this pelican gently relieved of its painful life. They assure me that it will be taken to a local vet, but as I walk away I imagine it already listed on tomorrow night's restaurant menu. All resolve and dignity, I have done my best for a pelican whose head was probably chopped off and thrown back into the sea.

A varicose leg appears before me and the cracked-tile

smile of a peanut vendor appears on the white sand. The beach is private, but a Mexican on a mission cannot be stopped. A beach at nighttime is silent with secrets – finally given a rest from those dreaded day-people. I, too, subside into fatigue, and it is a fatigue I now feel every moment of my life. By moonlight I stretch on the sand, alone, yet sets of eyes blink somewhere in the distance, like hunting dogs spotting lame prey. Too much happens in my life, and then months and months of nothing. I am always in the back of a car being taken somewhere, with all of my belongings labeled. As if words could ever be found to describe it! Yet the body drags the mind along, and we are fooled into believing that we ever have a choice. It is all done.

In 2010 the Queen of England is caught driving her own car without a fastened seat-belt, and she is nabbed by the usual morass of predatory photographers who, like birds of prey, bloodsuck her every move for their own profit. The newspapers headline is NOW, NOW, MA'AM!, whereas you or I would, of course, be humiliated and fined and jumped on and incarcerated or set alight for the very same conduct. The Queen, quite naturally, does not apologize for her seditious transgression in the year when 1,850 citizens (whom the Queen might fancifully believe are her 'subjects') are killed in British road accidents.

At the mercy of chance, I am alone in the South of France, spring having sprung on 2010 as I drive open-topped along the Sainte-Maxime Coastline road along to St Tropez, the singing voice of Kristeen Young at maximum volume as I tear along – she sounding like someone who had been indecently touched by a close relative in a darkened theater, and I an escapee from the petty world. I lodge at a glitzy hotel of higher-income commerce-hop-pers, all chivalrous respect and echoes of Coco. Wealthy French people kiss in public, but not in private, like those who put on display romantic affection that must be observed by others because it is untrue. Here, no one is considered apart from their appearance. Days pass and I speak to no one unless to explain my vegetarianism (whereas blood-spurting cannibalism demands no ques-tions). I sit alone in the steam room at the hotel spa. I rise to leave and I push the door open by gripping its handle. The monumentally heavy all-glass door shatters with a loud bang, sending me diving leftwards for protection as tiny shards of glass explode, bursting towards my face and body. Crumpled on the ground and now covered by glass I pull the emergency cord. Paramedics arrive and sprawl me out like a dissected rat as tiny particles of glass are pinched out from my legs and lower body. Humiliation is nothing when your powers of reflex have just spared you from blindness. The glass door had exploded due to the pressure of the heat within. *'You could 'ave been kill,'* says a Paramedic, and I smile a nothing smile, eyes reddened by Sassicaia. Ah yes, I could 'ave been kill.

As the unstable months of 2011 drew their final sighs we are in Mexico for six concerts. Over and over I watch Kirk Douglas in *Two Weeks in Another Town,* waking at odd hours of the night thinking that I am him. But I am not. His belly is flat and mine is fat. His frame is slender and his hair is strong. His clothes are the unlikely perfection that no truly busy human could adequately muster without three fussy Edward Everett Horton faithful fusspots at hand. Even now, I unwisely compare myself to those in the prime of their best. I live by such signals. I die by such signals. In *Two Weeks in Another Town*, Kirk Douglas darts about luxuriant Technicolor Rome – *my* ruined Rome – with all those blazing reds that I know too well, every inch a rich crypt. However little he wants it, he has fame and money and a catalogue of fur-lined women, a rubyfruit jungle at every turn. He has, I gather, endured a sanatorium and outlived a life-threatening depression, and having been a big Hollywood star his light has now gone out. Of course, for a star in descent, he is the very picture of prosperity and control. Something in me believes this story even though his carriage is weapon-strong, his face is power, there is no sign that depression had been his pillow, and no infirmities overlap. I cannot, for example, imagine this character surviving vertically in 1970s Manchester. *Two Weeks in Another Town* is Hollywood's idea of male depression – which, as you have already guessed, is nowhere near the real thing. In fact, it strikes me as a fitly perfection. Whenever a man sits he must arrange the box of gadgets between his legs, or at least be aware of how his rocks and stones fall. Any low-slung apparatus could be sat upon awkwardly and cause an unbecoming shriek. Kirk Douglas sits perfectly in *Two Weeks in Another Town*, never betrayed by tics and quirks, or by rough-hewn readjustments; his body inexperienced in misfortune, and polished to consummate perfection. The way a man uses his legs tells the entire story of the groin and the body above, because every move made by a man comes from the center, therefore a hug when the center doesn't meet is a hug with fear. How the zone between the legs is used, or unused, shows in everything that a man does. Most of the screen characters played by Kirk Douglas are concerned with ambition, and nothing else, because everything else is usually in its place already. He has a presumed authenticity in every move he makes. Interviewed on the *Dick Cavett Show* in the early 1970s, off-screen Kirk is much as you'd expect. He is what America likes to think of as its own experience; a boy born into nothing who becomes everything. Relaxed and solid, Kirk Douglas measures his words slowly, but the easy smile is power, and it becomes America having been born without American imprint. It is funny how those who least represent at birth can become those who most represent in later life. The amiable genius of Dick Cavett exemplifies trust and goodness used to clever purpose, and this gets the best out of Douglas, and we get to understand how what passes as self-esteem is really born out of sorrows and the fear of being put back to wherever you once unfortunately were. Kirk Douglas spent an anchored life in the grip of Satanic Hollywood, always looking like something to be dished up, always delivering gold-plated acting, yet strangely treated with scant respect from an industry to which he gave so much. His *'how deep it goes'* speech from *The Bad and the Beautiful*, his fate endured in *Lonely Are the Brave*, acting up and fully out to William Campbell's man-crush in *Man Without a Star* – *'You sure have a great saddle,'* says Campbell as he gives Douglas the once-over. It was a career of ten Oscar performances, yet minus those ten Oscars. With these thoughts, I awake in Monterrey in absolute panic, but I need fear nothing, as the cheer that awaits me at tonight's show drags doubts to heel. I appear to be more well known in Mexico than even in Sweden, Peru or Chile. Nothing the world holds could match the love awaiting me in Mexico City – two sold-out shows where my own voice goes unheard above the singing from the hall.

Let me kiss you has flag-waving meaning in Mexico, and each audience yawps out the words with a shivaree blast as I look out like a shepherd unable to restrain the haroosh. Arms and arms and chests and hands of Morrissey messages inked in for life – tattooed across nakedness, each one an essay, and it's all I can do to take deep breaths. A tattoo means I am always there – even when people shower, my words or pasty face will gaze up from soaped bodies. Puebla has sold out faster than any known concert in the history of the city. The youth of Puebla throw their bodies stagewards as an act of love. They give me the right to live.

I know it's over proves too much for flesh and blood – my flesh, my blood. *Scandinavia* is the stepping-back gasp, the new life saving the old. Mexico City has rendered me gasping for oxygen. The pollution trapped within the city has nowhere to go except into my lungs. I lie on the bed with two needles of steroids pumped into rump in order to get me through the next few days. Two nights at Guadalajara where everyone seems to be waiting, and everyone seems to be looking for me, and the crowds sing the songs in a way that tells me that these songs just might be all that they have. Parents hold their small children up to the stage, as if possibly born as a result of something I had said. Greater love hath no man than this. I am held. An earthquake has us fleeing the Puebla venue. As I run outside I look down and I am barefoot. We all gather in a parking lot, like Polish refugees waiting for someone to tell us where to go to die.

This microphone is my headstone

Puebla rumbles its never-turn-your-back-on-mother-earth warnings. Many of the world's victims live in Mexico, their poverty created by wretchedly rich governments of the civilized world; a poverty deliberately structured to keep the poor poor, and to keep Mexico unable to reach the vital interests of their border-neighbors. Coldly, coldly, the human race slides along – even now, in an age where presidents and prime ministers are generally seen as a threat to their own people – or, at its most tolerant, just a waste of time. A bubble has burst all over the world. In Mexico, people are not able to live, yet they smile throughout as they walk their eight-day pilgrimage for Our Lady of Guadalupe, reduced to pulling beads, caught up in the fear of not believing. There is a certain Mexican movement of the head, telling we from elsewhere that they know very well how they are thought not to matter. Because of this, they have abnormal strength and love, with anchored hearts beyond the imaginations of royal dictatorships. There are more stolen goods in either Buckingham Palace or the British Museum than the Mexican poor could ever get their hands on. Yet, the people of Mexico are largely unable to move or to progress, and although their toil and labor has built most of America, modern America does its utmost to keep them from joining in.

When you arrive at American Immigration you are reminded of the desperately compulsive fears of American authority. An unnecessary rudeness from Immigration officers is required in order to justify the gaping hole in American justice, and it belies the truth of the American people, and it thus spoils America. A disloyal American is one who questions their own government, which, certainly through the Bush era, begged constant examination. The infantile panic with which American Immigration officials shout loudly and humiliate gleefully is designed to exert strength, yet it trumpets cowardice and it fouls notions of patriotism. The louder they shout, the less the world wants to be like them. The louder they shout, the more they believe the world will respect them. They dare not know another way. Throughout Europe, borders of strength lead you on your way with admirable calmness; there is no need to destroy the soul at security checkpoints, and there is no need to make travelers feel defiled simply because they have turned up with their passports. This trigger-happy vacuum, so terrified of human touch, feeds every high-school shooting – an unfortunate link that no American politician can understand. Fame, fame, fatal fame. The US government proudly boasted Zero Tolerance and implemented the scheme with zero intelligence. Oh, why am I even thinking about all of this now, as I leave Mexico – each hour having struck with such beauty and sunlit magnificence? I have lost all respect for myself as I deny myself the joy of Mexico; the boy of 16 with my face tattooed across his belly; the honcho of 30 with STILL ILL tattooed across his chest. If I deny this love then I lie to myself about the world I know. In ministering angel Jesse, in godbrother Solomon, in the Boz who always saves the day, and in our newly joined rescuer Gustavo Manzur, I, too, have blood-bubbas – clansmen long searched for. I shall be undressed, washed, laid out and buried by Jesse; Gustavo will catch me in any fall, bringing me back to the point I had started from – I had known him for a lifetime after our first five-minute meeting, and the dead are dead, and the heart warms. Whenever I meet Gustavo we both automatically laugh because we both know that sooner or later one or both of us will say something funny, and human energy rings a timeless hum. Loyal to the mugwump, the band prefer mischief to limelight, and although no major label will sign us, these years are ours, locked together, and I stream out of you, not a matter of whether but of when. Take it as it is. I am no more unhappy than anyone else, and most humans are wretched creatures – cursed by the sadness of being. The world created me and I am here – never realizing that I am in love until it gets me into trouble.

For a year's-end concert at the Congress Theater in Chicago, the audience heaves with responding kindness, and I am immobilized by singing voices of love.

All along, my private suffering felt like vision, urging me to die or go mad, yet it brings me here, to a wintry Chicago street-scene in December 2011 – *I, a small boy of 52,* clinging to the antiquated view that a song should mean something, and presenting himself everywhere by way of apology. It is quite true that I have never had anything in my life that I did not make for myself.

As I board the tour bus, a fired encore is still ringing in my ears, and then suddenly a separated female voice calls out to me – full of cracked now-or-never embarrassment above the still Illinois winter atmosphere of midnight, and it was dark, and I looked the other way.

CREDITS: IMAGES

Grateful acknowledgement is given to the following for permission to reproduce copyrighted material.

Every effort has been made to contact copyright holders. The author and publisher would be glad to amend in future editions any errors or omissions brought to their attention.

p. 69: courtesy of Universal Music, photograph by Toshi;

p. 124: courtesy of James Maker;

p. 136: courtesy of Linder Sterling;

p. 198: courtesy of Warner Music Group, photograph by Jürgen Vollmer;

p. 246: courtesy of Warner Music Group, photograph by Linder Sterling;

p. 282: courtesy of Warner Music Group, photograph by Dean Freeman;

p. 369: courtesy of Nancy Sinatra;

p. 375: published by Universal Music (now BMG), photograph by Greg Gorman;

p. 419: published by Universal Music (now BMG), photograph by Fabio Lovino;

p. 445: courtesy of Universal Music, photograph by Jake Walters;

p. 454: courtesy of 'really nothing';

p. 459: courtesy of Svenja Brandenburg.

All other photographs are courtesy of the author and Margaret Dwyer. Page 1 shows Morrissey aged 4 at Lytham St Anne's, 1963.

CREDITS: WORDS

CREDITS: WORDS

Dolls c/o Gold Mountain Entertainment; lines by Victoria Wood © Victoria Wood. 'Oscar Wilde,' from *The Portable Dorothy Parker* by Dorothy Parker, edited by Marion Meade, copyright 1944 by Dorothy Parker. Copyright © 1973, 2006 by The National Association for the Advancement of Colored People. Used by permission of Viking Penguin, a division of Penguin Group (USA) LLC.

For lyric usage, Morrissey is represented by Warner-Chappell, to whom grateful acknowledgement is expressed.

ACKNOWLEDGEMENTS

to Damon Anacreonte, for encouragement

to Julia Riley, for always being everywhere

to Helen Conford, a steady scrutineer

to Tina Dehghani, always level

whatever is sung is the case